"This book on treatment planning stands out for its holistic approach. The co-editors selected some of the best scholars and practitioners in the play therapy field. I love the emphasis on the wide array of contributing factors and wider systems."

David A. Crenshaw, *PhD, ABPP,*
author and board-certified clinical psychologist

"*Play Therapy Treatment Planning with Children and Families* delivers just what the title describes and much more. The editors provide a thoughtful rationale for the importance of treatment planning, one that extends the plan to be a dynamic process, encompassing relevant contextual factors in the child's life. The editors have assembled seasoned practitioners to offer guidance and practical applications for treatment planning, ensuring that the book is useful across various presenting issues and theoretical orientations. The book will help practitioners craft holistic and high-quality plans to support the well-being of children and families!"

Anne Stewart, PhD, *Professor, Department of*
Graduate Psychology, James Madison University

"This is a book play therapists will keep handy for many years."

Richard Gaskill, *EdD, LPC, RPT-S*

PLAY THERAPY TREATMENT PLANNING WITH CHILDREN AND FAMILIES

Play Therapy Treatment Planning with Children and Families is a comprehensive guide that provides an integrative and prescriptive approach to creating customized treatment plans. It's an excellent textbook for graduate programs in social work, counseling, and family therapy and an invaluable guide for practicing clinicians in all settings.

After exploring and explaining the many modalities for treating children and adolescents, this book provides sample treatment plans using a variety of case vignettes. Chapters also take readers through a road map for case conceptualization, meeting with caregivers, problem identification, goal development, diagnosis determination, determination of interventions and termination, and much more.

Lynn Louise Wonders is a licensed professional counselor (LPC), certified professional counselor (CPCS), and registered play therapist-supervisor (RPT-S). She has provided clinical supervision, consultation, and training since 2010.

Mary L. Affee is a licensed clinical social worker (LCSW), a registered play therapist-supervisor (RPT-S), and holds a doctorate in education. She is the founder and clinical director of Horizon Integrated Wellness Group, a private practice in North Carolina.

PLAY THERAPY TREATMENT PLANNING WITH CHILDREN AND FAMILIES

A Guide for Mental Health Professionals

Edited by Lynn Louise Wonders and Mary L. Affee

Routledge
Taylor & Francis Group

NEW YORK AND LONDON

Designed cover image: Weekend Images Inc. © Getty Images

First published 2024
by Routledge
605 Third Avenue, New York, NY 10158

and by Routledge
4 Park Square, Milton Park, Abingdon, Oxon, OX14 4RN

Routledge is an imprint of the Taylor & Francis Group, an informa business

Library of Congress Cataloging-in-Publication Data
Names: Wonders, Lynn Louise, author. | Affee, Mary L., author.
Title: Play therapy treatment planning with children and families : a guide for mental health professionals / Lynn Louise Wonders and Mary L. Affee.
Description: New York, NY : Routledge, 2024. | Includes bibliographical references and index.
Identifiers: LCCN 2023044040 (print) | LCCN 2023044041 (ebook) | ISBN 9781032363646 (hbk) | ISBN 9781032363622 (pbk) | ISBN 9781003334231 (ebk)
Subjects: LCSH: Play therapy. | Play therapy—Methodology. | Medical protocols. | Patient-centered health care.
Classification: LCC RJ505.P6 W66 2024 (print) | LCC RJ505.P6 (ebook) | DDC 618.92/891653—dc23/eng/20231229
LC record available at https://lccn.loc.gov/2023044040
LC ebook record available at https://lccn.loc.gov/2023044041

ISBN: 9781032363646 (hbk)
ISBN: 9781032363622 (pbk)
ISBN: 9781003334231 (ebk)

DOI: 10.4324/9781003334231

Typeset in Baskerville
by Apex CoVantage, LLC

This book is dedicated to all the mental health professionals who provide therapy services for children and families now and for years to come. May this book provide you with valuable resources for case conceptualization and therapy planning.

CONTENTS

FOREWORD

How do we know whether or not we have arrived somewhere if we don't know where we are going or what the end point is, or even have a road map to help get us there? We wouldn't think of getting into our car and just heading out in any direction for that long-desired and hoped-for transformative trip without taking along our GPS system (be it on our phone or through another means). This is very true for working with children and families in therapy.

Our clients generally want exactly the same things in life as ALL people: they want to be able to thrive and not just survive. A high-quality treatment plan is an essential tool that can help in this process. And it is important that individuals have the ability to design their own road maps and yet have the knowledge of and feeling that there is a supportive and invested therapist who is walking beside them while they are on their journey and helping them to develop, facilitate, and keep track of their individualized road map.

In order for treatment to be successful, there needs to be the creation of an allied stance with families, and most importantly, to move beyond emphasizing problems to emphasizing competence; moving out of the role of expert and into the role of accountable ally; moving off of our professional "land" and onto the family's "turf," and out of the stance of teaching and into that of learning *with*. If we ever hope to help our clients change, in a meaningful way, we need to think about what works in therapy with regard to the working relationship. In *The Heart and Soul of Change. What Works in Therapy*, editors Hubble, Duncan, and Miller (1999) report four common factors for positive behavior change: Client Factors: 40% which included resources and influences such as persistence, faith, or a supportive relative; Hope and Expectancy: 15% which includes expecting to get better and do better; Model and Technique: 15% which included staff procedures, techniques, and beliefs; and most importantly, Relationship Factors: 30%, which was the strength of the alliance. To make therapy effective, we need to join with families in treatment planning and partner with them, giving the family a voice and choice and opportunities for involvement.

By bringing in the family and client into becoming involved in the treatment planning, it demonstrates a culture of respect, being listened to, and having their input valued and considered in treatment planning. Planning needs also to consider the family's readiness for involvement and their ability to assume tasks on behalf of their child. We must also include the child/teen client as an expert resource, respecting their voice and treating them as equal partners in creating a system of change. They need to be included in all meetings concerning them, and no idea is a "bad" idea, should they offer it, along with helping the child/teen become educated about all their choices, and most importantly, having transparent conversations with them. It becomes a "partnership," making decisions together, which leads to investment in the treatment process and in initiating their own treatment through their goals, objectives, and interventions.

Treatment plans need not only have a goal, an endpoint, but also the strengths related to the goal and the barriers to the goal, along with measurable objectives, interventions, services, and supports. The goals are the broader endpoint and help to express the hopes and dreams of the individual expressed in the child/teen's or parent/guardian's own words. The goals identify the hoped-for-destination to be arrived at through the services being offered. Goal development becomes a critical component in engagement and in creating a collaborative working relationship.

A lot goes into thinking about the goal and the more specific objectives of how to get there. For example, strengths, abilities, competencies, values and traditions, interests, hopes, dreams, motivation, resources, and assets, unique individual attributes, things that have worked well in the past, "natural supports" (e.g., family members, relatives, friends, community resources), and cultural influences are all woven into the tapestry of the treatment plan. But it is not complete if there is no consideration of what factors keep the person from their goals. Barriers such as skill development, environmental and familial factors, lack of resources, self-defeating strategies, threats to health and safety, and cultural factors need also to be spotlighted and addressed for a successful outcome.

And lastly, but far from the least, objectives must be stated in behaviorally measurable language, be time-limited, and clear for when we know the client has achieved the established objectives and the end has been reached. Objectives should capture the positive alternative to the current needs and challenges and work to remove barriers, build on strengths and address cultural issues. Objectives are like stepping stones along the path, bringing the client closer to attaining the broad goal. Objectives can be changed and updated as the plan is reviewed, and when all the necessary objectives have been achieved, then we have arrived at our destination, and the goal has been successfully met.

Writing treatment plans and conceptualizing them from a theoretical framework is not an easy task, and it requires nuance and takes practice, support, and guidance. How fortunate we are that there is now a volume exclusively devoted to the broad topic of treatment planning, illuminating the topic from a myriad of angles and lenses. Edited by Lynn Louise Wonders and Mary Affee, *Treatment Planning with Children and Families: A Guide for Mental Health Professionals* is the one resource all clinicians should have at their side and in their professional library. It is comprehensive, offering a rich variety that succeeds in meeting the need for an inclusive how-to book on writing detailed and relevant treatment plans with measurable objectives that will lead to effective outcomes. The book is divided into three sections: Foundations of Treatment Planning; Treatment Plans from Theoretical Models and Approaches; and Special Topics, Samples, and Resources. The editors have gathered an impressive array of chapter authors, experts on their topics and fields of interest, who openly share their wisdom and time-honored approaches to treatment planning with us.

Readers, you will delight in reading this well-crafted, comprehensive and contemporary volume. It will help guide you toward a richer treatment practice with more effective outcomes.

—Athena A. Drewes

REFERENCE

Hubble, M. A., Duncan, B. L., & Miller, S. D. (1999). *The heart and soul of change: What works in therapy*. American Psychological Association.

PREFACE

This is a contemporary treatment planning book that provides perspectives on how clinicians may conceptualize and develop plans for therapy through various lenses and with attunement to various special considerations. The book provides essential resources for mental health clinicians working with children and their families. After the editors' encountered repeated challenges of having to access multiple books for treatment planning resources, encountering gaps in treatment planning, training opportunities, and through years of providing clinical services, teaching master's level students, and training clinicians through continuing education about treatment planning, this book was conceived. The editors observed that many practicing clinicians did not receive thorough training on the topic of treatment planning specific to child clients and families in graduate school or in continuing education. This book is designed to represent a diversity of perspectives on the topic of planning for therapy by including contributing chapter authors who are experts on theories, models, and important points of view. The vision for this book was to provide a comprehensive text for clinicians in training as well as practicing therapists in the field of child and play therapy on the process of case conceptualization with an evolving road map for the course of therapy. The editors have sought to straddle the medical model and the growing need for more sensitivity, inclusivity, cultural humility, and avoidance of over-pathologizing children's mental health challenges. The book will help clinicians organize and formulate information collected and observed with clients to develop effective and measurable treatment goals and objectives that lead to effective outcomes. For all theoretical orientations from which clinicians provide services, this guide provides a golden thread of goal-directed treatment planning that is substantive and purposeful so that clinicians can be accountable to the efficacy and quality of the psychotherapy services being provided.

—Lynn Louise Wonders and Mary Affee

AN OVERVIEW OF THE TEXT

This book is organized into three parts.

Part 1 takes the reader through a thorough overview of contemporary, purposeful goal-directed treatment planning, including reasons for having a plan, a case for goals and objectives regardless of theoretical orientation, phases of therapy, the process of case conceptualization, human development, systemic and cultural considerations, and an introduction to the use of an integrative and prescriptive model for treatment planning.

Part 2 includes chapters authored by expert and revered therapists and trainers in the field of child and play therapy. The theories, models, and approaches were intentionally chosen as most closely representing the canon of theoretically based approaches to providing play therapy services for children and their families but also have gone beyond theories alone, considering that theories are not the only lens through which we approach therapy. Some particular models and approaches offer their own unique and important filter through which clinicians can shape the way therapy is delivered that may or may not be based upon a particular theoretical orientation. Each author's perspective and voice were honored and preserved while keeping this book section aligned with a sense of continuity. There are 17 chapters, each providing an overview of the theory, model, or approach and a fictional case study demonstrating the treatment planning process through the lens of the chapter's orientation.

Part 3 provides chapters that address special considerations during the treatment planning process, including special populations and circumstances. There are sample forms, documents, and resources included in this section of the book as well.

VOICES AND TONES

It's important to note that many voices contribute to this book, and each author's voice is their own. Some contributing authors have chosen to use the first person and some the third person when providing a narrative of their case studies. Some voices are more formal, and some more casual. The editors hope this lends to the spirit of representing variety and diversity of perspectives without removing the intention of flow and easy structure of the book. Due to variations in terminology and methods in the theory and method chapters, it was necessary to shift some of the original wording and organization to facilitate synthesis.

A WORD OF CARE AND CAUTION

It is always advisable to seek formal training, supervision, and consultation as the process of treatment planning can be complex, given every client and their presenting challenges and their biopsychosocial factors are unique. This book is not intended to be a stand-alone source but rather one that compliments further training, supervision, and consultation.

ACKNOWLEDGMENTS

FROM LYNN LOUISE WONDERS

The synergy Dr. Mary Affee and I experienced in formulating this book was remarkable. After I had been teaching about the importance of treatment planning in the field of play therapy when often there seemed to be a gap in this part of our field's education, Mary approached me, having realized the same need I had realized. She suggested we write a book and I jumped at the opportunity to join forces. I am grateful for Mary's gift of visioning and creativity! We've laughed and we've cried through this project and I'm grateful for every moment because we have both grown so much professionally through this project.

I want to acknowledge my husband Dennis Wonders whose support and patience through the process of writing and editing for this book has been invaluable.

I want to acknowledge one of my many beloved mentors Dr. Janet Courtney whose wisdom and experience with editing and writing books was a tremendous support from the very beginning of this process all the way through.

I also want to thank Judith Norman, my consultant in Synergetic Play Therapy® training and Lisa Dion, creator and teacher of Synergetic Play Therapy® who both inspired and supported me in being true and staying connected to my essential self throughout this process.

I most certainly stand on the shoulders of many giants. I am so grateful for my many mindfulness-based practice teachers over the past 30 years. My mindfulness practice personally and professionally carries me through all big and important projects such as this book. I have learned so much from many of the great contributors to this book, humble and grateful to now have them offering their expertise and wisdom to this book and to my revered colleagues who were gracious enough to lend their expertise to this book as well. I am so thankful for each and every one of you.

Lastly, I want to acknowledge all of the child and family therapists providing therapy services for your clients and leaning in to learn and grow as professionals. To all my many consultees, supervisees, and students over the years, I offer a deep bow of respect and gratitude for all you have done and continue to do to be the best therapists you can be.

FROM MARY AFFEE

With humility and gratitude, I want to thank our universe and the divine for the mystery, misery, and the magnificence of life.

I want to thank the clients who graciously and painfully shared their hardest moments and memories in life with me, for they have all made me a better human. I want to thank the children who taught me resilience and how to play in their deepest pain. I am thankful for the wisdom and the incredible insights I have gained in the service of helping others and teaching others.

I owe an extraordinary debt of gratitude to all the authors, for this book would not have been possible without all of you. Anna Moore, at Routledge, thank you for your patience and support. It was a pleasure and honor to work with you.

I want to thank Lynn Louise Wonders, for sharing in this incredible writing project, and for the journey of learning how to edit a book. Thank you for putting your heart and time into this entire project, and for putting up with me! I could not have done this without you.

Taylor Auslander, my newly hired administrative assistant. Taylor, the last few weeks of completing this book often felt insurmountable. I know the completion of many editing tasks would not have been possible without you. You are one of the most intelligent, tenacious, and incredible humans I am honored to know and work with. Thank you for showing up in my life! Courteney Matteson, my executive assistant, thank you for all your hard work and all the laughs during the last few weeks in the editing process around the long table. Cindy Yewdall, Office Manager at Horizon Integrated Wellness Group, PLLC. Thank you for caring so much and taking the initiative when I couldn't.

I want to thank my granddaughter Adalina Eve Torrey-Lerose, for teaching me patience and when to walk away from the computer, for our play is my respite from difficult days. My mother, Mary Buttafuoco-Aguilar, who taught me to never give-up. I am so proud of all you have accomplished. My daughter Mary Torrey, you have always been the reason I am where I am. You gave me purpose and inspiration to be better and do better from the day you were born-I love you. J. C. Moeller for challenging me, encouraging me, and spending time with Adalina so I could write and research.

I want to thank my mentors, Dr. John Demartini, Founder of the Demartini Institute®. I could write pages about how impactful your teaching is and how it has changed and continues to change my life for the better. You are an incredible human and I am thankful. Lisa Dion, Founder of Synergetic Play Therapy® Institute, for boldly doing life; you are an inspiration! Thank you for the brilliance of Synergetic Play Therapy®. Carmen Marzella, Founder of Marzella Law Group, PLLC. Thank you for your time, patience, support, and demonstrating that lawyers can operate with so much compassion.

ABOUT THE EDITORS

Lynn Louise Wonders has been licensed and certified as a professional counselor and supervisor in Georgia since 2007. She is a registered play therapist-supervisor, and since 2010 she has provided play therapy training, supervision, and consultation. She is the author of *When Parents Are at War: A Child Therapist's Guide to Navigating High Conflict Divorce & Custody Cases*, the therapeutic children's book series Miss Piper's Playroom, author of *Jule Moved to a New House and a New School, Jolie Wants to Go Swimming: A Lesson in Patience, Breathe: A Coloring & Activity Book*, co-author of *Spark and His Screenagains, Sammy Saw Something on the Screen*, and co-editor of *Nature-based Play & Expressive Play Therapies for Children & Families*. She is the co-editor and author of *Treatment Planning for Children and Families: A Guide for Mental Health Professionals*. Ms. Wonders has been a certified teacher of mindfulness meditation, Tai Chi, Qi Gong, and Yoga since 1995. She is a certified AutPlay® Therapist, a certified Pure Presence Practitioner, on track to be a Board Certified Coach providing Life Design Coaching, and a trained divorce and parenting coach. She is currently a psychology Ph.D. student at Saybrook University. Ms. Wonders is known for her efforts to curate mental health support resources for child and family therapists worldwide, for her international, engaging speaking and training, as well as her creative support by way of groups and individual clinical consultation. Ms. Wonders is the owner and director of Wonders Counseling Services, LLC and the founder and director of The Mindfulness-based Therapy Training Institute ™ and the Mindfulness-based Play Therapy™ transtheoretical approach to play therapy services.

Dr. Mary Affee is a licensed clinical social worker and a registered play therapist-supervisor. She has worked in the mental health field for more than 12 years and is the founder and clinical director of Horizon Integrated Wellness Group, PLLC, a practice that provides mental health services for children, adolescents, and families. Dr. Affee specializes in play therapy, and she is the President of the North Carolina Association for Play Therapy. Dr. Affee received the 2023 NASW-NC Social Worker of the Year award. In 2022, she was awarded the Emerging Leader National Award of Excellence from the Association for Play Therapy. In 2014, she received an Award of Excellence from the National Institute for Trauma and Loss in Children. Dr. Affee is the author of *Adalina's Mask*, co-author of *Adalina and Eli Play Together*, co-author of *Spark and His Screenagains* and *Sammy Saw Something on the Screen*. In April 2020, Dr. Affee volunteered her time and expertise to provide psychological first-aid to New York's first responders during the COVID-19 pandemic. She was interviewed several times by news outlets highlighting her efforts in promoting mental health interventions during the pandemic lockdown and her leadership in spearheading a statewide action for fair reimbursement for practitioners from United Healthcare. She has presented numerous workshops, training, and presentations to parents, teachers, professionals, and students. Dr. Affee teaches a summer creative and expressive play therapy course at Molloy University, and she is a field supervisor for the University of Mount Olive's Counseling Department and North Carolina State University's MSW program. She is also an advisory board member for Hope Connection International, where she facilitates free children's mental health groups, and for Carol's Hope, and serves on NASW-NC's Private Practice Work Group.

CONTRIBUTORS

Rachel Altvater Psy.D, RPT-S

Mary Affee Ed.D, LCSW, RPT-S

Timothy Baima Ph.D, LMFT

Ann Beckley-Forest LCSW-R, RPT-S

Felicia Carroll LMFT, RTP-S

Isabella Cassina TPS, CAGS, PhD Candidate in Expressive Arts Therapy

Rebecca Chow Ph.D, LPC, LCPC, RPT-S,

Janet Courtney Ph.D, LCSW, RPT-S

Lisa Dion LPC, RPT-S

April Duncan DSW, LCSW, RPT-S

Eliana Gil Ph.D, LMFT, RPT-S, ATR

Geoff Goodman Ph.D, ABPP, CST, CSAT-S, RPT-S

Paris Goodyear-Brown LCSW, RPT-S

Robert Jason Grant Ed.D LPC, RPT-S

Rita Grayson LCSW, RPT-S

Eric J. Green Ph.D, RSP, RPT-S, LPC-S

Cary Hamilton LMHC, RPT-S, CDWF

Rosalind L. Heiko Ph.D, RPT-S

Julia Krebs LCMHC

Eleah Hyatt LMFT, RPT

Rhonda Johnson LPC-S, LMFT-S, RPT-S

Susan Becker Kerley LPC, CPCS

Courteney Matteson LCMHC -A

Claudio Mochi RP, RPT-S

Sueann Kenney-Noziska LCSW, LISW, RPTS

Rosie Newman LMHC, RPT-S

Judith Norman LPC, LSC, RPT-S

Kurt Oster LCSW, ACSW, BCD

Kim Street LPC

Risë VanFleet Ph.D, RPT-S, CDBC, CAEBI

Lynn Louise Wonders LPC, RPT-S, CPCS

PART 1

FOUNDATIONS OF TREATMENT PLANNING

CHAPTER 1

PURPOSEFUL AND EFFECTIVE TREATMENT PLANNING FOR CHILDREN AND FAMILIES

Lynn Louise Wonders

INTRODUCTION

The process of planning for therapy begins the moment therapists meet a child's caregivers and continues throughout the child's and family's time in therapy. The treatment plan is not only a step in the required clinical record documentation; it is a multifaceted, ongoing process. To gain a complete understanding of a client's presenting circumstances, concerns, and challenges, a thorough intake is needed. As all the data is gathered, the therapist pieces the information together, formulating and conceptualizing the presenting case. Collaborating with the child and caregivers, the therapist develops an itinerary for the journey of therapy to include identification of the destination (goals), milestones to track progress toward the destination (objectives), and selection of vehicles and routes (interventions). Therapists learn these skills conceptually in graduate school, but it is not until working directly with clients that they can apply that knowledge meaningfully (Fairburn, 2011; Sperry & Sperry, 2020). Even with the most client-centered theoretical approach, the therapist needs to conceptualize what the client is experiencing, expressing, and needing for the most appropriate course of therapy (Sperry & Sperry, 2020).

Effective psychotherapy with children and their caregivers is built on a foundation of a therapeutic alliance rooted in the therapist's warm, welcoming, attentive, and reflective presence (Axline,1981; Halbur, 2011; Landreth, 2012; Ray, 2021). The therapeutic alliance is a trans-theoretical construct (Koole & Tschacher, 2016) and, therefore, the relationship between therapist and client(s) is believed to be essential and necessary for effective psychotherapy outcomes regardless of theoretical orientation or approach (Tschacher et al., 2015). While randomized controlled trials about the therapeutic alliance have yet to show that the relationship is the basis for effective therapy, research has demonstrated that the therapeutic alliance is strongly correlated with positive outcomes (Koole & Tschacher, 2016). This foundation of rapport, trust, and connection is optimal for working collaboratively with the child and caregivers (Treichler et al., 2021) to develop a therapy plan based on what the child and family are presenting (Stewart et al., 2022). Treatment planning is, ideally, a dynamic and fluid process that allows for collaborative adjustments as progress is tracked and as new information and needs may arise.

PHASES OF THERAPY

While various therapy models may differ, there are typically three phases of psychotherapy.

Phase 1: Connect, Gather, and Develop

In the first phase, caregivers and the therapist come together to begin forming the therapeutic alliance through authentic connection during the intake session and the first several

DOI: 10.4324/9781003334231-2

sessions to follow. Clinicians build rapport with the child and caregivers, gather information, assess, develop a case conceptualization, establish goals and objectives collaboratively, determine the approach to use, and choose interventions with the initial therapy plan.

Phase 2: Maintaining, Observing, and Adjusting

Here, the therapist's role is to maintain the therapeutic alliance and assess for progress, regression, and new needs that may arise as indicated by the nature of the child's play or by the client or caregiver report. In addition, the therapist consults closely with caregivers and may adjust the therapy plan to offer new interventions to meet the presenting needs of the child and the family system as needed. This phase continues until all needs have been addressed, objectives achieved, and goals are met.

Phase 3: Closure of Therapy

As objectives and goals are reached, the clinician, caregivers, and the child together bring the therapy to a close. In this phase, the therapist ensures ethical and appropriate termination so that the child and caregivers feel a sense of satisfactory completion, healthy goodbyes, and an easeful transition from therapy.

THE INTERSECTION OF RELATIONAL PSYCHOTHERAPY AND THE MEDICAL MODEL

The belief in the therapeutic alliance as essential and foundational for desired treatment outcomes in psychotherapy seems to conflict with the standard medical model (Koole & Tschacher, 2016). All theoretical orientations in the field of child mental health are ideally rooted in a strong therapeutic relationship (Landreth, 2012; Ray, 2021). This relational emphasis creates distinct differences between psychotherapy and medical services. In child and family counseling, those coming for therapy are referred to as *clients*, whereas in the medical field, the term is *patient*. In the medical field, a patient receives a treatment believed to cure the patient's problem with no need for a relationship between the patient and the medical practitioner (Koole & Tschacher, 2016). Contrarily, therapists providing mental health services rely upon the therapeutic alliance to create the necessary connection, rapport, and trust for the therapy to be most effective.

The standard medical model does not fit the broader case conceptualization process unique to psychotherapy (Gehart, 2015). A mental health professional needs to conduct a full intake that considers the context of the child client's multiple systems and lived experience for case conceptualization, but there is no need for a medical doctor to have a complete biopsychosocial understanding of the patient's life to treat the patient's medical problem.

Many mental health professionals find it challenging to operate from the medical model while honoring the therapeutic alliance. And yet assigning a diagnosis and maintaining a clinical record is a necessary reality for most therapists (Ray, 2021). Mental health professionals are required by third-party payers to establish *medical necessity* for the client's participation in psychotherapy (Stockton & Sharma, 2019). Medical necessity must be documented with particular language in the clinical record. To meet the requirement of medical necessity, services must be evidence-based and appropriate for diagnosing and treating a disorder (Wiger, 2020). While some clinicians have the privilege of providing services outside of the medical model and can, therefore, avoid diagnosis and goal setting, most families in the United States need to use their health insurance to participate in psychotherapy. As a result, mental health professionals paneled as providers with insurance companies and Medicaid must have one foot in the medical model and the other in their chosen theoretical orientation(s).

The concept of treatment planning was born out of the medical model, not from the original psychotherapy theorists (Gehart, 2015). According to Luepker (2022), the medical model has advantages:

1. The medical model provides a clear structure and legitimizes mental health services in the eyes of the managed healthcare system.
2. Competent recordkeeping can be a framework for supporting the therapeutic alliance from the start of therapy.
3. Recordkeeping can ensure continuity of care if the client is referred for other services.
4. Recordkeeping protects clinicians from accusations of poor quality of care or lack of professionalism.

PLAY THERAPY AND THE MEDICAL MODEL

Play therapy is considered the most appropriate modality for supporting children with mental and emotional health challenges (Ray, 2021; Wonders, 2021a). Just as in the greater field of psychotherapy, play therapy includes a variety of seminal and historical theoretical orientations (Wonders, 2021a). Establishing the medical necessity of play therapy during treatment planning and documentation may initially seem daunting, given the relational emphasis of all play therapy seminal theories and models. But play therapy can be supported as medically necessary because *one* of the many benefits of play therapy is that it supports children's acquisition of developmental milestones. According to the American Academy of Pediatrics, this meets the requirement of medical necessity (Giardino et al., 2022). Play is the natural way children access and explore their inner and outer worlds, make meaning of experiences, process perceptions and emotions, meeting physical, cognitive, and emotional milestones (Hancock, 2021; Rathnakumar, 2020). Play therapy provides children with a designated space and time to playfully explore, express thoughts and feelings, and gain a sense of empowerment through play (Landreth, 2012; Ray, 2011; Schaefer, 1993). Given the literature about the powers of play as children's natural means of growth, healing, and change (Bratton et al., 2005; Hughes, 2021; Schaefer & Drewes, 2013), therapists providing play therapy can feel confident that with proper documentation the use of play therapy can both satisfy theoretical orientation guidelines and medical model requirements.

While child therapists working within the required parameters of third-party-payers need to have one foot in the medical model, it is important, at the same time, to avoid pathologizing or stigmatizing children (Kohrt et al., 2020; Suhr & Johnson, 2022). When a child receives a potentially stigmatizing diagnosis, it may negatively color the child's self-view or influence negative perceptions of the child by those aware of the diagnosis in the family, school, or community. It is important to utilize the medical model's necessary aspects while discerning when assigning diagnoses. Additionally, therapists need to be aware of the pathologizing risks of using certain medical model terminology. Being sensitive and informed about various populations can inspire therapists to seek more inclusive terminology. One example of using inclusive terminology is to refer to the adults bringing the child to therapy as *caregivers* rather than *parents* because not all caregivers are parents. Often children are in foster care or raised by an aunt, uncle, grandparents, adult cousin, or older sibling. Additional inclusive terminology can help to avoid unnecessary pathologizing of the presenting challenges that many children face resulting from traumatic events, neurodivergence, or systemic barriers such as racism, antisemitism, and ableism. Traditional terminology is often used, such as *parent, treatment plan,* and *presenting problem* in this book but also may use more inclusive terms, such as *caregivers, therapy plan,* and *presenting challenges.* While the spirit of this book seeks to provide a broad and inclusive process of conceptualizing and planning for therapy with children and families, the terminology and perspectives contained herein are purposefully varied to harmonize requirements of managed healthcare documentation with efforts to avoid pathologizing children.

While some clinicians can work outside of the medical model to avoid diagnosing children altogether, it is more common that mental health providers participate as paneled insurance providers. Knowing how to use DSM-5-TR criteria to direct therapy without stigmatizing or unnecessarily pathologizing children is essential (Kohrt et al., 2020; Suhr & Johnson, 2022). While children's behaviors may seem to align with items on the symptom lists for various disorders in the DSM-5-TR, therapists might first consider the underlying reasons for the behavior and the context for an individual child through a non-pathological perspective (Probst, 2006).

DIAGNOSTIC IMPRESSION AS A GUIDE

At the beginning of therapy services, there is a presenting concern or challenge, often referred to, in traditional medical terminology, as the *presenting problem.* Rather than seeing it as a problem to be solved, however, a more inclusive way to frame this concept is to see it as a challenge through which the client can learn and grow in therapy. The presenting challenge most often motivates caregivers to seek therapy for the child. Identifying the presenting challenge will be one stepping stone on the path to determining a diagnostic impression, which provides a launch toward case conceptualization and the therapy planning processes (Schwitzer & Rubin, 2012; Wonders, 2021b). The root of *diagnosis* is the Greek word *diagignōskein,* which means *to distinguish* or *discern.* While the term *diagnosis* has since become associated with the scientific determination of pathology, it may be worth revisiting the root meaning to use the diagnostic process as a directional sign for the therapeutic journey toward the most optimal route to take rather than a fixed determinant. Doing so will aid in the effort to avoid pathologizing children and instead lead to seeking to understand underlying causes for behaviors and develop a plan to support the resolution of those underlying causes.

While listening for concerns and challenges, the clinician identifies symptomatic patterns that align with the diagnostic criteria outlined in the DSM-5-TR. While there has been discussion about perceived problems with the DSM-5 (Clark et al., 2017; Michelini et al., 2020; Wakefield, 2016; Yager, 2017; Ross & Margolis, 2019), we can mindfully employ symptomology and the diagnostic criteria as a starting point for conceptualization and therapy planning (Jongsma et al., 2014; Wonders, 2021b). The initial working diagnosis can be established early during therapy, pointing the clinician toward a path to gain a greater understanding of what the client is experiencing and needing through case conceptualization (Schwitzer & Rubin, 2012). Ideally, the child, caregiver(s), and therapist will work together to determine the presenting challenge on which the therapy will first focus (Hawley & Weisz, 2003; Zubernis et al., 2017). As the case conceptualization process unfolds, fluidity is important as often the presenting challenge can be merely a directional sign pointing to a bigger or deeper challenge (Wonders, 2021b). The initial diagnosis will sometimes change during case conceptualization and through treatment based on new information gained. The diagnosis, therefore, need not limit the course of therapy to one direction but rather serve as an initial cue guiding the therapist to begin shaping the course of therapy and the plan for best supporting a child's challenges while remaining flexible as needed if new information is presented.

CASE CONCEPTUALIZATION

Sperry and Sperry (2020) assert that case conceptualization is the one competency counselors most need subsequent to forming the therapeutic alliance. The authors define conceptualization as a process for developing a map that guides counselors in understanding and addressing the reasons for a client's presenting concerns. Case conceptualizations provide the landscape from which interventions can be chosen and applied to achieve therapy goals. According to Sperry & Sperry (2020), there are eight elements they call "the eight P's" that illustrate the elements of case conceptualization:

Presentation: symptoms, expressed concerns, therapist's observations

Predisposition: biological, psychological, and social factors

Precipitants: causative or coinciding stressors such as pain and trauma

Protective Factors and Strengths: secure attachment, coping skills, positive support systems

Pattern: predictable and persistent personality tendencies

Perpetuates: processes through which patterns are processed and perpetuated

Plan: goals, objectives, clinical decision-making, and ethical considerations

Prognosis: forecast for client's expected response to therapy

The case conceptualization or formulation process begins when caregivers first initiate therapy, and this process continues throughout the phases of therapy. The initial step occurs in the first phase of therapy and, more specifically, in the intake session. From there, the lion's share of the work happens in the intake process. The intake provides the opportunity for the therapist to gather multifaceted information that will evolve into a holistic framework of understanding what the child is experiencing currently, what has contributed to these experiences in the past, and how therapy can best support growth, development, relief, and healing (Thomassin & Hunsely, 2019).

THE INTAKE

As the therapist is meeting with caregivers, there are three processes practiced simultaneously: (1) building trust and rapport between the therapist and caregivers, (2) collecting information needed for case formulation, and (3) assessing for presenting concerns and other contributing factors. In the intake, the therapist connects with caregivers, hearing their concerns with empathy while also gathering essential information to begin case conceptualization. The therapist needs to inquire about all of the systems to which the client belongs (O'Connor & Ammen, 2013). If possible and appropriate, having conversations with as many of the people in the child's systems, such as other caregivers, teachers, and school counselors, can assist in conceptualization and aid in the course of treatment (Dowell & Ogles, 2010; O'Connor & Ammen, 2013). As clinicians gather information, the therapist will inquire about medical history, psycho-social history, and familial and social systems context, with sensitivity to cultural influences.

Biopsychosocial Intake Model

During the intake, the clinician can use a *biopsychosocial intake model* to understand how the history of physical, psychological, and social events has shaped the child's development (Zastrow et al., 2018). The form of biopsychosocial intake may differ depending on the theoretical approach from which a clinician is operating, but overall, a biopsychosocial approach considers factors that contribute to the conceptualization of every individual case. Using the biopsychosocial model has moved mental health professionals beyond seeing humans as only a mind and body; understanding clients' life experiences are multifaceted (Peterson et al., 2015). The domains found in a traditional biopsychosocial model can be expanded to include inquiry as to the child's use of and access to technology and time spent in nature, given recent research about the benefits of nature for children's mental health (Tillman et al., 2018) and the effects of digital technology on children's development (Chen et al., 2023; Santos et al., 2022; Siskind et al., 2022). The editors of this book have included examples of a multi-contextual biopsychosocial intake model along with a COVID-19 pandemic intake form, given the far-reaching impact of the pandemic on families everywhere (see Appendix A.2 and A.3).

Developmental Intake Model

When working with children in therapy, the developmental dimension is paramount. The therapist seeks information to conceptualize the child's developmental age that may or may not match the child's chronological age (Drobinin et al., 2022). The therapist may consult the CDC's developmental milestones resources (Zubler et al., 2022). Based on information gathered in the biopsychosocial assessment, the clinician can assess for normal, advanced, delayed, and deviant markers of development. Attuning to the child's past and current developmental milestones provides the therapist with essential information to prescriptively choose theoretical models, approaches, and ways to shape the therapy plan (Choo et al., 2019).

Temporal and Contextual Intake Model

Zubernis et al. (2017) introduced a case conceptualization model that hears the client's presenting challenges through a filter of contextual factors that influence the client's lived experience. The model emphasizes the relationship between the client's inner world (values, attitudes, beliefs, self-view) as experienced and expressed through the client's thoughts, emotions, and behaviors and the child's outer world (family, school, social, community, cultural systems). With this framework, the clinician considers when the issues began, what factors were at play then and now, whether there are patterns, and how the child's systems impede or contribute to the therapy progress.

Screening for Adversity in the Intake

The Adverse Childhood Experiences (ACEs) screening tool is a means to collect information about negative experiences that may have contributed to a child's experience of trauma (Watson, 2019). Meraj et al. (2022) recently introduced a new intake tool called Adverse Life Events Inventory (ALEI) that enhanced an existing mental health intake instrument, the interRAITM Child and Youth Mental Health instrument providing consideration of a wider variety of adverse events than the ACEs instrument. Clinicians can use tools such as these during the intake to consider how traumatizing experiences may contribute to a child's social, mental, and emotional health.

Cultural Humility in Case Conceptualization

Cultural humility, both an interpersonal and an intrapersonal process, is defined as an introspective, personal ongoing commitment to reflect on one's own cultural identity, learn about one's own cultural identity, seek to understand others' cultural backgrounds and identities, and examine one's own implicit biases (Lekas et al., 2020). With it, clinicians remain humble, curious, and respectful of all facets of people, and their cultures, including ethnicity, race, sexual orientation, gender, and ability status, without assumptions (Hook et al., 2015; Yeager & Bauer-Wu, 2013; Zhang et al., 2022). Through the processes of establishing rapport and gathering information through the developmental biopsychosocial intake with each client and their caregivers, therapists can invite caregivers and child clients to share anything they would like to share about their culture, background, and community that may help the therapist to understand their lived experiences. The ORCAStance (Openness, Respect, Curiosity, and Accountability) is a model designed to provide a means through which we can ensure therapeutic productivity and authentic connectedness even when there are differences between the therapist's culture and the client's culture (Grauf-Grounds & Rivera, 2020, p. 23). Positive therapy outcomes are connected to therapists' practice of cultural humility (Zhang et al., 2022).

Collaborating With Caregivers

From the first encounter with caregivers, the collaborative experience between therapist and caregivers ideally continues throughout the therapy process. Suppose clinicians do not have a method and plan for involving caregivers in the process of the child's therapy, taking time for careful intake and assessment with caregivers, and building rapport with caregivers. In that case, there runs a risk of premature termination of therapy on the part of caregivers (Novick & Novick, 2011). For the therapist to keep the child as the center of focus while working with caregivers, the therapist must engage parents in therapy from the beginning while knowing when to refer caregivers for individual therapy or relationship therapy if needed. Caregivers can be invaluable resources within the therapeutic process through all three phases of therapy. In addition to the initial intake and assessments, the therapist can create a predictable rhythm of connecting with parents between the child's sessions through parent-consultation sessions, status update report forms, parent-child dyad sessions, and family sessions. It is essential to have caregivers invested in the continuity of therapy through all three phases.

GOALS AND OBJECTIVES

It is common for therapists providing play therapy to remain fluid in ongoing assessment. Some play therapy approaches rely solely on the ongoing needs presented by the child and family to guide the therapy. At first glance, it might seem that having goals for therapy with children would contradict that more fluid approach. The determination of needs can be a variable and flexible process. Considering children's rapid growth and development, ongoing assessment is critical (O'Connor & Ammen, 2013), but this fluid process can also be problematic. Without goals and objectives, the therapy process can feel directionless, leaving the therapist to feel adrift. Developing a goal-focused framework for therapy anchored by objectives to measure progress alleviates aimless feelings, equipping clinicians to have targets, direction, and guideposts along the way. Flexibility and flow can exist within the structure of the treatment plan. Goal-directed planning identifies priorities collaboratively with the child and caregivers and provides a focused target for measurable results (Stewart et al., 2022). The treatment plan is a living document (Homeyer, 2023), as it can shift and change depending on the developments in therapeutic dynamics and variables along the way. The overarching goals of therapy can keep therapy focused while the objectives allow for measuring progress. Interventions couched in theoretical orientation are the mechanism through which therapy is delivered. They may be as simple as child-centered practices of tracking and reflecting in session or directive activities such as sandtray creation with prompts, games, or invitations to explore specific toys or activities in the playroom. With goal-directed treatment planning, the clinician may prescriptively choose the approach to therapy based on reflective inquiries such as: (1) Which approach has the most empirically supported evidence of efficacy with the presenting issues? (2) Which approach best matches the child's and family's sociocultural identity and values? (3) Which approach matches the clinician's competency levels?

As reflected in the variety of theory-based approaches to providing therapy for children in this book, there are many perspectives and differing opinions on how or whether to use goals and objectives. This author argues that it is possible to be true to any theoretical orientation or approach when providing therapy for children while finding creative ways to establish goals and objectives collaboratively.

Nurcombe's (2014) model, called *goal-directed treatment planning*, was originally developed to meet the needs of pediatric hospitalization that had moved toward shorter-term in-patient stays. The model can also be useful in providing structure and accountability in outpatient psychotherapy. Goal-directed treatment planning asks three questions: (1) What are we aiming to achieve in therapy? (2) How will the client reach that achievement in therapy? (3) How will we know the client is on track toward reaching the goal? The model provides a six-step process:

Step 1: Identify both problems and potentials in the client and their circumstances.

Step 2: Turn the problems around into goals.

Step 3: Estimate the time required to achieve the goals.

Step 4: For each goal, choose at least two objectives.

Step 5: For each goal, determine evidence-based, sociocultural appropriate interventions.

Step 6: For each goal and objective, create a means to monitor and measure progress. (p. 9)

Target dates are established for objectives to serve as benchmarks and to shape the timeline of the therapy plan, avoiding the overwhelmingness some caregivers may feel with no end in sight. Those target dates can be changed and moved when unexpected dynamics or circumstances arise during therapy.

The phrasing of the goals will reflect the desired change to the problem and the use of the potential, if applicable.

Example Goals

- Reduce the intensity of anxiety symptoms.
- Enhance the child's self-efficacy.
- Increase the frequency of fun and laughter.
- Reduce the frequency of impulsive behavior.
- Resolve internal conflict regarding parents' divorce.
- Foster more active listening in parent-child communication.
- Foster natural artistic ability.

Objectives are specific. In writing objectives, the clinician includes samples of actions or behaviors that can be observed while working toward the goals. Well-written objectives provide a concrete step for caregivers, therapist, and child to see progress. Without objectives, goals risk being nebulous, abstract, and overwhelming.

Example Objectives

- Client will use breathing techniques before taking tests and presenting book reports to mitigate anxiety symptoms.
- Parents will report client sleeps independently by March 30.
- Client will attend two birthday parties before the end of June to practice social anxiety symptom management.
- Client will demonstrate a positive self-concept by naming three newly named positive attributes in session for 10 sessions in a row.

CONCLUSION

The process of mapping out a therapy plan was not part of what the original psychotherapy theorists introduced when they presented their theories and models for practice. Yet, over time, treatment planning has become an important part of the standards for ethical clinical recordkeeping and a necessity for participation in the health care system. In keeping with the essential relational focus of all child therapy theories, the thorough conceptualization of a child's challenges presented in therapy supports a strong connection between therapist and client while guiding the development of goals and objectives for therapy. When a therapist can view the wholeness of a child in the context of their family, school, community, and cultural systems and seek to understand what is underlying the challenging experiences and behaviors, it is possible to meet the necessities of medical model mandates while honoring the therapeutic alliance and the process of conceptualizing and developing a road map for therapy.

Key Takeaways

- ♡ Therapeutic relationship is foundational to therapy with children.
- ♡ Planning for the therapy can be both fluid and structured.
- ♡ While often challenging, it IS possible to be true to one's theoretical orientation while also meeting requirements of the medical model.
- ♡ Developing a goal-focused framework for therapy anchored by objectives to measure progress provides aim and structure.
- ♡ The diagnosis is not necessarily an endpoint, but rather a starting point from which the therapist can begin shaping the course of therapy.
- ♡ Case conceptualization a holistic framework of understanding the child's lived experience and what the child most needs.
- ♡ Gathering information about the contexts of the child's various systems and collaborating with caregivers with cultural humility is essential.

REFERENCES

Axline, V. M. (1981). *Play therapy: The groundbreaking book that has become a vital tool in the growth and development of children* (Vol. 125). Ballantine Books.

Bratton, S. C., Ray, D., Rhine, T., & Jones, L. (2005). The efficacy of play therapy with children: A meta-analytic review of treatment outcomes. *Professional psychology: research and practice, 36*(4), 376. https://doi.org/10.1037/0735-7028.36.4.376

Chen, Y. Y., Yim, H., & Lee, T. H. (2023). Negative impact of daily screen use on inhibitory control network in preadolescence: A two-year follow-up study. *Developmental Cognitive Neuroscience*, 101218. https://doi.org/10.1016/j.dcn.2023.101218

Choo, Y. Y., Agarwal, P., How, C. H., & Yeleswarapu, S. P. (2019). Developmental delay: identification and management at primary care level. *Singapore Medical Journal, 60*(3), 119. https://doi.org/10.11622/smedj.2019025

Clark, L. A., Cuthbert, B., Lewis-Fernández, R., Narrow, W. E., Reed, G. M. (2017). Three approaches to understanding and classifying mental disorder: ICD-11, DSM-5, and the National Institute of Mental Health. Research Domain Criteria (RDoC). *Psychol Sci Public Interest, 18*(2):72–145. https://doi.org10.1177/1529100617727266

Dowell, K. A., & Ogles, B. M. (2010). The effects of parent participation on child psychotherapy outcome: A meta-analytic review. *Journal of Clinical Child & Adolescent Psychology, 39*(2), 151–162. https://doi.org/10.1080/15374410903532585

Drobinin, V., Van Gestel, H., Helmick, C. A., Schmidt, M. H., Bowen, C. V., & Uher, R. (2022). The developmental brain age is associated with adversity, depression, and functional outcomes among adolescents. *Biological Psychiatry: Cognitive Neuroscience and Neuroimaging, 7*(4), 406–414. https://doi.org/10.1016/j.bpsc.2021.09.004

Fairburn, C. G., & Cooper, Z. (2011). Therapist competence, therapy quality, and therapist training. *Behavior Research and Therapy*, *49*(6–7), 373–378. https://doi.org/10.1016/j.brat.2011.03.005

Gehart, D. R. (2015). *Theory and treatment planning in counseling and psychotherapy*. Cengage Learning. https://search.worldcat.org/title/Theory-and-treatment-planning-in-counseling-and-psychotherapy/oclc/920805943

Giardino, A. P., Hudak, M. L., Sood, B. G., Pearlman, S. A., & Committee on Child Health financing. (2022). Considerations in the determination of medical necessity in children: Application to contractual language. *Pediatrics*, *150*(3). https://doi.org/10.1542/peds.2022-058882

Grauf-Grounds, C., & Rivera, P. M. (2020). The ORCAStance as a practice beyond cultural humility. In C. Grauf-Grounds, T. S. Sellers, S. A. Edwards, H. S. Cheon, D. Macdonald, S. Whitney, & P. M. Rivera (Eds.), *A practice beyond cultural humility*. Routledge. https://doi.org/10.4324/9780429340901

Halbur, D. (2011). *Developing your theoretical orientation in counseling and psychotherapy*. Pearson. https://search.worldcat.org/title/developing-your-theoretical-orientation-in-counseling-and-psychotherapy/oclc/569538265

Hancock, D. (2021). The role of toys and games in helping children reach their milestones. *Journal of Health Visiting*, *9*(1), 22–28. https://doi.org/10.12968/johv.2021.9.1.22

Hawley, K., & Weisz, J. (2003). Child, parent, and therapist (dis)agreement on target problems in outpatient therapy: The therapist's dilemma and its implications. *Journal of Consulting and Clinical Psychology*, *71*(1), 62–70. http://doi.org/10.1037/0022-006X.71.1.62

Homeyer, L. E., & Bennett, M. M. (2023). *The guide to play therapy documentation and parent consultation*. Taylor & Francis. https://doi.org/10.4324/9781003258766

Hook J. N., Davis D. E., Van Tongeren D. R., Hill P. C., Worthington E. L. Jr., Farrell J. E., & Dieke P. (2015). Intellectual humility and forgiveness of religious leaders. *The Journal of Positive Psychology*, *10*(6), 499–506.

Hughes, F. P. (2021). *Children, play, and development*. Sage. https://eric.ed.gov/?id=ED512184

Jongsma, A. E., Peterson, L. M., McInnis, W. P., & Bruce, T. J. (2014). *The child psychotherapy treatment planner*. Wiley.

Kohrt, B. A., Turner, E. L., Rai, S., Bhardwaj, A., Sikkema, K. J., Adelekun, A., ... & Jordans, M. J. (2020). Reducing mental illness stigma in healthcare settings: Proof of concept for a social contact intervention to address what matters most for primary care providers. *Social Science & Medicine*, *250*, 112852. https://doi.org/10.1016/j.socscimed.2020.112852

Koole, S. L., & Tschacher, W. (2016). Synchrony in psychotherapy: A review and an integrative framework for the therapeutic alliance. *Frontiers in Psychology*, *7*, 862. https://doi.org/10.3389/fpsyg.2016.00862

Landreth, G. L. (2012). *Play therapy: The art of the relationship*. Routledge. https://doi.org/10.4324/9781003255796

Lekas, H. M., Pahl, K., & Fuller Lewis, C. (2020). Rethinking cultural competence: Shifting to cultural humility. *Health Services Insights*, *13*, 1178632920970580. https://doi.org/10.1177/1178632920970580

Luepker, E. T. (2022). *Recordkeeping in psychotherapy and counseling: Ethics, practice and supervision*. Routledge. https://doi.org/10.4324/9781003150008

Meraj, N., Arbeau, K., Fadiya, B., Ketelaars, T., St. Pierre, J., Swart, G. T., & Zayed, R. (2022). Introducing the Adverse Life Events Inventory for Children (ALEIC): An examination of adverse experiences and related impacts in a large clinical sample of children and youth. Traumatology. Advance online publication. https://doi.org/10.1037/trm0000385

Michelini, G., Palumbo, I. M., DeYoung, C. G., Latzman, R., & Kotov, R. (2020). Linking RDoC and HiTOP: A new interface for advancing psychiatric nosology and neuroscience. https://doi.org/10.31234/osf.io/ps7tc

Novick, K. K., & Novick, J. (2011). *Working with parents makes therapy work*. Jason Aronson. https://www.ncbi.nlm.nih.gov/pmc/articles/PMC2387115/

Nurcombe, B. (2014). Diagnosis and treatment planning in child and adolescent mental health problems. *IACAPAP e-textbook of child and adolescent mental health*. Geneva: *International Association for Child and Adolescent Psychiatry and Allied Professions. Accessed at http://iacapap. org/wp-content/uploads/A.*

O'Connor, K. J., & Ammen, S. (2013). *Play therapy treatment planning and interventions: The ecosystemic model and workbook* (2nd ed.). Elsevier/Academic Press. https://doi.org/10.1016/b978-0-12-373652-9.00017-0

Peterson, A. L., Goodie, J. L., & Andrasik, F. (2015). Introduction to biopsychosocial assessment in clinical health psychology. In F. Andrasik, J. L. Goodie, & A. L. Peterson (Eds.), *Biopsychosocial assessment in clinical health psychology* (pp. 3–7). Guilford. https://psycnet.apa.org/record/2015-10562-001

Probst, B. (2006). Re-framing and de-pathologizing behavior in therapy for children diagnosed with psychosocial disorders. *Child and Adolescent Social Work Journal, 23*, 487–500. https://doi.org/10.1007/s10560-006-0066-5

Rathnakumar, D. (2020). Play therapy and children with intellectual disability. *Shanlax International Journal of Education, 8*(2), 35–42. https://doi.org/10.34293/education.v8i2.2299

Ray, D. (2021). *Advanced play therapy: Essential conditions, knowledge, and skills for child practice.* Taylor & Francis. https://doi.org/10.4324/9780203837269

Ross, C., & Margolis, R. (2019). Research domain criteria: Strengths, weaknesses, and potential alternatives for future psychiatric research. *Molecular Neuropsychiatry, 5*(4), 218–236. https://doi.org/10.1159/000501797

Santos, R. M. S., Mendes, C. G., Marques Miranda, D., & Romano-Silva, M. A. (2022). The association between screen time and attention in children: A systematic review. *Developmental neuropsychology, 47*(4), 175–192. https://doi.org/10.1080/87565641.2022.2064863

Schaefer, C. E., & Cangelosi, D. M. (1993). *Play therapy techniques.* Jason Aronson Inc. https://doi.org/10.1176/ps.45.12.1243

Schaefer, C. E., & Drewes, A. A. (2013). *The therapeutic powers of play: 20 core agents of change.* John Wiley & Sons. https://doi.org/10.1002/9781119140467.ch3

Schwitzer, A. M., & Rubin, L. C. (2012). *Diagnosis & treatment planning skills: A popular culture casebook approach.* Sage. https://psycnet.apa.org/record/2011-24377-000

Siskind, D., Conlin, D., Hestenes, L., Kim, S. A., Barnes, A., & Yaya-Bryson, D. (2022). Balancing technology and outdoor learning: Implications for early childhood teacher educators. *Journal of Early Childhood Teacher Education, 43*(3), 389–405. https://doi.org/10.1080/10901027.2020.1859024

Sperry, L., & Sperry, J. J. (2020). *Case conceptualization: Mastering this competency with ease and confidence.* Routledge. https://doi.org/10.4324/9780429288968

Stewart, V., McMillan, S. S., Hu, J., Ng, R., El-Den, S., O'Reilly, C., & Wheeler, A. J. (2022). Goal planning in mental health service delivery: A systematic integrative review. *Frontiers in Psychiatry, 13*, 1057915. https://doi.org/10.3389/fpsyt.2022.1057915

Stockton, R., & Sharma, R. (2019). Advocacy, third-party Payers, and managed care. *Clinical Mental Health Counseling: Practicing in Integrated Systems of Care,* 243. https://doi.org/10.1891/9780826131089.0012

Suhr, J. A., & Johnson, E. E. (2022). First do no harm: Ethical issues in pathologizing normal variations in behavior and functioning. *Psychological Injury and Law, 15*(3), 253–267. https://doi.org/10.1007/s12207-022-09455-z

Thomassin, K., & Hunsley, J. (2019). Case conceptualization. *Treatment of Disorders in Childhood and Adolescence, 1*, 8–26. https://psycnet.apa.org/record/2019-19530-002

Tillmann, S., Tobin, D., Avison, W., & Gilliland, J. (2018). Mental health benefits of interactions with nature in children and teenagers: A systematic review. *J Epidemiol Community Health, 72*(10), 958–966. https://doi.org/10.1136/jech-2018-210436

Treichler, E. B. H., Evans, E. A., & Spaulding, W. D. (2021). Ideal and real treatment planning processes for people with serious mental illness in public mental health care. *Psychological Services, 18*(1), 93–103. https://doi.org/10.1037/ser0000361

Tschacher, W., Haken, H., & Kyselo M. (2015). Alliance: A common factor of psychotherapy modeled by structural theory. *Frontiers in Psychology, 6*, 421 . https://doi.org/10.3389/fpsyg.2015.00421

Wakefield, J. C. (2016). Diagnostic issues and controversies in DSM-5: Return of the false positives problem. *Annual Review of Clinical Psychology, 12*(1), 105–132. https://doi.org/10.1146/annurev-clinpsy-032814-112800

Watson P. (2019). How to screen for ACEs in an efficient, sensitive, and effective manner. *Paediatrics & Child Health, 24*(1), 37–38. https://doi.org/10.1093/pch/pxy146

Wiger, D. E. (2020). *The psychotherapy documentation primer*. Wiley. https://www.wiley.com/en-be/The+Psychotherapy+Documentation+Primer,+4th+Edition-p-9781119709930

Wonders, L. L. (2021a). Purposeful application of theory to case conceptualization and treatment planning. In J. Stone (Ed.), *Play Therapy and Telemental Health* (pp. 25–44). Routledge. https://doi.org/10.4324/9781003166498-2

Wonders, L. L. (2021b). Theoretical roots and branches of the evolving field of play therapy. In J. Stone (Ed.), *Play Therapy and Telemental Health* (pp. 2–24). Routledge. https://doi.org/10.4324/9781003166498-1

Yager, J., & Feinstein, R. E. (2017). Potential applications of the National Institute of mental health's research domain criteria (RDoC) to clinical psychiatric practice. *The Journal of Clinical Psychiatry, 78*(04), 423–432. https://doi.org/10.4088/jcp.15nr10476

Yeager, K.., & Bauer-Wu, S. (2013). Cultural humility: Essential foundation for clinical researchers. *Applied Nursing Research, 26*(4): 251–256. https://doi.org/10.1016/j.apnr.2013.06.008

Zastrow, C., Kirst-Ashman, K. K., & Hessenauer, S. L. (2018). Empowerment series: Understanding human behavior and the social environment (11th ed., pp.8–9). Cengage Learning US. https://bookshelf.vitalsource.com/books/9781337670722

Zhang, H., Watkins Jr, C. E., Hook, J. N., Hodge, A. S., Davis, C. W., Norton, J., ... & Owen, J. (2022). Cultural humility in psychotherapy and clinical supervision: A research review. *Counselling and Psychotherapy Research, 22*(3), 548–557. https://doi.org/10.1002/capr.12481

Zubler, J. M., Wiggins, L. D., Macias, M. M., Whitaker, T. M., Shaw, J. S., Squires, J. K., Pajek, J. A., Wolf, R. B., Slaughter, K. S., Broughton, A. S., Gerndt, K. L., Mlodoch, B. J., & Lipkin, P. H. (2022). Evidence-informed milestones for developmental surveillance tools. Pediatrics. https://doi.org/10.1542/peds.2021-052138

Zubernis, L., Snyder, M., & Neale-McFall, C. (2017). Case conceptualization: Improving understanding and treatment with the temporal/contextual model. *Journal of Mental Health Counseling, 39*(3), 181–194. https://doi.org/10.17744/mehc.39.3.01

CHAPTER 2

UNDERSTANDING THE CONTEXT OF HUMAN DEVELOPMENT IN TREATMENT PLANNING

Cary McAdams Hamilton

INTRODUCTION

Child therapists, who engage in the therapeutic powers of play and expressive therapies, acknowledge that each child has their path, way of being, and development that is unique to them. Respect for a child and the state of childhood begins when we understand that each child has a unique worldview. They are constantly transitioning between their perceived world and that of reality, where adults have power and the ability to influence how their growth is realized. Respecting each child's specific way of thinking and sensing, their perceptions, and how they experience being in the world is our starting point when getting to know them as therapists (Landreth, 2012). The unique aspects of every child must be front and center in the therapeutic healing process that occurs within the relationship of the therapeutic process (Ray, 2015). Research across professional fields confirms that developmental milestones follow a predictable pattern of growth (Osher et al., 2021; Ray, 2015; Szalavitz & Perry, 2010; Copple and Bredekamp, 2009). This sequential trajectory includes cognitive, physiological, socioemotional, communication, and learning. A child's personality develops through life experiences within their culture and on predictable timelines.

The assessment process with children and adolescents requires intensive information gathering from the caregivers about the child's observable developmental experiences. Clinicians must acquire information from the child's family, school, and medical professionals about their developmental milestones and experiences. In addition, a clinician must apply informed analysis of the neurobiological interpersonal factors at play in the inter/intrapersonal realms of the child or adolescent. Additionally, the clinician should be informed if the child or adolescent has experienced trauma and, more importantly, understand trauma's effects on human development.

Once the narrative and the components of the child's life are better understood, the clinician applies the lenses of the developmental theories, the research on trauma, neurobiological interpersonal factors, and, increasingly, the growing body of research on neurodivergence when determining a course of treatment. The intent of this chapter is to empower the reader to apply the various lenses and concepts of known human development in addition to theoretical lenses when creating and developing a treatment plan for children and adolescents.

HUMAN DEVELOPMENTAL PRINCIPLES

According to Maslow's hierarchy of needs, humans require food, shelter, and relationships with other humans. The developing child has the best outcomes when there is physical and emotional safety. The process is slowed and, in severe cases, stalled when their basic needs

DOI: 10.4324/9781003334231-3

are unmet. Without physical and emotional safety, a child will be limited in their capacity to learn, express, and develop new skills, as well as limit their ability to experience wellness (Gaskill & Perry, 2014; Ray, 2015; Copple & Bredekamp, 2009). The type of relational care provided by the caretakers determines how a child will develop interpersonal attachments as children and in their future relationships.

Most developmental theories present and define the stages of human growth. They focus on the progression of human development as growth occurs by passing through stages, achieving a level of mastery, personality development, and the meaning of self (Gaskill & Perry, 2014; Ray, 2015; Copple & Bredekamp, 2009). Development cannot be rushed. It can, however, be slowed. Research has shown that while many children move through stages at predictable time frames, many do not, yet they can achieve the same level of functioning by adulthood. It is the goal of the therapist to be aware of various stages and assess for challenges or barriers that are preventing the child from moving through the stage or, if more time is needed, for mastery of the current stage (Ray, 2015; Osher et al., 2018; Copple and Bredekamp, 2009). It is important to understand that a different developmental trajectory does not denote pathology or deficits. Rather, the difference indicates a need for further understanding and compassionate curiosity for their story. A child must develop at their own pace and not be rushed in the context of therapy, or therapy may be more harmful than successful. The therapist should accept the child's presentation as authentic to their lived experience and understand that their individualized development falls on a continuum with progress occurring at their own unique pace.

Trauma often creates hiccups in the developmental process. How a child responds to trauma is, in part, determined by how well their basic survival needs are being met. If a child is not getting what they need for survival, their energy will be focused on maintaining homeostasis versus having energy for growth. The functional impact and length of recovery are determined by the various aspects of the child's development occurring when the trauma occurs. Conversely, a child who experiences trauma but has food, shelter, and loving relationships, will still have the energy for developmental growth and resilience (Gaskill and Perry, 2014). Child development and the integration of the mind and body proceed naturally. Any attempt to speed up or alter the expected trajectory of a child's development from its natural pace could lead to significant struggles or impairments. Ray (2015) states, "As a child's body and physical ability grow, cognitive understanding becomes more abstract, and their emotional life becomes more complex." A child's emotional well-being can be placed in jeopardy, or, at the minimum, the progression of development evolution is delayed. A therapist's goal when creating a treatment plan is to glean the pertinent information to tailor interventions to meet the child's therapeutic needs (Ray, 2015).

Regardless of the developmental theoretical approach, treatment plans provide a guide based on the assessed needs and specific methods necessary to support healing and growth for the client. They outline proposed goals, time frames, and therapeutic modalities to treat the identified diagnosis or presenting problem. Treatment plans are flexible and require regular review with the client to know how and when changes are necessary and to track developmental growth.

DEVELOPMENTAL MODELS

This section will review the core human developmental models to provide a framework for a child's movement through the ages and stages of maturation. Additionally, it will provide a reminder of how societal and environmental contexts are invaluable components of assessing and treating children and adolescents. These models were developed over the last century and have been supported and adjusted with current research (Ray, 2015; Osher et al., 2018; Gaskill & Perry, 2014; Copple & Bredekamp, 2009). The impact of the neuroscience field on human development has created a significant understanding of brain phase development and the relational dynamics at play when looking at brain states in child development and maturation (Gaskill & Perry, 2014; Szalavitz & Perry, 2010; Kestly, 2014).

Maturational-Developmental Theory

One of the earliest developmental theorists was Arnold Gesell, who conducted research via observations of children from infancy to adolescence. Gesell noted that a child's development followed a cyclical pattern with periods of equilibrium and disequilibrium within established norms of each age in motor development, adaptive behavior, language, and personal-social behaviors. Gesell defined *equilibrium* as stages characterized by calm, compliance, and confidence, while children in "disequilibrium" stages may be explosive, fearful, and self-involved (Ray, 2015; Weizmann & Harris, 2012). Current practices continue to hold Gesell's observation and theory in practice when conceptualizing a child's development and are particularly notable in assessing a child's behaviors for treatment.

Gesell acknowledged that professionals must know children's growth patterns are unique. While a child may cycle through stages, it may not be at specified ages. Notably, children of any age will experience times of upset or imbalance within themselves and those around them. Therefore, behaviors or actions that are perceived as challenging are to be expected and seen as part of the human developmental experience. Being mindful of inter and intrapersonal relationships and experiences continue to determine the pace and level of integration occurring in the child's development at the time of assessment.

Erikson's Psychosocial Theory

Erik Erikson's psychodynamic psychosocial theory is founded on the belief that humans are motivated to develop socially and in relation to their environment (Ray, 2015; Copple & Bredekamp, 2009). Erikson's theory supposes that one's identity or personality is developed throughout the stages of human development. Erikson designated eight stages in the human lifespan. With each stage, there are specific psychosocial or emotional challenges. Sequential movement through the stages is accomplished by resolving the crisis of the prior stage. When developmental tasks are unresolved or prevented, the cumulative effect and timing of the failure in development create clinically significant pathology. Erikson's theory of development is foundational to case conceptualization and treatment planning for child therapists (Wonders, 2021).

Loevinger's Ego Development

American psychologist, Jane Loevinger, viewed ego development as internalizing social constructs and the development of conscience in making personal decisions. Loevinger theorized that the "ego" is in constant flux based on experiences and struggles. Loevinger believed that ego development emerges from the self's encounter with the world as it seeks to make sense of, interact with, and construct images of the world and relate to others within it. Personality development is acquired via successive freedoms, initially from personal impulses, followed by conventions and social pressures (Ray, 2015; Armstrong, 2020). Loevinger believed a human could theoretically operate from any stage, not wanting to set concrete ego development stages. "Loevinger introduced the idea that the essence of ego is the striving to master, understand, organize, and integrate experience and that one's sense of self or ego is in constant flux, depending on experiences and challenges" (Ray, 2015, p. 7). Loevinger's theory encourages child therapists to focus on the child's internal drive toward learning and mastery of self and understanding based on their lived context.

Piaget's Cognitive Theory

Jean Piaget is perhaps one of the best-known cognitive developmental theorists. Piaget determined that children learn by doing, and a child's reality is constructed based on experiences they have in their environment. His four stages of development: Sensorimotor (0–2 years), Preoperational (2–7 years), Concrete Operations (7–11 years), and Formal Operations (11 years–adult) are preceded by chronological age, brain development, and learned patterns of thinking as they become adults (Mercer, 2018). While age is part of Piaget's theory, it is the pace of life experiences and mastery of each stage that denotes progress. Piaget provides guidance and support for therapists to assess the child's cognitive development and presenting level of functioning based on their chronological age and perspective life experience.

Kohlberg's Moral Development

Lawrence Kohlberg's theory of moral development focused on applying cognitive reasoning to moral decision-making. Therefore, his interest lay not in the moral choice but in the person's process to reach their decision. Kohlberg's theory has three levels: Pre-conventional (infancy to preschool), Conventional (school age), and Post Conventional (adolescence to adulthood), consisting of six stages overall: Obedience and Punishment Orientation, Individualism and Exchange, Good Interpersonal Relationships, Maintaining the Social Order, Social Contract and Individual Rights, and Universal Principles (Mercer, 2018). Kohlberg did presuppose that the higher stages of moral development are "better" as they involve more complex and integrated cognitive processes. He was clear that higher moral development meant only morally superior thinkers, not better humans. Adults, therefore, are not morally superior to children; adults have adult levels of cognition, and children have child levels of cognition. To guide a child's development therapeutically, a therapist must first listen to a child's view or perspective to understand where they are on their path of moral development.

Vygotsky's Cognitive Development Theory

Lev Vygotsky made significant contributions with his cognitive development theory based on his term "zone of proximal development." In Vygotsky's view, children's cognitive development is affected by culture in two ways: by teaching children what to think and how to think (Scheithauer et al., 2022). Intellectual growth is a dialectical process in which problem-solving opportunities are provided through social agents such as siblings, caregivers, and teachers. Vygotsky called the difference between what children can and cannot do by themselves the "zone of proximal development." Much like the belief of child therapists in the therapeutic powers of play (Schaffer & Drewes, 2014), Vygotsky's developmental model determined that play is integral to child development as it liberates children to be their current age to reach higher levels of cognitive development without the confines of reality (Scheithauer et al., 2022; Ray, 2015). Vygotsky did not offer a stage theory of development, but his extensive research offered a greater understanding of the developmental processes that occur in the early stages of childhood (Ray, 2015). This theory is particularly valuable for child therapists seeking to use expressive and play therapy as their therapeutic process. It presupposes the need for creative whole-body expression for learning and developing.

Greenspan's Emotional Development

Stanley Greenspan determined that it was our emotional health and relationships that drive our behavior, thinking, and communication (Greenspan & Benderly, 1997). He built upon the theories of Erikson and Piaget, focusing on the significance of children's emotional lives in their development. Greenspan identified four areas or "milestones" all children need to navigate for emotional growth: self-regulation, relationships, reality and fantasy, and communication from birth to age 12 (Greenspan & Benderly, 1997). Like other developmental models, a child must achieve mastery over the challenges associated with each area or "milestone," noting that a child may need support to develop the mastery needed for each area. Greenspan was the first to use the concepts of kinesthetic, sensorimotor regulation, and relational connectedness to foster cognitive development and emotional resilience as part of a child's development (Greenspan & Benderly, 1997). These are key factors to address in conceptualizing therapeutic goals for children in treatment.

Attachment Theory

Attachment theorists, such as John Bowlby, Harry Harlow, and Konrad Lorenz, theorized that children are biologically hardwired to form attachments to other humans for survival (Stewart et al., 2014). It is the caregiver's responsiveness that fosters the biopsychosocial development of the child. Leading neuroscience researchers Bruce Perry, Daniel Siegel, and Allen Schore have agreed with the conclusion that the critical window of the development for attachment is between the ages of 0–5 years. Disruptions, trauma, and lack of attachment during this time lead to significant developmental consequences across all domains of life (Kestly, 2014; Stewart et al., 2014).

Bowlby's theory, derived from evolution theory, ethology, and cybernetics, provides evidence that human bonding is necessary for survival (Mellenthien, 2019; McLeod, 1970). Ainsworth later identified different attachment styles (Secure, Insecure-Avoidant, Insecure-Resistant, and Insecure-Disorganized) and defined the impact of each on human development and progression through the lifespan (Stewart et al., 2014; Mellenthien, 2019). Successive researchers and theorists reinforced these concepts with neuroscience confirming that attachment patterns established in early life, create significant neuronal patterns of integrated development (Kestly, 2014; Delahooke, 2019).

Regardless of the developmental theoretical approach, treatment plans provide a guide based on the assessed needs and specific methods necessary to support healing and growth for the client. They outline proposed goals, time frames, and therapeutic modalities to treat the identified diagnosis or presenting problem. Treatment plans are flexible and require regular review with the client to know how and when changes are necessary and to track developmental growth.

DEVELOPMENTAL MILESTONES OF HUMAN DEVELOPMENT

Human development in childhood means transformation and progression through the life stages. Traditional childhood developmental milestones are available from the Centers for Disease Control and Prevention (CDC) and the American Academy of Pediatrics (AAP). The research determined that 75% of children meet "standard" developmental milestones (Centers for Disease Control and Prevention, 2022). For each phase of human development: infant, toddler, preschooler, middle childhood, adolescent, and adult, there are four main areas, which include: physical, cognitive, social, and emotional, communication, and language. Like Gesell's theory, their milestones have alternating states of equilibrium and disequilibrium around specific ages that impact the emotions and behaviors in child development.

In initial interviews, clinicians must have concrete knowledge and awareness of human developmental milestones. It can be helpful to review the characteristics present in each age to address and assess if the client is: meeting, below, or above the presently known standard. Physical development includes maturation and growth, including body size, proportion, appearance, health, and perceptual abilities. Cognitive development is the maturation of thought processes and ways in which we obtain knowledge, develop an awareness of the world around us, and solve problems. Socioemotional development includes changes in personality, emotions, views of oneself, social skills, and interpersonal relationships with family and friends. Notably, each of these areas of development overlap and interact with each other in the context of the micro and macro environments a child is growing up in (Osher et al., 2018; Delahooke, 2019).

Human development consists of growth and decline, gains and losses, throughout the lifespan. Interpersonal dynamics, environmental contexts, and cultures leave a marked impact on a human's genetics, attachment, sensory profiles, ability to develop resilience, and adaptive functional patterns of life. Survival is at the core of human development, with the miraculous human brain as the conductor—the content and context of the life a brain experiences influence who we uniquely become in adulthood.

NEUROTYPICAL VS. NEURODIVERGENT DEVELOPMENT

While brains develop similarly, no two brains function just alike. Neurodiversity addresses the variations in the human brain, such as learning, mood, attention, sociability, and other mental functions, without assigning pathology and being neurodivergent means having a brain that works differently from the average or "neurotypical" person (Delahooke, 2019). Being neurodivergent is not considered a deficit but simply a difference in processing the world (Delahooke, 2019; Doyle, 2020).

Neurotypical individuals generally can navigate complex social situations, communicate well, establish social connections easily, and be in distracting environments without becoming overwhelmed (Grant, 2017; Doyle, 2020). Neurotypicals have acquired physical, verbal, cognitive, and social skills at the determined acceptable developmental milestones. As neurodivergence becomes more known and understood, ableist biases and sociocultural norms have yet to shift enough for the neurodevelopmental spectrum to be well accepted and understood.

Often neurodivergent humans, particularly children, rely on survival skills and the need for belonging to mask their neurodivergence to pass as neuronormative. During an assessment, their masking behavior can be confused as behavioral challenges, and the client risks being misidentified. Therefore, a clinician must keep an open mind for bias awareness and inclusive assessment of norms (Grant, 2023).

While working within the medical model (disability model), it is imperative to understand the world of the child and have social context awareness and family culture to be able to treat children within the present system of ableism. Grant (2023) states,

> We must continually commit to listening to, hearing, learning from, and contemplating the words, insights, and experiences of neurodivergent individuals. Therapists should strive to become non-ableist and affirming through a mindful and consistent pursuit to deconstruct society's conditioning and create new self-awareness. (p.1)

NEUROBIOLOGICAL INTERPERSONAL PRINCIPLES

Neuroscience is the combined disciplines of psychology and biology working in tandem. It describes human development and its functioning as understanding the relationship between body, mind, and relationships—called relations (Kestly, 2014; Siegel, 2016). Our internal human mechanism, the nervous system, drives our survival as humans and impacts how we interact with the dynamic elements of our lives. The nervous system creates human cognition and perception. Thus, when working with children, we must understand neurobiology and how it intersects and interacts with our thoughts, memory, cognition, perception, and function. Interpersonal neurobiology (IPNB) was developed by Dan Siegel and Allan Schore (Kestly, 2014; Delahooke, 2019). IPNB is the concept, founded on clinical evidence, that the human brain is continuously growing therefore, damage and healing occur throughout the lifespan. This continuous damage and healing process, creating new neurons and links, is called neuroplasticity. It is because of neuroplasticity that we know a child therapist can promote improved functioning if the child is in a respectful and compassionate environment and experiences internal and external regulation (Siegel, 2016; Kestly, 2014; Delahooke, 2019).

IPNB shares similarities with the Dynamic Maturational Model of Attachment and Adaptation (DMM). Both are transdisciplinary meta-models incorporating many fields of science to understand human functioning and are heavily reliant on attachment science and theory. The DMM grew specifically from Dr. Patricia Crittenden's research in attachment theory and her work with attachment founders Mary Ainsworth and John Bowlby. Applying IPNB and DMM in treatment planning allows for the convergence of modern sciences and historical theorists in creating a holistic developmental worldview of a child (Osher et al., 2018).

TRAUMA'S IMPACT ON HUMAN DEVELOPMENT

Trauma is defined as experiencing an event perceived as life-threatening and inescapable. The experience of trauma can have lasting adverse effects on functioning and mental, physical, social, emotional, or spiritual well-being. The impact of trauma on childhood is complex and multidimensional, varying with the stage of development a child is in when the event occurs. Knowing the "brain state" when the traumatic event occurs is fundamental to understanding and addressing the healing therapeutically in Dr. Bruce Perry's Neurosequential Model of Therapeutics (NMT). The NMT model forces clinicians to pay attention to a child's brain-mediated strengths and vulnerabilities (Gaskill & Perry, 2014). Humans are hardwired for connection; therefore, one's attachments and life experiences dramatically impact a developing brain's capacity to form resilience. The expressive and play-based therapeutic processes that innately engages the physiological sensations, emotions, and cognitions, in both verbal and nonverbal expressions, are particularly theoretically aligned to treating a child during their development. Where traditional psychodynamic or cognitive behavioral therapies strive to support the development of cognitive regulation and control in therapy, they fail to attune to the lower brain developmental stage children are experiencing, which is disorganized, underdeveloped, or even impaired. A neurodevelopmental-informed assessment and treatment plan will align with a child's general developmental stage and brain state reactivity, especially after a traumatic event (Gaskill & Perry, 2014; Delahooke, 2021).

CONCLUSION

This chapter intends to draw attention to the importance of understanding the role human development plays in the assessment of clients and the treatment planning process. No two humans develop in the same way. Scholars, practitioners, and researchers throughout the history of psychology have studied and theorized how our environments, genetics, the influence of culture, and traumatic events influence the development and, importantly, what those differences mean when assessing and treating a client. This research is ever-evolving. Emerging research in neuroscience, INPB, and the effect trauma has on the developing brain, will continue to influence a clinician's understanding of and creation of treatment plans focused on healing. The functionality of treatment plans can only exist if the foundational knowledge of how a child develops and the impact of the environment in which it develops is assessed for and considered in its creation.

Key Takeaways

- Children are constantly transitioning between their perceived world and that of reality, where adults have power and the ability to influence how their growth is realized.
- Developmental milestones follow a predictable pattern of growth.
- Clinicians need to acquire information from the child's family, school, and medical professionals about their developmental milestones and experiences.
- Clinicians' must apply informed analysis of the neurobiological factors at play in the inter/intrapersonal realms of the child or adolescent.
- Differences in developmental trajectories indicate a need for further understanding and compassionate curiosity.
- Treatment plans are flexible and require regular review with the client to know how and when changes are necessary to track developmental growth.
- The content and context of the life a brain experiences influence who a child uniquely becomes in adulthood.
- Therapists must understand neurobiology and interpersonal neurobiology in the context of human development.
- The functionality of treatment plans can only exist if the foundational knowledge of how a child develops and the impact of the environment in which it develops is assessed for and considered in its creation.

REFERENCES

Armstrong, T. (2020, January 31). *The stages of ego development, according to Jane Loevinger*. The American Institute for Learning and Human Development. Retrieved December 7, 2022, from https://www.institute4learning.com/2020/01/31/the-stages-of-ego-development-according-to-jane-loevinger/

Centers for Disease Control and Prevention. (2022, August 17). *CDC's Developmental Milestones*. Centers for Disease Control and Prevention. Retrieved December 7, 2022, from https://www.cdc.gov/ncbddd/actearly/milestones/index.html

Copple, C., & Bredekamp, S. (2009). *Developmentally appropriate practice in early childhood programs serving children from birth through age 8*. National Association for the Education of Young Children.

Delahooke, M. (2019). *Beyond behaviors: Using brain science and compassion to understand and solve children's behavioral challenges*. Pesi Publishers .

Doyle, N. (2020). Neurodiversity at work: A biopsychosocial model and the impact on working adults. *British Medical Bulletin, 135*(1), 108–125. https://doi.org/10.1093/bmb/ldaa021

Gaskill, R. L., & Perry, B. D. (2014). The neurobiological power of play: Using the neurosequential model of therapeutics to guide play in the healing process. In C. A. Malchiodi & D. A. Crenshaw (Eds.), *Creative arts and play therapy for attachment problems* (pp. 178–194). Guilford. https://psycnet.apa.org/record/2013-43568-011

Grant, R. J. (2017). *AutPlay therapy for children and adolescents on the autism spectrum: A behavioral play-based approach*. Routledge. https://doi.org/10.4324/9781315657684

Grant, R. J. (2023, March 3). *Play therapist: Your neurodiversity journey matters*. AutPlay Therapy. RetrievedDecember7,2022,fromhttps://autplaytherapy.com/play-therapist-your-neurodiversity-journey-matters/

Greenspan, S. I., & Benderly, B. L. (1997). *The growth of the mind and the endangered origins of Intelligence*. Perseus Books. https://doi.org/10.5860/choice.34-6548

Kestly, T. A. (2014). *The interpersonal neurobiology of play: Brain-building interventions for emotional well-being*. Norton. https://psycnet.apa.org/record/2014-37632-000

Landreth, G. L., & Teja, C. (2012). *Play therapy: The art of the relationship*. Routledge. https://doi.org/10.4324/9781003255796

Malchiodi, C. A., & Crenshaw, D. A. (2014). *Creative arts and play therapy for attachment problems*. Guilford. https://www.routledge.com/Creative-Arts-and-Play-Therapy-for-Attachment-Problems/Malchiodi-Crenshaw/p/book/9781462523702

McLeod, S. (1970, January 1). *What is attachment theory? Attachment theory: Bowlby and Ainsworth's theory explained*. Retrieved December 7, 2022, from https://www.simplypsychology.org/attachment.html

Mellenthin, C. (2019). *Attachment centered play therapy*. Routledge. https://doi.org/10.4324/9781315229348-3

Mercer, J. A. (2018). *Child development: Concepts and theories*. Sage.

Osher, D., Cantor, P., Berg, J., Steyer, L., & Rose, T. (2018). Drivers of human development: How relationships and context shape learning and development. *Applied Developmental Science, 24*(1), 6–36. https://doi.org/10.1080/10888691.2017.1398650

Osher, D., Cantor, P., Berg, J., Steyer, L., & Rose, T. (2021). Drivers of human development: How relationships and context shape learning and development 1. In The Science of Learning and Development (pp. 55–104). Routledge.

Ray, D. C. (2015). *A therapist's guide to child development: The extraordinarily normal years*. Taylor & Francis. https://doi.org/10.4324/9781315737959

Rudy, L. J. (2022, August 27). *Are you neurotypical or neurodiverse?* Verywell Health. Retrieved December 7, 2022, from https://www.verywellhealth.com/what-does-it-mean-to-be-neurotypical-260047

Schaefer, C. E., & Drewes, A. A. (2014). The therapeutic powers of play: 20 core agents of change. Wiley. https://onlinelibrary.wiley.com/doi/10.1002/9781119140467.ch3

Scheithauer, H., Hess, M., Zarra-Nezhad, M., Peter, C., & Wölfer, R. (2023). Developmentally appropriate prevention of behavioral and emotional problems, social-emotional learning, and developmentally appropriate practice for early childhood education and care: The Papilio-3to6

Program. *International Journal of Developmental Science, 16*(3–4), 81–97. https://doi.org/10.3233/dev-220331

Scheithauer, H., Hess, M., Zarra-Nezhad, M., Peter, C., & Wölfer, R. (2022). Developmentally appropriate prevention of behavioral and emotional problems, social-emotional learning, and developmentally appropriate practice for early childhood education and care: The Papilio-3 to 6 program. *International Journal of Developmental Science,* 1–17. https://doi.org/10.3233/dev-220331

Siegel D. J., & Bryson T. P. (2016). *The whole-brain child: 12 revolutionary strategies to nurture your child's developing mind.* Delacorte Press.

Stewart, A., Whelan, W., & Pendleton, C. (2014). Attachment theory as a road map for play therapists. In C. A. Malchiodi & D. A. Crenshaw (Eds.), *Creative arts and play therapy for attachment problems* (pp. 35–51. Guilford.

Szalavitz, M., & Perry, B. D. (2010). *The boy who was raised as a dog: And other stories from a child psychiatrist's notebook—what traumatized children can teach us about loss, love, and healing.* Basic Books.

Weizmann, F., & Harris, B. (2012). Arnold Gesell: The maturationist. In *Portraits of pioneers in developmental psychology* (pp. 1–20). Psychology Press. https://www.taylorfrancis.com/chapters/edit/10.4324/9780203806135-1/arnold-gesell-maturationist-weizmann-fredric-ben-harris

Wonders, L. L. (2021). Purposeful application of theory to case conceptualization and treatment planning. In J. Stone (Ed.), *Play Therapy and Telemental Health* (pp. 25–34). Routledge. https://doi.org/10.4324/97810031664

CHAPTER 3

CULTURAL IMPLICATIONS TO TREATMENT PLANNING FOR CHILDREN AND FAMILIES

Rebeca Chow

INTRODUCTION

Culture is full of rich histories and shared stories existing within the larger sociopolitical context that influences the power, privilege, and opportunities we have in everyday life. The child's cultural values, beliefs, practices, and attitudes in the counseling room shape their presenting challenge and determine the treatment plan. Culture is a complex concept because it constantly changes and evolves, making the treatment planning process unique to each individual and family (Chan et al., 2018). Faulkner et al. (2006) caution against attempting to provide one definition of culture but rather consider seven themes: (1) structure/pattern (culture as ideas, behaviors, symbols), (2) function (culture as a means for achieving an outcome), (3) process (culture as an ongoing process of social construction), (4) product (culture as a collection of artifacts), (5) refinement (culture as individual or group cultivation to higher intellect or morality), (6) group membership (culture as signifying a place or group of people, including a focus on belonging to a place or group), and (7) power or ideology (culture as an expression of group-based domination and power). To understand culture in treatment planning, clinicians must remain nonjudgmental in listening to the child and family's perspective while identifying how to address, reduce, manage, or resolve the client's presenting challenge.

MULTICULTURAL ORIENTATION FRAMEWORK IN TREATMENT PLAN

Connecting a treatment plan with a theoretical framework is essential for providing effective mental health services from a cultural perspective. The Multicultural Orientation (MCO) framework can be used to understand how different cultural identities interact to shape a child and family's experience. The MCO framework recognizes that individuals have multiple identities and that these identities interact with each other to create unique experiences of oppression and privilege (Davis et al., 2018; Zhang et al., 2022). From this theoretical framework, the client and the therapist interact and influence one another to co-create a relational experience and inclusive therapeutic environment. Rather than being a comprehensive therapeutic model that outlines the nature of psychopathology/ health, personality, and so on, the MCO framework supplements existing psychotherapy models (e.g., cognitive-behavioral therapy, interpersonal, psychodynamic, or systems). This framework outlines a therapist's "way of being" in session (cultural humility), a way of recognizing and responding to cultural markers in the session (cultural opportunities), and a way of understanding the self in these moments (cultural comfort) (Davis et al., 2018; Ray et al., 2022; Rigg et al., 2020).

DOI: 10.4324/9781003334231-4

Based on the MCO framework, while creating a treatment plan, the culturally humble therapist strives to use opportunities in the session to develop cultural comfort for engaging various clients' cultural identities during treatment. The therapist's professional responsibility is to engage cultural humility by accepting his or her inability to know everything and demonstrating respect for those who do know (i.e., family members or support system) (SoHoo, 2013; Ray et al., 2022). Hook et al. (2017) defines cultural humility as "an awareness of one's limitations" to understand the client's cultural background and experience… and an interpersonal stance that is other-oriented rather than self-focused regarding the cultural background and experience of the client" (p.9). The therapist incorporates the child and family's identities, backgrounds, and experiences into an effective treatment plan through cultural humility. When creating a treatment plan, the therapist engages in the four practices of cultural humility (Chan et al., 2018):

1. Acknowledging and understanding cultural differences: cultural humility requires that practitioners recognize and respect the cultural differences between themselves and their clients regarding language, values, and beliefs. Therapists should strive to understand the cultural contexts that shape the lives of the child and/or family and be open to learning about differences between their own cultural background and that of their clients.

2. Engaging in self-reflection: practitioners must be willing to engage in ongoing self-reflection and self-critique as part of their treatment planning process. This includes reflecting on their biases and attitudes and considering how their cultural background may shape how they perceive and respond to the client's presenting challenge.

3. Establishing cultural safety: cultural safety involves creating an environment where clients feel respected, valued, and understood. The therapist should strive to create a safe space by using appropriate language and avoiding assumptions or stereotypes.

4. Adapting treatment strategies: practitioners should be open to adapting their treatment approaches to better serve the child and/or family. This may involve incorporating culturally specific resources and practices into treatment plans or using evidence-based treatments for specific cultural groups. Practitioners need to be flexible and responsive to their clients' multiple identities.

Cultural humility requires an acknowledgment of one's biases and privileges, which is essential to understand the challenges faced by individuals from different cultural identities. Increasingly, the counseling field is acknowledging the work and assertions of intersectionality scholars (Davis et al., 2018) who argue that no identity or experience(s) associated with identity exists in isolation; instead, all identities, as well as their affiliated privileges and oppressions, are interlocking, coexisting, and fluid. For example, a Caucasian, middle-aged, single mom therapist will need to reflect on how her cultural identities, biases, and privileges will impact the treatment plan process as she is working with a 7-year-old bilingual Latina child who immigrated to the United States with her father, who is pursuing an engineering degree and was recently diagnosed with depression? Significantly, a therapist's reflection on his or her cultural identities, biases, and privileges can help foster a sense of trust that enriches the therapeutic relationship and treatment plan process.

INTERSECTIONALITY AND TREATMENT PLAN

During the case conceptualization stage, the therapist considers the complexities of the child and family's cultural identities. Crenshaw (1989) developed the term intersectionality initially to address various aspects of oppression, which co-occur within an individual based on their multiple identities and social locations. Intersectionality in treatment planning is the idea that a child and family's identity is not just a single category but a combination of multiple intersecting identities. These identities may include gender, race, ethnicity, culture, class, sexual orientation, and ability, among others. These identities and how they intersect with one another can create unique experiences during treatment. The interplay between identities, privilege, and oppression will impact a child and family's presenting problem (Syed, 2008). For example, a newly arrived migrant with limited English language proficiency would face more significant challenges in adapting to the culture, seeking employment, school, and a place to live compared to members of their ethnic group who speak English as a first language, who nevertheless are still facing disadvantages in contrast to white, middle-class families.

Designing a carefully prepared treatment plan that acknowledges the child's and/or family's intersecting identities while assessing, diagnosing, and establishing goals assures that the mental health services will align with the child's presenting challenge and increase the likelihood of success (Brinkman et al., 2020; Sue et al., 2009; Schwitzer & Rubin, 2015). For instance, when working with a 10-year-old child struggling with anxiety, the therapist must consider the different identities that interact while creating an effective treatment plan. In this case, an intersectional approach to treatment would involve looking at the child's life holistically, including their age, gender, birth order, culture, ethnicity, socioeconomic status, and grade in school to name a few. The therapist and child would begin by exploring the child's current situation and identifying any cultural identity factors contributing to his or her anxiety. Once the child and the counselor have identified any contributing factors, they can begin to develop a plan of action. This might involve addressing any home or environmental issues, such as providing the child with additional support or resources or helping them develop better coping skills and learn better ways to handle stress. Additionally, understanding the child's multiple cultural identities provides a cultural opportunity. Cultural opportunities are "markers that occur in therapy in which the client's cultural beliefs, values, and other aspects of identity could be explored" (Owen et al., 2016).

Cultural opportunities can be integrated into the four core components of treatment planning: (1) behavioral definition of the presenting challenge, (2) goals for change, (3) therapeutic interventions, and (4) outcome measures of change (Schwitzer & Rubin, 2015).

BEHAVIORAL DEFINITION OF THE PRESENTING CHALLENGE

The first element of treatment planning is the behavioral definition. This is the process of identifying the child and family's variety of problems, interests, areas of growth, and other needs and addressing those that can be reasonably achieved in counseling. Defining the presenting challenge from an intersectionality framework can assist the therapeutic alliance and uncover any underlying issues or concerns that may not have been initially discussed. In other words, valuing how the child and/or family's different identities may be affected as part of their presenting challenge is imperative to individualize the treatment plan to serve the client best (Sue & Sue, 2016). Because of this, clinicians need to be aware of relevant contextual information stemming from a child's and family's identities. For example, uncontrollable crying and headaches are symptoms of panic attacks in some cultures, while difficulty breathing may be the primary symptom in other cultures. Understanding such distinctions will help therapists more accurately capture how the client experiences challenges in everyday life.

GOALS FOR CHANGE

The second element of treatment planning is the goals for change. This is the process of setting goals that will help the child and/or family reach their desired outcomes. Goal setting can be challenging, especially involving a client's culture. Cultural identities are influential in shaping an individual's perception of change. They can create barriers that prevent or hinder progress; or a source of strength, providing a sense of identity, purpose, and direction (Ray et al., 2022). The impact of cultural identities on the client's perception of change is complex and multi-dimensional. One way in which cultural identities impact a client's perception of change is through language. Language can be a powerful tool for conveying and sharing meaning, values, and beliefs (Sue et al., 2009). It can also be a source of misunderstanding and misinterpretation. For example, a child's culture may be heavily influenced by his or her family's religious beliefs. If a therapist is unaware of this, they may use language that is not appropriate or respectful of the child's beliefs. This could lead to a breakdown in communication and impede the client's progress.

Cultural identities also shape a client's perception of change through values and beliefs, and they can be a source of conflict when a child's values conflict with a proposed change (Rigg et al., 2020). For example, a family may strongly believe in traditional gender roles. If the proposed treatment goal is for the child to explore his or her gender identity, the therapist must create a safe and accepting environment. As the therapist shares the proposed treatment goal with the caregivers, the therapist ensures a space where the child can explore their gender identity without fear of judgment or rejection. During the caregiver meeting, the therapist should also be prepared to answer questions and discuss different gender identities and expressions from a culturally sensitive and informed perspective. In addition, the therapist must be sensitive to the client's values and beliefs and work to understand how the proposed treatment goal can affect the family system.

THERAPEUTIC INTERVENTIONS

The third element of treatment planning is therapeutic interventions. This is selecting interventions based on a theoretical framework to help the child and family reach their goals. Integrating cultural identities and experiences within interventions can improve the accessibility, retention, congruence, and efficacy of treatment plan goals (Bryant-Davis, 2019; Owen et al., 2017; Sue et al., 2009). When counselors choose therapeutic interventions as a cultural opportunity to explore the child's identities in-depth, they understand how their values and perspectives within their professional community impact their theoretical framework. Furthermore, the therapist can initiate cultural conversations when they feel it is warranted and therapeutically wise (Owen et al., 2016). For example, if a 16-year-old, heterosexual high school student mentions that she was born and raised in Kansas by her single mother, her presenting concern centers around adapting to a new school after her mother remarried. A therapist might explore what being "born and raised in Kansas" means for the client with an expressive art collage. Another direction could be to explore how being raised by a single mother has impacted her view of gender roles, societal norms related to a traditional view of family, and issues of social class as opposed to her current blended family experience.

OUTCOME MEASURES FOR CHANGE

The fourth element of treatment planning is the outcomes. This is the process of determining the measures that will be used to demonstrate the client's progress. Outcome measures are generally selected based on the objectives of the intervention and the population being served (Clauss-Ehlers et al., 2019). Change can be evaluated through outcome measures such as a client self-report, caregiver reports, and in-session therapist observation (Kuo et al., 2020; Schwitzer & Rubin, 2015). These methods are beneficial because they provide a more comprehensive and holistic assessment of the child and/or family's experiences and allow the therapist to assess their cultural comfort (Clauss-Ehlers et al., 2019; Owen et al., 2017). In addition, encouraging the child to provide their perspective and input on outcomes creates a cultural opportunity to explore the child's unique strengths, helping him or her learn to recognize and appreciate his or her accomplishments from a culturally affirming perspective.

Engaging caregivers in this process can provide additional insight into the client's experiences and their level of functioning outside the counseling room. Furthermore, in-session therapist observations can allow the therapist to assess their cultural comfort. Cultural comfort refers to the therapist's thoughts and feelings that emerge before, during, and after sessions about the client's cultural identities and culturally focused context (Owen, 2017; Davis et al., 2018). Ultimately, these methods are better outcome measurements from an MCO and intersectionality standpoint since these frameworks focus on understanding a child's and family's unique circumstances.

CONCLUSION

Creating a treatment plan that considers the therapist's "way of being" (cultural humility) and context-specific behaviors associated with creatively exploring the client's multiple intersecting identities (cultural opportunities) while finding outcome measures of change (cultural comfort) is essential for maintaining a successful therapeutic relationship. In this way, the therapist can ensure that the treatment plan is informed by the child and/or family's multiple intersecting identities and that clients feel comfortable and respected throughout the therapeutic process.

Key Takeaways

- ♥ The child's cultural values, beliefs, practices, and attitudes in the counseling room shape their presenting challenge and determine the treatment plan.
- ♥ To understand culture in treatment planning, clinicians must remain nonjudgmental in listening to the child and/or family's perspective.
- ♥ The MCO framework recognizes that individuals have multiple identities and that these identities interact with each other to create unique experiences of oppression and privilege.
- ♥ The MCO framework supplements existing psychotherapy models.
- ♥ The therapist incorporates the child and/or family's identities, backgrounds, and experiences into an effective treatment plan through cultural humility.
- ♥ Cultural humility requires an acknowledgment of one's biases and privileges, which is essential to understand the challenges faced by individuals from different cultural identities.
- ♥ The interplay between identities, privilege, and oppression will impact a child and/or family's presenting problem.
- ♥ The therapist must be sensitive to the client's values and beliefs and work to understand how the proposed treatment goal can affect the family system.
- ♥ Therapists must understand neurobiology and interpersonal neurobiology in the context of human development.
- ♥ The functionality of treatment plans can only exist if the foundational knowledge of how a child develops and the impact of the environment in which it develops is assessed for and considered in its creation.

REFERENCES

Brinkman, B., & Donohue, P. (2020). Doing intersectionality in social justice oriented clinical https://doi.org/10.1037/tep0000274training. *Training and Education in Professional Psychology, 14*(2), 109–115. https://doi.org/10.1037/tep0000274

Bryant-Davis, T. (2019). The cultural context of trauma recovery: Considering the posttraumatic stress disorder practice guideline and intersectionality. *Psychotherapy, 56*(3), 400–408. https://doi.org/10.1037/pst0000241

Chan, D. N., & Band, M. P. (2018). Privilege and oppression in counselor education: An intersectionality framework. *Journal of Multicultural Counseling and Development, 46*(1), 58–73. https://doi.org/10.1002/jmcd.12092

Clauss-Ehlers, C., Hunter, S. J., Roysircar, G., & Tummala-Narra, P. (2019). APA multicultural guidelines executive summary: Ecological approach to context, identity, and intersectionality. *The American Psychologist, 74*(2), 232–244. https://doi.org/10.1037/amp0000382

Crenshaw, K. (1989). Demarginalizing the intersection of race and sex: A black feminist critique of antidiscrimination doctrine, feminist theory, and antiracist politics. *Feminist Legal Theory: Readings in Law and Gender, 1989*(1), 139–167. https://doi.org/10.4324/9780429500480-5

Davis, D., C., Owen, J., Hook, J. N., Rivera, D. P., Choe, E., Van Tongeren, D. R., Worthington, E. L., & Placeres, V. (2018). The multicultural orientation framework: A narrative review. *Psychotherapy (Chicago, Ill.), 55*(1), 89–100. https://doi.org/10.1037/pst0000160

Faulkner, S. L., Baldwin, J. R., Lindsley, S. L., & Hecht, M. L. (2006). Layers of meaning: An analysis of definitions of culture. In J. R. Baldwin, S. L. Faulkner, M. L. Hecht, & S. L. Lindsley (Eds.), *Redefining culture: Perspectives across the disciplines* (pp. 27–52).Lawrence Erlbaum. https://doi.org/10.4324/9781410617002

Hook, J. N., Davis, D., Owen, N. J., & DeBlare, C. (2017). *Cultural humility: Engaging diverse identities in therapy.* American Psychological Association. https://doi.org/10.1037/0000037-000

Kuo, S. K., & Huang, S. (2020). Developing clinical trainees' multicultural counseling competencies through working with refugees in a multicultural psychotherapy practicum: a mixed-methods investigation. *International Journal for the Advancement of Counselling, 42*(3), 249–268. https://doi.org/10.1007/s10447-019-09392-8 https://doi.org/10.1007/s10447-019-09392-8

Owen, J., Tao, K. W., Drinane, J. M., Hook, J. N., Davis, D. E., & Kune, N. F. (2016). Client perceptions of therapists' multicultural orientation: Cultural (missed)opportunities and cultural humility. *Professional Psychology: Research and Practice, 47*, 30–37. http://dx.doi.org/10.1037/pro0000046

Owen, J., Drinane, J., Tao, K. W., Adelson, J. L., Hook, J. N., Davis, D., & Fookune, N. (2017). Racial/ethnic disparities in client unilateral termination: The role of therapists' cultural comfort. *Psychotherapy Research, 27*, 102–111. http://dx.doi.org/10.1080/10503307.2015.1078517

Ray, D. C., Ogawa, Y., & Cheng, Y. J. (2022). *Multicultural play therapy: Making the most of cultural opportunities with children.* Routledge https://www.taylorfrancis.com/books/edit/10.4324/9781003190073/multicultural-play-therapy-dee-ray-yumiko-ogawa-yi-ju-cheng

Rigg, K., & Tao, K. W. (2020). Problematic systems: Applying a Multicultural Orientation Framework to Understand "Problematic Members." *Professional Psychology, Research, and Practice, 51*(3), 278–283. https://doi.org/10.1037/pro0000277

Schwitzer, A. M., & Rubin, L. C. (2015). Diagnosis and treatment planning skills: *Popular culture casebook approach.* Sage. https://psycnet.apa.org/record/2015-27931-000

SoHoo, S. (2013). Humility within culturally responsive methodologies. In M. Berryman, S. SoHoo, & A. Nevin (Eds.), *Culturally responsible methodologies* (pp.199–219). Emerald Group.

Sue, D., & Sue, D. (2016). *Counseling the culturally diverse: Theory and practice.* Wiley https://psycnet.apa.org/record/2002-06787-000

Sue, S., Zane, N., Nagayama Hall, G. C., & Berger, L. K. (2009). The case for cultural competency in psychotherapeutic interventions. *Annual Review of Psychology, 60*, 525–548. http://dx.doi.org/10.1146/annurev.psych.60.110707.163651

Syed, J. (2008). Employment prospects for skilled migrants: A relational perspective. *Human Resource Management Review, 18*(1), 28–45. https://doi.org/10.1016/j.hrmr.2007.12.001

Victoria Government. (n.d.). *Census Publications.* Retrieved from https://www.multicultural.vic.gov.au/population-and-migration/victorias-diversity/

Zhang, H., Watkins, C. E., Jr., Hook, J. N., Hodge, A. S., Davis, C. W., Norton, J., & Owen, J. (2022). Cultural humility in psychotherapy and clinical supervision: A research review. *Counselling and Psychotherapy Research, 22*(3), 548–557. https://doi.org/10.1002/capr.12481

CHAPTER 4

APPROACHES FOR CASE CONCEPTUALIZATION AND TREATMENT PLANNING

Lynn Louise Wonders

INTRODUCTION

The multifaceted process of case conceptualization and planning for therapy requires therapists to be prepared to explain what and why they do what they do in therapy. Theoretical orientation has historically been the basis from which therapists in training have gone about understanding what is happening for the client and the planning and practice of therapy. Theoretical orientation is to psychotherapy what roots are to a tree. But many branches have grown from those historical and seminal theories, including various models, approaches, and considerations for providing psychotherapy for children. Additionally, there are many schools of thought to consider when examining what it is that lends to therapy efficacy.

THEORETICAL ORIENTATION

The American Psychological Association (n.d.) defines *theoretical orientation* as "an organized set of assumptions or preferences for given theories that provides a counselor or clinician with a conceptual framework for understanding a client's needs and for formulating a rationale for specific interventions." The belief that theoretical orientation guides and supports the process of case conceptualization, goal setting, and treatment planning both inside and outside of therapy sessions is a long-standing position (Berman, 2018). Psychotherapy theories are developed to provide explanations for why humans behave as they do and how therapy can best support people. To ensure effective and ethical child therapy services, clinicians must understand how seminal psychotherapy theories, models, and approaches inform the way clinicians go about facilitating the most viable and appropriate plan for therapy (Stewart, 2014). Traditionally therapists have been encouraged to begin the work of therapy by learning and focusing on one theoretical model. A chosen theory shapes the manner through which therapists view the client's world and provide perspectives that help the clinician to understand the challenges the child faces. Theory determines the degree to which the therapy will be client-led or how much the therapy will be guided or directed by the therapist's clinical discernment and intervention (Wonders, 2021). In child psychotherapy, clinicians must consider both the developmental age and stage of the child as well as the nature of the child's attachment to and with caregivers. Any theoretical orientation a child therapist operates from will naturally consider those elements and incorporate related factors into the process of treatment planning.

The theories that rely on a purely humanistic and client-centered approach purport that the resolution for the client's challenges will naturally emerge from within the client without any direction from the therapist as long as the child experiences a therapeutic alliance that is unconditionally accepting, warm, and affirming (Landreth, 2012; Mullins & Rickli, 2014;

DOI: 10.4324/9781003334231-5

Ray, 2021). And other theoretical orientations agree on the essential element of the thera-peutic alliance (Wonders, 2021) but also see the therapist as the holder of clinical knowledge and, therefore, the facilitator of experiences in therapy (Leggett & Boswell, 2017; Wonders 2021). Integrative approaches to therapy may prescriptively select one, two, or even multiple theoretical approaches from a combination of non-directive and directive approaches based on the presenting challenges and systemic context of each individual client (Schaefer, 2001; Wonders, 2021). While there may be conflicting opinions about whether the therapeutic relationship, by itself, is all that a client needs for healing, growth, and change, the unifying belief in all play therapy seminal theories is that the trusting, emotionally safe therapeutic relationship is foundational and essential (Lugo, 2017; Wonders, 2021). Relational connec-tions established and maintained on a foundation of trust combined with the child's play are believed to be connected to positive treatment outcomes (Kottman & Meany-Wallen, 2018).

BEYOND THEORETICAL ORIENTATION

There are a number of varying perspectives that argue for differing determinants of therapy efficacy beyond theoretical orientation. Meta-analyses show that there is little evidence to support the efficacy of one theory over another (Gehart, 2015; Lambert, 1992). So, if it is not theoretical orientation we consider when measuring outcomes, what do we consider instead? Some assert that *competency* is the only threshold clinicians need to meet to provide effective psychotherapy (Fairburn & Cooper, 2011). Others argue that much progress has been made to show that it is *evidence-based treatment* that is most important for effective therapy (Zilcha-Mano et al., 2022). The *common factors* proponents argue that the effectiveness of therapy is more to do with certain elements found in all theories and not a result of what is unique in any specific theory (Cuijpers et al., 2019; Laska et al., 2014). In the field of psy-chotherapy, two movements have influenced an effort to go beyond theoretical orientation for case conceptualization and treatment planning: *competency* and *research* (Gehart, 2015).

THE COMPETENCY MOVEMENT

The competency movement in mental health challenges the traditional one-lens theoretical approach so that the presenting needs of every unique client are more likely to be matched (Gehart, 2015). Fairburn and Cooper (2011) explain therapist competence as the measure of knowledge and skills the therapist needs to deliver psychological services. Competency-based training and competency assessment measures, used to determine and address gaps in skills, have been demonstrated effective in various healthcare settings (Kohrt et al., 2020). If a clinician operates from a competency orientation, it is essential to be trained and skilled in the interventions used with clients but also to be culturally sensitive, informed, and respon-sive with clients while engaging in ongoing self-inquiry as to their own cultural identity and biases (Gehart, 2015; Gorczynski et al., 2021). While it is essential to meet a threshold of competency, there is no end to learning and developing professionally; thus, the need for continuing education requirements for mental health professionals (Vasquez, 2011). According to Gehart (2015), there are several topics under the umbrella of competency to which all therapists must be committed: (1) cultural, (2) research, (3) laws and ethics, and (4) person-of-the-therapist issues.

Cultural Competency

Clinicians practice cultural humility by remaining curious about and respectful of all facets of clients and their cultures, which includes race, ethnicity, gender, sexual orientation, and ability status, without making assumptions (Zhu et al., 2022). Cultural competency requires the therapist to recognize they are never fully competent but constantly seek competency with each client's cultural context (Gehart, 2015; Gorczynski, 2021).

Research Competency

Clinicians have a duty to stay current with the latest research as it applies to their clients' presenting challenges and the practice of therapy. It is important for clinicians to engage in continuing education for competency in evidence-based models and interventions fitting for working with specific populations and issues (Gehart, 2015; Sprenkle, 2003; Vasquez, 2011).

Legal and Ethical Competency

It is critical that therapists are well informed about their state and federal laws and ethical tenets that guide the mental health profession. Every major professional organization in the mental health field has its own ethical code, and therapists are required to receive ethics training during every renewal cycle of licensing for good reason. There are also state and federal laws that overlap some of the ethical tenets, such as confidentiality, mandated reporting, and scope of practice, just to name a few (Gehart, 2015; Weaver, 2019).

Person-of-the-Therapist Competency

This area of competence speaks to personal character and a way of being in the role of therapist. Clinicians are responsible for their own personal development and consciousness of how their personal challenges might inadvertently spill over into a client's therapy, potentially causing harm. While it is difficult to measure a clinician's quality of presence with clients, it is an important area of competency a therapist needs to prepare for and maintain (Gehart, 2015).

THE RESEARCH MOVEMENT

Two areas within the research have challenged the notion of a one-theory approach to providing psychotherapy services, and those areas are evidence-based research and common factors research. The common factors research demonstrates that it is the common elements in all theoretical orientations that contribute to the efficacy of treatment, and the evidence-based treatments research supports prescriptively choosing specific theories and forms of therapy to match with specific presenting problems or symptoms to ensure desired outcomes (Emmelkamp et al., 2014; Goodheart et al., 2006; Gehart, 2015).

Evidence-based Treatment Research

Based on an ongoing effort by the American Psychological Association (the APA) to ensure the efficacy of practice, the APA first established categories that described empirically supported therapies or *evidence-based therapies* (APA, 1993; Chambless et al., 1996; Gehart, 2015). Then, in 2005, the APA published survey results indicating such training requirements in empirically supported therapies were impractical and that revisions were needed to the criteria and the logistics (Woody et al., 2005). Efforts continue today to establish ways to ensure mental health services are empirically supported (Ecker et al., 2022), and there can be need for evidence-based practice (Zilcha-Mano et al., 2022). Cook et al. (2017) found when therapists integrate empirically based research into clinical practice rather than rely solely on personal preference for one theoretical model, and there is a higher likelihood that best-fitting interventions and practices will be used for the particular client's presenting needs.

Often, therapists new to providing child psychotherapy services make the error of moving too hastily into directive interventions without first gathering and considering contextual information about the child, the family, and the child's lived experience. The first steps in planning for therapy include careful exploring, examining, and synthesizing information about the client and then establishing goals to direct the therapeutic process (Wonders, 2021). A prescriptive approach to child therapy planning permits the clinician to selectively choose theoretical orientation(s) and interventions that may be the most appropriate response to the child's presenting symptoms and degree of severity (Schaefer, 2001; Wonders, 2020).

Common Factors Research

There is a model that argues that the efficacy of therapy results from *common* or *universal factors* found in all therapies. Those factors include the therapeutic alliance between the patient and the therapist, hope and expectation on the client's part that therapy will help, and specific interventions that reinforce the client's hope and expectations of therapy (Cuijpers et al., 2019). Sprenkle & Blow (2004) urge that this common factors approach should not dismiss theoretical orientations and therapy models but reframe their purpose to support a clinician's ability to actualize the common factors. Another way to understand this is to see a theoretical orientation to ensure clinician competency rather than seeing any one theory as the only way for a client to have optimal and desired outcomes from therapy (Gehart, 2015).

PRESCRIPTIVE TREATMENT PLANNING

While it can be useful and appropriate for clinicians to apply one chosen theoretical model in the therapy room, it can also be problematic if all child clients are viewed through only one lens (Kaduson et al., 2020). Schaefer (2015) described prescriptive play therapy as consciously pulling from a variety of theories and approaches and then customizing the therapy plan to fit the needs of the individual client as supported by the empirical evidence, clinical experience, context, and preference of the client, and underlying reasons for the presenting challenges. A prescriptive approach to treatment planning focuses on clearly identifying what will be most beneficial for a client and selecting an approach, model, theoretical orientation(s), and interventions accordingly (Beutler et al., 2005). Zilcho-Mano et al. (2022) found that both evidence-based data and theory can be used together to tailor the therapy to fit the presenting needs of each individual client. The terms *prescriptive* and *integrative* are often conflated because when using a prescriptive approach, the clinician may integrate two or more theories to design the treatment plan. However, being prescriptive does not necessarily mean being integrative.

Being prescriptive or eclectic should not be an arbitrary mixing of theories and interventions (Beutler et al., 2005). This is why counselors in training are often encouraged to choose one theoretical orientation, study and practice it well before mixing in other theories and approaches. With ample training, practice, and supervision, however, therapists can be well-versed in various theoretical models to have a well-stocked tool chest to pull from to meet the needs of each client (Goldstein & Stein, 1976; Kaduson et al., 2020). There is value in learning multiple psychotherapy theories and models rather than operating only from one. Abraham Maslow (1966) said, "If the only tool you have is a hammer, you tend to see every problem as a nail."

The term *technical eclecticism* means that the methods and interventions used in therapy do not need to be tied to the theories from which they originally were developed and that therapeutic interventions can be chosen based on the degree to which they fit with a particular client rather than on the basis of the therapist's theoretical orientation (Norcross & Beutler, 1986; Beutler & Hodgson, 1993). Technical eclecticism emphasizes *interventions* and is not to be confused with theoretical integration, common factors approach, or any "haphazard eclecticism" (Beutler & Hodgson, 1993).

Prescriptive eclecticism pulls effective methods from across theoretical orientations, matching methods to particular client needs and purposefully organizing those methods into a plan for implementation (Norcross & Beutler, 1986; Kaduson et al., 2020). We could look at one client case through multiple theoretical lenses and develop various treatment plans depending on the views of each theory and the methods used in each theoretical model. Prescriptivism is a matter of pulling what fits best for this particular client. Being prescriptive requires the therapist to keep a finger on the pulse of the child's sense of connection to the therapist and the therapy every step and adjust the plan as needed. There is a dynamic and fluidly responsive element of prescriptive treatment planning. Being prescriptive involves ongoing observation, reading the client in the therapy room, and watching and listening to the non-verbal and verbal feedback the child provides.

CHOOSING SPECIAL APPROACHES AND MODELS

In the process of conceptualizing what is happening for child clients, there are many unique models built upon theoretical orientation(s) that are designed to create optimal therapeutic fit for the individual needs of child clients and their caregivers. Clinicians may, for example, choose FirstPlay® if working with a child age 0–3 or TraumaPlay® if a child has come to therapy with a trauma history. If working with an autistic child, the therapist would want to utilize a neurodiversity-affirming approach to therapy, such as AutPlay® and perhaps a Digital Play Therapy™ approach if the child is most comfortable interacting with digital games and communication methods. Choosing a particular approach to therapy or a specific model is done so prescriptively after a thorough intake and formulation of all the presenting information.

CONCLUSION

While theory is foundational to the psychotherapist's training, professional development, and ability to develop case conceptualization and a treatment plan, it's worthwhile to consider that competency, common factors, and evidence-based practice are equally important. There is a time and a place for being prescriptive in the treatment planning process because every individual client has unique needs. Being prescriptive and having a focus on common factors, competency, and research does not preclude the use of theory. The whole of conceptualizing and planning for therapy provides myriad perspectives and considerations. Clinicians will do well to examine the breadth of perspectives when approaching the therapy planning process for children and their families.

Key Takeaways

- ♡ There are many schools of thought to consider when examining what it is that lends to therapy efficacy.
- ♡ Psychotherapy theories are developed to provide explanations for why humans behave as they do and how therapy can best support people.
- ♡ Theory determines the degree to which the therapy will be client-led or how much the therapy will be guided or directed by the therapist's clinical discernment and intervention.
- ♡ The unifying belief in all play therapy seminal theories is that the trusting, emotionally safe therapeutic relationship is foundational and essential.
- ♡ Some assert that competency is the only threshold clinicians need to meet in order to provide effective psychotherapy, while others believe it is the common factors found in all therapy or the evidentiary basis for the treatment that matters most.
- ♡ A prescriptive approach to treatment planning focuses on clearly identifying what will be most beneficial for a client and selecting an approach, model, theoretical orientation(s), and interventions accordingly.
- ♡ Prescriptive eclecticism pulls effective methods from across theoretical orientations, matching methods to particular client needs and purposefully organizing those methods into a plan for implementation.

REFERENCES

American Psychological Association. (n.d.). *APA dictionary of psychology*. American Psychological Association. Retrieved March 13, 2023, from https://dictionary.apa.org/theoretical-orientation

American Psychological Association. (1993, October). Task force on promotion and dissemination of psychological procedures: A report adopted by the Division 12 Board. https://doi.org/10.1037/e550782009-001

Berman, P. S. (2018). *Case conceptualization and treatment planning: Integrating theory with clinical practice*. Sage. https://us.sagepub.com/en-us/nam/case-conceptualization-and-treatment-planning/book246809

Beutler, L. E., & Hodgson, A. B. (1993). Prescriptive psychotherapy. *Comprehensive handbook of psychotherapy integration* (pp. 151–163). https://doi.org/10.1007/978-1-4757-9782-4_12

Beutler, L. E., Consoli, A. J., & Lane, G. (2005). Systematic treatment selection and prescriptive psychotherapy: An integrative eclectic approach. *Handbook of psychotherapy integration* (Vol. 2, pp. 121–143). Oxford University Press. https://doi.org/10.1093/med:psych/9780195165791.003.0006

Chambless, D. L., & Hollon, S. D. (1998). Defining empirically supported therapies. *Journal of Consulting and Clinical Psychology, 66*, 7–18. https://doi.org/10.1037/0022-006x.66.1.7

Cook, S. C., Schwartz, A. C., & Kaslow, N. J. (2017). Evidence-based psychotherapy: Advantages and challenges. *Neurotherapeutics, 14*, 537–545. https://doi.org/10.1007/s13311-017-0549-4

Cuijpers, P., Reijnders, M., & Huibers, M. J. (2019). The role of common factors in psychotherapy outcomes. *Annual review of clinical psychology, 15*, 207–231. https://doi.org/10.1146/annurev-clinpsy-050718-095424

Ecker, A. H., O'Leary, K., Fletcher, T. L., Hundt, N. E., York-Ward, K. M., Kauth, M. R., ... & Cully, J. A. (2022). Training and supporting mental health providers to implement evidence-based psychotherapies in frontline practice. *Translational Behavioral Medicine, 12*(1), ibab084. https://doi.org/10.1093/tbm/ibab084

Emmelkamp, P. M., David, D., Beckers, T., Muris, P., Cuijpers, P., Lutz, W., ... & Vervliet, B. (2014). Advancing psychotherapy and evidence-based psychological interventions. *International Journal of Methods in Psychiatric Research, 23*(S1), 58–91. https://doi.org/10.1002/mpr.1411

Fairburn, C. G., & Cooper, Z. (2011). Therapist competence, therapy quality, and therapist training. *Behaviour Research and Therapy, 49*(6–7), 373–378. https://doi.org/10.1016/j.brat.2011.03.005

Gehart, D. R. (2015). *Theory and treatment planning in counseling and psychotherapy.* Cengage Learning. https://search.worldcat.org/title/theory-and-treatment-planning-in-counseling-and-psychotherapy/oclc/920805943

Goldstein, A. P., & Stein, N. (1976). HYSTERIA. Prescriptive Psychotherapies, 204. https://doi.org/10.1016/b978-0-08-019506-3.50024-x

Goodheart, C. D., Kazdin, A. E., & Sternberg, R. J. (2006). *Evidence-based psychotherapy: Where practice and research meet* (pp. xi–295). American Psychological Association. https://doi.org/10.1037/11423-000

Gorczynski, P., Currie, A., Gibson, K., Gouttebarge, V., Hainline, B., Castaldelli-Maia, J. M., ... & Swartz, L. (2021). Developing mental health literacy and cultural competence in elite sport. *Journal of Applied Sport Psychology, 33*(4), 387–401. https://doi.org/10.1080/10413200.2020.1720045

Kaduson, H. G., Schaefer, C. E., & Cangelosi, D. (2020). Basic principles and core practices of prescriptive play therapy. *Prescriptive play therapy: Tailoring interventions for specific childhood problems* (pp. 3–13). Guilford Press. https://psycnet.apa.org/record/2019-54604-001

Kohrt, B. A., Schafer, A., Willhoite, A., Van't Hof, E., Pedersen, G. A., Watts, S., ... & van Ommeren, M. (2020). Ensuring quality in psychological support (WHO EQUIP): Developing a competent global workforce. *World Psychiatry, 19*(1), 115. https://doi.org/10.1002/wps.20704

Kottman, T., & Meany-Walen, K. K. (2018). *Doing play therapy: From building the relationship to facilitating change.* Guilford. https://psycnet.apa.org/record/2018-25969-000

Landreth, G. L. (2012). *Play therapy: The art of the relationship.* Routledge. https://doi.org/10.4324/9781003255796

Laska, K. M., Gurman, A. S., & Wampold, B. E. (2014). Expanding the lens of evidence-based practice in psychotherapy: a common factors perspective. *Psychotherapy, 51*(4), 467. https://doi.org/10.1037/a0034332

Leggett, E. S., & Boswell, J. N. (2016). *Directive play therapy. Theories and techniques.* Springer. https://doi.org/10.1891/9780826130662.0001

Maslow, A. H. (1966). *The psychology of science: A reconnaissance.* Harper and Row.

Mullin, J. A., & Rickli, J. M. (2014). *Child-centered play therapy workbook: A self-directed guide for professionals: a self-directed guide for professionals.* Research Press. https://psycnet.apa.org/record/2014-12061-000

Norcross, J. C., & Beutler, L. E. (1986). A prescriptive eclectic approach to psychotherapy training. *Journal of Psychotherapy Integration, 10*, 247–261. https://psycnet.apa.org/record/2000-05897-002

Ray, D. C. (2021). *Advanced play therapy: Essential conditions, knowledge, and skills for child practice.* Routledge. https://www.researchgate.net/publication/286756041_Advanced_Play_Therapy_Essential_Conditions_Knowledge_and_Skills_for_Child_Practice

Schaefer, C. (2001). Prescriptive play therapy. *International Journal of Play Therapy 10 57–73*. https:// doi.org/10.1037/h0089480

Schaefer, C. E., & Drewes, A. A. (2015). *Prescriptive play therapy. Handbook of play therapy* (pp. 227–240). Wiley. https://doi.org/10.1002/9781119140467.ch10

Sprenkle, D. H. (2003). Effectiveness research in marriage and family therapy: Introduction. Journal of Marital and Family Therapy, 29(1), 85–96.

Sprenkle, D. H., & Blow, A. J. (2004). Common factors and our sacred models. *Journal of Marital and Family Therapy, 30*(2), 113–129. Portico. https://doi.org/10.1111/j.1752-0606.2004. tb01228.x

Stewart, A. L., & Echterling, L. G. (2014). *Therapeutic relationship* (pp. 157–169). Wiley.

Vasquez, M. J. (2011, February 1). Lifelong learning: An ethical responsibility for all psychologists. *Monitor on Psychology, 42*(2). https://www.apa.org/monitor/2011/02/pc

Weaver, C. M., & Meyer, R. G. (2019). *Law and mental health: A case-based approach*. Guilford. https:// psycnet.apa.org/record/2019-48087-000

Wonders, L. L. (2020). Play therapy for children with selective mutism. Prescriptive play therapy: Tailoring interventions for specific childhood problems. In H. G. Kaduson, D. Cangelosi, & C. E. Schaefer (Eds.), Prescriptive play therapy: Tailoring interventions for specific childhood problems (pp. 92–104). Guilford. https://psycnet.apa.org/record/2019-54604-006

Wonders, L. L. (2021). Purposeful application of theory to case conceptualization and treatment planning. In J. Stone (Ed.), *Play Therapy and telemental health* (pp. 25–44). Routledge. https://doi. org/10.4324/9781003166498-2

Woody, S. R., Weisz, J., & McLean, C. (2005). Empirically supported treatments: 10 years later. *The Clinical Psychologists, 58*, 5–11. https://doi.org/10.1037/e533302009-003

Zilcha-Mano, S., Constantino, M. J., & Eubanks, C. F. (2022). Evidence-based tailoring of treatment to patients, providers, and processes: Introduction to the special issue. *Journal of Consulting and Clinical Psychology, 90*(1), 1. https://doi.org/10.1037/ccp0000694

Zhu, P., Liu, Y., Luke, M. M., & Wang, Q. (2022). The development and initial validation of the cultural humility and enactment scale in counseling. *Measurement and Evaluation in Counseling and Development, 55*(2), 98–115. https://doi.org/10.1080/07481756.2021.1955215

PART 2

TREATMENT PLANNING FROM A VARIETY OF THEORETICAL ORIENTATIONS, MODELS, AND APPROACHES

CHAPTER 5

AN ADLERIAN PLAY THERAPY APPROACH TO TREATMENT PLANNING

Susan Becker Kerley and Erica Wassenaar

INTRODUCTION

Alfred Adler, the founder of Individual Psychology, is often considered the father of modern therapy (Watts & Bluvshtein, 2020). Adler's roots began with Freud and Jung before he split off to develop his own holistic theory. Adler was the first to consider the social context in which an individual lives in conceptualizing treatment. In collaboration with and continued by Rudolf Dreikurs, Adler was the first to include community in treatment through groups, presentations, and consultations (Sweeney, 2019). Notably, Adler never received credit for his foresight, wisdom, and contributions to the field (oh, the irony…he was also the first to describe the concept of inferiority complex). Terry Kottman (Kottman & Meany-Walen, 2016) applied Adlerian theory to play therapy in the mid-1980s, and Adlerian Play Therapy (AdPT) was born.

ADLERIAN PLAY THERAPY

Primary tenets of AdPT include:

- People are socially embedded and have a need to belong.
- All behavior is goal-directed.
- A person's perception of reality is subjective.
- We are each whole, unique beings who cannot be separated into parts (Kottman & Meany-Walen, 2016).

AdPT continues to grow its research base and has been shown to be an effective, measurable treatment, applicable to diverse individuals, groups, cultures, genders, and presenting clinical issues (Dillman Taylor, & Kottman, 2019; Meany-Walen & Kottman, 2017).

PHASES OF ADPT

AdPT is made up of four phases:

1. Building the relationship
2. Exploring the child's lifestyle and functioning at life tasks
3. Helping the child gain insight
4. Reorienting/reeducating the child

DOI: 10.4324/9781003334231-7

Adler promoted an egalitarian relationship with clients, fostering a sense of agency and choice (Sweeney, 2019). Adlerian play therapists hold the utmost belief that every child can find better ways of coping, improve their sense of belonging, and become meaningful contributors to society (Reviews, 2016). One unique differentiating factor of AdPT is that power and decision-making are shared (e.g., by including the child in the cleaning-up process and taking turns deciding on activities and interventions). AdPT is a positive, strengths-based approach built on encouragement and mutual respect. The application of the phases is illustrated in the case study presented in the following sections.

Treatment planning organically grows out of conceptualization. It is a reiterative process: as we conceptualize, the therapist learns more information about the client's lifestyle from the relationship, various interventions, and frequent consultation and collaboration with the primary adults in the child's life. The therapist creates customized therapeutic interventions best to meet the needs of the child and system. It is not a "one size fits all" approach. Creativity is essential to the process.

CASE SCENARIO

Charlie was an 8-year-old boy in second grade. Charlie's parents sought out therapy after Charlie's teacher expressed concerns regarding his ability to focus, sit still, and stay on task, and frequent visits to the school clinic, complaining of stomach pain and headaches.

Initial Intake

In AdPT, the initial intake involves two parts: meeting with caregivers and meeting with the child. Building trust and an egalitarian relationship take precedence. Charlie's parents noted that he experienced somatic symptoms at school and home, starting early in the school year. Charlie's history at school included being placed in a gifted cluster classroom in kindergarten with a warm and nurturing teacher, much like his mother. He was tested for the gifted program on his teacher's recommendation and was accepted, along with much of his class. First grade was relatively unremarkable. In second grade, he was separated from some of his core group of friends and placed in a classroom with a teacher who was stricter and less nurturing than his previous teachers and lifelong caregivers.

Case Conceptualization

As illustrated in Figure 5.1 below, lifestyle components provide the initial basis for case conceptualization. Charlie's family atmosphere was authoritative. His parents were well-educated and knowledgeable about parenting. The home was structured, organized, and routine based. The structure helped Charlie feel valued and capable.

Birth order is an important concept in AdPT. Charlie was the younger of two boys, with a brother, Trevor, who was 18 months older. Charlie was nearly the same size as Trevor, and the two were often thought to be twins. This often resulted in adults mistaking him for being older and holding him to higher standards than he was developmentally capable of achieving. His brother had the same second-grade teacher Charlie had. Trevor's personality was nearly night and day from Charlie's. Trevor was quiet,

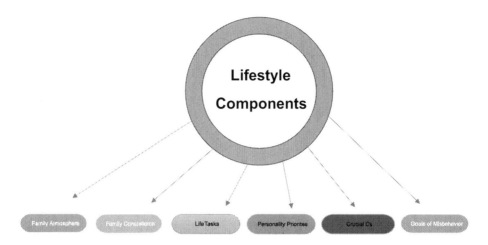

Figure 5.1 Lifestyle Component © Kottman, T., & Meany-Walen, L. (2016). *Partners in play* (3rd ed.). American Counseling Association

compliant, a rule follower (often typical of firstborns), and did not create disruptions. Charlie, on the other hand, had high levels of energy. After meeting with the parents, the therapist consulted with the teacher, who directly stated she expected Charlie to be more like Trevor and visibly expressed frustration when reporting how often she needed to redirect him.

Assessment Process

Further assessment includes Charlie's functioning with the five major life tasks described in Figure 5.2. Evaluating these areas revealed that Charlie felt discouraged towards school and at home. The therapist consulted with Charlie's teacher to get a better understanding of his assets and challenges. The parents, teacher, and therapist were all involved in gathering information on Charlie's current functioning.

Personality priorities develop when children encounter experiences they feel their usual coping skills cannot handle (Kfir, 2011). At this point, Charlie was frustrated with his difficulty complying with his teacher's expectations and sometimes at home. Charlie was a pleaser and did not like to disappoint others. He struggled with staying on task, and his parents (both superiority personality priorities) had relatively high expectations. His brother did not give him the attention he desired, nor shared his intense interests. He felt like he only counted when others were happy with his behavior.

Charlie's advanced intellect created another challenge for him. He observed and understood behaviors of others and himself that were difficult to control. At the same time, he had age-appropriate social and emotional skills. Charlie struggled to understand why his parents and teachers focused so much on his perceived flaws and shortcomings, while Trevor typically received praise and positive attention for his compliance. As a pleaser, this was especially troublesome for Charlie. Although his parents tried to treat both sons equally, now that his teacher openly compared Charlie to Trevor, he was beginning to experience more significant emotional and behavioral challenges.

School

Refers to a person's primary means of contributng to society and can include school, household chores, and volunteer actvites.

Family

Refers to how the person gets along with other family members.

Friendship

Connectng socially with others and enjoying connecton with others is an important life task and evaluates a person's social interest.

Self

Added by Harold Mosak, to determine how well the person is developing an acceptng relatonship with the self, as well as self-awareness.

Spirituality

Adlerians have added developing a relatonship to something greater than the self.

Figure 5.2 Life Tasks © Kottman, T., & Meany-Walen, L. (2016). *Partners in play* (3rd ed.). American Counseling Association

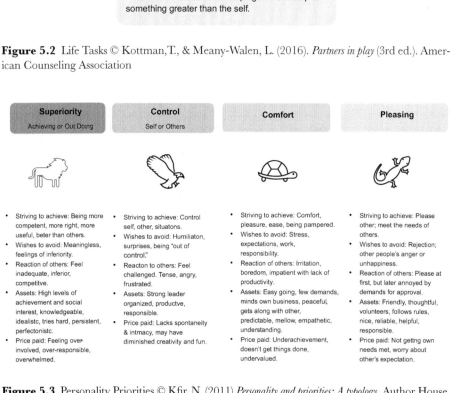

Superiority Achieving or Out Doing	Control Self or Others	Comfort	Pleasing

- Striving to achieve: Being more competent, more right, more useful, beter than others.
- Wishes to avoid: Meaningless, feelings of inferiority.
- Reaction of others: Feel inadequate, inferior, competitve.
- Assets: High levels of achievement and social interest, knowledgeable, idealistc, tries hard, persistent, perfectonistc.
- Price paid: Feeling over involved, over-responsible, overwhelmed.

- Striving to achieve: Control self, other, situatons.
- Wishes to avoid: Humiliaton, surprises, being "out of control."
- Reacton to others: Feel challenged. Tense, angry, frustrated.
- Assets: Strong leader organized, productve, responsible.
- Price paid: Lacks spontaneity & intmacy, may have diminished creativity and fun.

- Striving to achieve: Comfort, pleasure, ease, being pampered.
- Wishes to avoid: Stress, expectations, work, responsibility.
- Reaction of others: Irritation, boredom, impatient with lack of productivity.
- Assets: Easy going, few demands, minds own business, peaceful, gets along with other, predictable, mellow, empathetic, understanding.
- Price paid: Underachievement, doesn't get things done, undervalued.

- Striving to achieve: Please other; meet the needs of others.
- Wishes to avoid: Rejection; other people's anger or unhappiness.
- Reaction of others: Please at first, but later annoyed by demands for approval.
- Assets: Friendly, thoughtful, volunteers, follows rules, nice, reliable, helpful, responsible.
- Price paid: Not gettng own needs met, worry about other's expectation.

Figure 5.3 Personality Priorities © Kfir, N. (2011) *Personality and priorities: A typology*. Author House. Kottman, T., & Meany-Walen, L. (2016). *Partners in play* (3rd ed.). American Counseling Association

Identifying Problems and Diagnosis

Continuing the assessment process leads to identifying problems and potential diagnoses. The therapist considered Charlie's level of functioning on the Crucial Cs, detailed in Figure 5.4.

The therapist used a Likert scale to evaluate where Charlie fell in the four import-ant areas that, once mastered, would lead to feelings of self-worth and positive social

Secure		Not Secure
I feel secure I can reach out I can make friends I can cooperate	Connection	I feel insecure I am more susceptible to peer pressure I seek attention I compete
I feel competent I have self-control and self-discipline I am self-reliant	Capable	I feel inadequate I try to control others I become dependent
I feel valuable I can make a difference I contribute	Count	I feel insignificant I may try to hurt back
I feel hopeful I am willing to try I am resilient	Courage	I feel inferior I may give up

Figure 5.4 Crucial C's © Lew, A,. Bettner, B. L. (1996). *A parent's guide to understanding and motivating children.* Connexions.

interest. Notably, Charlie was struggling with feeling capable and courageous the most. He was typically low in all the Crucial Cs, with connection likely his strongest leveraged to build up the others. While he felt capable academically, he struggled to feel like he could meet the expectations of the adults in his life. He exhibited many characteristics of attention deficit hyperactivity disorder (ADHD) and met the diagnostic criteria, and he showed signs of developing an anxiety disorder. His mom reported that he had recently started following her out of the classroom, crying when she left after volunteering. This was a new behavior.

All behavior is purposeful, and exploring the goals of misbehavior is a vehicle for helping to understand and alleviate misbehavior. Figure 5.5 illustrates the four goals of misbehavior Adlerians consider. Charlie was likely in the category of proving inadequacy, perhaps a way of avoiding trying to continuously contain his ADHD and anxiety symptoms. The adults in his life reported feeling helpless about how to best support him.

All the components of Adlerian Play Therapy culminate in helping the therapist identify the client's lifestyle convictions, private logic, and mistaken beliefs. Lifestyle convictions (typically out of the child's awareness) represent the phenomenological perspective through which the client filters everything that happens. Some of these convictions may be "mistaken beliefs" (inaccurate, faulty, or self-defeating convictions), and the child will "act as if" they are all true (Kottman & Meany-Walen, 2016). These are often conceptualized visually in a chart and include:

- I am…
- Others are…
- The world is…
- I must be…
- Others must be…
- Therefore, I must…

Child's Goal	Child's Feelings	Child's Actions Active	Child's Actions Passive	Adult's Feelings	Child's Reactions to Correction
Attention Needs more positive attention	I only count when I am being notice or serve	Bothers others Shows off. Minor mischief Class clown Needy	Shy Uptight 'I can't" Messy Anxious Lazy Vain clingy	Annoyed Coaxes Reminds Involved Attentive Busy	Temporary halt of behavior when given attention, but later resumes behavior. wants to be helpful. Ask questions
Power Needs age-appropriate power, responsibility, & autonomy	I only count when I am dominating or when you do what I want you cannot control me	Argues Contradicts Tantrums Dishonest Defiant Power Struggle Disrespectful	Lazy Stubborn Disobedient "Forgets." Does little or no work Passive aggressive	Anger Challenged Preachy Threatened Provoked	Escalates behaviors when punished; works harder to be the boss, show you cannot be the boss
Revenge Needs to protect self; needs to make sure nobody gets close	People hurt me. I can't be liked. I need to push others away to stay safe	Malicious Violent Bad loser Cruel Steals Wets bed Hurts others Bully	Moody Pouty Threatens Withdraws	Hurt Wants to get even; wants to withdraw	Becomes even more hurtful and escalates pushing others away
Proving Inadequacy Needs to keep expectation of others low	I can't do anything right, so I won't try to do anything at all, I am not capable	Suicide	Won't try Gives up Wants to be alone Discourage	Helpless Does not know what to do and may give up	Feels even worse Stops even small efforts

Figure 5.5 Goals of Misbehavior © Kottman, T. (2021) Beginning Adlerian Play Therapy handouts. Unpublished manuscript. Reprinted with Permission.

Charlie appeared to believe he was a failure, unlike other kids, and only likable when he could control his behavior and emotions. He felt he must be flawed, unable to control himself, and should be able to control himself. In sessions, Charlie gave up easily when faced with a difficult task, yet he frequently sought approval from his therapist. This bind created significant difficulties for him and was beginning to manifest as extreme worry and physical symptoms of anxiety.

Setting Goals

Therapy goals for Charlie included helping him develop insight into his behavior and inner world, which then translated into progress towards adaptive lifestyle convictions, healthier private logic, stronger Crucial Cs, improvement in life task functioning, and shifting his feelings of inadequacy and helplessness. Providing his parents and teacher with support, psychoeducation, and strategies to support Charlie were also critical goals. Session goals are referred to as Little A agendas, and therapy goals are Big A agendas. Therapists develop flexibility with the Little As and keep the Big As in mind at all times (Kottman & Meany-Walen, 2016).

Establishing Measurable Objectives

Therapists help children like Charlie gain increased self-awareness by facilitating the development of insight. Therapists offer tentative hypotheses about behavior by identifying and communicating underlying motivations and goals (i.e., metacommunication). Encouraging change and inviting action were essential goals to help Charlie "reorient" to life by understanding his private logic, correcting basic mistakes in thinking, feeling, and acting, and learning new skills (Meany-Walen & Kottman, 2017; Reviews, 2016). Therapists challenge, support, and practice with clients to develop the courage it takes to make life changes based on their newly discovered insights. Encouragement and metacommunication are foundational tools used throughout all phases of AdPT.

Frequent and regular consultations were utilized with parents, teachers, and other important adults in Charlie's life to obtain feedback and monitor progress. Some examples may include reducing the number of trips to the nurse's office in school, gradually increasing Charlie's ability to focus and complete tasks, and providing opportunities for Charlie to feel valued without having to please others. Crucial Cs are monitored on a Likert scale in the therapy room to assess progress over time. Additionally, the therapist looks at the frequency of mistaken beliefs expressed and how the child is functioning in various environments and with life tasks.

Theoretically Based Interventions

An appealing aspect to many AdPT providers is that interventions are based on improving the major lifestyle components. There is a clear structure and purpose designed in the approach that invites the therapist and client to mutually design creative interventions. Interventions can include sandtray, storytelling, bibliotherapy, art therapy, tabletop games, and even video games. As Charlie was intellectually gifted, interventions that naturally appeal to that strength could be developed. He was an avid dinosaur lover and could recite the names, Latin translations, and even the periods in which certain dinosaurs lived. Using dinosaur metaphors in therapy appealed to Charlie. Puppet shows with dinosaurs were used to practice new skills and teach new information. Creating a dinosaur family genogram helped the therapist, and Charlie understand family dynamics, strengths, and areas for improvement. Writing a story together with dinosaurs as the main characters helped identify and teach ways for Charlie to improve his mistaken beliefs. As Charlie was very active and needed to move his body, incorporating movement and creating a theatrical play and song with choreographed motions met his body's physical needs while helping to strengthen his executive functioning skills and improve frustration tolerance. Teaching him breathing techniques was adapted into "dino breaths" or "dino breathing fire.".

Collaborating With the Client and Caregivers in Therapy Planning

Working with the parents to narrow down primary goals (which will ideally have a beneficial cascading effect) is referred to as helping them identify their "stake in the ground," their most important goal. The Adlerian concept of "connection before correction" (Nelson, 1987) is taught, modeled, and monitored. As discussed previously, important adults in Charlie's life were incorporated into his treatment from the beginning. Family sessions were designed to improve family cohesion and demonstrate that while Charlie may be different from his brother, he was no less important. A variety of useful forms are available in the book *Partners in play* (Kottman & Meany-Walen, 2016) and online.

Tracking Progress

Monitoring progress is directly tied to goals. Progress in Adlerian Play Therapy is a fluent process, a constant assessment of the presenting issues and progress toward treatment goals. Improvement in Charlie's Crucial Cs was an important indicator of progress, as is the development of social interest. Movement in his personality priorities toward healthier functioning was another indicator of progress. Goals of misbehaviors shifted to more positive goals by reducing his feelings of helplessness. He began substituting positive convictions for mistaken beliefs and common sense for private logic to reduce self-defeating behaviors and learn positive behaviors. Progress was seen in his ability to use skills (e.g., social, negotiation, communication, assertiveness, taking appropriate responsibility for behavior, etc.). Changes in the targeted behaviors and beliefs were observable through his play (e.g., play themes, willingness to try without a guarantee of success) and verbal patterns (e.g., expressions indicating healthier private logic, increased frustration tolerance, and less reliance on needing to please others). Charlie began to generalize new ideas and skills for positive behaviors, thoughts, and feelings outside the playroom as evidenced by parent, teacher, and child reports of improvement, along with therapist observations.

Termination Process Strategies

As goals are met, treatment will move into the termination phase. Encouragement and a "strengths bombardment" are often used to celebrate progress and mark the end of therapy. A strengths bombardment includes any creative way of providing the child with a remembrance of their growth, progress, and assets. It may be made collaboratively with the client and can include the family. Some examples include a t-shirt written with all of Charlie's strengths in Sharpie, a blank white dinosaur stuffed animal with his strengths written on it, or a special story created together and recorded or written. A reminder to Charlie and his parents was included to that "booster" sessions may sometimes be needed as ongoing development will include new complexities in self and the environment. A thank you card was given to parents, highlighting how much effort they have put into the process and how they have been an integral part of the success. Other collaborative sources (e.g., teachers, school counselors, coaches) participating in Charlie's treatment were also recognized and acknowledged.

CONCLUSION

The preceding presents a broad overview of AdPT. The reader is encouraged to seek out additional information to learn more about birth order, the complexities of lifestyle components, the importance of early recollections, and a myriad of AdPT concepts that extend beyond the scope of this chapter.

Key Takeaways

- As a holistic approach, AdPT looks at both strengths and areas in need of improvement, along with the various environments in which behavior is displayed.
- AdPT has been shown to be an effective measurable treatment, applicable to diverse individuals, groups, cultures, genders, and presenting clinical issues.
- Adler promoted an egalitarian relationship with clients, fostering a sense of agency and choice.
- In AdPT power and decision-making are shared.
- The therapist creates customized therapeutic interventions to best meet the needs of the child and system. It is not a "one size fits all" approach.
- Creativity is essential to the process.
- Personality priorities develop when children encounter experiences they feel their usual coping skills cannot handle.
- All behavior is purposeful, and exploring the goals of misbehavior is a vehicle for helping to understand and alleviate misbehavior.
- All the components of Adlerian play therapy culminate in helping the therapist identify the client's lifestyle convictions, private logic, and mistaken beliefs.
- Encouragement and metacommunication are foundational tools used throughout all phases of AdPT.

REFERENCES

Dillman Taylor, D., & Kottman, T. (2019). Assessing the utility and fidelity of the Adlerian play therapy skills checklist using qualitative content analysis. *International Journal of Play Therapy*, *28*(1), 13–21. https://doi.org/10.1037/pla0000082

Kfir, N. (2011). *Personality and priorities: A typology*. Author House.

Kottman, T., & Meany-Walen, K. (2016). *Partners in play* (3rd ed.). American Counseling Association. https://doi.org/10.1002/9781119272205

Meany-Walen, K. K., & Kottman, T. (2017). Adlerian play therapy: Practice and research. In R. L. Steen (Ed.), Emerging research in play therapy, child counseling, and consultation (pp. 100–111). Information Science Reference/IGI Global. https://doi.org/10.4018/978-1-5225-2224-9.ch006

Nelsen, J. (1987). *Positive discipline*. Ballantine Books.

Reviews, C. T. (2016). *Studyguide for theory and treatment planning in family therapy: A competency-based approach by Gehart, Diane r., ISBN 9781285456430*. Cram101.

Sweeney, T. J. (2019). *Adlerian counseling and psychotherapy* (6th ed.). Routledge. https://doi.org/10.4324/9781351038744

Watts, R. E., & Bluvshtein, M. (2020). Adler's theory and therapy as a river: A brief discussion of the profound influence of Alfred Adler. *The Journal of Individual Psychology*, *76*(1), 99–109. https://doi.org/10.1353/jip.2020.0021

(2015). Appendix G: Lifestyle conceptualization and treatment plans. In T. Kottman and K. Meany-Walen (Eds.), *Partners in play: An Adlerian approach to play therapy* (3rd ed.). Wiley Online Library

CHAPTER 6

TREATMENT PLANNING FOR ANIMAL ASSISTED PLAY THERAPY™

Risë VanFleet

INTRODUCTION

In the past decade, the involvement of animals in therapeutic work has expanded considerably, although it existed long before. The acceptability of professionals working alongside a dog, cat, horse, or other animal has grown rapidly, and in some cases, the practice of "taking one's nice family pet" into therapeutic or educational environments has been rather haphazard. There are training and registration programs for therapy animal teams, but many focus on visitation and social support programs more than on animals included in professional work. An overview of the field can be found in numerous books and articles (e.g., Chandler, 2017; Fine, 2019; Tedeschi & Jenkins, 2019), or in organizations centering on Animal Assisted Interventions (AAI), such as the International Association of Human-Animal Interaction Organizations (https://iahaio.org).

After an initial 20 years of individual research and development, two credentialed play therapists, Risë VanFleet (USA) and Tracie Faa-Thompson (UK), formed a collaboration in the early 2000s to further develop a unique approach to animals in play therapy. Their vision was unique in that it not only combined values and principles from play therapy and animal-assisted therapy but incorporated important features of other disciplines such as ethology, anthrozoology, animal science, behavior and learning, motivation, and animal welfare. Early workshops titled Animals in Play Therapy™ quickly became Animal Assisted Play Therapy™, and numerous articles, chapters, and two award-winning books shared information with other therapists (VanFleet, 2008; VanFleet & Faa-Thompson, 2017).

Animal Assisted Play Therapy™ (AAPT) can be used in conjunction with non-directive or more directive forms of play therapy, and it can be applied to a variety of problem areas for individuals, families, and groups. It is also applicable to children, youth, and adults of all ages. It is a trans-theoretical approach in that it can be used by professionals with different theoretical orientations as well as by those with integrative theoretical orientations.

This contribution discusses some of the unique features of AAPT that must be considered in treatment planning. A definition and the guiding principles are followed by descriptions of the preparation needed by therapists and how the fundamentals of AAPT are woven into the treatment planning process. In general, AAPT is an adjunct treatment approach, as animals are never expected to work full-time, and it meshes well with many other modalities.

DEFINITION, PRINCIPLES, AND PREPARATION

AAPT has been defined as the,

> . . .integrated involvement of animals in the context of play therapy, in which appropriately trained therapists and animals engage with clients primarily through systematic playful

DOI: 10.4324/9781003334231-8

interventions, with the goal of improving clients' developmental and psychosocial health, while simultaneously ensuring the animal's well-being and voluntary engagement. Play and playfulness are essential ingredients of the interactions and the relationship. (VanFleet & Faa-Thompson, 2017, p. 17)

The guiding principles of AAPT place equal emphasis on the well-being of humans and animals. In short, they represent (a) reciprocal respect, (b) physical and emotional safety, (c) agency and voluntary choices for all involved, (d) acceptance of clients and animals for who they are, (e) the use of animal-friendly training methods, (f) a focus on the relationship, not control, (g) encouragement of growth and empowerment, (h) a process orientation to therapy, and (i) grounding in terms of lifespan development, clinical intervention, play therapy, ethical practice, and humane animal treatment. While many practitioners would likely agree with these more abstract concepts, the real challenge comes in being in the human-animal relationship and the therapist-client relationship at all times. It is for this reason that a substantial amount of training and preparation is needed for this work.

While it is, unfortunately, a common practice for therapists to "take their friendly family pet" to work with them, this is risky and violates the boundaries of practice. Far too many things can go wrong, and it is not a given that a happy animal at home will be happy working in clinical or educational work or in busy settings such as schools (Lewis et al., 2022). Stressed animals can become ill, or they can react defensively such as by biting. Neither of these outcomes is acceptable in this work. Instead, the animal must be selected carefully and then matched to the right environment and type of work to suit his or her personality and preferences. AAPT uses a rather different approach to this process, borrowing the child development concept of goodness-of-fit (VanFleet, 2020, 2022b). This work also requires numerous competencies on the part of the professional. Not only must they be competent in play therapy, but they must understand a great deal about animals, including species-specific body language, how to train using positive reinforcement-based methods, what the natural behaviors are of the species and the individual animal, and how to build a reciprocal relationship with the animal so as to then help their clients do so. They must be very skilled in a variety of play therapy approaches and know how to bring an animal into that environment and facilitate sessions in ways that strengthen clients' progress toward goals while always attending to the animals' needs as well. How they practice AAPT depends in large part on several factors described in the next section that relate to treatment planning.

TREATMENT PLANNING IN AAPT

Considerations

Animals involved in therapeutic or educational work can be unpredictable, just as clients can be, especially children. Practitioners of AAPT must be able to split their attention between clients and the animal (reading the body language of both) and develop proactive attention skills to see potential problems and intercede before they occur. They must also be creative and use unexpected behaviors therapeutically, and specifically, in service of the client's goals. Because of these complexities, treatment planning that includes AAPT requires considerable additional learning.

Basic case formulation must be comprehensive and caring in tone, and it must inform the treatment plan developed in conjunction with the client or the client's family. VanFleet (2022a) has detailed the case formulation process she has used in a variety of settings since 1978.

Detailed information about the goal areas of AAPT is in VanFleet & Faa-Thompson (2017). AAPT's five major goal areas are (1) self-efficacy, (2) attachment and relationship, (3) empathy, (4) self-regulation, and (5) specific problem resolution, which includes a wide range of presenting problems.

Even animals well-suited to play-based work are not expected to work all day. Young animals not yet in adulthood are not expected to work at all. In general, dogs might work 2 hours per day and 2 to 3 days per week, usually with a day off in between. Dogs sleep 14 to 17 hours each day, so work hours are limited, and the dogs need to be at home or in a room separate from the office or playroom. They should not be crated more than a couple hours each day as well.

Treatment Planning Details

The intake process described in the Filial Therapy chapter in this book is the same one used to determine what treatments are best suited to the problem. The establishment of goals and objectives are not dependent on AAPT being used. AAPT is a modality that can take many different forms, so once a client's goals are known, it can be considered as one form of intervention. It is at this level of the process that the rest of this chapter describes.

After the intake and assessments, the methods to be used to help clients reach their goals are considered. This, too, is part of the treatment planning process. AAPT might be appropriate for a wide range of treatment goals, and there are AAPT resources that can help determine this (VanFleet & Faa-Thompson, 2017, 2019a). The *Manual of AAPT Techniques* (VanFleet & Faa-Thompson, 2019) offers 45 play-based AAPT interventions, but most importantly each one describes the purpose and participants for which it is designed, followed by what is needed to prepare the animal appropriately. This helps practitioners determine if a particular activity is suitable for the client's needs or the personality of the animal.

WHAT AAPT INTERVENTION TO USE?

AAPT can be done in a non-directive play therapy manner, or it can be done using varying levels of structure (VanFleet et al., 2019). There are prepared interventions, such as in the manual noted above, or practitioners can create their own. This is part of AAPT training for professionals. To select or create the best AAPT intervention, therapists must consider four critically important factors. These are described briefly below.

1. **Consider the client's goals**. This is done when planning interventions, but also during AAPT sessions, as the therapist's facilitation or use of metaphors is derived from client goals. Client needs and goals are always kept in mind.

2. **Consider the animal's personality, preferences, and skills**. AAPT is heavily focused on therapists first developing a great relationship with their animals. They get to know who they are and what they like, what they prefer to avoid, and what motivates them. They understand many features, such as energy levels, patience, curiosity, initiation, emotional reactions, sociability, persistence, and resilience. The forms that play therapy takes are myriad, so the goodness-of-fit concept considered earlier comes back into play here. One would not expect a very energetic, active dog to engage in quiet, slow activities in most cases. While a dog

without much patience might be suitable for a short activity where a client could help the dog be more patient (since that would be the client's goal), it would not be beneficial for the dog to have to show much patience all the time. At all times, the animal's choices and motivations are taken into account when determining how best to use AAPT to meet client goals.

3. **Consider the therapist's theoretical orientation and usual ways of working**. Here, the therapist's own skills and style of working come into play as well. If a play therapist prefers working in a non-directive, less structured manner, and their dog is more suited to directive play therapy, the therapist needs to consider if they have the competencies to switch to the dog's style during AAPT. While stretching one's learning to expand to new methods is valuable, there are limits, so the therapist's orientation is considered.

4. **Consider the environment in which the session occurs**. Adding an animal means that more space is needed. Spatial aspects are very important for most animals. AAPT is more active than traditional forms of animal-assisted therapy, and interventions involving obstacle courses, dramatic imaginary scenes, and teaching an animal a new behavior all require more space. Also, the playroom must have a "safe space" that humans may not invade. This might be a bed under a desk, a cat tree, or an area in the corner of the room. This also means more space is needed. Some AAPT must take place outdoors. Almost all equine activities are done outdoors in horses' natural environments, but there are many canine interventions suitable for outdoors as well if there is sufficient privacy and safety can be maintained for all. When considering interventions to meet a particular goal, the therapist will need to think about hindrances in the environment. Another key area that relates to the therapeutic environment is the use of props. The animals must be comfortable with them, as well as the clients, and there must be sufficient space for the animal to always have an exit route and the freedom to use it.

These four factors are always kept in mind, both in the initial treatment planning process and throughout therapy. It can be difficult to weave them all into the process simultaneously, but that is precisely what is needed in AAPT to ensure ethical services to clients and excellent animal well-being.

CASE SCENARIO

The case that follows represents a composite of several families involved in AAPT. All identifying information has been changed to protect the privacy of the children and families. It represents a typical case where AAPT is used, however. The child's name was Leo and he was 9 years old.

Family system factors

Leo was, at the time, in foster care. He was removed from his mother's home when he was 6 years old because his mother's live-in boyfriends were beating him when they got drunk. His mother had a choice to make, and she chose to let him go. Leo had been living with his current foster family for 9 months and had made a good adjustment overall. There were five other adopted children in the family, three boys and two girls. Leo's foster parents, Joan and Curt, were willing to consider adopting Leo eventually, too. Three of his siblings in the foster home were older than he was. The family was well known in the foster care system as one which was loving but had good boundaries as well. The children were encouraged to explore their own interest areas, and Leo was very interested in animals. The family had taken him to a wildlife rehabilitation center where he could see how injured or homeless animals were taken care of and then released back into the wild.

Cultural Factors

Leo was Caucasian from an impoverished urban environment where he lived the first 6 years. He was exposed to gang violence, as well as physically and verbally abusive treatment by at least two of his mother's live-in boyfriends. He was placed in foster care where he did not adjust readily. He did things behind the parents' backs, stole money, and carelessly broke home items. He was in two placements where a negative pattern emerged with which the foster parents became very frustrated with his behavior, and he became sneaky and hid things from them. He was then moved to his current family. He went through a short period of pushing the boundaries, but Joan and Curt handled this better than previous foster caregivers had. He seemed to relax in the more rural setting and responded positively much of the time to the affection they showed him. The foster parents were Caucasian, and the five adopted children were of mixed race. The parents were aware of diversity and cultural considerations and worked to ensure that the children all got along together.

Social System Factor

Leo had been involved with child protection services for 4 years, three of which had involved his placements. He had trouble relating to other children and he struggled in school, likely because he had been enrolled in three different schools in the past three years. In his current placement, Joan and Curt had indicated to social service caseworkers that if Leo's mother's parental rights were terminated, they would be open to adding a sixth child to their family.

Presenting Issues

Leo showed signs of complex trauma with occasional emotional outbursts, some "sneaky" behaviors including taking money from his foster mother's purse, impulsivity, fear of loud noises attributed to the gunshots he had heard in his early years. His quality of sleep suffered due to night terrors. Despite increasing efforts, his school performance was poor. Leo flinched if someone raised their arm too quickly. Most of the time he was cooperative and interested in all the family members, and he began playing more with his siblings at home. His previous isolating behavior began to decrease.

Initial Intake/Assessment

The intake process included collateral information from the child protective agency, a meeting with the adoptive parents plus a family play observation in the same manner as described in the Filial Therapy chapter in this volume.

Case Conceptualization/Problems/Diagnosis

With Leo's repeated traumas, unstable environments, and uncertainty throughout his life, he was insecure in his attachments, and yet he maintained hope for a safe, loving family. His demeanor was sweet, and he was surprisingly thoughtful of others, given his history. His presenting issues were typical of children in foster care. Because of his range of challenges, it was determined that he would benefit from child-centered play therapy (CCPT) to help him express his feelings and work through some of his bad experiences. If he responded well to CCPT, Filial Therapy could help him connect in safe and significant ways with his foster parents with potential adoption in mind. More directive and prescriptive play therapy approaches could be used to address some of his behavioral problems that were sequelae of his deprivations and harsh treatment. Following a short course of CCPT and with Filial Therapy well underway, AAPT was viewed as a useful adjunct treatment. The primary theories relevant to Leo's case conceptualization are developmental/attachment for safety and connection, humanistic for acceptance and empathy, and cognitive-behavioral for the behavioral manifestations, all of which would be delivered as play therapy.

Setting Goals

It was clear that his most pressing needs were to strengthen his sense of safety, to assist him in building a more secure attachment, to provide opportunities to work through the feelings associated with his traumatic experiences, and to improve executive functioning skills such as focus, thinking before acting, and overall behavioral regulation.

Establishing Measurable Objectives

Examples of measurable goals for Leo and his parents follow:

1. Leo will talk with his parents about his feelings of frustration or fear when they occur to help eliminate the destruction of household items.
2. Leo will develop three coping skills for use when he has strong unpleasant feelings such as fear, anxiety, anger, and frustration.
3. Leo will demonstrate improvements in executive functioning skills of focus, inhibition and restraint, and problem-solving.
4. Leo will engage in prosocial behaviors when interacting with others, including showing an understanding of their feelings.
5. Leo's foster parents will keep a brief record of the times and situations in which he tells them he is having unpleasant feelings.
6. Leo's foster parents will learn the Filial Therapy parent skills and use them in daily life.
7. Leo will demonstrate how to greet a dog safely, how to obtain consent from a dog, how to use positive approaches to teach a dog at least three new behaviors.

Planning Theoretically Based Interventions

Several of these goals require a sense of safety and relationship, so CCPT was chosen as the initial intervention as this is suited to providing the child with empathy and acceptance, the foundations of trust, as well as with reparative experiences within the safety of play. Many children play out trauma and attachment themes, including metaphors for threat and rescue, power and control, mastery, and relationships of victim and victimizer as well as family relationships. After 15 CCPT sessions with the therapist, his parents and the therapist will evaluate his progress in the play sessions and at home. This will overlap with the training phase of Filial Therapy. Parents will alternate their supervised FT sessions with the therapist's CCPT sessions for approximately 4 weeks, after which the parents will continue all the non-directive play sessions, continuing under the therapist's direct supervision and then moving to home but still with the therapist's supervision.

As the parents take over the non-directive play sessions via FT, the therapist will incorporate more directive play therapy interventions to help with his development of the specific skills noted above. This will include AAPT, during which Leo will learn to build a mutual relationship with the play therapy dog. This relationship-building will include attention to the goals of developing empathy and better self-regulation, and the specific objectives of greeting a dog safely, using consent testing to consider what the dog wants, and how to use positive reinforcement to teach the dog new behaviors, all within the context of playful interactions.

Collaborating with Caregivers In Treatment Planning

The parents are involved at all times in treatment planning, as described in the FT chapter in this volume (VanFleet, 2023). They are also involved in conducting FT sessions in the office and eventually at home. Furthermore, when the AAPT sessions begin, Leo will invite them to join him with the dog while he demonstrates the things he has learned and has taught the dog. This will provide them with insight as to how this approach helps Leo develop competence and confidence in several areas that can eventually be applied at home without an animal.

Tracking Progress

Progress is tracked after each session in terms of play theme/behavior changes within the playroom and at home. Parents will be involved at least every other session to discuss this, and a more complete evaluation session is to be held every 5 to 10 sessions. Progress is determined by actual behavior change and movement toward the goals.

Termination

This is determined jointly by the therapist and Leo's foster parents at the point that they see sufficient improvement, and movement toward goal acquisition that they can manage further development on their own at home. Typically, the AAPT portion of this intervention lasts 6 to 12 sessions.

CONCLUSION

Animal Assisted Play Therapy™ (AAPT) was developed with consideration of and full attention to the core needs of animal therapy partners as well. There are added complexities of treatment planning and the need for specific preparation and advanced thinking required in AAPT. Treatment planning must consider the child's or family's goals while simultaneously incorporating the animals' needs throughout the therapeutic journey.

Key Takeaways

- Animal Assisted Play Therapy™ (AAPT) can be used in conjunction with non-directive or more directive forms of play therapy, and it can be applied to a variety of problem areas for individuals, families, and groups. It is also applicable to children, youth, and adults of all ages.
- AAPT is an adjunct treatment approach, as animals are never expected to work full-time, and it meshes well with many other modalities.
- The guiding principles of AAPT place equal emphasis on the well-being of humans and animals.
- The animal must be selected carefully and then matched to the right environment and type of work to suit his or her personality and preferences.
- Practitioners of AAPT must be able to split their attention between clients and the animal (reading the body language of both) and develop proactive attention skills to see potential problems and intercede before they occur.
- AAPT's five major goal areas are (1) self-efficacy, (2) attachment and relationship, (3) empathy, (4) self-regulation, and (5) specific problem resolution.
- AAPT can be done in a non-directive play therapy manner, or it can be done using varying levels of structure.
- There are added complexities of treatment planning and the need for specific preparation and advanced thinking required in AAPT.

REFERENCES

Chandler, C. K. (2017). *Animal assisted therapy in counseling* (3rd ed.). Routledge. https://doi.org/10.4324/9781315673042-8

Fine, A. H. (Ed.). (2019). *Handbook on animal-assisted therapy* (Vol 5). Elsevier/Academic Press.

Lewis, H., Grigg, R., & Knight, C. (2022). An international survey of animals in schools: Exploring what sorts of schools involve what sorts of animals, and educators' rationales for these practices. *People and Animals: The International Journal of Research and Practice, 5*(1), Article 15. https://www.researchgate.net/publication/349517957_Iss_1_Article_2_People_and_Animals_The_International_Journal_of_Research_and_Practice_People_and_Animals

Tedeschi, P., & Jenkins, M.A. (2019). *Transforming trauma: Resilience and healing through our connections with animals.* Purdue University Press. https://doi.org/10.2307/j.ctv2x00vgg

VanFleet, R. (2008). *Play therapy with kids and canines: Benefits for children's developmental and psychosocial health.* Professional Resource Press. https://search.worldcat.org/title/191898232

VanFleet, R. (2020). Assessment of therapy animals: Using a goodness-of-fit conceptualization. *Blog of the International Institute for Animal Assisted Play Therapy,* Retrieved April 19, 2020, https://iiaapt.org/assessment-of-therapy-animals-using-a-goodness-of-fit-conceptualization

VanFleet, R. (2022a). *Case formulation guide for professionals working with children and families* (3rd ed). Play Therapy Press. Retrieved from https://www.academia.edu/13621799/The_Case_for_Using_Animal_Assisted_Play_Therapy_

VanFleet, R. (2022b). Professional decision making in Animal Assisted Play Therapy™: How the goodness-of-fit model impacts practice. *Blog of the International Institute for Animal Assisted Play Ther-*

apy®, *October 2022*. Retrieved from https://iiaapt.org/professional-decision-making-in-animal-assisted-play-therapy-how-the-goodness-of-fit-model-impacts-practice/

VanFleet, R. (2023). A filial therapy approach to treatment planning. In L. L. Wonders & M. Affee (Eds.), *Treatment planning for children and families: A guide for mental health professionals* (pp. 000). Routledge.

VanFleet, R., & Faa-Thompson, T. (2017). *Animal assisted play therapy*. Professional Resource Press. https://iiaapt.org/the-distinctiveness-of-animal-assisted-play-therapy/

VanFleet, R., & Faa-Thompson, T. (2019). *Manual of animal assisted play therapy techniques*. Play Therapy Press. https://risevanfleet.com/product/animal-assisted-play-therapy-new/

VanFleet, R., Fine, A. H., & Faa-Thompson, T. (2019). Application of animal-assisted interventions in professional mental health settings: An overview of practice considerations. In A. H. Fine (Ed.), *Handbook on animal-assisted therapy* (Vol. 5, pp. 225–248). Elsevier/Academic Press. https://doi.org/10.1016/b978-0-12-815395-6.00015-8

CHAPTER 7

AN AUTPLAY® APPROACH TO
THERAPY PLANNING

Robert Jason Grant

INTRODUCTION

AutPlay® is a neurodiversity-affirming and informed framework for integrating play therapy theory designed to support the mental health needs of neurodivergent children ages 3–18 including autistic children, those with ADHD, social anxiety, sensory differences, learning differences, and developmental and physical disabilities (Grant, 2023). AutPlay® integrates psychotherapy theories, various play therapy models, and relational approaches together in a collaborative protocol to support children and adolescents in achieving gains with mental health needs. In the AutPlay® model, parents and children are considered partners in the process of therapy, working along with the therapist.

AutPlay® Therapy is designed to value the child as a unique individual, highlighting their strengths while guiding areas of intervention to address the needs of the child and family. The therapeutic powers of play and the core change agents (Schaefer,1993; Schaefer & Drewes, 2009) are utilized to address a range of potential presenting needs, including emotional regulation challenges, social navigation needs, engagement and connection, anxiety and fear, sensory challenges, executive functioning, depression, and self-esteem concerns, trauma issues, advocacy, stigmatization, identity appreciation, the social model of disability, autonomy, inclusion needs, and parent/child relationship struggles (Grant, 2023).

PHASES OF THERAPY

AutPlay® rests on a foundation in the neurodiversity paradigm and integrates play therapy and other approaches as beneficial for the individual child. Three phases of therapy guide the AutPlay® framework:

1) **Intake and Assessment Phase**—much this phase of therapy takes place in the first three to four sessions with the focus on building a relationship and supporting the child in becoming familiar with the therapist and the playroom. Therapeutic relationship development is a core change agent within the therapeutic powers of play and the AutPlay® Therapist will be dedicated to relationship-building practices at the beginning of therapy and throughout the duration. During this first phase, there is a process of assessment that includes AutPlay® inventories provided to the caregivers, a parent-child observation, and a play-based child observation session. Areas of the child's lived experience are examined in the assessment phase, including social navigation, emotional awareness, regulation needs, connection ability, sensory processing differences, ways of communicating, unwanted behaviors, family support, medical and psychological conditions. The therapist talks to the child and caregivers about the reasons for therapy so goals can be set collaboratively, and the therapist can develop a therapy plan.

DOI: 10.4324/9781003334231-9

2) **Structured Play Intervention Phase**—there is no limit to the number of sessions during this phase as each child and family's presenting needs are unique. Generally, the higher the needs, the more sessions will be required for this phase of therapy. In this phase, a therapist may implement the Follow Me Approach (FMA), which is designed for children with limited or no interaction or engagement. The FMA is uniquely designed to meet these children where they are and assist in building relationship, connection, and engagement. Structured play interventions may also be chosen to address needs tied to the therapy goals. Parents and child are introduced to various play interventions by the therapist so that parents can implement the interventions at home with their child. Therapy goals are periodically revisited approximately every 3 to 6 months to track progress. As therapy goals are achieved, new goals are established until therapy reaches a point of completion.

3) **Termination Phase**—This phase of therapy normally is accomplished in three sessions. The therapy plan is reviewed with parents and child, and it is established that therapy goals have been accomplished and there are no new goals. The final session is scheduled, and during that final session, there is a graduation party for the child providing a celebration of all the child and family have accomplished.

This chapter presents an example of therapy planning with a neurodivergent child client from an affirming perspective using AutPlay® Therapy protocol for intake, assessment, and goal planning.

THERAPY PLANNING PROCESS

Note on Affirming Terminology

Throughout this chapter, *therapy planning* will be used instead of *treatment planning*. Neurodivergence is an identity (a difference), not something to be fixed, cured, or erased. An autistic child is not in therapy because they are autistic; they would be in therapy because they have mental health needs such as regulation issues, anxiety, trauma, social navigation needs, etc. It is these needs that are targeted in the therapy process, not autism. In the therapy process, goals are not designed to make the child less autistic or look more neurotypical. Unfortunately, the historical view has been to "treat" autism and other neurodivergence as a disease that needs a cure (erase the neurodivergence, make them look neurotypical, and ignore the real mental health needs). This ableist approach has caused harm to many neurodivergent individuals creating negative self-worth, anxiety, depression, and trauma issues (Cage & Troxell-Whitman, 2019; Mandy, 2019).

The Intake and Assessment Phase

Being with, learning about, and building relationships with the child and family.

Session 1

In session one, the therapist meets with the parents only to conduct a general intake process which includes completing intake paperwork and any legal documents. The example will highlight a 12-year-old autistic child named Ronan. He was brought to therapy by his parents, who stated that he would not talk to them, and anytime they brought up friend situations or Ronan's feelings, he would get angry at them. They were concerned about his lack of social interest and involvement. They also felt that Ronan seemed depressed and anxious. They stated they were bringing him to therapy so he could have "someone to talk to." Both of Ronan's parents participated in the intake session, completing all necessary documents, and reviewing informed consent.

The therapist provides a brief education on neurodiversity-affirming processes, including asking the family if they have any language preference regarding diagnosis and/or neurodivergence. The therapist also gives the parents any AutPlay® inventories to complete and return in session two. Ronan's parents did not have any preference regarding autistic language, so it was established that the therapist would use identity-first language (autistic child). Ronan's parents were given the AutPlay® Social Navigation Inventory and AutPlay® Emotional Regulation Inventory.

During the initial session, the therapist also collects information on the child and family and all relevant documents, including any previous psychological evaluations, sensory evaluations, and IEP documents. Ronan's parents provided background information, presenting issues, and a copy of a previous psychological evaluation with a diagnosis of autism spectrum disorder.

At the end of session one, the therapist explains that at least one parent and the child will participate in session two, and this session will include a child/parent observation playtime.

Session 2

In session two, the therapist collects the AutPlay® inventories from the parents. The therapist takes the child on a tour of the facility, including all playroom(s) and office spaces that may be used.

The therapist then facilitates a child/parent play observation in a playroom setting or in their office—whatever space is appropriate. The therapist observes through monitor equipment or stations themselves in one corner of the room. The observation should last approximately 25–30 minutes. The family play observation is a tool designed to gain further information about the child (play preferences, communication style, social preferences, etc.) and to help identify therapy needs and therapy approaches. The therapist joins the child and parent in their playtime after the observation time is over.

Ronan attended the session with his mother. It was explained to Ronan that he was going to have a play-activity time with his mother. He chose to go into the sandtray room and complete a sandtray with his mother. Ronan and his mother seemed to enjoy completing the tray together. They communicated with each other and shared some humor and fun moments. It was observed that the mother did initiate control over the process on several occasions, and Ronan tended to withdraw and become quieter when this happened. The therapist finished the session by asking them some follow-up processing questions and how they felt spending time together creating the tray.

Session 3

In session three, the therapist continues to focus on relationship development and helping the child become familiar and comfortable with the facility and the therapist. The Therapist facilitates a child play observation in a playroom or office setting. The parents do not need to participate but can observe via the monitor or in a corner of the playroom. The child play observation is another tool designed to gain further information about the child and possible therapy needs. The observation should last approximately 45 minutes.

Ronan chose to return to the sandtray room. He asked the therapist for a prompt, unsure of what to create in the sand. The therapist invited Ronan to create a sandtray about himself and his life. Taking most of the session to work on his tray, Ronan was intensely focused on his process, and when finished, he shared with the therapist the meaning of his tray. He shared that the figure in the middle was himself, and the four areas around the middle were different people and parts of his life. Ronan furthered that he felt stressed and anxious because people in his life did not understand him. At the end of session three, the therapist explained to Ronan that the next session would involve deciding on goals for the therapy plan and that he and his parents would be included in the process. This affirming piece gives the neurodivergent child a voice in their therapy.

Identifying problem(s) and diagnosis, setting goals, and establishing measurable objectives

Session 4

The therapist meets with the parents and child to discuss observations and AutPlay® inventories and address any questions. The parents and child are asked to join the therapist in establishing therapy goals with the child having an active voice. One to three priority goals are agreed upon. Then the therapist will consider what has been learned about the child's neurotype to conceptualize which play therapy approach best fits to support the child in therapy. Any remaining time in the session is utilized for the therapist and child to continue developing rapport.

Ronan, his parents, and the therapist agreed that one priority goal would be anxiety reduction in social situations, and a second priority goal would be for Ronan's parents to better understand Ronan's neurodivergence, how his brain operated, and to find value in his differences.

The Structured Play Intervention Phase

Planning theoretically based interventions and collaborating/including client and caregivers in therapy planning and progress tracking.

In this phase, play therapy approaches, and interventions were implemented to address the established therapy goals. The level of parent and/or family involvement is also established. Much of the direction in this phase is determined by information gathered in the Intake and Assessment Phase. The therapist may move forward with a more non-directive approach, may begin implementing structured play interventions to address specific needs, or may do some combination. This will depend heavily on the individual child—their needs, their play preferences, their support level, their age, the totality of their self, and how much or little parent participation is available. The therapist will want to conceptualize this plan and be open to adjustments, changes, and feedback from the child and parent (Grant, 2023).

Play therapy approaches and interventions must also be filtered through a neurodiversity-affirming and non-ableist lens. The therapist must ensure that therapy approaches are not supporting problematic constructs such as masking, camouflaging, and devaluing identity. They must also be cognizant of addressing common neurodivergent needs such as the double empathy problem, empowerment, and self-advocacy. This is the time that family involvement is also considered. Does the therapeutic approach need to be family therapy or some other version of parent/family involvement—regular parent consultations, parent training, etc.? Much of this will be decided by the therapist consulting with the parents and child for the best fit considering the therapy needs and the child's spectrum of presentation.

It was decided that Ronan would participate in therapy once per week. One week would be an individual session with Ronan, and the next would be a family session with Ronan and his mother (the father could not participate due to scheduling conflicts). The individual sessions with Ronan would incorporate more structured play interventions designed to help him address social anxiety and improve his self-worth and neurodivergent identity. The family sessions would focus on improving the relationship and common understanding between Ronan and his mother, involve parent training regarding neurodiversity, and how to recognize and support Ronan as a neurodivergent teen.

Tracking progress

In the AutPlay® Therapy framework, therapy goals are periodically reviewed (every 3 to 6 months) to ensure that progress is being made toward goals. This often involves meeting with the parent and child to review the goals and discuss progress. This can also involve re-administering any initial AutPlay® inventories completed during the Intake and Assessment Phase.

At the five-month point of therapy, the therapist, Ronan, and his mother met to discuss progress toward the original therapy goals. All agreed that Ronan had improved with his social anxiety and anxiety dysregulation in general. Ronan had begun to explore more social-related outlets that he found interesting. Ronan's mother had made improvements in understanding Ronan and appreciating his presentation and style as opposed to trying to make him more like herself and the other family members. It was decided that Ronan and his mother would continue with therapy as therapy goals were not fully realized.

The Termination Phase

Ending the therapy experience with affirmations, empowerment, and celebration.

The Termination Phase will typically begin with the therapist initiating the transition. As the therapist becomes aware that therapy goals have been achieved and maintained, they should have a session with the child and parent to discuss the termination of therapy. The Termination Phase usually consists of three sessions. The first session introduces the idea to the child and parent to elicit a discussion about the readiness for therapy to end. The therapist can determine the appropriateness of having the child present or not for this session. The therapist should review the therapy goals and discuss whether therapy goals have adequately been accomplished. The therapist should make sure there are no other therapy goals to work on at this time. It is important to note that the initial therapy plan will likely be updated by the therapist, child, and parent throughout the Structured Play Intervention Phase, with new goals being added as others are accomplished.

After approximately 10 months of participating in weekly sessions, the therapist met with Ronan and his mother to discuss the completion of therapy goals and the possible termination of therapy. It was agreed that Ronan had completed his original therapy goals. His social-related anxiety had greatly decreased. He was now initiating with friends (of his choosing) to do things with them when and how he desired. He had also joined the football team at this school and was enjoying it. Ronan's mother and father were both doing well with understanding Ronan and appreciating his neurodivergence. His mother reported they were still working on this but had greatly improved and were dedicated to continued growth. It was decided that there were no new goals to work on, and therapy would be terminated. The therapist established two more sessions, one for a termination activity and the last one for a graduation celebration (see Appendix B.3).

CONCLUSION

The AutPlay® Therapy framework is designed for working with neurodivergent children and their families. Mental health professionals, especially child therapists, have historically not been involved in the therapy planning process and the healing needs of neurodivergent children. AutPlay® provides a unique and needed perspective on how to integrate play therapy theory and approaches for working with children across the spectrum of presentation from low support to high support needs.

Key Takeaways

- ♥ AutPlay® is a neurodiversity-affirming and informed framework for integrating play therapy theory.
- ♥ AutPlay® supports the mental health needs of neurodivergent children ages 3-18 including autistic children, those with ADHD, social anxiety, sensory differences, learning differences, and developmental and physical disabilities.
- ♥ AutPlay® rests on a foundation in the neurodiversity paradigm and integrates play therapy and other approaches as beneficial for the individual child.
- ♥ An autistic child is not in therapy because they are autistic; they would be in therapy because they have mental health needs. Goals are not created to make the child less autistic or look more neurotypical.
- ♥ The therapist must ensure that therapy approaches are not supporting problematic constructs such as masking, camouflaging, and devaluing identity.
- ♥ Therapists must be cognizant of addressing common neurodivergent needs such as the double empathy problem, empowerment, and self-advocacy.

REFERENCES

Cage, E., & Troxell-Whitman, Z. (2019). Understanding the reasons, contexts, and costs of camouflaging for autistic adults. *Journal of Autism and Developmental Disorders*, *49*(5), 1899–1911. https://doi.org/10.1007/s10803-018-03878-x

Grant, R. J. (2023). *The AutPlay® therapy handbook: Integrative family play therapy with neurodivergent children*. Routledge. https://doi.org/10.4324/9781003207610

Mandy, W. (2019). Social camouflaging in autism: Is it time to lose the mask? *Autism*, *23*, 1879–1881. https://doi.org/10.1177/1362361319878559Schaefer, C. E. (1993). *The therapeutic powers of play*. Jason Aronson. https://psycnet.apa.org/record/1993-97847-000

Schaefer, C. E., & Drewes, A. A. (2009). The therapeutic powers of play and play therapy. *Blending play therapy with cognitive behavioral therapy: Evidence-based and other effective treatments and techniques* (pp. 3–15). Wiley https://doi.org/10.1002/9781118269701.ch1

CHAPTER 8

A CHILD-CENTERED PLAY THERAPY APPROACH TO TREATMENT PLANNING

Rosie Newman

INTRODUCTION

Child-centered play therapy (CCPT) is one of the most common theoretical approaches for working with children (Lam•bert et al., 2005). CCPT is defined as a "dynamic interpersonal relationship with a child . . . and a therapist, trained in play therapy procedures, who provides selected play materials and facilitates the development of a safe relationship for the child . . . to fully express and explore the self . . . through the child's natural form of communication" (Landreth, 2012, p. 11). CCPT has been shown to be an effective therapeutic approach for social, emotional, and behavioral challenges (Baggerly et al., 2010; Lin & Bratton, 2015).

CCPT is informed by the principles of the person-centered approach postulated by Carl Rogers in the 1940s (Rogers, 1942). This approach emphasizes the importance of a relationship founded in empathic understanding, genuineness, and unconditional positive regard as the key agents of change in therapy (Jayne & Ray, 2015; Kaimaxi & Lakioti, 2021; Kolden et al., 2018). The goal of therapy is not to solve a problem but to facilitate a growth-promoting environment so that the client can become more integrated and authentic, allowing them to respond to challenges in new and healthier ways (Landreth, 2012; Rogers, 1951, 1951). Axline (1947) applied Rogers' person-centered philosophy to children with her eight basic principles of non-directive play therapy. Briefly, these espouse that the therapist is genuinely warm and accepting of the child; believes in the child's wholehearted ability to act responsibly; does not direct the play or conversation; and does not attempt to hurry the process (Axline, 1947).

The theoretical constructs of CCPT directly discourage the therapist from leading the conversation, pathologizing through diagnosis, dictating the direction of therapy, or presuming to know what the child needs (Axline, 1947; Landreth, 2012; Ray, 2011; Rogers, 1959). However, clinical settings require a problem or diagnosis that meets medical necessity to receive funding for services (Wampold 2001; Wiger, 2021). This can be antithetical to the healing properties of CCPT and can make treatment planning challenging.

Dee Ray (2011) speaks to this dilemma, offering guidance for CCPT therapists on behavioral assessments for caregiver benefit, diagnostic and administrative purposes, without eliminating the person-centered healing properties of change essential to the play therapy process. Building on Ray's (2011) work, differentiating between the measurable objectives and therapeutic work in play therapy allows the therapist to fully attune to the child's feelings and needs without the pressure of focusing on the problem or symptoms in play sessions. This can be achieved by creating a treatment plan that separates the quantifiable behavioral *symptom objectives* that can be addressed with caregivers and other stakeholders from qualitative internal *growth objectives* that are observed in CCPT sessions (Newman, 2020). This separation allows the therapist to fully attune to the child's feelings and needs without the pressure of focusing on the problem or symptoms. The interconnected relationship between these two types of objectives exemplifies how change occurs in CCPT—that *internal growth leads to external behavioral change*.

DOI: 10.4324/9781003334231-10

The following case study shows how identifying and tracking parallel but interrelated growth and symptom objectives is congruent with CCPT theory, with standards of care within the medical model, and, most importantly, with the theoretical constructs of how change occurs in CCPT. The case example is based on a case from clinical practice; however, some information has been significantly disguised to eliminate the possibility of identification.

CASE SCENARIO

Sonia is a 7-year-old biracial/bicultural Mexican-American child assigned female at birth. Sonia lives with her mother, father, and four-year-old brother and is in second grade at a local public school. Sonia's family is well-resourced financially, with adequate social support from family and friends. Sonia's mother sought play therapy to address Sonia's emotional outbursts, which were causing her family to "walk on eggshells" around her.

INITIAL INTAKE

During the parent-only intake with Sonia's parents, the therapist inquired about early life events, developmental milestones, and present concerns to begin formulating the goals for therapy and a diagnosis for billing purposes (Wiger, 2021). The therapist began building rapport with Sonia's parents, asking questions to understand the context of their experience and frustrations with parenting Sonia. In addition, the therapist focused on acquiring information about Sonia's behavioral issues, including frequency and intensity/duration, to formulate the symptom objectives of the treatment plan.

Sonia's parents stated that Sonia was experiencing intense emotional outbursts daily, lasting over two hours, when she didn't get her way. She was quick to anger, struggling to follow directions at school, and "bossing around" her peers and younger sibling. These challenges began about 3 years ago but have increased significantly since Sonia started her new school 3 months prior. They indicated that their goals for therapy were to increase the harmony at home, so they no longer feel like they're walking on eggshells around Sonia and for Sonia's behavior and peer relations at school to improve.

Case Conceptualization

From the initial intake, the therapist created a working hypothesis based on CCPT theory: Sonia's basic needs for connection, understanding, and worth were disrupted when her sibling was born, and again when she started a new school. Sonia may also have internalized negative beliefs about her self-worth, others, and the world which led to these emotional outbursts (Rogers, 1959). Following CCPT principles, the therapist aimed to create an environment of safety, an attuned relationship, and an understanding of Sonia and her experience. This would allow Sonia to increase her ability to trust herself and improve her flexibility, problem solving, self-regulation, resiliency, and ability to tolerate distress, allowing her to respond to upsets in a more authentic, regulated way.

In addition, the therapist maintained an awareness of Sonia's Mexican-American culture when providing support and psychoeducation to her parents to help them understand the feelings and needs beneath Sonia's anger. This was important to increase Sonia's overall feelings of being understood and, in turn, decrease her problematic behaviors.

Identifying Problem(s) and Diagnosis

The therapist separated Sonia's behavioral symptom objectives (e.g., decrease emotional outbursts) from internal growth objectives (e.g., increase self-regulation) in her treatment plan (see Appendix B.4). For diagnostic purposes, Sonia met the DSM-5–TR criteria for Adjustment Disorder, Unspecified due to her recent transition to a new school and the disproportion between her behaviors (level of distress) and the intensity of the stressors (American Psychiatric Association, 2022).

Assessment Process

The therapist conducted a traditional biopsychosocial intake using the Pediatric Symptom Checklist (PSC; Jellinek et al., 1999) and information collected from the parents in the intake. This process included creating a basic genogram to understand relevant medical and mental health family history and learning more about the family's support system. The assessment process consisted of five sessions: the initial intake with Sonia's parents, three CCPT sessions with Sonia, and then a parent meeting to discuss progress and develop the treatment plan.

Setting Goals

According to Landreth (2012), having specifically defined goals is counter to the CCPT theory of change and can therefore impede the client's process of growth. However, there are two key reasons for specifying treatment goals. First, most therapists must define a long-term goal and short-term measurable objectives, and provide a diagnosis, to meet the requirements of clinical settings (Wiger, 2021). Second, creating symptom-focused goals and objectives increases caregiver buy-in and enables therapists to explain the treatment plan in an "understandable manner" as emphasized in the Association for Play Therapy's (2022) *Best Practices*.

Establishing Measurable Objectives

Symptom objectives are quantitatively measurable objectives primarily based on the caregiver report from the initial intake. Growth objectives are qualitatively measurable objectives based on the therapist's conceptualization about the child's internal needs. Here are examples of both for Sonia:

- *Symptom objectives:* (a) decrease outbursts from daily to 4–5 times per week and decrease duration from 2 hours to 30 minutes or less; (b) decrease noncompliant behavior at school from daily to 3–4 times per week; (c) decrease "bossy" behaviors with peers and younger sibling from daily to 4–5 times per week.
- *Growth objectives:* (a) increase sense of self, self-regulation, frustration tolerance, flexibility, and problem solving; (b) increase social awareness, social engagement, healthy boundaries, and reciprocity in play.

Planning Theoretically Based Interventions

CCPT interventions consisted of 45–55-minute weekly play therapy sessions along with caregiver-only consultations every 3–6 weeks to assess progress toward symptom objectives not directly observed in play therapy sessions.

Collaborating With Client and Caregivers in Planning and Progress Tracking

In the initial intake, Sonia's parents reported the frequency and duration or intensity of Sonia's problematic behavior, which was used to establish symptom objectives and serve as a baseline for tracking progress. In subsequent caregiver sessions, parents reported the frequency and duration of Sonia's behaviors. The therapist shared with caregivers the progress toward growth objectives as observed during play sessions.

Tracking Progress

The following treatment summary outlines Sonia's play behaviors. It demonstrates how the therapist assessed and documented Sonia's progress toward symptom objectives (ascertained in caregiver-only sessions) and growth objectives (observed in play therapy sessions). A full play therapy session progress note appears in Appendix C.6.

In the first two play therapy sessions, Sonia entered the playroom cautiously and was slow to warm and engage with the therapist. She wanted to know the rules, asking questions such as, "Can I play with the ball?" After, the therapist shifted the responsibility to Sonia by saying, "You're wondering if it's okay to [blank]. In here, Sonia, you get to decide," Sonia began to show excitement at her newfound ability to make decisions in the playroom. By the third play therapy session, Sonia enthusiastically said, "I am going to decide to do [blank], then [blank] and [blank]!" This change in her demeanor showed an increased sense of relational safety with the therapist and increased trust in herself (see Table 8.1).

In the first caregiver follow-up, Sonia's parents reported that Sonia's outbursts still occurred daily, but Sonia seemed quicker to recover (improved duration). They reported that the bossy behavior remained frequent with no positive reports from school. The therapist shared that in play therapy Sonia started making progress toward organizing her internal world and began to trust herself, likely enabling her to regulate more quickly during outbursts (see Table 8.2).

In sessions four through six, Sonia chose to play catch with the therapist and then spent most of the time creating ball mazes. She explained that these mazes were "so hard," and she did not think the ball would make it. When the ball went outside of the maze, she exclaimed,

Table 8.1 Assessing Progress Toward Growth Objectives: Play Sessions 1–3

Growth Objective	Progress
Increase sense of self	Progress evidenced by decisively choosing how to spend play time rather than asking therapist

Table 8.2 Assessing Progress Toward Symptom Objectives: First Caregiver Follow-Up

Symptom Objectives	Progress
Decrease outbursts from daily to 4–5 times per week; decrease duration from 2 hours to 30 minutes or less per parent report	Now "quicker to recover" (less than 1 hour)

"Oh boo!" and tried again. Her increasingly regulated responses and willingness to try again demonstrated progress toward self-regulation, flexibility, and problem solving (see Table 8.3).

In sessions seven through nine, Sonia continued making mazes. She began involving the therapist in their creation and giving the therapist a turn to drop the ball down the maze. She asked the therapist whose turn it was and created a counting system on the whiteboard to track whose turn it was to add something to the maze and to run the ball through. This showed progress toward her growth objective of social awareness, social engagement, and reciprocity in play (see Table 8.4).

In the second caregiver follow-up, parents reported less frequent and shorter outbursts. They also reported that Sonia had been "nicer" to her friends and siblings with a newfound ability to play together successfully. The therapist shared that Sonia demonstrated social awareness and reciprocity in play by involving the therapist, which showed progress toward internal and relational growth (see Table 8.5).

In play therapy sessions 10 through 13, after a few minutes of creating mazes, Sonia began to create scenes in the dollhouse, where the doll family was preparing for the birth of a baby. The doll parents were "stressed out" and the older son got to play a lot of video games. The shift from mastery-based play (i.e., maze) to symbolic play (i.e., dollhouse) showed progress toward internal strength and safety and toward self-regulation (see Table 8.6).

In the third caregiver session, Sonia's parents reported that Sonia showed more empathy toward her sibling and was less quick to anger and more likely to find another solution. In

Table 8.3 Assessing Progress Toward Growth Objectives: Play Sessions 4–6

Growth Objectives	Progress
Increase self-regulation, frustration tolerance, flexibility, and problem-solving skills	Progress evidenced by ability to create new mazes when previous ones did not work

Table 8.4 Assessing Progress Toward Growth Objectives: Play Sessions 7–9

Growth Objectives	Progress
Increase self-regulation, frustration tolerance, flexibility, and problem-solving skills	Progress evidenced by creating tracking system for taking turns
Increase social awareness, social engagement, healthy boundaries, and reciprocity in play	Progress evidenced by involving therapist in maze-making and turn-taking

Table 8.5 Assessing Progress Toward Symptom Objectives: Second Caregiver Follow-Up

Symptom Objectives	Progress
Decrease outbursts from daily to 4–5 times per week; decrease duration from 2 hours to 30 minutes or less per parent report	Now 6x/week, lasting about 45 minutes
Decrease "bossy" behaviors with peers and brother from daily to 4–5 times per week per parent report	Sonia has been "nicer" more frequently

Table 8.6 Assessing Progress Toward Growth Objectives: Play Sessions 10–13

Growth Objectives	Progress
Increase sense of self	Progress evidenced by ability to go deeper into symbolic processing of new baby in the dollhouse
Increase self-regulation, frustration tolerance, flexibility, and problem-solving skills	Progress evidenced by shift in play from mastery to symbolic play in the dollhouse

Table 8.7 Assessing Progress Toward Symptom Objectives: Third Caregiver Follow-Up

Symptom Objectives	Progress
Decrease outbursts from daily to 4–5 times per week; decrease duration from 2 hours to 30 minutes or less per parent report	"Less quick to anger and easier to find another solution" per parent report
Decrease noncompliant behavior at school from daily to 3–4 times per week per teacher and parent report	"Fewer testing behaviors" per teacher report
Decrease "bossy" behaviors with peers and brother from daily to 4–5 times per week per parent report	"Showed more empathy" per parent report

addition, her teacher reported fewer testing behaviors and an increased ability to complete work. Sonia's parents expressed new insight about the emotional difficulty Sonia must have experienced when their second child was born. Without disclosing details of the play, the therapist shared that Sonia was showing the increased internal organization of her world, self-regulation, and an expanded window of tolerance to explore more difficult and previously overwhelming feelings in play (see Table 8.7).

Termination Process Strategies

Following the CCPT model, no direct interventions were provided to end treatment except for honoring the child's relationship in therapy with the option to create a special art project to take home. The therapist also wrote Sonia a card to express appreciation of the relationship and Sonia's growth in therapy over time.

CONCLUSION

Sonia's case illustrates a method for assessing progress toward symptom objectives in caregiver sessions and growth objectives in play sessions. This separation of the two types of objectives allowed the CCPT therapist to focus on the child, their play, and the relationship in play sessions rather than the caregivers' agenda. The therapist could trust that the caregivers' concerns about symptoms would be addressed through the theory of change; that internal growth will lead to behavioral change. By utilizing this dual process of objectives, the therapist was able to communicate to Sonia's parents how play therapy was helping her increase internal strength, and the parents were able to understand Sonia's external change in symptoms as a result of the internal growth.

Key Takeaways

♡ CCPT is informed by the principles of the person-centered approach postulated by Carl Rogers in the 1940s.

♡ The goal of therapy is not to solve a problem but to facilitate a growth-promoting environment so that the client can become more integrated and authentic, allowing them to respond to challenges in new and healthier ways.

♡ The theoretical constructs of CCPT directly discourage the therapist from leading the conversation, pathologizing through diagnosis, dictating the direction of therapy, or presuming to know what the child needs.

♡ Clinical settings require a problem or diagnosis that meets medical necessity to receive funding for services and this can be antithetical to the healing properties of CCPT and can make treatment planning challenging.

♡ Differentiating between the behavioral symptom objectives and the growth objectives in play therapy allows the therapist to fully attune to the child's feelings and needs without the pressure of focusing on the problem or symptoms in play sessions.

♡ Internal growth leads to external behavioral change.

REFERENCES

American Psychiatric Association. (2022). *Diagnostic and statistical manual of mental disorders* (5th ed. text rev.). https://doi.org/10.1176/appi.books.9780890425596

Association for Play Therapy. (2022). *Play therapy best practices*. Retrieved fromhttps://cdn.ymaws. com/www.a4pt.org/resource/resmgr/publications/best_practices.pdf

Axline, V. M. (1947). *Play therapy*. Ballantine Books.

Baggerly, J., Ray, D. C., & Bratton, S. (Eds.). (2010). *Child-centered play therapy research: The evidence base for effective practice*. Wiley. https://doi.org/10.1002/9781118269626

Jayne, K. M., & Ray, D. C. (2015). Therapist-provided conditions in child-centered play therapy. *The Journal of Humanistic Counseling, 54*(2), 86–103. https://doi.org/10.1002/johc.12005

Jellinek, M. S., Murphy, J. M., Little, M., Pagano, M. E., Comer, D. M., & Kelleher, K. J. (1999). Use of the Pediatric Symptom Checklist to screen for psychosocial problems in pediatric primary care: A national feasibility study. *Archives of Pediatrics & Adolescent Medicine, 153*(3). https://doi.org/10.1001/archpedi.153.3.254

Kaimaxi, D., & Lakioti, A. (2021). The development of congruence: A thematic analysis of person-centered counselors' perspectives. *Person-Centered & Experiential Psychotherapies, 20*(3), 232–249. https://doi.org/10.1080/14779757.2021.1938179

Kolden, G. G., Wang, C.-C., Austin, S. B., Chang, Y., & Klein, M. H. (2018). Congruence/genuineness: A meta-analysis. *Psychotherapy, 55*(4), 424–433. https://doi.org/10.1037/pst0000162

Lambert, S. F., LeBlanc, M., Mullen, J., Ray, D., Baggerly, J., White, J., & Kaplan, D. (2005). Learning more about those who play in session: The National Play Therapy in Counseling Practices Project (Phase I). *International Journal of Play Therapy, 14*(2), 7–23. https://doi.org/10.1037/h0088900

Landreth, G. L. (2012). *Play therapy: The art of the relationship* (3rd ed.). Routledge. https://doi.org/10.4324/9781003255796

Lin, Y.-W., & Bratton, S. C. (2015). A meta-analytic review of child-centered play therapy approaches. *Journal of Counseling & Development, 93*(1), 45–58. https://.org/10.1002/j.15566676.2015.00180.x

Newman, R. (2020). *Child-centered documentation: Treatment planning and assessing progress*. [PowerPoint presentation]. Seattle Play Therapy Training Center.

Ray, D. C. (2011). *Advanced play therapy: Essential conditions, knowledge, and skills for child practice*. Routledge. https://doi.org/10.4324/9780203837269

Rogers, C. R. (1942). *Counseling and psychotherapy*. Houghton Mifflin.

Rogers, C. R. (1951). *Client-Centered Therapy*. Houghton Mifflin.

Rogers, C. R. (1959). A theory of therapy, personality, and interpersonal relationships, as developed in the client-centered framework. In S. Koch (Ed.), *Psychology: A study of a science. Vol. 3. Formulations of the person and the social context* (pp. 184–256). McGraw-Hill.

Wampold, B. E. (2001). *The great psychotherapy debate: Models, methods, and findings*. Lawrence Erlbaum. https://doi.org/10.4324/9780203893340

Wiger, D. E. (2021). *The psychotherapy documentation primer* (4th ed.). Wiley.

CHAPTER 9

TREATMENT PLANNING FROM A COGNITIVE BEHAVIORAL PLAY THERAPY PERSPECTIVE

Sueann Kenney-Noziska

INTRODUCTION

Cognitive Behavioral Play Therapy (CBPT) (Knell, 1993, 2009, 2011) is a contemporary approach to play therapy with roots in Cognitive Therapy (Beck, 1963, 1964, 1967, 1976) in combination with behavioral therapies. CBPT operationalizes the constructs of Cognitive Behavioral Therapy (CBT) into a play therapy framework, given that the developmental levels of children and adolescents limit the use of the traditional verbal approaches to CT and CBT. CBPT is widely used in mental health to treat various presenting problems with diverse populations. It has a broad research base supporting both efficacy and effectiveness.

CBPT is based on the foundation that our patterns of thinking, feeling, and behaving are interconnected and influential in our experiences. CBPT aims to shift thought patterns, conscious and unconscious beliefs, attitudes, and behavior to facilitate improved overall functioning. Cognitive interventions encompass psychoeducation, positive self-talk, cognitive coping, cognitive restructuring, and problem-solving. Behavioral interventions include modeling, relaxation training, systemic desensitization, exposure, and contingency management (e.g., positive reinforcement, praise, shaping).

In contrast to more traditional approaches to play therapy, CBPT requires a more directive role for the therapist to achieve and sustain progress and treatment goals. Initially conceptualized as a briefer treatment approach, CBPT can be modified for children and adolescents who have experienced complex, interpersonal traumatic, or abusive events. The therapeutic relationship creates a lived experience for the client in which they encounter empathy, congruence, and unconditional positive regard (UPR). Like child-centered Play Therapy (CCPT) (Ray, 2011), the relationship is a crucial change agent in CBPT.

CBPT occurs in four phases: introduction, assessment, treatment, and termination. (Knell & Dasari, 2016). Although treatment planning is an ongoing process, in CBPT, it typically begins and is intertwined with the introduction and assessment phases. Treatment planning should include referral information as well as input from the client, parent(s)/caregiver(s), child/adolescent, teacher reports, and other relevant information from collateral sources (Cavett, 2015). If trauma is involved, a standardized assessment measure of posttraumatic stress symptoms and other common problems should be utilized (Smith et al., 2019).

CASE SCENARIO

Sophia is a 12-year-old Hispanic female who enters treatment due to symptoms of depression. Treatment was initiated by her mother, who called the therapy office seeking outpatient services. She described Sophia as "depressed" and "withdrawn." Per the mother, Sophia's teacher also has noticed Sophia appears to be experiencing "depression," and there has been

DOI: 10.4324/9781003334231-11

a slight decline in grades over the past few months. The mother denies any precipitating events or identified stressors. Sophia has never received therapy, nor did she receive any services at school.

Family System Factors

Sophia resides with her 33-year-old mother (Selena), 16-year-old half-brother (Stephan), 13-year-old half-sister (Carolina), and 2-year-old half-sister (Angelica). She had intermittent phone contact with her biological father (45), who resides in another country. Sophia has not seen her father since she was 4 years old. During the initial session with Sophia, she stated: "My dad has a new family," referring to the fact that her father remarried and has three children who reside with him and his wife.

Sophia's mother was 25 years old, and her father was 37 when she was born. There is a 12-year age difference between her mother and father. Her parents were never married. Her father works for a construction company as a frontline laborer. He does not pay child support or provide any financial support for Sophia.

Sophia's mother is a single parent who worked from home as a remote scheduling specialist for a medical center. She worked approximately 30 hours per week with somewhat flexible work hours. The mother reported having a series of "baby daddies" and described them all as "deadbeat dads." She was currently in a relationship with a man she had dated for 9 months. This man lived outside the home. According to Sophia's mother, the couple was engaged and expected to marry within the following year.

Cultural Factors

In CBPT, it is essential to consider culture broadly and inclusively. Cultural influence expands far behind race and ethnicity. It also includes religion, socioeconomic status, geographical area of residence, generational influences, and other factors. For a broad conceptual framework for understanding cultural influences, refer to Hays (2016). Pertinent cultural factors for Sophia included ethnicity, national origin, generational influences, patriarchy, collectivism, socioeconomic status, and religion.

The family self-identified as "Mexican." Sophia's maternal grandparents were first-generation immigrants. They composed the ethnic majority in the community where they lived. The entire family resided in a small community in the southwestern portion of the United States. Their community was economically limited.

The grandparents were Spanish-speaking, whereas Sophia, her mother, and her siblings were bilingual English-Spanish. The family structure was patriarchal (i.e., the father or a male elder had authority over the family). There was a strong sense of collectivism (i.e., characterized by respect for parental authority and solid, interdependent ties where family preservation supersedes individualistic independence). The grandparents have maintained many of their traditional Mexican customs and identity. Sophia described them as "old fashion Mexicans," whereas Sophia, her mother, and siblings were more acculturated and identified with Mexican and American culture and traditions. They all resided on the same acreage of property with separate houses for the grandparents, Sophia's family, and the maternal aunt and her family.

Socioeconomically, the family was low-income and underprivileged. They had less money, education, and resources than the other community members. The family received food stamps, and the children were insured through Medicaid. Sophia attended a designated Title 1 school (i.e., a minimum of 40% of attending students must qualify for free or reduced lunch). They were economically marginalized and resided in a small community.

The nuclear and extended family were Jehovah's Witnesses and attended the local Kingdom Hall. There was a long, strong following of faith in the family system. The grandparents actively participated in the faith, and the mother was raised as a Witness. However, the mother chose to turn away from religion during adolescence after having her first child at 17. The mother and children had recently returned to the faith. Sophia was not raised practicing despite strong familial roots in the Jehovah's Witnesses denomination. Nevertheless, she was significantly exposed to the faith through her grandparents and other extended family members.

Social System Factors

Social systems, the interrelationship between individuals, groups, and institutions, were relatively complex for Sophia and her family. Although an ethnic majority in her small community, Sophia and her family were ethnic minorities in the country where they reside. Additionally, they lived in a conservative Catholic community, contrasting several of their religious beliefs. The family did not value educational attainment. Sophia's mom did not complete high school and had only a 10th-grade education. Both of her older siblings struggled significantly in school. As noted, Sophia's grades had declined, albeit she reported that she enjoyed school and liked her teacher.

She was in the 6th grade and transitioned to a predominantly White Catholic middle school in a neighboring community the next academic year. Sophia was not in special education, nor did she exhibit any behavioral difficulties in the educational setting.

Sophia's mother reported hesitancy regarding mental health treatment as it was against the grandparent's wishes and inconsistent with the family's religious convictions. Even if Sophia struggled with severe depression, a recommendation for psychotropic medication would be incongruent with the family's religious beliefs. Fortunately, her current functioning level did not indicate the need for medicine as a first-line intervention.

Assessment in CBPT

In CBPT, assessment involves formal and informal evaluation measures. The Children Depression Inventory 2 (CDI-2) (Kovacs, 2011) was the formal measure utilized. Derived from the Beck Depression Inventory (BDI), CDI-2 is a 28-item self-report scale for assessing depressive symptoms in children and adolescents. It contains a total score, two scales (emotional problems and functional problems), and four subscale scores (negative mood/physical symptoms, negative self-esteem, interpersonal problems, and ineffectiveness). The CDI-2 has three reports (assessment, progress, and comparative) to monitor treatment progress.

The CDI-2 scores were elevated for the total score, emotional problems, and negative self-esteem. Interpersonal problems were significantly elevated. This suggested that Sophia may have had difficulties interacting with others, felt lonely, and believed she was unimportant to her own family. Scores were consistent with her depressed and withdrawn clinical appearance.

The informal assessment component consisted of three play therapy interventions. The Puppet Sentence Completion Task (Knell & Beck, 2000), Color Your Heart (Goodyear-Brown, 2022), and About Me Puzzle (Lowenstein, 2002) were utilized with Sophia. Completed sentence stems included: My sister… "gets more attention than me"; I am… "not loved"; I don't under-stand…"why I have to be Mexican"; and When I see other kids…"I'm jealous they get to cele-brate." Through the Color Your Heart and About Me Puzzle activities, Sophia processed feeling unloved by both parents, jealousy toward her younger sister for receiving "all the attention." And confusion as her family's Mexican American cultures and traditions often conflicted with the Mexican and Jehovah's Witnesses traditions and beliefs of the family system at large.

Presenting Issues

There was no "single" identified stressor for Sophia's withdrawn, depressed mood. Instead, a complex network of familial, religious, and Mexican heritage influences was combined into an intricate web. She felt unloved by both parents, was struggling to accept her new religious convictions, and found herself struggling to embrace her self-identity as a "Mexican Ameri-can" with such strong family roots in Mexican culture.

Diagnostically, Sophia did not meet the criteria for Major Depressive Disorder but did appear to have a depressed mood and withdrawal as a result of adjusting to her develop-mental stage and the complex collusion of her cultural- and self-identity. Subsequently, she was diagnosed with Adjustment Disorder with Depressed Mood (American Psychological Association, 2022). The adjustment was to the multiple transitions she was experiencing as she progressed from childhood to adolescence. She must address and integrate numerous issues to maneuver her world. In essence, she was adjusting to life. It wasn't straightforward for a Mexican American preadolescent female to know how to simultaneously find her way in a patriarchal environment and learn new doctrines of strict religion.

CBPT TREATMENT PLANNING

Drawing from CBT (Beck, 2021), the principles of CBPT treatment planning are based on the following: (a) diagnostic evaluation and cognitive formulation of the disorder(s), (b) general treatment strategies for that disorder, (c) clinician conceptualization of the client, (d) client aspirations, strengths, values, and senses of purpose, and (e) obstacles the client is facing in achieving their goals.

Overall Treatment Plan

- Reduce depression; increase understanding of self; increase self-acceptance.

Values and Goals
- Values: Family, school, Mexican American culture
- Goals: "I want to belong;" "I want to understand myself better."

Potential Obstacles
- Feelings of depression.
- Self-criticism.
- Negative self-talk.
- Doesn't want her mother involved in treatment.

Potential Interventions
- Psychoeducation regarding depression.
- Psychoeducation regarding the cognitive triangle.
- Reduce depressed mood.
- Increase positive emotions with a combination of positive experiences and mastery.
- Connect with family or other support people in a comfortable manner for the client.
- Increase awareness of cognitive distortions, particularly around her perception of self within her various cultural influences.
- Facilitate the client's ability to identify, challenge, and reframe cognitive distortions.

OPERATIONALIZING THE CBPT TREATMENT PLAN

In CBPT, directive play therapy interventions are purposeful and clinically grounded. Given her age and functioning, Sophia presented consistent with her chronological age. From a CBPT perspective, she had metacognition and the ability to think about her thoughts. This typically developed around age eight years. This opened many avenues to use play and other expressive media. Play therapy, bibliotherapy, games, puzzles, drawing, storytelling, puppets, and sandtray were utilized in CPBT to reach clear, established goals.

CBPT pulls from the therapeutic powers of play, as delineated by Schaefer and Drewes (2014). Therapeutic powers commonly associated with CBPT include direct teaching, indirect teaching, self-expression, abreaction, creative problem-solving, and social competency. When abuse or trauma has been experienced, catharsis, counterconditioning of fears, and stress inoculation are often associated with CBPT.

Trauma-informed CBPT has become a preferred treatment approach for children and adolescents impacted by abusive and traumatic events. CBPT can be integrated with the core components of evidence-based trauma treatment (National Child Traumatic Stress Network, 2022). It is also consistent with the evidence-based Trauma-Focused Cognitive Behavioral Therapy (TF-CBT) protocol as delineated by Cohen et al. (2006, 2017). TF-CBT is deemed effective for pediatric posttraumatic stress symptoms as well as secondary posttraumatic outcomes such as depressive, anxiety, and grief symptoms (Thielemann et al., 2022).

CONCLUSION

For the past 30 years, CBPT has been utilized with children and adolescents from various backgrounds and diverse presenting issues. CBPT provides a blueprint for integrating principles of CBT with play. Within a play therapy paradigm, CBPT facilitates the development of more adaptive thoughts and behaviors. It incorporates research-based interventions, including psychoeducation, cognitive restructuring, systematic desensitization, modeling, and relaxation training. Treatment plans are modified as needed for each client.

CBPT is a seminal play therapy theory that is developmentally accessible and appropriate for children's and adolescents' verbal and cognitive levels. It has a substantial research base supporting both efficacy and effectiveness. It is readily adaptable to be trauma-focused and integrated into the core components of evidence-based treatments (NCTSN, 2022) and the TF-CBT protocol (Cohen et al., 2006, 2017).

Key Takeaways

✩ CBPT operationalizes the constructs of Cognitive Behavioral Therapy (CBT) into a play therapy framework, given that the developmental levels of children and adolescents limit the use of the traditional verbal approaches to CT and CBT.

✩ CBPT aims to shift thought patterns, conscious and unconscious beliefs, attitudes, and behavior to facilitate improved overall functioning.

✩ The relationship is a crucial change agent in CBPT. CBPT requires a more directive role for the therapist to achieve and sustain progress and treatment goals.

✩ Treatment planning should include referral information as well as input from the client, parent(s)/caregiver(s), child/adolescent, teacher reports, and other relevant information from collateral sources.

✩ In CPBT, it is essential to consider culture broadly and inclusively. Cultural influence expands far behind race and ethnicity. It also includes religion, socioeconomic status, geographical area of residence, generational influences, and other factors.

✩ Therapeutic powers commonly associated with CBPT include direct teaching, indirect teaching, self-expression, abreaction, creative problem-solving, and social competency.

✩ CBPT can be integrated with the core components of evidence-based trauma treatment.

REFERENCES

American Psychiatric Association. (2022). *Diagnostic and statistical manual of mental disorders* (5th ed., text rev.). https://doi.org/10.1176/appi.books.9780890425787

Beck, A. T. (1963). Thinking and depression: Idiosyncratic content and cognitive distortions. *Archives of General Psychology, 42*, 441–447.

Beck, A. T. (1964). Thinking and depression. *Archives of General Psychology, 10*, 561–447.

Beck, A. T. (1967). *Depression: Clinical, experimental, and theoretical aspects*. Harper Row.

Beck, A. T. (1976). *Cognitive therapy and emotional disorders*. International University Press.

Beck, J. S. (2021). *Cognitive behavior therapy: Basics and beyond* (3rd Ed.). Guilford. https://psycnet.apa.org/record/2020-66930-000

Cavett, A. M. (2015). Cognitive-behavioral play therapy. In D. A. Crenshaw & A. L. Stewart (Eds.), *Play therapy: A comprehensive guide to theory and practice* (pp. 83–98). Guilford. https://psycnet.apa.org/record/2014-41947-006

Cohen, J. A., Mannarino, A. P., & Deblinger, E. (2006). *Treating trauma and traumatic grief in children and adolescents*. Guilford. https://psycnet.apa.org/record/2006-11899-000

Cohen, J. A., Mannarino, A. P., & Deblinger, E. (2017). *Treating trauma and traumatic grief in children and adolescents* (2nd ed.). Guilford. https://psycnet.apa.org/record/2017-07340-000

Goodyear-Brown, P. (2022). *Big behaviors in small containers: 131 trauma-informed play therapy interventions for disorders of dysregulation*. PESI.

Hays, P. A. (2016). *Addressing cultural complexities in practice: Assessment, diagnosis, and therapy* (3rd ed.). American Psychological Association. https://doi.org/10.1037/14801-000

Knell, S. M. (1993). *Cognitive-behavioral play therapy*. Routledge. https://doi.org/10.1037/e549312011-006

Knell, S. M. (2009). Cognitive behavioral play therapy: Theory and applications. In A. A. Drewes (Ed.), *Blending play therapy with cognitive behavioral therapy: Evidence-based and other effective treatments and techniques* (pp. 117–133). Wiley. https://psycnet.apa.org/record/2009-04903-006

Knell, S. M. (2011). Cognitive-behavioral play therapy. In C. E. Schaefer (Ed.), *Foundations of play therapy* (2nd ed.) (pp. 313–328). Wiley. https://doi.org/10.1002/9781119140467.ch6

Knell, S. M., & Beck, K. W. (2000). Puppet sentence completion task. In K. T. Gitlin-Wiener, K. Sandgrund, & C. Schaefer (Eds.). *Play diagnosis and assessment* (pp.704–721). Wiley. https://doi.org/10.4324/9781315181349-5

Knell, S. M., & Dasari, M. (2016). Cognitive-behavioral play therapy for anxiety and depression. In L. A. Reddy, T .M. Files-Hall, & C. E. Schaefer (Eds.), *Empirically based play interventions for children* (pp. 77–94). American Psychological Association. https://doi.org/10.1037/14730-005

Kovacs, M. (2011). *Children's depression inventory* (2nd ed.). Multi-Health Systems. https://doi.org/10.1037/t00788-000

Lowenstein, L. (2002). *More creative interventions for troubled children and youth.* Champion.

National Child Traumatic Stress Network (NCTSN) (2022). Core components of trauma-informed interventions. Retrieved December 4, 2022 from http://www.nctsn.org/resources/topics/treatments-that-work/promising-practices

Ray, D. C. (2011). *Advanced play therapy: Essential conditions, knowledge, and skills for child practice.* Routledge. https://doi.org/10.4324/9780203837269

Schaefer, C. E., & Drewes, A. A. (2014). *The therapeutic powers of play: 20 core agents of change* (2nd ed.). John Wiley & Sons. https://doi.org/10.1002/9781119140467.ch3

Smith, P., Dalgleish, T., & Meiser-Stedman, R. (2019). Practitioner review: Posttraumatic stress disorder and its treatment in children and adolescents. *Journal of Child Psychology and Psychiatry, 60*(5), 500–515. https://doi.org/10.1111/jcpp.12983

Thielemann, J. F. B., Kasparik, B., König, J., Unterhitzenberger, J., & Rosner, R. (2022). A systematic review and meta-analysis of trauma-focused cognitive behavioral therapy for children and adolescents. *Child Abuse & Neglect, 134.* https://doi.org/10.1016/j.chiabu.2022.105899

CHAPTER 10

A DIGITAL PLAY THERAPY™ APPROACH TO THERAPY PLANNING

Rachel A. Altvater

INTRODUCTION

Digital Play Therapy™ (Stone, 2022) is a therapeutic modality incorporating digital technologies in playfully engaging ways to assist clients in working through psychological distress. As Stone (2022) explains, "It is a component of a fundamental belief system regarding the respect and acceptance of a client's culture, combined with solid play therapy tenets" (p. 14). Digital Play Therapy™ offers clients a comfortable and familiar method for therapeutic connection, processing, exploration, and release. Present-day and future generations of children are digital natives, so they only know a world with rapidly growing immersive technologies, and much of youth's play and entertainment lies within technological screens. Incorporating digital tools in therapy will assist clinicians in gleaning greater insight into clients' inner and outer worlds, thus affording opportunities to meet them where they are, comprehend their methods of communication, and offer a therapeutic holding space rooted in genuine consideration for and connection to their interests.

Therapeutic modalities are specified methods of treatment, whereas theoretical orientations are a system of ideologies that conceptualize and aim to mitigate psychological suffering. In play therapy, there are two overarching theoretical frameworks—non-directive and directive. Non-directive aligns with humanistic theory, and directive includes various approaches that follow seminal psychological theories (Schaefer, 2011). Digital Play Therapy™ can be incorporated with any non-directive or directive therapy, as it is just another carefully selected tool available for projective expression and communication among all other play therapy tools within a virtual or in-person therapeutic play space. Digital tools are to be carefully selected based on a firm understanding of the theory the clinician is operating from; clinicians are to follow the core tenets of their chosen orientation, and digital tools are to be intentionally utilized in a way that the chosen framework encourages to foster therapeutic change.

This therapy planning guide follows the humanistic framework. While the core tenets of this model primarily follow child-centered/non-directive play therapy principles and interventions (Axline, 1969; Landreth, 2012), there are slight differences from traditional methods due to a clinician's typical lack of familiarity with many of these ever-growing and changing digital platforms in sessions. Depending on developmental abilities and the use of verbal dialogue in sessions, questions specifically pertaining to gameplay, digital worlds, and avatars are typically asked to enhance the conceptualization of therapeutic symbols, metaphors, and themes. Since the focus of humanistic theory is to allow the client to lead the session, there are frequent times that clients introduce unfamiliar digital play spaces to the clinician. This often leads to a sense of clinician uncertainty and perceived incompetence. Since play therapy often relies on working through thematic material, developing a firm understanding of what is presenting within the digital therapeutic play is necessary.

DOI: 10.4324/9781003334231-12

Providing a sense of permissiveness and offering clients opportunities to teach and enhance mastery further support the humanistic approach to treatment. Oftentimes, clients enjoy providing more in-depth information about their digital gaming spaces, as this tends to be an area of deep passion and interrelatedness.

CASE SCENARIO

Embry, a 9-year-old non-binary child, was referred for services due to heightened anxiety, particularly at night. It was reported that their anxiety typically presents as overwhelming hypothetical scenarios about death that result in rumination and emotional discomfort. Embry also struggled with unrealistic beliefs about how others perceive them in social relationships. The intensification of these difficulties resulted in long, tearful conversations with their caregivers every night and ongoing challenges with delayed and interrupted sleep. Embry was referred for services to receive further psychological assistance in processing and developing coping mechanisms to mitigate anxiety symptoms.

Embry began identifying as "not a boy" in kindergarten, which was followed by a period of confusion around what that meant. Their immediate family was supportive in encouraging them to wear, play, and live in a way that aligned with their true self. Their continued self-concept development evolved to gender identification as non-binary at the end of second grade.

Embry was reportedly verbal, articulate, insightful, and a quick learner. They are intellectual, which leads to deep thought and, at times, information overload. They became bored quickly and rarely felt challenged or would need to invest much effort, so they often easily became stressed when things were arduous. It was postulated that their current anxieties felt complex and unmanageable, as they were not easily resolvable. Embry's caregiver indicated that their sarcastic sense of humor with peers was often misunderstood, and they did not understand why others wouldn't comprehend the humor. Their advanced intellectual abilities seemingly resulted in incongruent social experiences and led to them thinking that others did not like them, which exacerbated social discomfort and overall anxiety.

Embry recently began to experience a noticeable increase in existential anxiety. It was reported that there were no major losses or significant illnesses or injuries to trigger fears of death. However, ongoing coronavirus pandemic public health safety concerns and an intensification in awareness of racial discrimination and injustices, war and genocide, and mass shootings in schools and the community, with some specifically targeting LGBTQIA+ individuals, seemingly contribute to heightened awareness and concern for the welfare of self and others.

THERAPY PLANNING PROCESS

Initial Intake

Incorporate questions in the intake about the utilization of technology. The following questions, derived from Altvater (2021), offer a foundational assessment of client interest, digital citizenship, screen time, and safety.

Children/Adolescents

1. What is your earliest memory of screen time?
2. How much time a day/week do you spend on the Internet, social media, and gaming?
3. What do you spend most of your time doing during your screen time? What do you think makes you spend the most time here?
4. What is/are your favorite games/apps to play? How come?
5. Tell me all about [insert game/app the client enjoys].
6. What is your favorite character and/or what character would you say you identify most closely with in [insert game/app the client enjoys]? What are their strengths and weaknesses?
7. What social media sites do you [and your friends, if applicable] use? Tell me as much or as little as you would like to share about [insert social media account name(s)].
8. What are some positive experiences you have encountered during screen time? Negative experiences?
9. What are your caregiver's rules and limits surrounding your screen time?
10. What do you know about Internet safety?

Caregivers

1. How much time a day/week do you and your child spend collaboratively and independently on the Internet, social media, and gaming?
2. How familiar are you with what your child is playing/doing online? Share any information that you know about how they spend their screen time.
3. Is your child presently encountering any difficulties related to screen time? If so, explain in as much detail as possible what is occurring.
4. What are your rules and limits surrounding screen time?
5. What does your child know about Internet safety? (pp. 177–178)

Embry expressed in the initial intake that they favored popular games in Roblox; however, they did not have opportunities to connect with peers despite them reportedly playing the same games. Screen time was closely monitored and limited by their caregivers. Upon further exploration, it was discovered that they and their siblings shared devices, which impacted the length of screen time for fairness, and their caregivers were concerned about what they could access online. Embry openly shared that they were aware of inappropriate content online and knew not to venture into the perilous areas of the Internet.

Embry's caregivers expressed limited knowledge about their screen time and gameplay. They indicated that they have parental controls on devices to limit access to content and provide set times for screen time for each child. They acknowledged that due to Embry's challenged social relationships, they believed the play offered alternate opportunities for social engagement, but they were unsure of the specifics of how Embry was spending their time in the digital realm.

Case Conceptualization

From a humanistic perspective, a client's presenting concerns emerge because their internal conditions of worth led them to disconnect from their true self. This disconnect leads to incongruence, anxiety, internally impaired locus of control, and a compromised ability to become self-actualized (Rogers, 1951). Individuals learn to act in certain ways when they are rewarded or valued for certain behaviors, and then conflict arises when they choose external over internal acceptance. This struggle between external expectations of who they should be and internal experiences of who they truly are creates a sense of false identity and a disconnect from the true self (Rogers, 1951).

Embry's general anxiety was a normal and expected human response to both real and perceived threats. It was likely exacerbated by a lack of connections to others, especially their peer group, as they were present in Erikson's (1950) psychosocial stage of Industry vs. Inferiority. Social interactions and a sense of capability and competence are the primary focuses in a child's life during this stage of development. Children would avoid situations and social support, mistrust others, struggle to initiate relational experiences, and feel discouraged and inferior if they encountered social challenges during this time. Embry likely felt disconnected from their true self due to perceptions of rejection from others and subsequent distancing and isolation which perpetuates the lack of close connections with others. At the time of intake, it did not appear that their gender identity further contributed to feelings of rejection and disconnect from the self, as their family was supportive and discrimination or rejection concerns were denied.

Assessment Process

Employed play in assessment and treatment provided a developmentally necessary method to meet the unique needs of children (Bratton et al., 2005; Landreth, 2012). Children under age 11 often think concretely, as they have not yet developmentally mastered abstract thinking (Piaget, 1962). This advanced form of thinking was necessary to formulate and comprehend many verbal communications (Bratton et al., 2005; Piaget, 1962). Due to the child's preference for and interactions with digital toys, it was advantageous to implement them in the assessment process to provide additional insights into presenting and underlying concerns.

During the assessment phase of therapy, when the clinician continued to gather clinical information through non-directive play, Embry and the clinician engaged in digital play with several of the competitive- and fear-based Roblox games discussed in the initial intake. They frequently made unkind remarks about others in the gaming space, often reflecting on other players' lack of intellect. Of note, the commentary was provided in the HIPAA-compliant teletherapy platform with only the clinician present, so no comments were heard by other players. It became readily apparent through their gaming interactions that they distanced from and rejected others, seemingly feeling like they could only rely on themselves, as evidenced by not participating in team activities and seeking resources alone. Embry reflected on a lack of trust toward and connection with others.

Identifying Problems and Diagnosis

Mental health diagnoses are provided after careful consideration of presenting concerns, gathering comprehensive background information, and conducting a clinical assessment, which may expand over the course of several sessions. In regard to conceptualizing and incorporating digital play in therapy, it is essential that clinicians remain mindful of how their personal beliefs and level of comfort influence their perspective. While screen time can be a valid concern, sometimes unhealthy use is actually a method of coping or avoiding a more deep-rooted psychological concern. Prior to categorizing digital tools as a problem, enter this space with a client to uncover more about what is occurring here for them to develop a clearer view of their challenges. If clients feel a sense of disconnect or rejection from the clinician due to their personal biases, it could significantly hinder the therapeutic relationship and treatment progress.

After a thorough clinical assessment, Embry received the following diagnoses:

F41.1 – Generalized Anxiety Disorder

Z60.9 – Other Problem Related to Social Environment

Setting Goals

Goals were chosen carefully considering the client's diagnostic concerns and effective methods for relieving their psychological distress. In digital play, it is helpful to align gaming goals with therapeutic goals. For example, with Embry, goals for confronting anxiety-provoking situations in fear-based gameplay and building trust and forming meaningful relationships in team and role-playing gameplay was seemingly a more comfortable, projective experience to address their concerns from a safe enough distance in therapy.

Establishing Measurable Objectives

Clinicians assessed needs, established practical goals, and then identified objectives focused on reduction of symptoms and level of psychological distress. Objectives were actionable steps that supported the overarching therapy goals. Clinicians utilized their theoretical framework as a guide to clearly delineate what would be implemented in sessions to reach specified target areas in play therapy treatment.

Planning Theoretically-Based Interventions

As defined by Rogers (1951), in humanistic therapy, rapport with and acceptance by the clinician facilitates the client's own self-acceptance. The clinician created a growth-promoting environment through congruence, unconditional positive regard, and accurate empathetic understanding. Through therapy, the goals were for the client to see themself as whole and complete, to be authentic, to become emotionally competent, to relate to others in a way that they are able to balance personal beliefs and respect for difference, to heal the past, and to achieve honesty and autonomy. The clinician helped the client discover how they could personally reach self-awareness and self-actualization.

In non-directive play, the client takes the lead, so interventions are chosen by the client. Play therapists utilize non-directive play therapy techniques of tracking, reflection of content, and reflection of feeling (Landreth, 2012). Embry had the power and control to choose each digital tool that was implemented in session. During digital play, the clinician provided the same non-directive methods as used in traditional play therapy services. Aforementioned, some direct questioning is provided about the gameplay for clarification of what is occurring to enhance conceptualization.

Collaborating with Client and Caregivers and Progress Tracking

It is recommended that clients and caregivers remain active participants in the therapy planning and tracking process. Younger children might struggle with clearly understanding and articulating problem areas and engaging in a verbal needs assessment. However, the client was typically an active participant in their play so that clinicians could gain insight into the inner workings of their psyche through play-based assessment and treatment, incorporating both verbal and nonverbal indications in therapy planning and progress tracking. The level of caregiver involvement will vary depending on client needs and caregiver engagement. A general rule of thumb is to meet with caregivers every 4–6 weeks. Meeting more frequently is sometimes desired by caregivers; however, with play therapy, it takes several sessions to identify recurrent thematic material more clearly. All caregivers are encouraged to reach out with pertinent updates and/or if they want to converse further about sessions. Providing overarching themes versus detailed session content is a beneficial way to balance confidentiality while including caregivers in therapy.

Older clients typically want increased privacy, so progress tracking and regular check-ins might become a bit more challenging. Embry did not want clinician to connect with their caregivers much, so their caregivers respectfully offered more space. During one session, there was an idea presented by Embry to increase connections with peers the clinician recommended including their caregivers at the start of the following session to communicate and advocate for these desires, as additional support from them was needed.

Tracking Progress

Progress in play therapy is tracked through client and caregiver self-reports and ongoing evaluation of dynamic play experiences. It is recommended to schedule parent check-ins for ongoing assessment of behavioral, emotional, and relational changes. During the working through stage of play therapy, there will typically be movement/change in the play interactions, and the metaphors and themes will often begin to tell a clearer story about the child's psychological inner workings. Assessing how gaming progress in digital play parallels therapeutic goals is a beneficial way for clinicians to uncover how the digital realm is supporting therapy progress.

Termination Process Strategies

A beneficial method of incorporating digital play in the termination process is by using gaming as a metaphor for their therapeutic experience. Clinicians can liken the process of therapy to the beginning, middle, and end of a digital game. When there are clear connections between game play and client difficulties and the client is emotionally and cognitively able to bridge the connection between a character/avatar and their experiences, the content can be further reflected on in sessions. Highlighting introductory uncertainties, anxieties, and challenges, utilization of supports and resources, the process of transformation and enhancement of skills, and overcoming the obstacles and succeeding can provide a beneficial roadmap and facilitate the termination process (see Appendix B.5).

CONCLUSION

Theoretically sound therapy planning continues to expand as the field of psychology develops a more refined understanding of variations in the human condition. While well-established, traditional evidence-based, and research-informed methods of therapy remain effective, more frameworks and methodologies are developed, explored, and practiced to meet the ever-evolving needs of humans. Innovative methods are historically initially met with resistance due to uncertainty and unfamiliarity, and then they often eventually transform into the new gold standards of treatment. The digital era has significantly impacted countless aspects of present-day existence. Inevitably, this sociocultural transition pervades human psychology, and thus play therapy services. This chapter offers careful therapy considerations and provides a clinical example to guide clinicians on how to connect to intricate aspects of digital native children's lives in a clinically sound manner. Incorporating digital tools in therapy assists modern children in working through their challenges with an approach that is familiar and comfortable for them. The Digital Play Therapy TM therapeutic modality provides clinicians with the framework and skills to meet children where they are and affords opportunities to speak through their modern facilitator of language.

Key Takeaways

- ♡ Present-day and future generations of children are digital natives.
- ♡ Digital Play Therapy™ can be incorporated with any non-directive or directive therapy.
- ♡ Digital tools are to be carefully selected based on a firm understanding of the theory the clinician is operating from.
- ♡ If a child's preference for and interactions with digital toys are indicated, it is advantageous to implement them in the assessment process to provide additional insights into presenting and underlying concerns.
- ♡ Questions specifically pertaining to gameplay, digital worlds, and avatars are typically asked to enhance the conceptualization of therapeutic symbols, metaphors, and themes.
- ♡ Providing a sense of permissiveness and offering clients opportunities to teach and enhance mastery further support the humanistic approach to treatment.
- ♡ Specific questions offer a foundational assessment of client interest, digital citizenship, screen time, and safety.
- ♡ While screen time can be a valid concern, sometimes unhealthy use is a method of coping or avoiding a more deep-rooted psychological concern.
- ♡ Assessing how gaming progress in digital play parallels therapeutic goals is a beneficial way for clinicians to uncover how the digital realm is supporting therapy progress.

REFERENCES

Altvater, R. A. (2021). The culture of technology and play therapy. In E. Gil & A. Drewes (Eds.), *Cultural issues in play therapy* (2nd ed., pp. 172–190). Guilford Press. https://psycnet.apa.org/record/2021-46047-009

Axline, V. M. (1969). *Play therapy* (rev. ed.). Houghton-Mifflin.

Bratton, S. C., Ray, D., Rhine, T., & Jones, L. (2005). The efficacy of play therapy with children: A meta-analytic review of treatment outcomes. *Professional Psychology: Research and Practice, 36*(4), 376–390. https://doi.org/10.1037/0735-7028.36.4.376

Erikson, E. H. (1950). *Childhood and society*. Norton.

Landreth, G. (2012). *Play therapy: The art of the relationship* (3rd ed.). Routledge. https://doi.org/10.4324/9781003255796

Piaget, J. (1962). *Play, dreams and imitation in childhood*. Norton.

Rogers, C. (1951). *Client-centered therapy: Its current practice, implications and theory*. Constable.

Schaefer, C. E. (Ed.). (2011). *Foundations of play therapy* (2nd ed.). Wiley.

Stone, J. (2022). *Digital play therapy: A clinician's guide to comfort and competence* (2nd ed.). Routledge. https://doi.org/10.4324/9780429001109

CHAPTER 11

USING A FAMILY SYSTEMS APPROACH TO ASSESSMENT AND TREATMENT

Eliana Gil and Timothy Baima

INTRODUCTION

A Family Systems approach to therapy assumes that all behavior makes sense in the context of relational patterns. A child's challenges are often a response to distressing gridlocked relational dynamics such as fusion, triangulation, coalitions, and/or ineffective hierarchies (Minuchin & Fishman, 1981; Satir, 1983). Systemic theory postulates that the presence of a problem stabilizes the larger family system in some way. For example, when a child is triangulated into emotional distance between parents, their presenting problem may provide one or both parents with a focal point to avoid distress in their relationship. Systemic theory predicts that treating a child's symptoms without attending to the larger family dynamics will reinforce the triangulation in the family. Therefore, Family Systems models of treatment endeavor to facilitate sustainable change by transforming the relational dynamics in which the child and presenting issues are immersed. Furthermore, culturally attuned systemic therapists explore how family dynamics are linked to broader social institutions, cultural norms, and systems of power and oppression (Hardy, 2016; McDowell et al., 2002).

Historically Family Systems approaches prioritized relational transformation so much that the needs of individuals were often overlooked, particularly in the case of children. The thinking was that if the system no longer requires the presence of a problem, the child's problem will disappear (Wachtel, 2004). Systemic theory maintains the view that "the whole is more than the sum of its parts." Therefore, a system cannot be understood by separating and analyzing each part. Instead, the whole system must be observed. However, understanding the system is not mutually exclusive with understanding the individuals in that system (Gil, 2006; Wachtel, 2004). We suggest that assessment include the interaction of three lenses: (1) Self (individual issues for each child); (2) Family System (relational patterns and opportunities for attachment); and (3) Social Systems (social relationships outside the home, and dynamics of power and oppression).

While Family Systems models of treatment have long included playfulness, interventions have largely served as ways to teach, enactments used for assessment, or ice-breakers designed to get families talking. A relatively small body of work highlights the value of play in and of itself as a therapeutic means to restructure problematic family dynamics, promote secure bonding, and facilitate healing (e.g., Booth & Jernberg 2010; Gil, 2015; Daley et al., 2019). This chapter embraces the power of play as useful for assessment and treatment.

CASE SCENARIO

Brody was an 8-year-old boy who had developed school refusal and whose grades had dropped significantly. He had an African American mother, Monique, a Caucasian father, Alexander, and a ten-year-old brother, Alex.

DOI: 10.4324/9781003334231-13

Initial Intake

We suggested that the systemic intake begin by meeting with the parents. This positions therapists to achieve several foundational therapeutic objectives to a systemic treatment approach including:

- Developing a strong therapeutic alliance with the parent(s).
- Ensuring a thorough assessment of the parents' understanding of the presenting problem.
- Assessing and validating parents' attempts to address the issue so far, and learning their perspective on what has and hasn't worked and why.
- Providing parents with an empathetic context to vent frustrations about their child (Wachtel, 2004).
- Assessing dynamics in the parental subsystem; and
- Reframing the presenting issue as relational and recruiting parental investment in a systemic treatment trajectory.

In the initial intake, the tension between Alexander and Monique was palpable. Each parent seemed to want to appear more professional and sensitive than the other, and each jockeyed to suggest ways the other parent may be a part of the problem. However, both agreed that there had been a tremendous amount of tension in the home recently because 6 months prior, Monique had discovered that Alexander was having an affair. While they were careful to avoid talking about the affair with the kids, they often discussed divorce, and Alexander had moved out of the home for 2 months. At the time of intake, they were seeing a couples therapist who was helping them process the affair. Alexander wanted to save the relationship, and Monique was open to this outcome, but uncertain and hurt.

Monique stated that Brody always wanted more attention from his father, but Alexander seemed closer to Alex, who is lighter skinned. Father identified this as a racist accusation, adding it was a typical example of the kind of nonsense mother made up to make him look bad. Father felt that mother was hard on Brody and pushed him, noting that she was "controlling" with everyone. Mother said that she wouldn't push Brody so much (to do schoolwork, for example) if Alexander held up his end. Both parents described their early courting relationship as "blah," and agreed that had Monique not been pregnant with Brody, they would not have married.

Assessment Process

The most optimal family play assessment activities are designed so that clinicians can observe individual expression, systemic dynamics, and the connection between the family and society with an emphasis on power dynamics. Family play therapists bring the whole family together to observe relational dynamics. As therapists join with the family, they witness how the system operates before endeavoring to reshape relational dynamics (Minuchin & Fishman, 1981). Therapists may also meet with subsystems to zoom in on one aspect of a family and then return to whole-family meetings to observe those dynamics in the context of the whole. Because so much occurs simultaneously in family play sessions, therapists are strongly encouraged to watch video recordings of sessions as part of an assessment process.

I met with the parents again to assess their ability to work towards being more unified as parents, even if they decided to dissolve their marriage. I asked Monique and Alexander to pick a miniature that showed their relationship when it was at its best. I wanted to focus some on this couple's strengths, but the activity reinforced the unstable beginnings of their relationship. Mother picked a fire hydrant and said she was always putting out fires that he created. Father picked an adult holding a little girl's hand and stated that from the outset, Monique wanted to be taken care of as if she was a child. Given that I had asked them for miniatures that described their relationship at its' best, I noted that they had a quid pro quo early on: Mom was the resource to Dad, capable of solving whatever problems came up. Father was able and willing to be the caretaker to his wife, and both had played their roles with clarity. Amazingly, their anger became a little less intense as they noted that neither of them started out with a level playing field, that is, each of them brought some expectation that was difficult to meet. The couple agreed to sign a release of information so I could coordinate treatment with their couple's therapist.

Assessment then moved to family sessions. The therapist facilitated a family play geno-gram in which family members were asked to select miniatures that expressed some thoughts and feelings about each family member, including themselves. Family play genograms are a powerful intervention that often reveal numerous individual, family, and social dynamics by objects chosen, how they are arranged, what people say about them, and how each family member responds (Gil, 2016; McGoldrick et al., 2020). Since a thorough description of all of the assessment information that can be gained from a single-family play genogram would exceed the page constraints of this chapter, just a few highlights are described below.

The alliance between Alexander and Alex became clear when the father chose a playful puppy for his son and Alex chose a vet feeding a puppy with a bottle for his dad. Additionally, both placed their objects facing each other on the genogram. Alexander chose Spiderman for Brody and said that he is capable of doing amazing things. While this sounded like an encour-aging statement, the therapist thought about Spiderman losing his father figure in Uncle Ben and wondered if Alexander overestimated Brody's independence while missing his vulnerability. The therapist also wondered about the significance of Spiderman being completely covered up, head to foot, particularly after Monique's statements about Alexander favoring his fairer-skinned son. Monique's choice of a boy playing guitar for Alex led to some discussion of Alex's interests and attributes. This choice stood in contrast to her choice of a cute mythical creature for Brody, about which she said, "He's adorable and cuddly, and he calms me down when I'm upset, but he's also a mischievous little troublemaker!" For his mom, Brody chose two cats playing with each other and talked about his closeness with his mom. The therapist noted that these cats are entangled with one another, and one cat seems to be swatting the other, suggesting a combination of closeness and conflict. A discussion of this miniature revealed that Brody had been sleeping with his parents more nights than not for the past three years, ever since he expressed distress about starting kindergarten three years prior. Alexander often slept in Brody's bed to have more space. Monique chose an octopus for herself, saying that it captures how busy she feels, and Brody placed her octopus in a plastic container and added water. The therapist noted how this act seemed to simultaneously suggest a way to care for the octopus while also containing and isolating it. Further indications of power dynamics showed up in the parents' selections for each other. Alexander chose a Black princess in an eloquent gown, saying, "She's my African princess," to which Monique visibly cringed and looked away. Monique chose a large football player for Alexander, saying he likes football. The therapist noted that the miniature was near twice the size of any other chosen for the family and he was in full gear with his hand extended, which may have indicated dominance, power, and difficulty getting through that exterior shell.

Case Conceptualization

As previously indicated, the description of the two sessions using miniatures highlights just a few examples of the type of powerful material that can come to the surface. Repeated symbolic themes and exchanges eventually revealed that this family had been hurting for a long time. Brody's parents did not have a strong, loving foundation for marriage and entered marriage because of Brody's impending birth. Thus, both parents see Brody as the cause of this precipitous union. Monique's parents criticized her for getting pregnant, and for giving up her career aspirations. Monique felt that her parents, extended family, and friends had negative attitudes about her marrying a white man and called the authenticity of her Blackness into question. Her feeling of needing to justify herself to Black friends and family increased a sense of isolation—not only in terms of family distress but also for much-needed support when she experienced racism at work. Monique especially took issue with Alexander's way of shrugging off racist comments from his family or jokes from cousins and siblings as merely outdated ways of thinking. Monique's pain in learning about Alexander's infidelity was compounded by the fact that he had developed a relationship with a white woman who was in the same field she had given up to take care of her children.

Brody was unable to process the range of emotions he had about his parents' conflict. In this family, one child appeared to be favored over the other, and the father did state that Alex looked more like he did when he was a child. With some pride, he said, "Alex is the spitting image of me when I was his age... If you put two pictures together of us, you won't know who's who." When I asked Dad who Brody looked like, he said, "No clue." The therapist hypothesized that this couple had avoided a great deal of emotionally demanding relational work through triangulation. The marriage and parenting began under duress, with neither parent ready to take on the responsibility of being partners and/or cooperative parents, and they had not formed a sense of identity as a couple nor shared meaning about their lives together. Alexander had initially moved away from Monique and towards his career, a move he justified as necessary for financial support. Monique had tried to get Alexander to be more involved as husband and father yet found that being honest with him only seemed to elicit his defensive distancing. Frustrated and heartbroken, she too pulled away from the marriage and invested energy in her kids—much to the expense of her own career aspirations. This triangulation likely accounted for at least part of Brody's distress 3 years back when he started kindergarten. As Monique grew closer to Brody through attempts to comfort him, she became increasingly critical of Alexander for being distant and uninvolved. Brody seemed to have internalized his mom's frustration and acted out whenever Alexander did make attempts to connect with Brody. Alexander experienced Brody's distress as tantamount to being rejected by him and began to invest his energy into Alex, who was happy to have his full attention. After the infidelity was revealed, Monique clung more tightly to Brody as a source of comfort, further deteriorating a healthy hierarchy in that relationship, and Monique began to experience Brody's school refusal and dropping grades as a betrayal. The school refusal drew Alexander and Monique together as they attempted to find solutions to help Brody overcome anxiety and provided the parents with a distraction from recent marital distress.

The therapist understood Brody's school refusal and dropping grades as a response to relational dynamics in the family. Based on this hypothesis, the following diagnoses were given:

F43.23 Anxiety Disorder with mixed anxiety and depressed mood

V61.20 Parent-Child Relational Problem

Setting Goals and Measurable Objectives

In a Family Systems approach, goals for treatment are rooted in the assumption that the mental health of children is inseparable from larger family and social systems, and the quality of attachment bonds. Goals and objectives focus on restructuring systems as well as targeting specific symptoms. To set goals that are consistent with a family system's theoretical framework, it is essential to remember that a child's mental health is inseparably connected to the larger family system and the quality of that child's attachment bonds. Therefore, family play therapists may develop goals and objectives that focus on restructuring the family system as well as targeting specific symptoms. A challenge for family system practitioners is to be able to articulate how each goal, objective, and intervention addresses the presenting problem and diagnosis, whomever they are working with in any given session; the individual child, the whole family, or a subsystem in the family (e.g., parents). While family system therapists may work with the whole family, subsystems, or individuals in a family, they ought to be able to articulate how each goal, objective, and intervention addresses the presenting problem and diagnosis. Therapy progresses in a nonlinear fashion and therapists may address multiple goals simultaneously or focus on them in any order. Specific goals and objectives for Brody and his family are included in the sample treatment plan (see Appendix B.6). The reader will note that interventions are integrated with measurable objectives. This is because simply engaging in an intervention can be an indication of increased relational flexibility, even as the intervention serves to facilitate further restructuring of the family system (see Appendix B.6 for Sample Treatment Plan).

Planning Theoretically Based Interventions

Systemic interventions may involve psychoeducation and strategizing with parents, as well as individual and family play sessions. Ideally, interventions and strategies are designed to complement one another. For example, the strategy to have Alexander take Brody to school positions Alexander to be the person who provides Brody with comfort and encouragement and supports some separation between Brody and Monique. Family sessions that facilitate the expression of emotion, and Theraplay activities between Brody and his father, increase the likelihood that Brody will experience his dad as a source of comfort (Booth & Jernberg, 2010). When Brody internalizes comfort and encouragement from his dad, Alexander feels enhanced competence as a father and experiences Brody as less rejecting of him.

It is vital that therapists construct play interventions that support both individual expression and family interaction. Examples of such interventions can be found in books such as *Play in Family Therapy*, second edition (Gil, 2015), and *Family Play Therapy* (Schaefer & Carey, 1994).

Tracking Progress

Progress is assessed by a combination of self-report and observation.

Termination Strategies

Termination will begin to be addressed when treatment goals are met regarding the presenting problem (for example, the child attends school three out of five days a week initially; the child will attend school every day eventually). However, once presenting problems decrease, it is important to see if the family will maintain this new homeostasis, or if a new default strategy will show up that reflects another unmet family need. Thus, our clinical role is to notice how things improve and what changes emerge as things get better. Eventually, when all goals have been addressed and progress has been at least 80%, termination can start in earnest, usually gradually decreasing treatment appointments.

CONCLUSION

From a systemic theoretical orientation, a child's symptoms are viewed in the context of the larger family dynamics. Without this perspective, there is a risk of reinforcing dysfunctional patterns in the family. Sustainable change can be supported by transforming the relational dynamics within the family system that may contribute to a child's presenting issues. When a child's behavior is singled out as the presenting problem, a Family Systems approach, with expressive therapies integrated, can support the clinician's development of a treatment plan to address the family dynamics and thereby address the child's presenting problems.

Key Takeaways

- ♥ Family systems models of therapy seek to promote sustainable change by transforming the relational dynamics that create, sustain, or in some way contribute to a child's presenting issues.
- ♥ A Family Systems approach to therapy assumes that all behavior makes sense in the context of relational patterns.
- ♥ Assessment can include the interaction of three lenses: 1. Self (individual issues for each child); 2. Family System (relational patterns and opportunities for attachment); and 3. Social Systems (social relationships outside the home, and dynamics of power and oppression).
- ♥ The power of play is useful for assessment and treatment.
- ♥ Family play therapists bring the whole family together to observe relational dynamics. As therapists join with the family, they witness how the system operates, before endeavoring to reshape relational dynamics.
- ♥ To set goals that are consistent with a family systems theoretical framework, it is essential to remember that a child's mental health is inseparably connected to the larger family system and the quality of that child's attachment bonds.
- ♥ Systemic interventions may involve psychoeducation and strategizing with parents, as well as individual and family play sessions.

REFERENCES

Booth, P., & Jernberg, A. (2010). *Theraplay: Helping parents and children build better relationships through attachment-based play*. Jossey-Bass. https://eric.ed.gov/?id=ED424491

Daley, L. P., Miller, R. B., Bean, R. A., & Oka, M. (2019). Family system play therapy: An integrative approach. *American Journal of Family Therapy*, *46*(5), 421–436. https://doi-org.paloaltou.idm.oclc.org/10.1080/01926187.2019.1570386

Gil, E. (2006). *Helping abused and traumatized children: Integrating directive and non-directive approaches.* Guilford. https://doi.org/10.1007/s10560-008-0144-y

Gil, E. (2015). *Play in family therapy* (2nd ed.). Guilford. https://psycnet.apa.org/record/2014-44088-000

Gil, E. (2014). Individual and family play genograms. In C. F. Sori, L. L. Heckler, & M. E. Bachenberg (Eds.). *The therapist's notebook for children and adolescents: Homework, handouts, and activities for use in psychotherapy.* Routledge. https://doi.org/10.4324/9781315867304-14

Hardy, K. V. (2016). Toward the development of a multicultural relational perspective in training and supervision. In K. V. Hardy & T. Bobes (Eds.), *Culturally sensitive supervision and training: Diverse perspectives and practical applications* (pp. 3–10). Routledge. https://doi.org/10.4324/9781315648064-1

McDowell, T., Knudson-Martin, C., & Bermudez, L. M. (2002). *Socioculturally attuned family therapy: Guidelines for equitable theory and practice* (2nd ed.). Routledge.

McGoldrick, M., Gerson, R., & Petri, S. (2020, 4th Ed). *Genograms: Assessment and treatment.* Norton. https://doi.org/10.4324/9781003216520-9

Minuchin, S., & Fishman, H. C. (1981). *Family therapy techniques.* Harvard University Press. https://doi.org/10.2307/j.ctvjnrtsx

Satir, V. (1983). *Conjoint family therapy* (3rd ed., rev. and expanded). Science and Behavior Books. https://doi.org/10.1093/sw/10.4.119

Schaefer, C. E., & Carey, L. (Eds.) (1994). *Family play therapy.* Rowman & Littlefield.

Wachtel, E. F. (2004). *Treating troubled children and their families.* Guilford. https://www.guilford.com/books/Treating-Troubled-Children-and-Their-Families/Ellen-Wachtel/9781593850722

CHAPTER 12

A FILIAL THERAPY APPROACH TO TREATMENT PLANNING

Risë VanFleet

INTRODUCTION

Ever since Filial Therapy was first conceived in the 1950s and then developed and researched by Drs. Bernard and Louise Guerney, it has inspired other similar interventions that are useful in their own right. This chapter will center on their original family model that remains in active use today. The author of this contribution studied in graduate school directly with both of the Guerneys in the early 1980s and fully certified by the Guerneys' organization as a therapist, supervisor, and instructor. The author is well-equipped to represent its approach to treatment planning having taught it to thousands of clinicians through the intervening decades.

WHAT IS FILIAL THERAPY?

Filial Therapy (FT) was the brainchild of Dr. Bernard Guerney and his wife, Dr. Louise Guerney, both clinical psychologists after they had been trained in child-centered play therapy (VanFleet et al., 2010) recognizing that parents had been left out of many treatment models. At the time, it was common for parents, and especially mothers, to be blamed for the problems of their children so they were not typically included in treatment. As the field of family therapy evolved since the 1960s, it became clearer that the benefits of individual treatment of children without the support of a nurturing environment from parents might not endure. The Guerneys wondered if parents could learn to conduct non-directive play sessions with their own children, under the tutelage and supervision of therapists, in a manner that might extend the benefits of play-based interventions indefinitely. Early research showed that parents could learn to conduct non-directive play sessions on par with therapists, and with therapist support, could implement them to improve parent-child and whole family relationships that supported positive change for children.

Relevant to this pursuit are two major shifts in thinking by the Guerneys that took two or more decades to begin to be accepted by the mental health community: (1) the use of a psycho-educational model rather than a medical model of intervention with children and families, and (2) the concept that family members could help each other by serving as the primary change agents for other family members (in the case of Filial Therapy, the parents serving as change agents for their children), with proper therapist support, in ways that yielded more efficient and effective outcomes. Nearly six decades of continuing research have shown FT to do just that. It has some of the best evidence for positive outcomes of any play therapy approach (Bratton et al., 2005; Grskovic & Goetze, 2008; Topham et al., 2011; VanFleet et al., 2005).

FT has been described in detail elsewhere (Guerney, 2003; Guerney & Ryan, 2013; VanFleet, 1994, 2014; VanFleet & Guerney, 2003). In short, it is based on a psycho-educational model that is theoretically integrated in unique and powerful ways. It is

DOI: 10.4324/9781003334231-14

grounded in the full integration of the following theories: psychodynamic, humanistic, behavioral, interpersonal, cognitive, developmental/attachment, family systems (Cavedo & B.G.Guerney, 1999; Ginsberg, 2003; L.F. Guerney & Ryan, 2013; Topham & VanFleet, 2011; VanFleet, 1994, 2014). One might ask how all these theories, with their rather different assumptions and underpinnings, could reside together in a single approach, and the answer lies in the psychoeducational, rather than the medical, model of helping people.

In short, a psychoeducational model posits that most behavioral, social, or emotional difficulties for people arise from lack of knowledge or skill or the ability to apply relevant knowledge or skills. Intervention, therefore, is based on thorough assessment followed by the provision of the necessary knowledge, skills, and application of these to the person's situation. While children often do this naturally in the playroom when given the chance, focus is also placed on helping parents develop the skills needed to build stronger relationships with their children. Therapists teach parents how to conduct child-centered, non-directive play sessions with their own children, supervise them as they do this until they become highly skilled, and then help parents transition the play sessions as well as everyday life use of the skills to the home setting.

FT is also a play-based approach, resting on the knowledge of the vast importance of play for healthy child development. Ginsburg (2007) wrote in a definitive clinical report for the American Academy of Pediatrics, "play … is essential to the cognitive, physical, social, and emotional well-being of children and youth" (p. 183). Child-friendly forms of mental health intervention are therefore based on the use of play. In the case of FT, the choice is to use non-directive play interactions, not only because of the evidence-based benefits for children but also because these types of interactions provide parents with the tools to enhance their attunement and attachment with their children while simultaneously strengthening parents' abilities to guide their children's development using similar practices. FT helps parents come together to offer what Baumrind (1971) labeled as authoritative parenting, considered the form that is most likely to lead to healthy child development in a variety of areas. Similarly, in terms of attachment theory, it helps parents offer a secure base and ways they can develop secure attachment/parenting styles (Bifulco & Thomas, 2012).

Skills and Sequence of Filial Therapy

In FT, therapists teach and hone four primary skills that parents use within the non-directive play sessions with their own children. These are structuring, empathic listening, child-centered imaginary play, and limit-setting. Parents learn to use these in three training sessions with the therapist that includes behavioral rehearsal (role-plays), reinforcement of improving parent skills, and feedback for continuing improvement. Then parents begin to hold dyadic play sessions with their own children, one by one, under therapist supervision. Each one is followed by a feedback session that helps shape parent competence and confidence. After four to six supervised play sessions, the therapist and parent determine when the home play sessions, once per week per child, begin, and the parents report back to the therapist to ensure that all goes smoothly. Part of the process is helping parents identify and understand children's play themes in their sessions, and ensuring that parents feel good about the process while working through any reactions to the play that they might have. Parents are capable of learning the play session skills to a high level.

TREATMENT PLANNING IN FILIAL THERAPY

From the first contact by phone or email, practitioners of FT are aware of relationship-building with parents. They use many of the same skills with parents during all interactions as they eventually help parents use them with their children. During the first intake meeting in person, therapists use ample empathic listening to ensure they understand parents' concerns and to reassure parents that they are being understood. While they ask questions needed to get a full picture of the child, much of that meeting is done without taking notes while the parents are there. Notes are written afterward. This is to strengthen the interpersonal focus of the interaction. There should be warmth and caring expressed to the parents, and the therapist restates, in summary form, the parents' primary concerns, often reframed in the form of what parents would like to see in the future. Thus begins a very collaborative process toward a treatment plan. Whenever possible, any forms needed to gather additional developmental, behavioral, or family information are given to parents to complete prior to the next session. This allows the first interactions to be interpersonal rather than impersonal, as paperwork often seems.

During the second session, a "Family Play Observation" (FPO) is held. The parents bring all their children into the playroom and simply have a playful time with the whole family. Nothing has been taught to parents at this point—it's still part of the assessment. The therapist observes these interactions among family members from an observation area or the corner of the room using peripheral vision. After approximately 20 minutes of the FPO, the therapist meets with the parents/caregivers only and asks the question, "With what just happened there, what things were similar or dissimilar to what happens at home?" Parents usually respond with their own observations which the therapist empathically reflects. Key questions and observations of the therapist are also discussed with parents afterward, once again accompanied by ample empathic listening. More information on this valuable assessment tool is included in VanFleet (2014).

It is at this stage that more specific goals and objectives are discussed, often in a third meeting with parents only. If FT is the treatment of choice, it is explained and discussed in detail, or if FT is part of a multimodal process, that is discussed as well. Therapists ensure that parents play an active role in developing the plan—collaboration is essential. Once the treatment plan is developed, FT begins with the training phase for parents as described earlier. This entire process is described more fully in L.F. Guerney & Ryan (2013) and VanFleet (2014).

CASE SCENARIO

Case Background

The case that follows represents a composite of several families involved in FT. All identifying information has been changed to protect the privacy of the families. It represents a typical FT case, however.

Name of Client: Rondanna, known as Rondie

Age of Client: 5 years

Family System Factors

This was an intact African American family, parents Mike and Claire, 14-year-old brother, Jamal. The family has functioned well in the past, and Jamal and Rondie have typically gotten along well together. Both parents were employed full-time. Mike was a computer programmer and Claire worked as a receptionist in a local dentist's office. Both sets of grandparents lived nearby and occasionally took part in childcare when needed. Jamal was doing well in school and participated in local sports. Rondie was scheduled to start half-day kindergarten in 3 months at the time of the intake. Rondie was diagnosed with insulin-dependent diabetes 6 months prior to the family seeking services. The family lived in a middle-income neighborhood in a small town environment and reported friendly relationships with neighbors.

Cultural Factors

The parents reported that their neighborhood was "somewhat diverse," with African American and other diverse families comprising approximately a quarter of the homes. They reported that they were active in the community and sought out activities, festivals, and musical events that were affirming of their racial and cultural identities. They did not feel ostracized or discriminated against in their community.

Social System Factors

Jamal and Rondie had local friends and Mike and Claire were friendly with neighbors. . They have been pleased with their local school system. Jamal has done well and is about to start ninth grade. The family did not know anyone else with a child with diabetes in their area, but has met others at the clinic they periodically attend. Rondie's upcoming school enrollment was a concern primarily due to her diabetes management needs.

Presenting Issues

The parents had few concerns prior to Rondie's diagnosis of insulin-dependent diabetes (Type 1). The diagnosis had hit everyone hard, and Mike and Claire were eager to help Rondie cooperate with blood tests and insulin injections. They were fully aware and somewhat anxious about, the implications of having good blood glucose control in the early days and years of Type 1 diabetes. Rondie had to be hospitalized prior to the diagnosis due to exceptionally high blood glucose levels, and this was traumatic for her and her parents. Her brother had been involved as the family learned together what they needed to do, and he tried to help when needed. Presenting issues centered on Rondie's poor emotional and behavioral adjustment to the demands of diabetes management. She resisted injections, blood testing, and dietary restrictions, often throwing tantrums. Mike and Claire described feeling out of control and were terrified about Rondie's well-being. They also noted that as family attention turned to Rondie's diabetes and resultant behaviors that Jamal was getting less of their attention. They were at a loss about how to adapt to Rondie's diabetes.

Initial Intake

The Filial Intake process described earlier was implemented. The initial meeting with Claire and Mike revealed high levels of stress and frustration, and they covered Rondie's behavior pre- and post-diagnosis. The therapist listened empathically to their intense emotions and asked additional questions to acquire a clear understanding of Rondie's overall health and development as well as the development of her diabetes. Family development through the years was also covered in some detail. The therapist, experienced with chronic illness in children, reassured the parents that she would help them reduce their stress and help them all adapt to this new reality.

Assessment

The therapist suggested a Family Play Observation as part of the assessment process, and all four family members attended. Rondie was shy, hiding behind her mother upon entering the office, but once in the playroom, she excitedly explored all the various toys. Claire showed Rondie items of interest, and Mike followed them around the room as well. Jamal went to a small chair in the corner of the room, and although he watched the rest of the family with interest, he did not participate. He seemed to be somewhat uncomfortable.

At the end of the 20-minute FPO, Jamal and Rondie went to a private play area of the waiting room while the therapist met with the parents. The therapist asked the usual questions about what they had noticed. They mentioned how excited Rondie was, and how nice it was to see her acting "normal" again. They also noted that Jamal seemed awkward, and chalked that up to his age. They reported that while the play time for Rondie was similar to her personality and interactions prior to her diagnosis, they had not seen her as a happy child since. Their home battles had taken over. In addition, they reported they had had more parenting disagreements than usual. The therapist then discussed their goals and began the process of recommending FT.

Case Conceptualization

This appeared to be a high-functioning family that had experienced some traumatic experiences as they encountered a difficult health challenge. All family members had experienced considerable stress and anxiety about the lifestyle changes required of them as well as the potential for complications in the future that could be damaging for Rondie. The therapist's conceptualization came primarily from a family systems point of view, looking at every level of the presenting issues: Rondie, Jamal, both parents, extended family, neighborhood, community, and school. This was not an individual child matter so much as it was a family matter. Rondie was likely feeling a loss of control, intrusions in several aspects of her life, much greater denial of things she enjoyed prior to the diagnosis, and possibly noticeable changes in how people in her extended family and community behaved toward her, which is common in these cases (VanFleet, 1985). The parents were experiencing life-and-death level worries about their daughter and trying to find the right balance of watchfulness and allowing her to be a normally developing 5-year-old. They also were experiencing some tensions in their relationship as they tried to find this balance. It appeared that Jamal was trying to be helpful during this big change in the family dynamics, and likely feeling left out as the focus of family life now centered on diabetes and its management. Family relationships were disrupted. The potential solutions would require attention to the needs of all family members so they could better support each other and resume a less conflictual daily life.

Identifying Problems and Diagnosis

The conceptualization above, based on full collaboration with the family and a holistic examination of the situation, discusses the range of problems being faced by the family, viewed through a systems lens. Because FT is not based on a medical model, diagnosis is not always needed for social, emotional, and behavioral issues, but given the full picture, an adjustment "disorder" with mixed emotional features would be relevant.

Setting Goals

The primary goals for the family was to (1) help Rondie adapt to and cooperate with her diabetes management, (2) help the parents express their feelings and find points of agreement and balance in their parenting that incorporates diabetes but does not allow it to rule their lives, (3) return attention to Jamal and his interests and needs, and (4) have all family members enjoy each other once again and engage in pleasant activities that all of them could enjoy. The family also had medical goals that would be resolved by helping Rondie with her emotional reactions and as they worked more closely with the medical personnel who could help them.

Setting Measurable Objectives

These included a decrease in the incidence of tantrums and arguments about diabetes to two per week; seeing Rondie develop at least three coping strategies to use when she was frustrated; to see Rondie express her feelings in words rather than throwing household items, screaming, and hitting her parents; to give Jamal one-to-one parent time at least 15 minutes per day; as a family to select and engage in one activity per week that is enjoyable for all of them; and for the parents to take at least 15 minutes per day to discuss the diabetes management to ensure they were in agreement and handling things consistently.

Planning Theoretically Based Interventions

With the family systems considerations in mind, and also incorporating the needs of individual members, the pre-diagnostic functioning, and the developmental needs of the children and family as a whole, it seemed that FT would be an ideal intervention to help address this family's goals. In VanFleet (2014), the goals of FT for children, parents, and the family as a whole listed on pages 16–17 clearly fit with the needs and goals and objectives of this family. Because of its systemic nature and ability to resolve these types of presenting problems, FT was the only intervention deemed necessary for this family. The rationale for this lies in matching the early descriptions of FT in this contribution with the needs of the family.

Collaborating/Including Client and Caregivers

As noted earlier, it is inherent in FT to use an extremely collaborative approach to every step of the treatment. Parents are seen as the primary change agents for their own children, and therapists teach them skills that will help and how to apply them in unique situations. FT has always been based on a fully collaborative model.

Tracking Progress

It is the author's longtime practice to regularly check in with parents or caregivers, no matter what type of interventions are being used. In FT, the parents are there at every meeting, and the therapist invites and listens to their views. Parents know what is happening at home, school, and community, and a dialogue each week that covers the play sessions and themes also includes how the parents perceive how the child is doing at home. The true test of progress is when the parents report that they are seeing improvements in the goals and objectives.

Termination Process Strategies

FT is a self-limiting form of therapy. Parents typically report progress after three or four play sessions, and by the time the parent-child play sessions are moved to the home, there is typically considerable progress. During the home session phase, a deliberate generalization of the skills learned is included as home play sessions are also reviewed and skills and understanding of play themes by parents are honed. For a family such as described here, it would be expected that the primary problems would be resolved or nearing complete resolution after 17 to 20 one-hour sessions.

CONCLUSION

Filial Therapy is one of the most powerful play-based interventions designed for children and their parents using a psychoeducational approach to strengthen families and resolve problems. Through training and supervision by the Filial Therapist, parents become the primary change agents for their own children as they learn to conduct special dyadic non-directive play sessions with their children. Filial Therapy is a flexible intervention that can be used as a single intervention, or in tandem with other interventions.

Key Takeaways

- ♡ Filial Therapy is a play-based psychoeducational model based on the belief that family members can be the agents of change for other family members.
- ♡ Filial Therapy is grounded in psychodynamic, humanistic, behavioral, interpersonal, cognitive, developmental/attachment, and family systems theories.
- ♡ Therapists teach parents how to conduct child-centered, non-directive play sessions with their own children, supervise them as they do this until they become highly skilled, and then help parents transition in the play sessions as well as everyday life use of the skills to the home setting.
- ♡ Parents are taught skills for structuring empathic listening, child-centered imaginary play, and limit-setting.
- ♡ Because FT is not based in a medical model, diagnosis is not always needed for social, emotional, and behavioral issues.
- ♡ It is inherent in FT to use an extremely collaborative approach to every step of the treatment. The true test of progress is when the parents report that they are seeing improvements in the goals and objectives.
- ♡ Filial Therapy is a flexible intervention that can be used as a single intervention or in tandem with other interventions.

REFERENCES

Baumrind, D., (1971). *Current patterns of parental authority. Developmental Psychology, 4*(1, Pt 2), 1–103. https://doi.org/10.1037/h0030372

Bifulco, A., & Thomas, G. (2012). *Understanding adult attachment in family relationships: Research, assessment and intervention.* Routledge. https://doi.org/10.4324/9780203094556

Bratton, S. C., Ray, D., Rhine, T., & Jones, L. (2005). The efficacy of play therapy with children: A meta-analytic review of treatment outcomes. *Professional Psychology: Research and Practice, 36*(4), 376–390. https://doi.org/10.1037/0735-7028.36.4.376

Cavedo, C., & Guerney, B. G. (1999). Relationship enhancement (RE) enrichment/problem-prevention programs: Therapy-derived, powerful, versatile. In R. Berger & M. T. Hannah (Eds.), *Handbook of preventive approaches in couples therapy* (pp. 73–105). Brunner/Mazel. https://doi.org/10.1037/0735-7028.36.4.376

Ginsberg, B. G. (2003). An integrated holistic model of child-centered family therapy. In R. Van-Fleet & L. F. Guerney (Eds.), *Casebook of filial therapy* (pp.21–47). Play Therapy Press. https://psycnet.apa.org/record/2012-03903-010

Ginsburg, K. R. (2007). The importance of play in promoting healthy child development and maintaining strong parent-child bonds. *Pediatrics, 119*, 182–191. https://doi.org/10.1542/peds.2006-2697

Grskovic, J. A., & Goetze, H. (2008). Short-term filial therapy with German mothers: Findings from a controlled study. *International Journal of Play Therapy, 19*, 39–51. https://doi.org/10.1037/1555-6824.17.1.39

Guerney, B. G., Jr. (2003). Foreword. In R. VanFleet & L. F. Guerney (Eds.), *Casebook of filial therapy* (pp. ix–xi). Play Therapy Press. https://risevanfleet.com/product/casebook-of-filial-play-therapy/

Guerney, L. F., & Ryan, V. M. (2013). *Group filial therapy: A complete guide to teaching parents to play therapeutically with their children.* Jessica Kingsley. https://us.jkp.com/products/group-filial-therapy

Topham, G. L., & VanFleet, R. (2011). Filial therapy: A structured and straightforward approach to including young children in family therapy. *The Australian and New Zealand Journal of Family Therapy, 32*(2), 144–158. https://doi.org/10.1375/anft.32.2.144

Topham, G. L., Wampler, K. S., Titus, G., & Rolling, E. (2011). Predicting parent and child outcomes of a filial therapy program. *International Journal of Play Therapy, 20* (2), 79–93. DOI:10.1037/a0023261. https://doi.org/10.1037/a0023261

VanFleet, R. (1985). *Mothers' perceptions of their families' needs when one of their children has diabetes mellitus: A developmental perspective* [Unpublished doctoral dissertation]. Pennsylvania State University.

VanFleet, R. (1994, 2014). *Filial therapy: Strengthening parent-child relationships through play* (1st & 3rd ed.). Professional Resource Press. https://doi.org/10.1037/v00975-001

VanFleet, R., & Guerney, L.F. (2003). *Casebook of filial therapy.* Play Therapy Press. https://risevanfleet.com/product/casebook-of-filial-play-therapy/

VanFleet, R., Ryan, S. D., & Smith, S. K. (2005). A critical review of filial therapy interventions. In L. Reddy, T. M. Files-Hall, & C. E. Schaefer (Eds.), *Empirically-based play interventions for children* (pp. 241–264). American Psychological Association. https://doi.org/10.1037/11086-012

VanFleet, R., Sywulak, A. E., & Sniscak, C. C. (2010). *Child-centered play therapy.* Guilford. https://www.academia.edu/43146180/Child_Centered_Play_Therapy_book_

CHAPTER 13

A DEVELOPMENTAL APPROACH TO TREATMENT PLANNING FOR INFANTS WITH FIRSTPLAY® THERAPY

Janet A. Courtney

INTRODUCTION

There are few models in play therapy that directly meet the unique developmental needs of infants and young children. FirstPlay® Infant Play Therapy is an approach that assists to specifically address the challenges of intervening with children ages birth to three years of age. Founded, by Janet A. Courtney in the late 1990s (Baldwin et al., 2020; Courtney, 2020; Courtney et al., 2017), it is an attachment-based, parent-infant manualized model that combines first-play touch-based activities along with therapeutic storytelling. First-Play® is an alchemy of several different underlying theories and models including Developmental Play Therapy, *Modern* Attachment Theory (Schore & Schore, 2012), Filial Therapy, Ericksonian-based storytelling (Courtney & Mills, 2016), mindfulness practice, and the literature and research pertaining to neurobiology, touch, infant massage, and infant mental health. Utilizing the *FirstPlay® Parent Manual©*, trained practitioners model, guide, facilitate, and supervise parents to provide attuned touch to their infants and children to build healthy attachment relationships.

Foremost, FirstPlay® Therapy is an adapted Developmental Play Therapy (DPT) model. Developmental Play Therapy was formulated in the 1960s by play therapy pioneer, Viola Brody and is considered a close cousin to Theraplay (Jernberg & Booth, 2001; Brody, 1997; Courtney & Gray, 2014). Although Brody did not specifically work with infants, her approach worked with children at the pre-symbolic level of play with a focus on the importance of touch to the attachment relationship. The healing value of caring touch was considered by Brody to be a core component to the attachment relationship as it assisted a child to develop an inner sense of "I" or "home" within. From this place, children can positively develop an inner sense of life choice decision-making. Touch is now known to play a key role in the development of interpersonal relationships beginning with early attachment and bonding processes (Courtney & Nolan, 2017; Courtney & Siu, 2018; Jackson & McGlone, 2020). In DPT, the nurturing and joyful *touch* interactions between an adult and child, including rocking, singing, developmental fun activities, and gentle cradling was viewed as intrinsically healing (Courtney & Gray, 2014). Brody (1997) advised that children who missed those crucial developmental stages in early life (through neglect, for example) can be helped by an attuned caretaker or practitioner to experience those joyful touch interactions by re-creating the first-play opportunities necessary for them to return to an earlier stage of development and "pick up what they need and bring it forward to the present" (p. 9).

Another central foundation for FirstPlay® is Filial Play Therapy that was developed in the 1960s by Louise and Bernard Guerney (Guerney, 2015). However, instead of the Filial model of parents receiving training in Client Centered Play Therapy techniques, FirstPlay® practitioners provide direct instruction to parents related to the gentle touch storytelling techniques

DOI: 10.4324/9781003334231-15

as outlined in the *FirstPlay® Parent Manual©*. As in Filial Play Therapy, the parents are viewed in FirstPlay® as the "change agent" and are empowered to implement the nurturing touch interactions with their own child as guided by the FirstPlay® practitioner. This is accomplished by practitioners demonstrating the touch-based activities on a baby-doll—a common parent training method used in infant mental health. At the same time, practitioners also model, instruct, facilitate, and supervise parents to use the techniques with their infant. Note, this is a change from DPT where the caring touch activities were provided directly by the therapists. Parents are thus empowered to securely provide attuned and nurturing touch to their infant as facilitated by the FirstPlay® practitioner. Thus, as in Filial Therapy, the key factor in First-Play® is that the parent-infant relationship is seen as the curative factor.

The next section will introduce a FirstPlay® Infant Play Therapy case study and how the treatment planning process helps guide the interventions and outcomes.

CASE SCENARIO

Presenting Problem

Foster parents Ana and Tom were seeking therapy as they were recently informed that they would be able to adopt the child in their care who was now 18 months old. Prior to this time, there was a possibility that Baby Jake might be placed back with his biological mother. During the initial intake, the foster parents reported that they were instructed in their foster training course, "Not to get too close to the children they were fostering as they may be going back to their biological parents." Following this advice, the foster parents made an effort to avoid bonding with Baby Jake as they did not want to jeopardize the attachment relationship with the biological mother as warned. As a result, the foster parents expressed deep pain about the disconnected relationship and the resulting behavioral problems with Baby Jake that they now faced. For example, if they tried to hold him, he would push them away and not want to be held. Because of this, Ana expressed that she was experiencing a lot of anxiety around the whole situation which was very upsetting for her. They both felt a love for Baby Jake and wanted to adopt him but realized they needed support to better build the attachment relationship. Ana stated that she has the support of her mother that has helped her through some of her feelings and has also been there to help with Baby Jake.

I spoke with them about the FirstPlay® model with foundations in Developmental Play Therapy and how this can support the building of attachment in relationships through developmental type touch-based activities and storytelling. They understood that most of the interventions did not involve the use of toys but were interactive experiences to grow the parent-child attachment relationship through joyful singing and playful developmental games. They were open to learning FirstPlay® and agreed to attend the next session without Baby Jake so that they could practice some of the activities first before we met together with Baby Jake.

Treatment Planning in FirstPlay® Therapy

The *FirstPlay® Therapy Parent Practitioner Manual* (Courtney, 2017) outlines a six-session curriculum that acts as a guiding framework for a suggested treatment plan. Each section of the curriculum sets forth the "steps of implementation" and "tips of facilitation." Table 1 is a

Table 13.1 FirstPlay® Six Session Curriculum Utilized in the Treatment Planning Process

Session 1-Introduction to FirstPlay®
The purpose of the first session is to gain a detailed background of the case situation and to introduce parents to the FirstPlay® model and to then review the introductory material found in the first few pages of the *FirstPlay® Parent Manual©* along with the consent forms.

Session 2-Live FirstPlay® Demonstration
In the second session practitioners teach parents the FirstPlay® Infant Therapy techniques using the *Baby Tree Hug©* story in the *FirstPlay® Parent Manual©* and video-record the demonstration part of the session for a review at the next planned session.

Session 3-FirstPlay® and Video-Recording Review
The focus of this session is assessing the parent's capacity to respond to their infant's cues, reinforcing techniques learned, and having parents demonstrate and show the practitioner what they have practiced with their baby related to the *FirstPlay® Parent Manual©*. The FirstPlay® story activities will be modeled and practiced together in the session. This session will also include a review of selected portions of the video-recording that happened within the previous session.

Session 4-FirstPlay® activities, clinician, and parent lead
In the fourth session practitioners encourage parents to share more about their early attachment and play experiences. Now that parents have a foundation for FirstPlay®, the practitioner can ask about songs and games that the client played during their childhood or that are familiar to them. It is during this session that the practitioner introduces the FirstPlay® activities found in the *FirstPlay® Parent Manual©*.

Session 5-FirstPlay® the parent is the instructor
In this session, parents take the lead as the instructor. Parents can choose to guide the practitioner in the process, or if another caregiver is present such as a grandmother, father, or friend, they can demonstrate to that person the FirstPlay® story and activities.

Session 6-FirstPlay® Putting it all together
In this final session, practitioners will be reviewing the course curriculum including the *Baby Tree Hug©* techniques, and FirstPlay® activities and any of the information discussed in the past five sessions.

summary of each session. Although the case in this chapter did not exactly follow this outline, it is offered to give the reader a general sense of how the curriculum can act as a guiding springboard to use as a baseline for creating a customized treatment plan. Therefore, it is a suggested outline and practitioners can modify this as deemed appropriate for each family.

In addition to the above FirstPlay® curriculum, there are four important components to consider when considering treatment planning with infants (Nowakowski & Powers, 2020). First, we need to consider the observation of the parent-infant dyad. From an infant mental health perspective, the parent-infant relationship is prioritized rather than focusing solely on either the baby or the parent. This acknowledges the interdependence that exists between parents and their infants. Second, because infants are rapidly changing in development from day to day, we pay close attention to the infant milestones and follow the lead of the infant for what they are showing us behaviorally. Third, families must be engaged with the utmost of respect from a resiliency-focused and strength-based perspective to create a sense of safety in a warm welcoming environment of empathy and compassion. Last, treatment planning must involve a co-created treatment plan of agreement, meaning that the parent is viewed as the "expert" on themselves and the infant. The creation of a treatment plan must therefore reflect the parent's input and desire to participate. With these components in mind, the following initial treatment plan was created.

Chapter Case Study Initial Plan

Following the initial meeting with the foster parents, a second appointment was arranged to review the *FirstPlay® Parent Manual®* and to teach a few of the FirstPlay® activities prior to an appointment with Baby Jake.

- Observe the attachment relationship between Baby Jake and the foster parents during their first session together.
- Meet with Baby Jake conjointly with the foster parents for weekly sessions to model, guide, and supervise nurturing and joyful FirstPlay® activities between Baby Jake and the foster parents.
- Build a relationship of safety and trust with Baby Jake and to support the attachment relationship with the foster parents.
- Help guide the foster parents to establish safe boundaries, practice limit setting, and create a daily FirstPlay® schedule for Baby Jake.
- Process with the foster parents any feelings of guilt and pain regarding Baby Jake's placement with them.
- To bridge the FirstPlay® activities to the home environment for a prescribed three daily brief intervals of FirstPlay® activity implementation for each parent.
- Include Ana's mother in the therapy sessions so she can participate in the developmental games when she is with Baby Jake.
- Bibliotherapy and therapeutic psychoeducation videos: recommend relevant parenting books and psychoeducational videos so Ana and Tom can learn more about their situation in relationship to the attachment literature and other foster parents with similar experiences.
- Coordinate with the foster care social worker as needed to support the family as they transitioned from foster parents to adoptive parents.
- Explore the possibility of including the grandmother in some of the sessions as appropriate.
- Administer the Generalized Anxiety Disorder-7 Scale (GAD-7) with the foster mother.
- Record a session with the intention of reviewing with the foster parents to gain insight into the dynamics of their relationship with Baby Jake.

Sample Documentation Following the Second Appointment

The foster parents returned to the next appointment and advised that they had gotten the books and watched the recommended videos. They stated the information was helping them to better understand Baby Jake. I explored in more detail with the foster parents their journey with Baby Jake, including holidays, and his connection to other relatives. They attended church weekly, and they shared that they had a lot of support from the congregation. They also disclosed they were unable to conceive, despite fertility treatment attempts, and decided to become foster parents with the hope they could possibly be able to adopt a child through that avenue. I felt an overwhelming heartfelt compassion for this family. During this session the foster parents were introduced to the *FirstPlay® Parent Manual©* intended to familiarize them with some of the FirstPlay® activities that we would be doing together with Baby Jake during the next planned session with him present. I discussed with them the healing power of touch to the attachment relationship and the respectful significance of "asking permission" of Baby Jake before we do the touch-based activities. I also reviewed the importance of parental self-regulation and how to calm, relax, and connect as I guided them in the "Rainbow Hug" mindfulness activity. The scores from the Generalized Anxiety Disorder scale completed by the foster mother indicated moderate anxiety. However, it was assessed as a situational anxiety related to the stress of the current situation as the mother had not had any anxiety prior to fostering Baby Jake. Ana was not interested in pursuing the need for pharmaceutical intervention. A call was placed to the foster care worker for a follow up status report. Baby Jake will be attending the next session.

Impressions: Although the past several months had placed a strain on their relationship, the foster parents appeared supportive of each other and held a shared vision to work on building the attachment relationship with Baby Jake. They cared deeply for Baby Jake and were willing to invest in the therapy process to make the necessary changes and to prepare to transition as adoptive parents.

Table 13.2 Case Study Objectives and Treatment Plan in Action for the First Six Sessions

Session Type	Goals and Objectives	FirstPlay® Intervention
Session 1: Intake with the foster parents	Gather background history, assessment, and formulate treatment plan. Assess parents' own experiences of touch and expectations for therapy. Co-create a treatment plan together.	Following the FirstPlay® curriculum for Session 1 found in the *FirstPlay® Parent Practitioner Manual©*.
Session 2 Foster parents together	To increase foster parent familiarization of the FirstPlay® model by reviewing the manual and experiencing for themselves some of the touch-based activities and processing their experiences. Educate the foster parents on how to provide sensitive and attuned caring touch.	Introduced four (4) FirstPlay® touch-based activities that were role played by the foster parents in session. Implemented the *Rainbow Hug* guided mindfulness activity.
Session 3 Foster parents with Baby Jake. Parts of session were recorded	Create a safe holding environment for Baby Jake. Increase co-regulation in the parent-infant dyad and to support respectful experiences of touch through the asking of "permission" for engagement. Observe the attachment relationship and the developmental milestones of Baby Jake. Facilitating the need to follow the lead of the infant. Video-record parts of the session to review in the next session. Support transition of the FirstPlay® activities to daily practice within the home.	*FirstPlay® Parent Manual©* portions of the *Baby Tree Hug©* were demonstrated.

(Continued)

Table 13.2 (Continued)

Session Type	Goals and Objectives	FirstPlay® Intervention
Session 4 Foster Mother with Baby Jake (Foster father was not present)	Review parts of the video with foster mother to increase parental reflective capacity and attunement. Increase foster mother's ability to appropriately read and respond to Baby Jake's behavioral cues. Increase co-regulation and attunement. Guided foster mother in the *Magic Rainbow Hug* story.	Introduced part of *The Magic Rainbow Hug©* story.
Session 5 Grandmother attended with foster mother	Empowering foster mother to take the lead to guide the grandmother in the FirstPlay® © techniques. To support extended family members to be part of the healing play process.	Reviewing the *Baby Tree Hug©* story.
Session 6: Check-in session with Foster Parents	Assess current progress in therapy with foster parents. Support parental confidence and sustain progress at home on-going. Evaluate for further sessions and to co-create an on-going treatment plan.	Reviewed some of the specific FirstPlay® © activities that were being played at home.

Six Week Check-In Session with Tom and Ana

After six weeks of therapy, I met with Tom and Ana without Baby Jake present to discuss how they and Baby Jake were progressing. Ana stated that Baby Jake was now coming to her for affection (hugs and cradling time), which he had rejected in the past. He was cooperating more with simple commands during transitions—such as being more willing to clean up toys or not resisting brushing his teeth or bath time. Meals were less of a "battle" and he was going to sleep better at night with fewer tantrums during the day. What was most significant was when Tom shared the following: "I feel like for the first time I have a relationship with Baby Jake, and the other day when I walked in the door from work, Baby Jake excitedly came running to the door because I was home saying, 'Daddy's home, Daddy's home!' He was happy to see me." When Tom shared this story, he choked up and put his head in his hands and began to cry. He stated, "He never did that before. Now he is happy to see me." He realized there had been a major shift in their relationship and he was feeling more bonded to Baby Jake.

Final Case Discussion

When Tom shared about Baby Jake's new greeting behaviors, I realized that something very profound had happened. In Attachment Theory, we are always interested in the reunions and how parents and children come together after a separation—even brief momentary ones can be significant. Therefore, to recognize the growth in Baby Jake's attachment in just a few weeks was very heartwarming and affirming. Tom and Ana became co-creators and partners in the therapy and treatment planning process that led to the final outcomes of change. It was the foster parents' determination to put in the time and effort daily and their trust in the process of implementing new behaviors with Baby Jake that ultimately made the difference. Ana and Tom were empowered to be the "change agents" in Baby Jake's therapy. Baby Jake had to also learn to trust Tom and Ana to meet not just his physical needs but also his emotional needs— which is what he had missed in his early infancy development due to abuse and neglect. Therapy continued with the foster parents and Baby Jake and within a few months, the adoption process was finalized, and we celebrated Baby Jake's adoption together.

CONCLUSION

FirstPlay® Infant Play Therapy is a trans-theoretical approach with special attention to developmental and attachment theories that assists to specifically addressing the challenges of intervening with children from birth to 3 years of age. The FirstPlay® six-session curriculum acts as a guiding framework for a suggested treatment plan. Additionally, the four important components of treatment planning with infants include (1) The observation of the parent-infant dyad, (2) the infant developmental milestones, (3) the creation of a sense of safety in a warm holding environment of empathy and compassion, and (4) a co-created treatment plan of agreement where the parent is viewed as the "expert" on themselves and the infant.

Key Takeaways

- ♡ FirstPlay® addresses the challenges of intervening with infants ages 0-3.
- ♡ First Play® is an attachment-based parent-infant model that combines first-play, touch-based activities along with storytelling.
- ♡ In FirstPlay® parents are viewed as the "change agent" and are empowered to use nurturing touch with the child as guided by the FirstPlay® practitioner.
- ♡ FirstPlay® practitioners provide instruction to parents related to gentle touch and storytelling techniques as outlined in the FirstPlay® Parenting Manual.
- ♡ There is a six-session curriculum that acts as a guiding framework for a suggested treatment plan. Each section of the curriculum sets forth "the steps of implementation" and "tips for facilitation."
- ♡ The parents-infant relationship is prioritized rather than focusing solely on either the baby or the parent.
- ♡ Close attention is given to infant milestones and following the lead of the infant for what they are showing behaviorally.
- ♡ Treatment planning must involve a co-created treatment plan agreement.
- ♡ Families must be engaged with respect from a resiliency-focused and strength-based perspective with empathy and compassion.

REFERENCES

Baldwin, B. B., Velasquez, M., & Courtney, J. A. (2020). FirstPlay® therapy strengthens the attachment relationship between a mother with perinatal depression and her infant. In J. A. Courtney (Ed.). *Infant play therapy: Foundations, models, programs, and practice* (pp. 83–100). Aronson. Routledge. https://doi.org/10.4324/9780429453083-6

Brody, V. A. (1997). *The dialogue of touch: Developmental play therapy* (2nd ed.). https://doi.org/10.1037/h0090232

Courtney, J. A. (2017). *FirstPlay® parent practitioner manual*. Developmental Play & Attachment Therapies, Inc.

Courtney, J. A. (2020). *Introduction infant play therapy: Foundations, programs, models and practice*. Routledge. https://doi.org/10.4324/9780429453083

Courtney, J. A., & Gray, S. W. (2014). Phenomenological inquiry into practitioner experiences of developmental play therapy: Implications for training in touch. *International Journal of Play Therapy, 23*(2), 114–129. http://dx.doi.org/10.1037/a0036366

Courtney, J. A., & Mills, J. C. (2016, March). Utilizing the metaphor of nature as co-therapist in StoryPlay®. *Play Therapy, 11*(1), 18–21.

Courtney, J. A., & Nolan, R. D. (2017). *Touch in child counseling and play therapy: An ethical and clinical guide*. Routledge. https://doi.org/10.4324/9781315628752

Courtney, J. A., & Siu, A. F. Y. (2018). Practitioner experiences of touch in working with children in play therapy. *International Journal of Play Therapy, 27*(2), 92–102. http://dx.doi.org/10.1037/pla0000064

Courtney, J. A., Velasquez, M., & Bakai Toth, V. (2017). FirstPlay® infant massage storytelling: facilitating corrective touch experiences with a teenage mother and her abused infant. In J. A. Courtney & R. D. Nolan (Eds.), *Touch in child counseling and play therapy: An ethical and clinical guide* (pp. 48–62). Routledge. https://doi.org/10.4324/9781315628752-4

Guerney, L. F. (2015). Foreword. In E. Green, J. N. Baggerly, & A. C. Myrick (Eds.), *Counseling families: Play-based treatment*. Rowman & Littlefield. https://rowman.com/ISBN/9781442244047/Counseling-Families-Play-Based-Treatment

Jackson, E., & McGlone, F. (2020). The impact of play on the developing social brain: New insights from the neurobiology of touch. In J. A. Courtney (Ed.), *Infant play therapy: Foundations, models, programs and practice* (pp. 18–36). Routledge. https://doi.org/10.4324/9780429453083-2

Jernberg, A., & Booth, P. (2001). *TheraPlay: Helping parents and children build better relationships through attachment based play* (2nd ed.). Jossey-Bass. https://www.biblio.com/book/theraplay-helping-parents-children-build-better/d/1486911075

Nowakowski-Sims, E., & Powers, D. (2020). Trauma-informed infant mental health assessment. In J. Courtney (Ed.), *Infant Play Therapy* (pp. 67–79). Routledge. https://doi.org/10.4324/9780429453083-5

Schore, A. N., & Schore, J. R. (2012). Modern attachment theory: The central role of affect regulation in development and treatment. In A. N. Schore (Ed.), *The science of the art of psychotherapy* (pp. 27–51). Wiley. https://doi.org/10.1007/s10615-007-0111-7

CHAPTER 14

A GESTALT APPROACH TO TREATMENT PLANNING

Felicia Carroll

INTRODUCTION

The word *Gestalt* is peculiar to most new clients and practitioners. Among many fundamentals, Gestalt Therapy is rooted in the neuroscience of Gestalt Psychology in the early 20th century and is confirmed by the developments in current neurobiology and studies in neuroscience (Siegel, 2007). *Gestalt* refers to the unifying, organizing, principle of integration found in all of nature and, for our purposes as child therapists, in human experience and organismic behavior.

Frederick Perls (1948), one of the primary founders of Gestalt Therapy wrote, "The criterion of a successful treatment is the achievement of that amount of integration that leads to its own development" (p. 52). Fundamental principles of Gestalt Therapy such as holism, organismic regulation, Gestalt formation (organization of figure/ground), and the process of awareness to closure support the assumption that each child will function in a way that meets the child's physical, and emotional, social, intellectual, and spiritual needs. The child strives to complete situations from moment to moment, paving the way toward healthy growth and development. The child's behavior is purposeful, balanced, and integrated, flowing from one experience to another.

When the child is unable to interact in his environment with ease because of a lack of appropriate support or is overwhelmed with a circumstance in life and is unable to assimilate experience, the child's sense of self becomes fragmented, lacking in cohesion. The energy that was used for ongoing construction and development of the self becomes engaged with internal splits and conflicts. Such childhood experiences result in the child developing a sense that "something is wrong about me," or "with me," or even more fragmenting, "I am wrong." In their efforts to maintain homeostasis or equilibrium in non-supportive life circumstances the child struggles with shame, unassimilated introjects, and a faulty sense of themselves and their relationships with others. The child organizes their sense of who they are according to these ideas and loses their spontaneous, purposeful involvement in life. The symptoms that bring a child into therapy are indicative of this disturbance of integration. (Carroll, 2009; Carroll & Orozco, 2019). The Gestalt therapist asks, how can I assist this child to achieve healthy integration in order to restore their path of wholesome development?

Oaklander (2015), in *Windows To Our Children*, brought together the Gestalt theoretical approach with the modalities of childhood play. Later in, *Hidden Treasure* (2006), she highlighted what is called the therapy process, which is a non-linear relational process that provides experiences to strengthen the organismic functioning of the child. This approach provides a way of working with children that strengthens their sense of self by utilizing many interventions that encourage the sharpening of the senses, learning direct and productive ways of getting needs met, understanding emotional expression, and becoming more accepting of the various aspects of being a whole person. The purpose of Gestalt Play Therapy is

DOI: 10.4324/9781003334231-16

to provide experiences and support so that the child can return to her unique and rightful process of growth and development. The general experience of healthy functioning is a readiness to trust in the ongoing, self-regulating powers of the organism.

As Oaklander (1993) offered in workshops, "I am not about fixing kids, but restoring healthful functioning." Healthful functioning requires relationships with others that respond to the child's organismic needs (at each stage of development) with just enough environmental support to allow for the development of self/other support. Children rely on their familial and community relationships for support as they take on the tasks of each stage of development. It is when children are brought for psychotherapy that we know that relational support and resources are not present or hindering the child from organizing physical, intellectual, and emotional experiences resulting in the symptoms that cause concern.

Assessment, diagnosis, and treatment planning in Gestalt Play Therapy are ongoing processes throughout the therapeutic encounter with a child and family, social and community resources. Assessment is about the gathering of information by observation, anecdotes, reports, and the child's self-reporting. This making sense of the symptoms and other information, can result in a category or a diagnosis (a *Gestalt*), that is informed by the theoretical perspective of psychopathology.

All variables and perspectives of those involved are taken into consideration as the initial, "step one" of a treatment strategy is co-developed with the child, parents, and others who may be consulted, such as pediatricians and school psychologists. Gestalt Play Therapy is a relational, co-creative process of growth and restoration that is responsive to each child with unique circumstances and events, therefore, there is no standard treatment plan or interventions.

The relationship between the therapist and the child is the scaffolding of support that allows the child and family to proceed. Our relationship is established through mutuality, authenticity, presence, and trustworthiness on my part (Carroll & Orozco, 2019; Wheeler & McConville, 2002). As one young client once remarked, "You are different from my other therapist."

"Oh, how so?"
"I don't know exactly, you're just more real somehow."

As a therapist, I do not put on a role or play a character. With discretion, I am who I am in our relationship in the present moment. Establishing such a "between-ness" occurs over time. Another young client commented, "I didn't trust you when I first came here because you were a stranger."

"You had to get to know me."
"Yes."
"I'm so glad that we are here, together, now."
"Me, too."

CASE SCENARIO

My relationship with Amanda began with a telephone call from her father letting me know that his wife, Amanda's mother, had died 2 months ago and that Amanda was not doing well at school and was withdrawn at home. Amanda was 6 years old and her first-grade teacher had recommended play therapy that might be helpful to her. Her father had learned from the teacher that she cried each day and gave no explanation for her sadness. The teacher knew about her mother's death and recognized that Amanda was having a difficult time adjusting to the first-grade routine.

Initial Intake

It is my practice to meet with parent(s) to learn more details about seeking out a child therapist. Prior to our meeting, the parents are provided with a disclosure statement which includes an explanation of confidentiality with exceptions and requirements for any needed reporting. After discussing with me these legal and financial matters and the issues that are of concern to them, they sign a consent form that states their responsibilities as parents in the therapeutic process. With these clarifications and understandings, we begin our working alliance which is an integral necessity for an effective therapy process. I meet with parents in this initial meeting without the child in order to establish this relationship and to provide parents with an opportunity to discuss any concerns, history of the family, other medical issues, medications, other members of the household, or any other relevant information. I determine that other assessments may be needed, such as medical checkups. The parents may decide that I am not the right professional for them or the child. Meeting without the child protects the child from anxiety and uncertainty and possible shaming from the parent/therapist discussions.

Amanda's father explained that Amanda's mother had battled with stomach cancer since Amanda was 4 years old. His grief and sense of loss were apparent as he spoke of his concerns for Amanda's grief and her emotional withdrawal, described as disengaged with him or her friends. She did enjoy being with her dog and playing video games. She slept with a few bad dreams. She was always a picky eater. He knew she needed more support than he knew how to provide. We set the next appointment for me to meet with Amanda.

In my first session with a child, I focus on engaging with the child with the support of the parent(s) being present. I acknowledge that I have met previously with her parents and that I have learned some things about her. I met Amanda who was shy as she walked into the office surrounded by shelves of sandtray figures, comfortable chairs, and a large stuffed dog at her feet. I acknowledged that I knew her name. I asked her if she knew my name, what my job is, and why her father wanted her to see a therapist. That was the beginning of her participation in setting the purpose and goals for our time together. It was also important that I let her know what I have learned about her in my previous conversations with her dad. I asked if she understood what his concerns were and if she agreed or disagreed with what her dad had said. During this first meeting, I explained confidentiality and the exceptions to Amanda.

After this introduction, I usually ask the parents to return to the waiting room so that the child and I can begin looking around the playroom and getting started with an activity that will allow us to enjoy our time together. At the conclusion of this session, I ask the child if they are willing to return so that we can see what we want to do together about her and her parents' concerns. In this way, the child assumes some responsibility for participating in her therapy. Amanda agreed to come again after we played a fun, non-competitive game.

These two initial sessions are so essential in establishing the presenting issues, observing interactions among family members, and beginning my assessment and case formulation. More importantly, this time is for creating working alliances and communication with parents and children.

Assessment Process

After several initial sessions, Amanda's situation with the loss of her mother remained figural. I sensed her loneliness as she no longer had the person who was the organizing center of her young life. Her mother's prolonged illness, the family's efforts with medical treatments, and the final days with home hospice had certainly caused developmental trauma. I was concerned about her need for withdrawing from friends and activities. I recognized this behavior as an indication of her persistent bereavement and difficulty in organizing her sense of self, and yet, I wanted to understand it further. I observed that she was not very responsive to her father's expressions of affection and bonding with her. Dysthymia Early Onset Mild described many of her symptoms of disinterest and withdrawal, possibly prolonged bereavement. Her symptoms had been present for the last year of her mother's illness. I was encouraged that her interest in our time together was strong and hopeful that she would respond well to our therapeutic relationship and time together.

Sample Treatment Plan Goals

- Initiate working alliance with the child's father in setting goals and support for therapeutic interventions.
- Create a relationship with the child so that trust and hopefulness can develop.
- Focus on developing a cohesive narrative that allows the child to create meaning to her mother's death.
- Restore supportive attachment with father.
- Throughout provide activities that are supportive of healthful, integrated organismic functioning and well-being. Restore a spontaneous, playful, and creative expression.
- Confer with father, teacher, and my clinical observation about the child's progress toward developmental milestones.
- Set closure date/sessions for assimilation, integration, and celebration with child and family.

Measuring Progress

The therapy process in Gestalt Play Therapy is non-linear. Each interaction with a child provides a feedback loop that suggests the next co-created interactions. As such I don't work from the concept of "measurable objectives." Instead at each session, I am aware of the child's flow of energy, use of senses, body, problem-solving, enjoyment, laughter, and creative experiments. I assessed how she uses her contact skills; how articulate she is; how energetically she engages with the therapeutic materials; how she is able to use the projective process for self-awareness. I am especially interested in patterns of verbal and behavioral interruptions of her activities and conversations with me (Wheeler & McConville, 2002).

Planning Theoretically Based Interventions

In Gestalt Play Therapy the process of therapy is an integrated, bi-focused endeavor that develops out of the creative interactions of child and therapist. One focus is on the presenting symptoms which are indications that she is interrupting, and constricting her organismic process which has become the patterns of physical, social, emotional, and intellectual symptoms that indicate creative adjustments of the child in her life situation. Her therapy included activities that aroused energy such as *Rough and Tumble Play* (Panksepp & Biven, 2012); games that provided opportunities to problem solve, make choices, share ideas, opinions, and life experiences; engaging in sensory stimulation (clay, paints,); projective, symbolic modalities (sand tray and story cards); and having fun and laughing together, living with the unexpected (Oaklander, 2015; Carroll, 2012; Carroll & Orozco, 2019).

Another focus is on the immediate life circumstances and support the child is receiving. Amanda was overwhelmed by the trauma of her mother's illness and death. Her symptoms were an indication of her organismic attempts to absorb and integrate this trauma at the same time her organism was developing through other significant tasks such as the challenges of first grade without her mother's support. In this case, I had periodic sessions with her father along with reports from her teacher as to her adjustments at home and school and made recommendations on how to best support her.

Amanda remained reluctant to talk about her mother. I decided that having a cohesive narrative or story about her mother's life, illness, and death would support her in talking about her mother in a supportive therapeutic relationship. I knew that having a concrete book with the story of her mother would provide her with a needed opportunity for making sense of this complex experience. A narrative provides a child with perspectives that are more available to integration than through spoken language alone. The narrative utilizes the networking dynamics of storytelling structure, language, autobiographical memory, and imprecise emotional description (Mills & Crowley, 2014; Cossolino, 2002).

Collaborating and Planning Theoretically Based Interventions

I proposed the book/narrative to her father in our follow-up meeting. I would need his help in providing pictures, background events, etc. With his support for the narrative, I proposed the project to Amanda. For the first time, I saw a genuine smile and enthusiasm at the idea of a book about her mother. Something opened in her as she selected a pink album that would hold the pages of the narrative. Amanda immediately drew a picture of herself with her mother and father for the cover.

Tracking Progress

A portion of each session was devoted to developing the narrative, which included pictures and photos. Amanda became more energized, often asking as she came into the session what we would be writing that day. She became more talkative and less withdrawn.

After several weeks, as we were writing about the memorial service for her mother, Amanda unexpectedly became quiet. Then, in almost a whisper, she disclosed, "Daddy is glad that Mommy is dead."

"How do you know that Amanda?"
"I heard him at the memorial."

"What did he say?"

"He said that he was glad that she was not hurting and that she was dead."

"Oh. There are so many feelings when someone we love dies."

"But he is glad. That is why I cry every day so I remember Mommy."

As we talked, I heard Amanda's hurt, anger, and anguish in her tone of voice and physical tension. I touched her hand, and we sat in silence. Then I asked Amanda if it would be all right for me to talk with her father about what she heard. She agreed.

In that moment I realized that Amanda had lost her mother and her father. How was it possible for her to receive comfort and love from someone who is "glad" that the most important person in her world had died? I began to understand the quiet isolation she had created for herself which put her at risk of developing a way of being that separated her from the intimate emotional connections with family and friends.

I met with her father and then we met together with Amanda. With my guidance, he told her that what she had heard was true. He explained that he knew that her mother was suffering and fighting every day to get better. But she got so weak and tired that she could not fight anymore. Amanda sat quietly listening. Then he said, "I love Mommy so much and I miss her so much each day, just like you do. What I said at the memorial was that I was glad that she was not hurting and needed to fight her cancer all the time. She didn't want to leave us, Amanda, but her cancer was so strong, and she got too weak. I couldn't help her. The doctors couldn't help." As he cried, Amanda crawled into her father's lap and they held each other for several moments.

In her next session, Amanda and I finished her narrative about her mother's death and the memorial. She wrote a "letter" to her mother and put it in her book entitled, "Remember Mommy." Her father wrote her a poem with these words, "Even though we know you're never coming back, we will remember." Out of session, they created a ritual and went together to her mother's favorite camping site and planted a tree.

Termination Strategies

Closure is an important time in Gestalt Play Therapy. It is a time that can take several sessions for assimilating, and making sense of the experiences and the changes that have occurred. This is done with the child, parent(s), and others significant to the child's ongoing development. My practice is not to make the therapeutic experience less meaningful by tapering down the sessions. We anticipate our closure and celebrate in some manner all that we have shared.

After the session with her father, Amanda began to relax. She became more spontaneous both in our sessions and at school. The daily crying ended and she began making friends in her class. In a follow-up session, Amanda and I sat together as we read to her father the narrative we had written. Together they looked at the pictures she had drawn and the photos. With her book held in one hand, they left my office holding hands.

As the close of the school year approached, I talked with Amanda and her father about the closure of our sessions. We set a date after the beginning of the next school year. Her father and I decided to stay in therapy through the first anniversary of her mother's death. After a summer vacation, Amanda came in and brought her book. I was especially glad to hear that she was looking forward to second grade.

CONCLUSION

The Gestalt therapist seeks to assist the child to achieve healthy integration to restore their path of wholesome development. In Gestalt Play Therapy the integrated process develops out of the creative interactions between child and therapist. Gestalt Play Therapy is a relational, co-creative process of growth and restoration that is responsive to each child with unique circumstances and events. Every treatment plan will differ as it is tailored to the unique presenting needs of each child and family.

Key Takeaways

- ♡ Gestalt refers to the unifying, organizing principle of integration found in all of nature and, for our purposes as child therapists, in human experience and organismic behavior.
- ♡ The child's behavior is purposeful, balanced, and integrated, flowing from one experience to another. When the child is unable to interact with ease, the child's sense of self becomes fragmented, lacking in cohesion.
- ♡ The symptoms that bring a child into therapy are indicative of this disturbance of integration.
- ♡ The Gestalt therapist asks, "How can I assist this child to achieve healthy integration to restore their path of whole development?
- ♡ The purpose of Gestalt Play Therapy is to provide experience and support so that the child can return to her unique and rightful process of growth and development.
- ♡ A treatment strategy is co-developed with the child, parents, and others who may be consulted.
- ♡ The relationship between the therapist and the child is the scaffolding of support that allows the child and family to proceed.
- ♡ The therapy process in Gestalt Play Therapy is non-linear.
- ♡ In Gestalt Play Therapy, the process of therapy is an integrated, bi-focused endeavor that develops out of the creative interactions of child and therapist.

REFERENCES

Carroll, F. (2009). Gestalt play therapy. In K. O'Connor & L. Braverman (Eds.), *Play therapy: Theory and practice: A comparative presentation* (pp. 283–314). Wiley. https://psycnet.apa.org/record/2010-04804-007

Carroll, F. (2012). Every child's life is worth a story. In J. Chang (Ed.), *Creative interventions with children: A transtheoretical approach* (pp. 187–191). Family Psychology Press. https://vsof.org/wp-content/uploads/2022/07/child_life_story.pdf

Carroll, F., & Orozco, V. (2019), Gestalt play therapy. *Play Therapy, 14*(3), 36–38.

Cozolino, L. (2002). *The neuroscience of psychotherapy: Building and rebuilding the human brain.* Norton.

Mills, J. C., & Crowley, R. J. (2014). *Therapeutic metaphors for children and the child within.* Routledge. https://doi.org/10.4324/9781315886237

Oaklander, V. (1993). I don't fix kids. *Workshop handout.*

Oaklander, V. (2006). *Hidden treasure: A map to the child's inner self.* Karnac. https://doi.org/10.4324/9780429475528

Oaklander, V. (2015). *Windows to our children: A Gestalt therapy approach to children and adolescents.* Gestalt Journal Press. https://www.abebooks.com/signed/Windows-Children-Gestalt-Therapy-Approach-Adolescents/13587652993/bd

Panksepp, J., & Biven, L. (2012). *The archaeology of mind: Neuroevolutionary origins of human emotions.* Norton. https://doi.org/10.4324/9781315668505-26

Perls, F. (1948). Theory and techniques of personality integration. In J. Stevens (Ed.), *Gestalt is...* (pp. 45–55). Real People Press. https://doi.org/10.1176/appi.psychotherapy.1948.2.4.565

Siegel, D. (2007). *The mindful brain: Reflection and attunement in the cultivation of well-being.* Norton. https://www.ncbi.nlm.nih.gov/pmc/articles/PMC2527776/

Wheeler, G., & McConville, M. (Eds.) (2002). *The heart of development: Gestalt approaches to working with children, adolescents and their worlds. Vol 1: Childhood.* Analytic. https://doi.org/10.4324/9781315781976

CHAPTER 15

A JUNGIAN APPROACH TO TREATMENT PLANNING

Eric J. Green and Kim Powell Street

INTRODUCTION

Both play therapy and sandplay therapy provide children with the opportunity to use symbols (i.e., toys and other materials) to communicate their thoughts, feelings, fantasies, and experiences, where toys are their words and play is their language (Landreth, 2012; Mitchell et al., 2013). For most children, play is the only way to express and communicate their difficulties; often it is not until adolescence that words are used in therapy to express or share internalized struggles. Jungian Play Therapy with children is a depth psychology approach that utilizes symbols to uncover and allow for the tangible expression of the unconscious. Historically, Jungian analysis has been utilized with adults by assisting with individuation in the second or later half of life. In recent years, however, Jungian therapy has gained more prominence in utilization with children, specifically in the context of sandplay therapy (Heiko, 2018; Kalff, 1971), Jungian child analysis (Punnett, 2022) and Jungian Play Therapy (Green, 2012).

Carl Gustav Jung was born on July 26, 1875 in Kesswyl, Switzerland. The relationship to the symbolic life or how individuals relate to the symbols inside themselves was the crux of Jung's psychology and theory of *individuation*, a lifelong inner journey of self-discovery. A Jungian approach to counseling children focuses on the psyche's role in child personality development (Green, 2009). *Psyche* is defined as the child's center of thought that regulates conscious experiences, such as behaviors and feelings. Jung (1951) explained the evolving nature of the child's psyche in accordance with the collective unconscious and how it influences the process of individuation. Individuation characterizes a progress from psychic fragmentation towards wholeness—the acknowledgment and reconciliation of opposites within an individual. Fordham (1994) took this a step further and stated that childhood, not just the latter part of adult life as Jung stated, is a time of individuation. In children, the growth process revolves around the ego separating from the Self. In late adulthood, growth occurs from the re-integration and alignment of the Self with the ego.

Children's symbols or *archetypes* are bipolar structures comprised of (a) spiritual energy, and (b) feelings associated with culturally specific images in human behavior that may appear in children's dreams, fantasies, and mythology, such as Earth Mother, Trickster, and Wise Old Man. A *self-healing archetype* is an innate symbol that promotes healing by recognizing and achieving a balanced communication between the ego and the Self. The *ego* is the seat or faculty of reasoning, and the *Self* is the central organizing archetype that embodies the ego aligned with the personality. In this chapter's case study, Muriel identified his self-healing archetype as a butterfly. A blue butterfly sand miniature was present in several of Muriel's sand pictures.

Both Allan (1997) and Green (2009) adapted Jungian theory to play therapy, or Jungian Play Therapy (JPT), and identified JPT as a beneficial treatment modality when counseling

DOI: 10.4324/9781003334231-17

elementary school-aged children fixated to or regressing from archetypal complexes. Additionally, several qualitative investigations and anecdotal data obtained through case study analyses have demonstrated JPT as a potentially beneficial therapeutic modality with young children who are struggling with difficult feelings and behaviors (Allan, 1997; Green, 2007). The next section contains a fictional case study involving Muriel, an 8-year-old African American male, including the treatment plan and primary Jungian technique, sandplay, utilized.

CASE SCENARIO

Muriel was an 8-year-old African American male located in the southern United States (this is a fictional case study). Muriel was referred to therapy by this teacher because she noticed he was isolating himself from his peers and appeared sad and withdrawn. His grades were beginning to decline precipitously in three of his seven subjects. Muriel's parents were middle-class, both worked in the local church ministry, and were eager to get their son mental health treatment to resolve his current psychological challenges.

APPLICATION OF JUNGIAN THEORY TO TREATMENT PLANNING

In this section, the authors will apply the Jungian Play Therapy theoretical model, specific to utilizing sandplay, a Jungian intervention, to Muriel's case.

Intake

In the initial intake, the therapist will meet with the child to establish a comfortable and safe environment for the child. It is important for the child to feel that they can establish a connection with the therapist so that the therapist can hold all the feelings of the child. We hold so they can contain. The Jungian therapist has a welcoming and caring approach, while not being the person in charge of the therapy but collaborating and relating to the client. The therapist should be genuine and accepting (Green, 2007). Children can often take much longer to fully engage with an adult because they are testing out the relationship to ensure that they are psychologically, physically, and socially safe. Therapists must be their real and authentic selves to sufficiently help a child feel as though they belong.

Muriel was initially reluctant to begin therapy and appeared stoic and apprehensive as evidenced by his lack of eye contact and barely audible voice The therapist greeted the child by bending down to his level, and warmly introducing himself by saying, Hello Muriel. Welcome to play therapy. I'm not the type of doctor that will give you a shot. I help kids sometimes if they are feeling sad or lonely, or maybe they have a hard time making or keeping friends. Sometimes I help kids if their grades are dropping, and they maybe don't feel that good about themselves anymore. I do that through play. You will come here once a week for about 45 minutes. We will talk sometimes if you're up to it, and we will play. And you get to choose what we play. Lots of kids enjoy doing sandplay, which is one of the many activities I have here at the clinic. Whatever you tell me or whatever we talk about will be between us, unless someone is trying to harm you, or you try to hurt yourself. Then we will talk to your parents together and let them know what's going on to keep you safe. Most kids come here for a few months to a year or so. I'll be meeting with your parents once every few weeks to help them learn different ways to communicate and support you so you can start feeling better as well. Do you have any questions at all? If not, let's go tour the playroom.

After this introduction, Muriel warmed up slightly to the idea of play therapy as evidenced by his partial smile and walking toward the playroom energetically. The intake usually lasts 1–3 sessions and involves psychometric tests as indicated to assist with diagnosis, multiple discussions with parents about the collaborative nature of therapy and their participation in the treatment planning process, and the limits of confidentiality with a minor. I explained to his parents that while they have a legal right to know everything that Muriel and I discuss in our play sessions, it would create a more cohesive atmosphere if they did not question him after the session. I assure them that if I uncover anything urgent or crisis-related, I will discuss it with them immediately. I also let them know that I will be updating them with general progress notes every week that I meet with Muriel, and that I will be meeting with them approximately every three weeks independent from Muriel's play sessions for parent consultation to improve communication and support at home with their child.

Case Conceptualization

To conceptualize this case, I examined Muriel's presenting problems, family/social/and cultural factors, and presenting issues. Muriel appeared to be a highly anxious child, so I administered the SCARED interest inventory, an assessment tool to gauge Muriel's level of anxiety. He scored high on the assessment, and his anxious presentation was validated by his parents, schoolteacher, and my observations during his play. He expressed feeling uneasy a lot of the time, had nightmares frequently, and was nervous in social situations. His anxiety affected him negatively in his home, social, and school performance. I diagnosed Muriel with generalized anxiety disorder. Muriel needed a creative, non-threatening mechanism to share and release the negative emotional valence from his generalized anxiety and fears.

Assessment and Diagnosis

In assessment, Jungian-oriented therapists meet with parents to gain more perspective about why the child is coming to therapy. It is important to learn about any pressure that the child may be experiencing from external contexts (i.e., peers, family life, or school). The therapist can also ask the child why they are coming into therapy to see if they identify any issues. Jungian play therapists can utilize drawings, creating mandalas, analysis of play themes, and sandplay in their work with children to assist them in diagnosis, prognosis, assessment, and treatment planning. The process of amplification of symbols is an important part of assessment in JPT; children are asked to talk about a certain symbol that they may have used in play, whether it be through drawing or sandplay. For example, Muriel's first few drawings involved a monster dinosaur to depict his fear. The therapist can also ask the child additional questions about the symbols. For instance, I asked Muriel what story the symbol of the dinosaur was telling, and what he was thinking or feelings as he drew the picture. This could also apply to symbols that may have appeared during a dream that the child may have had (Allan, 1997). During this process, I am listening to Muriel and hearing him in a nonjudgmental way. By utilizing empathic therapeutic micro-skills, such as head nods, eye contact, and supportive statements, I demonstrate to Muriel that he is being heard and that it is okay to talk about the feelings he is having (if he chooses to) within therapy.

Jungian therapists look at the children's play and try to identify themes and the self-healing symbols depicted in their sandplay. Once the child has drawn a symbol or has used a certain symbol in sandplay, the child may be asked to amplify that symbol by talking more about it. The therapist may ask questions related to how the child interprets that symbol. The important thing is that the therapist should not make assumptions about what the symbol means, but instead, curiously ask questions to tease out the child's meaning of the symbol. Therapists never share their interpretations with children, especially in sandplay.

Assessment can also be accomplished by observing what the child does in therapy. The therapist can interpret the various mediums that a child might use, as well as the colors used. The therapist can also look for themes that the child may use to signify archetypes. Once the presenting issues and conceptualization of the problem have been completed, the therapist can move toward setting goals with the child and parents.

SETTING GOALS AND MEASURABLE OBJECTIVES

One of the goals in JPT is to help the child with individuation. Put simply, individuation involves helping the child develop their personality through the liminal space where psyche and symbol are enacted (i.e., sandplay) (Green, 2009). Within the playroom, Muriel is encouraged to express those symbols in artwork, play, and within the sand while the therapist adopts an analytical attitude. The goal of using the analytical attitude is to help the child move from outright impulsiveness to a symbolic life (Green, 2009). Jungian play therapists notice and expound on the symbols, which is where they believe that emotions are contained. For example, through therapy, Muriel can move from paralyzing fears to manageable concerns, which would be a healthier expression of the polarity within that emotion. Managing anxiety can produce more positive feelings, including increasing Muriel's' self-esteem. When children can express negative emotions, such as anger, through symbolic work, they are able to then turn that emotion into an expression of empowerment.

The overarching goal of Jungian Play Therapy is activating the individuation process. The process is facilitated through an analytic attitude. I would honor the images Muriel produces in sandplay and other creative expressions in the playroom so that he can regulate his impulses and maintain an equilibrium of energy flow between his inner and outer worlds. The goal of individuation is operationalized through the transformation of symbols—the process of the child's symbols being generated throughout therapy. Jungian play therapists observe symbol production and transformation in children throughout the clinical process.

Another goal of JPT that may differ from other paradigms is to *ground* the child back to the external reality at the end of each session through yoga or mindfulness. The transition to yoga at the end of a play session helps the child move from impulse and action to metaphor and symbol to calmness and feeling "okay."

After the first few weeks of intake and assessment, we would begin goal setting. Muriel's goals would be measurable and time specific. For instance, I would start with these three initial goals: (1) to build a safe, trusting, nonjudgmental, warm, therapeutic relationship with Muriel so that the transference may be activated within the first month of therapy, (2) use sandplay and other Jungian techniques, including play therapy, to allow for the expression of Muriel's unconscious and conscious thoughts and feelings each week, and (3) decrease Muriel's anxiety on a Likert scale from his self-reported "4.5/5" to a "3.5/5" within three months.

Interventions

Sandplay therapy, within the context of play therapy, allows a child to create an imaginative world by placing miniatures in a tray (19.5 × 28.5 inches with a depth of 3 inches), half-filled with fine-grained, sterilized white sand and painted blue on the inside to give the impression of water and/or sky. Dora Kalff (1971), the founder of sandplay therapy, articulated that sand represents instinct, nature, and the healing power of Mother Earth. The miniatures on nearby shelves stimulate the child's imagination and represent many aspects in the child's world. The child's choice of miniatures helps the therapist to symbolically understand the issues that are displayed in the sand (Mitchell et al., 2013). Two trays are available in sandplay therapy, so the child will have a choice of wet (damp) sand or dry sand. Photographs of the sandplay scene, taken by the therapist after the child has left the therapy session, provide a permanent and ongoing record of the child's internal process (Mitchell et al., 2013). Thus, sandplay serves as a window into the client's inner world and provides the opportunity to express a myriad of feelings, unspoken thoughts, and even the unknown. Sandplay scenes may be created quickly, in as little as ten minutes, or take the entire play therapy session. Usually, a sandplay picture is not created at every therapy session; it is the child's choice when, and if, to use sandplay.

A sandplay process is unique to each child. We accept the uniqueness of the individual and their ways of coping with their lives, and in Muriel's case, stress. It is within this safe "space" that the healing of the inner psychological wound can occur; the Self can be activated, and the inner child re-discovered with all its potential for creativity and renewal. In sandplay the therapist does not play in the sand with the child but rather remains the holder of the *vas* (or the blank slate) (Punnett, 2022). The therapist sits in a chair nearby watching; some therapists will use notepads and take notes and draw images of the child's sand picture. After Muriel would indicate he is finished with his sand picture, I would say, "Is there anything you'd like to share about your sand picture? There's no right or wrong way to do that. And you don't have to if you don't want. It's completely up to you." The sand picture is left intact until the child leaves. For instance, after Muriel would complete his sand picture, and we discuss it (if he chooses to), then after he leaves the session, I would place the symbols from the sand creation back on the shelves. Muriel would not witness this as it would be like destroying an artist's product in front of them. I want Muriel to leave with the image intact. I would collate images of Muriel's sand pictures over a large expanse of time and analyze them by their progression in correlation to his healing. Utilizing sandplay, play therapy, completing issue-specific workbook exercises to assist the child with developing coping skills for his anxiety, and working with his parents would all culminate in the treatment plan in the section below.

Collaborative Treatment Planning with Caretakers and Progress Tracking

JPT's treatment plan with Muriel involves three steps: (1) counseling the child 45 minutes per week in an emotionally and physically safe environment using play therapy; (2) conducting one filial or family play therapy session with the child's family or caretakers every three weeks or so; and (3) consulting with a multidisciplinary team of school and community-based professionals to provide holistic care. These would be shared with and done in consultation with his parents. Figure 15.1 is an illustration of a sample treatment plan for Muriel's case presentation from a Jungian perspective. Progress would be tracked and codified every two

Figure 15.1 Sample Treatment Plan from a Jungian Approach

months or so by conducting intermittent and informal scaling questions on anxiety with Muriel, observations and/or check-ins with teachers, consultations with parents regularly, and improvement in grades. Also, I would review my progress notes on Muriel regularly to track his psychological progress (Figure 15.2).

Termination Process Strategies

When determining the appropriate time for termination, many children will know instinctively when therapy should conclude. This typically occurs when they can contain and manage disastrous and delightful feelings and images simultaneously. Interestingly, many children will disclose to their caretakers close to the time that the analyst decides to terminate. Muriel shared with his mother after about 8 months of therapy, "I don't think I need to see Dr. Green every week anymore. Maybe every other week would be OK. I'm feeling less anxious and happier now." Sometimes, children will tell a therapist directly, "I don't think we need to play anymore. I feel better about myself." From a Jungian perspective, the child's Self leads the ego down into the wounding and ascends to the healing. The ego becomes of sufficient strength to dissolve the therapeutic alliance. It is important to remember to make

DATE:	February 11, 2022
RE:	Muriel Progress Note
TYPE:	Individual Play Therapy
CONTENT:	Muriel reported having a fun time in Mississippi last weekend with his family and he commented that his anxiety decreased. Muriel completed a sand picture. He commented that it was a word where people were fighting back against the monsters and dragons and winnings.

THEORY:	Jungian
PARENT CONSULTATION:	Mother reported Muriel was more outgoing on their trip to Mississippi to visit relatives and that his nightmares decreased.
NEXT STEPS:	We will begin the workbook "What to Do When you Worry Too Much" by Dawn

Figure 15.2 Sample Clinical Progress Note

terminations a celebratory, positive experience. They should permit children to freely express their feelings and say "goodbye" in concrete or symbolic methods. Muriel, his mother, and I ate his favorite mint chocolate chip cookies for our last session, discussed his progress over the past several months of treatment, and left the door open should he ever want to return and need additional time in the playroom.

CONCLUSION

Sandplay therapy and play therapy offer children the opportunity to communicate their thoughts, feelings, fantasies, and experiences nonverbally through use of symbolic objects in the presence of an accepting and supportive therapist. The fictional case of Muriel articulates the treatment planning process along with the psychogenic healing power of play and sandplay with children in Jungian Play Therapy. The use of the

Jungian technique, sandplay, enabled Muriel to overcome his irrational fears, improve self-esteem, and create cohesive and clear communication within his familial and peer relationships.

Key Takeaways

- ✪ Jungian play therapy with children is a depth psychology approach that utilizes symbols to uncover and allow for the tangible expression of the unconscious.
- ✪ Psyche is defined as the child's center of thought that regulates conscious experiences, such as behaviors and feelings. The symptoms that bring a child into therapy are indicative of this disturbance of integration.
- ✪ Individuation characterizes progress from psychic fragmentation towards wholeness—the acknowledgment and reconciliation of opposites within an individual.
- ✪ Children's symbols or archetypes are bipolar structures comprised of spiritual energy and feelings associated with culturally specific images in human behavior that may appear in children's dreams, fantasies, and mythology.
- ✪ Jungian play therapists can utilize drawings, creating mandalas, analysis of play themes, and sandplay in their work with children to assist them in diagnosis, prognosis, assessment, and treatment planning.
- ✪ The process of amplification of symbols is an important part of assessment in JPT. The therapy process in Gestalt Play Therapy is non-linear.
- ✪ Jungian therapists look at the children's play and try to identify themes and the self-healing symbols depicted in their sandplay.
- ✪ Jungian play therapists notice and expound on the symbols, which is where they believe that emotions are contained.

REFERENCES

Allan, J. (1997). Jungian play psychotherapy. In K. J. O'Connor & L. M. Braverman (Eds.), *Play therapy: A comparative presentation* (2nd ed., pp. 100–130). Wiley.

Fordham, M. (1994). *Children as individuals*. Free Association Books. https://catalogue.nla.gov.au/catalog/499510

Green, E. (2007). The crisis of family separation following traumatic mass destruction: Jungian analytical play therapy in the aftermath of Hurricane Katrina. In N. B. Webb (Ed.), *Play therapy with children in crisis: Individual, Group, and Family Treatment* (3rd ed., pp. 368–388). Guilford. https://psycnet.apa.org/record/2007-14176-017

Green, E. J. (2009). Jungian analytical play therapy. In K. O'Connor & L. Braverman (Eds.), *Play therapy theory and practice: Comparing theories and techniques* (2nd ed., pp. 142–178). John Wiley. https://psycnet.apa.org/record/2010-04804-000

Green, E. J. (2012). The Narcissus myth, resplendent reflections, and self-healing: A contemporary Jungian perspective on counseling *high*-functioning autistic children. In L. Gallo-Lopez & L. Rubin (Eds.), *Play based interventions for children and adolescents with Autism spectrum disorders* (pp. 177–192). Routledge. https://www.taylorfrancis.com/chapters/edit/10.4324/9780203829134-11/narcissus-myth-resplendent-reflections-self-healing-eric-green

Heiko, R. (2018). *A therapist's guide to mapping the girl heroine's journey in sandplay*. Rowman and Littlefield. https://psycnet.apa.org/record/2019-44975-000

Jung, C. G. (1951). The psychology of the child archetype. In H. Read, M. Fordham, & G. Adler (Eds.), *The collected works of C. G. Jung* (Vol. 9). Princeton University Press.

Kalff, D. M. (1971). *Sandplay: Mirror of a child's psyche*. Browser.

Landreth, G. (2012). *Play therapy: The art of the relationship* (3rd ed.). Routledge. https://doi.org/10.4324/9781003255796

Mitchell, R. R., Friedman, H., & Green, E. J. (2013). Sandplay. In E. J. Green & A. Drewes (Eds.), *Integrating play therapy and expressive arts with children and adolescents* (pp. 92–116). Wiley. https://www.wiley.com/en-es/Integrating+Expressive+Arts+and+Play+Therapy+with+Children+and+Adolescents-p-9781118527986

Punnett, A. (Ed.). (2022). *Jungian child analysis: Cultural perspectives*. Analytical Psychology Press. https://junginla.org/product/jungian-child-analysis/

CHAPTER 16

KALFFIAN SANDPLAY IN ASSESSMENT AND THERAPY PLANNING

Rosalind L. Heiko

INTRODUCTION

Sandplay's roots can be traced back to four aspects and traditions which the founder, Swiss analyst Dora Kalff, conceived as a comprehensive practice. Sandplay accesses unconscious and conscious processes using a collection of symbolic figures, sand, water, and delineated trays within an attuned therapeutic relationship (called the co-transference) to access the internal healing capacity of the psyche (Kalff, 2020; Roesler, 2019). These roots include joining with Margaret Lowenfeld's seminal work in London at the Institute for Child Psychology using wet and dry trays filled with sand as well as toys available to place in them; working with Carl and Emma Jung directly and studying analytic theory; embracing Asian contemplative practice; and an engagement with spirituality and spiritual growth (i.e., connecting to the numinous, that which we find to be more than ourselves). According to Martin Kalff, his mother "…recognized that the intrapsychic process revealed in children's creations in the sand corresponded to the process that Jung had described as individuation. In agreement with Margaret Lowenfeld, she called her approach 'sandplay,' which, drawing on Jungian psychology, developed more and more its own form" (Kalff, 2020, p. 108).

These four roots combined to form a unified theory of the psychic process in the sandplay of a heroic journey. Kalff believed the therapeutic nature of the relationship between therapist and client, using the relational space of the sandtrays, water, and symbols (miniature figures), could address the wounding and suffering clients must examine in their quest for healing. Sandplay is a "… self-directed, hands-on creative work by the client without interference or interpretation" over the tray by the therapist (Freedle et al., 2020, p. 130) within what Kalff termed the "free and protected space." Kalffian Sandplay is a trauma-sensitive approach, activating multiple brain systems which engage neuroplasticity and neural integration processes in meaning-making narratives and journeys (Freedle, 2022; Roesler, 2019; Wiersma et al., 2022).

Freedle reported that "…there is a significant and growing body of qualitative and quantitative research that establishes sandplay therapy as an evidence-based therapy for children and adults with a variety of emotional and behavioral problems "(2022, p. 134). Wiersma et al.'s meta-analysis of international sandplay studies concluded that

> …The consistent effectiveness of sandplay therapy across domains in the present analysis might lie in its multisensory, symbolic, less verbal, and actively experiential approach … Sandplay appears to lower the threshold for the initiation of psychotherapy and provides people that have barriers to verbal expression with a safe, direct, and contained means to access and work through difficulties. (2022, p. 209)

Roesler's (2019) overview of sandplay therapy's evidence base concluded that "… in the process of transforming emotional content into a sandtray picture, clients can directly

DOI: 10.4324/9781003334231-18

modify and change their inner thoughts and emotions, restructuring their inner world and establishing order ..." (p.85). Sandplay therapy

> [C]hanges the focus of therapy away from solely verbal communication or cognitive insight ... for trauma victims it seems to offer the opportunity to address the psychological problems in a very indirect and nonconfrontational way, thus preventing the client from re-traumatization ... offer[ing] an innovative and transdiagnostic approach for reducing psychopathology and increasing well-being. (Roesler, 2019, p. 93)

CASE SCENARIO

Initial Intake

Theo was ten years old at the time of referral by a colleague who knew I specialized in Kalffian Sandplay. Theo experienced multiple foster family placements after their biological parents' rights were terminated at age 5. Little information was shared with the adoptive parents about early development, although it was postulated that both Theo's biological parents had been addicted to substances. After parental termination of rights, Theo was initially placed with a highly fundamentalist couple, who were physically and emotionally abusive to Theo. Unluckily, Theo was then placed in a series of foster homes. Theo's early education and academic experiences had been haphazard at best. Theo had been compelled to participate in a number of individual therapies and often silently refused to engage with therapists. Their newly adoptive parents described them as dysregulated, sullen, refusing to cooperate with performance demands at school and home, unwilling to accept being part of a new family, and sometimes physically aggressive, although not in the school setting.

Case Conceptualization

Theo was diagnosed by a former therapist with clinical depression, oppositional-defiant disorder, dysregulation, and anxiety. The adoptive parents indicated that "paperwork somewhere" placed Theo on the autism spectrum, although there was no clear evaluation data to support this.

When conceptualizing presenting issues for a client in Kalffian Sandplay, the client's cultural background, social-emotional connections, and possible structural racial and minority inequalities become vital considerations to understanding the client's family history, dynamics, and interactions. Children in foster care are at a higher risk of developing mental health disorders when compared with their peers (Papovich, 2019). Study findings of abuse and subsequent trauma during many foster care placements were also reported in the literature, concluding this has long-term impact and consequences emotionally, socially, academically, and behaviorally for these children (Papovich, 2019).

Kalffian Sandplay focuses on the whole person of the client and their web of influences, not solely on assessment and therapy of an individual child's behaviors. The lens I use is attachment which provides a trauma-sensitive approach. Theo's multiple foster placements, challenging early development, and the termination of their relationship with their biological parents led me to hypothesize that Theo had experienced trauma after trauma. Feeling clinically depressed, anxious, dysregulated, irritable, sullen, angry, oppositional, and hostile are all expressions of traumatic stress—and all of these behaviors had been reported as issues for Theo.

Assessment Process

Typically, I meet with a child and their family members as a unit for the first session. For an adolescent, I flip that expectation and meet with the teen first, then the family together for the next session. Meeting the adolescent first can help to establish a measure of agency and trust, subsequently welcoming the family as a whole. At that first meeting I explain that I'd like to introduce the space (both a family consultation room with a couch and comfortable chairs) and the sand room/play room next to it, as well as share my role (to listen and try to understand what's happening in the family and with the child/adolescent) and ask about what is challenging and what is easy. I say that I am like a river guide. I have worked with lots of families, and I know the currents and channels, but I don't know the way this family likes to flow. I assert that I am not going to "fix" anyone—people are not toasters, and I am not going to "repair" anyone. I then ask "Why are you here?" to each person present. I pursue the question in depth, asking "Why are you here on Earth? What are you here to learn?" if the initial answers solely focus on "problem behaviors" on the part of the child or teen. This initial session is crucial in terms of establishing containment, relational attunement, and expectations.

Once we develop a therapy plan going forward, I apply the Sandplay Journey Map© (Heiko, 2018) to assess and chart client journeys through the sandplay process. During this process, the client confronts and integrates their shadow material and the tension of opposite needs, emotions, and experiences within what Joseph Campbell referred to in story and myth as The Hero's Journey (1972). During this process, trays that symbolize the "constellation of the Self" (i.e., the experience of the beauty and treasure of the internalized self, the numinous) become more integrated and peaceful as centered representations emerge.

One method of mapping sandwork uses the Sandplay Journey Map© (Heiko, 2018) in four gateways/phases. The initial gateway is "Pathways." Here clients make the decision to undertake their journey to face their fear of the "unknown." The second gateway is "Discernment," where clients face many of their fears and courageously begin to address the tensions and shadow aspects of trauma and suffering in their psyche. A "Centering" in the middle phase of the journey reveals the beauty of their inner "light" and Self. The third gateway is "Harmony," where the client begins to integrate those challenges and tensions to balance their values and needs. The last gateway is "re-turn," where clients symbolically appreciate their courage, strengths, and the connections they value with others.

Assessment continues throughout the implementation of attuned work with the family and client. This includes regular meetings with caregivers and meetings as needed for initial assessment and later follow-up with adjunct caregivers such as school staff, psychiatrist, pediatrician, and related health care providers (i.e., after-school caregivers or tutors, physical or occupational therapists, speech pathologists, or caregiving relatives). Figure 16.1 illustrates this comprehensive model of assessment and therapy planning from this Kalffian Sandplay perspective.

Identifying Problems and Diagnosis

Theo and their parents initially identified problems related to getting along at home, emotional battles over Theo's completing chores, handling Theo's escalating aggression, and speaking respectfully to each other when stressed. The family indicated that they wanted to

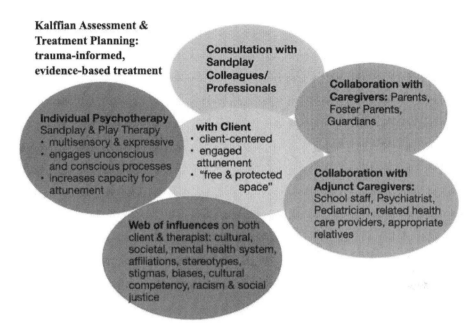

Figure 16.1 Model of Assessment and Therapy Plan from a Kalffian Perspective

learn to manage de-escalating and disengaging when tensions arose in difficult conversations and how to manage expectations. Theo wanted to begin working in the sand room immediately, as most children and teens do when offered a way to express themselves through creative play without having to use words.

Working in sandplay requires knowledge of healing and wounding themes through images that represent symbolic language in the trays and how these themes can affect the client's representation of their struggle (Rogers-Mitchell & Friedman, 2017). Observing Theo's play and sand trays, I could identify themes of trauma with regard to the unjust and abusive therapy he received at the hands of previous adoptive families. Theo's trays resounded with the experience of being unprotected from exposure to violence and aggression; feeling empty, isolated, and confined; as well as demonstrating his feelings of hopelessness.

I arranged for a consultation with the family's pediatrician and referred Theo to a psychiatrist as well as a neuropsychologist for a full evaluation. The psychiatrist hesitated to put Theo on any medication until the full evaluation was completed and then carefully added antidepressant medication to Theo's regimen. The neuropsychologist did not identify Theo as being on the spectrum; although his finding was that some of Theo's behaviors were off-putting, with a presentation of cognitive rigidity, social constraint, and difficulties with attachment. The neuropsychologist and I agreed that trauma and its attendant sequelae served as the current diagnosis for Theo. There were some neurodivergent academic and learning issues that the adoptive parents and I began to address with Theo's school staff regarding the need for Section 504 plan accommodations.

Setting Goals and Establishing Measurable Objectives

Trusting the relational field between therapist and client, that connection of shelter, active listening, and holding, is central to Kalffian Sandplay.

> It is not essential for us as therapists to understand everything that's happening in the tray at the time of the client's creation, or make verbal links to the client between the symbol material and what is happening in the client's everyday life (the process called "*interpretation*") … the struggle to understand during the client session may interfere with learning about the client's experience of their story and their emotions during a session. It's all a process of "… a mutual coming to understand," as Bradway and McCoard (1997, p. 28) pointed out when [Bradway was] reviewing her own trays ten years after completing her process with Dora Kalff. (Heiko, 2018, p. 14)

Kalffian Sandplay relies on ritual and ceremony to set the therapeutic environment apart from everyday life and concerns, allowing the client to enter a "liminal space" within the therapeutic container. When clients move out of the waiting area, they enter a hallway filled with pictures from my travels and a large dreamcatcher. With no doorways between rooms, they can then choose to enter left or right. I make sure I never sit where I am blocking the client's way in or out. We begin the sessions with breathwork and sometimes a guided meditation, as well as using EMDR® buzzies, which are used to help with self-regulation. It is all the client's choice.

Theo eagerly placed the buzzies in their socks as they came into the sand room. They seemed to enjoy the feeling of ease it brought. We ended sessions with candle lighting and the opportunity to take a shell from a jar gathered from my walks on one of the NC beaches. Theo let me know right away the drink and (healthy) snack they most enjoyed. I provided those for them each time they came, so there was predictability.

After an initial assessment session, we began working on therapy goals and objectives. Utilizing the Neurosequential Model of Therapeutics (Perry & Dobson, 2013), helped to focus on Theo's key strengths, which were their persistence, intelligence, curiosity, and interest in pursuing a heroic journey. Therapy goals centered on:

1. Addressing their displacement and trauma.
2. Reducing their reactivity and perceived/realistic abandonment.
3. Developing better emotional and behavioral regulation skills.
4. Discovering and utilizing their inner resources as well as their capacity for connection.

Planning Theoretically Based Interventions

Kalffian Sandplay was the focus of Theo's therapeutic work. Theo bent over the trays, keeping me in sight at all times. As they became more comfortable with me, they moved around the trays, sometimes allowing themselves to have their back to me. Theo initially worked on two trays at a time, moving back and forth in their narrative, sharing voluminous sand stories. I carefully wrote these down, noticing that Theo often paused to look over to make sure I was getting everything they said. Toward the end of their sandplay process, Theo consolidated and integrated the images into just one tray.

Theo also played with rocket balloons for anger management on days they were particularly overwhelmed, working in clay, humming their own songs while creating trays, and drawing. All of these activities, including the sandwork, were initiated by Theo.

Collaboration in Therapy Planning with Client and Caregivers

I continued to meet once monthly with adoptive parents, and with the entire family once quarterly during the time Theo was in therapy, while continuing to engage in individual therapy with Theo. Family work included resource development "homework assignments" to engage adoptive parents and Theo in brief, structured, enjoyable activities; family therapy around challenging situations and past ruptures; and adoptive parent check-ins online, by phone, and in person.

Consultation: Collaboration in Therapy Planning with Sandplay Professionals

Kalffian Sandplay practice requires regular meetings in consultation with professional colleagues to ensure a continued capacity to engage deeply with the emotions involved in the co-transference, as well as sharing clinical material and digital sandtray slides for discussion (occurring with the understanding and authorization of both Theo and his adoptive parents). I met regularly in both group and individual consultations with sandplay colleagues.

Progress Tracking in Therapy Planning with Client and Caregivers

A major issue for Theo was being asked to call his adoptive parents "Mom" and "Dad." He preferred to call them by their first names. This caused a rift in the relationship. Many family sessions were spent trying to address the needs of all family members; and in helping Theo's adoptive parents to understand how difficult it was to demand he addresses them as his parents from the beginning of their relationship without first developing a secure attachment or making that decision for himself.

There were healing themes in Theo's therapeutic progress. His sandtrays became more integrated, demonstrating mastery and self-confidence, with symbolically healthy protected boundaries, and a willingness to entertain more realistic interactions with figures. Images of nurturance and growth began to emerge over time, and centering trays that contained circular shapes with central gatherings occurred as well. I regularly reviewed my clinical notes, Sandplay Session Notes, VERDO Evaluation Sheet (see Figure 16.2) and Individual Tray Description forms; as well as sandtray images in consultation with sandplay colleagues to keep current and focused on his therapy goals.

The VERDO Evaluation Sheet tracks five aspects of sandtray creation: Vision (e.g., the problem statement and what resources were available to meet those challenges; and what obstacles needed to be overcome in particular trays), Emotion (e.g., what was manifested during the creation of this tray), Relationship (e.g., co-transference images, symbols and archetypal energies), Dynamics (e.g., themes and self-symbols), and Organization (e.g., regulated/unregulated, how well integrated, how space was handled, if there was any use of water), as well as which of the four gateways in the map was the focus of a particular session (see Figure 16.2).

The Sandplay Therapy Session Note can be used when documenting sandplay sessions for insurance purposes (see Figure 16.3), delineating symptomatology, intervention modalities, play themes, and a brief content summary.

This form can document individual tray creation from all areas of the tray, indicating which objects/symbols were used and where they were placed, so that the tray can be thoroughly documented for consultation.

Termination Process Strategies and Conclusion

Kalffian Therapy relies on a developmental approach to continued care. Often traumatized youth will re-engage in therapy following significant life events or experiences which re-activate the trauma response. After two years of therapy, Theo made fewer trays focusing on more abstract images of battle scenes won, reaching for peace. We adjusted their sessions to every other week, then every month, following a discussion with Theo and their adoptive parents. After two and a half years, Theo was able to transform their fears, dysregulation, and disconnection into connection with friends, a more affectionate relationship with their adoptive parents, the capacity to recover more easily when frustrated, and the ability to share insights about their difficulties. Theo began participating more in family activities, as well as showing interest in joining an after-school program in music. Theo was ready to end this piece of work with me (what I call the "turn of the wheel") when the relationship with their adoptive parents became more settled.

Theo came in one day and made one last tray: a family eating and playing at a picnic. Outside in the woods, a cheerful-looking house beckoned. The therapy goals were met, and it was time to end, for now. We scheduled a final session. When a sandplay process comes to a close, it is time for an ending ritual. Theo and I each lit a candle and said some words that came to mind, about what we hoped for each other. We shared a chocolate treat and Theo's favorite drink. Then Theo made their choice of a pewter pocket pebble engraved with the word "hope" from a jeweled bag of treasures. I held the suite door open for Theo and his adoptive dad to pass through. On their way out the door, Theo looked back, met my eyes, and nodded, once. I smiled and thought: A bright and loving future to you, dear Theo.

Conclusion

Kalffian Sandplay provides a reliable and substantive theoretical basis for play-based expressive therapy assessment and therapy planning. Kalffian Sandplay, a trauma-informed and evidence-based therapy for children and teens, emphasizes "the free and protected space" within the therapeutic relationship and activates the healing energies inherent in symbolic language in the creation and neural integration of sandtray imagery. The case presentation of Theo illustrates a guide from case conceptualization and assessment in identifying salient presenting problems and dynamics through to therapy planning and termination outcomes. Kalffian Sandplay allowed Theo to successfully process challenging issues of dysregulation, depression and traumatic experiences in foster care and adoption through attuned therapeutic engagement and case collaboration with parents and adjunct professionals.

TRAY DESCRIPTION

BACK | **MIDDLE** | **FRONT**

OBJECTS USED:

_____

_____

_____

_____

_____

_____

_____

PLACEMENT:

_____

_____

_____

_____

_____

_____

_____

_____

_____

Gate 1 Pathways: Choosing to Journey
Gate 2 Discernment: Facing Fear & Embodying Courage
Center Illumination: Constellating the Self
Gate 3 Harmony: Reconciling Tensions & Integrating Shadow
Gate 4 Re-Turn: Appreciating Abundance

Figure 16.2 Sample Clinical Progress: VERDO Evaluation Sheet

Sandplay Therapy Session Note

Client: _____ **DOB:** _____

Date: _____ **Provider Signature:** _____

CPT Billing Code: ____(New Client) Diagnostic Interview (90791) ____Individual Regular (90834) ____Individual Lengthy (90837) _____Individual Brief (90832) ____Family with Child (90847) _____Family without Child (90846)

Treatment goals:

1.

2.

3.

Recently Reported Symptoms (* = increasing symptoms):

____panic attacks ____OCD ____anger outbursts ____sleep disturbances ____substance abuse ____hallucinations ____self-harming behaviors ____suicidal ideation/gesture ____disregulated mood ____running____other:_____

Present Symptoms:

Mood/Affect: ____sad ____hopeless ____angry ____scared ____anxious ____happy ____shy other:

_____

Cognitive State: ____distractable____concentrational difficulty ____suicidal ideation ____organized other:

_____

Behavior: ____compulsions/obsessions present ____cooperative ____resistant ____openly oppositional ____dissociated ____demonstrating attachment difficulties ____aggressive other:

_____

Energy Level: ____regulated ____overly high ____overly low/fatigued ____other: _____

Assessment/Intervention Modalities:

____cognitive-behavioral therapy ____directive play therapy ____non-directive play therapy ____sandplay ____expressive art/craft work ____life-skills training ____social skills training ____parenting skills ____facilitative attachment ____EMDR ____structuring compliance ____reflecting feelings ____reflecting content ____anger release activities ____developing attachment behaviors ____facilitating creative problem-solving ____role playing ____empathic attunement ____self-regulation other:_____

Client Play Themes:

____bridging danger ____diffusing anger ____mastery vs.powerlessness ____grief & loss ____attachment formation ____expressing negative emotions ____nurturing acts ____handling anxiety ____expressing good vs. bad internal beliefs ____identity formation ____negative/shadow self ____world exploration ____safety ____woundedness ____trust ____boundary exploration ____hiding and finding ____clarifying discipline/rule setting ____clarifying parenting & child roles ____other:_____

Session Content Summary:

Client Response to therapy: ____Excellent ____Good ____Fair ____Poor

Participation: ____Excellent ____Good ____Fair ____Poor

____developed alliance ____increased healthy expression of feelings ____crisis intervention ____discussion of collaboration with collateral professionals ____introduced/reinforced skills ____performed risk assessment ____gained insight ____monitored client ____intro/reinforced parenting skills other:

_____

Notes:

Figure 16.3 Sample Clinical Progress: Sandplay Session Note (Adapted from Karen Wheeler)

EVALUATING SANDTRAYS USING VERDO:

Vision | Emotion | Relationship | Dynamic | Organization

VISION

· In the first tray or trays, what is the Problem Statement:
· What strikes me as manifesting in this tray?
· What Obstacles need to be overcome?
· What Resources are available?

NOTES FOR SESSION:

_____

EMOTION

· What emotion(s) does the client manifest, either non-verbally or verbally, throughout the session
· During the creation of this tray, what emotions do I sense in myself?
· When the tray is completed, what do I feel in the presence of the client when I breathe deeply and slowly to center myself?

_____
_____
_____
_____
_____

RELATIONSHIP

· What do I notice about the co transference which emerges in this session?
· Are there any symbols the client has chosen that come from my childhood, I have made, or are especially meaningful to me at this stage in my life?
· Are there any symbols the client identifies verbally or puts into the tray that could be figures representing our relationship, such as the Sage, Healer, Magician or Wise Woman/Senex?

_____
_____
_____
_____
_____

DYNAMIC

· What themes are emerging in this tray?
· What active manifestations of the psyche appear here?
· Do I detect any potential self-symbols in the creation of this tray?
· What might I name this tray (even if the client has already named it, would I give it a different name?

_____
_____
_____
_____

ORGANIZATION

· How is the tray organized?
· Is it a tray representing a regulated or unregulated emotional stater
· How is the space and the sand handled?
· Is the tray dry? Wet? Flooded?
· How many of the elements (earth, air, water, fire) are represented in this tray?
· How are the symbols differentiated, if symbols are used?

_____
_____
_____
_____

Gate 1 Pathways: Choosing to Journey
Gate 2 Discernment: Facing Fear & Embodying Courage
Center Illumination: Constellating the Self
Gate 3 Harmony: Reconciling Tensions & Integrating Shadow
Gate 4 Re-Turn: Appreciating Abundance

Figure 16.4 Sample Clinical Progress: Individual Tray Description

Key Takeaways

- ❁ Sandplay accesses unconscious and conscious processes using a collection of symbolic figures, sand, water and delineated trays within an attuned therapeutic relationship that utilizes symbols to uncover and allow for the tangible expression of the unconscious.
- ❁ Kalff believed the therapeutic nature of the relationship and the relational space of the sandtrays, water and symbols (miniature figures) could address the wounding and suffering clients must examine in their quest for healing Individuation characterizes progress from psychic fragmentation towards wholeness—the acknowledgment and reconciliation of opposites within an individual.
- ❁ Kalffian Sandplay is a trauma-sensitive approach activating multiple brain systems. Jungian play therapists can utilize drawings, creating mandalas, analysis of play themes, and sandplay in their work with children to assist them in diagnosis, prognosis, assessment, and treatment planning.
- ❁ Kalffian Sandplay focuses on the whole person of the client and their web of influences, not solely on assessment and therapy of an individual child's behaviors.
- ❁ Working in sandplay requires knowledge of healing and wounding themes through images that represent symbolic language in the trays.
- ❁ Trusting the relational field between therapist and client, that connection of shelter, active listening, and holding, is central to Kalffian Sandplay.
- ❁ Kalffian Sandplay relies on ritual and ceremony to set the therapeutic environment apart from everyday life and concerns.
- ❁ Kalffian Therapy relies on a developmental approach to continued care.

REFERENCES

Bradway, K., & McCoard, B. (1997). *Sandplay: Silent workshop of the psyche*. Routledge. https://doi.org/10.4324/9780203977576

Campbell, J. (1972). *The hero with a thousand faces*. Princeton University Press. https://doi.org/10.2307/537371

Cunningham, L. (2013). *Sandplay and the clinical relationship*. Sempervirens Press. https://doi.org/10.4324/9781315656748-14

Freedle, L. R. (2022). Sandplay therapy: An evidence-based therapy. *Journal of Sandplay Therapy*, *31*(1), 129–136. https://doi.org/10.4324/9781315656748-12

Freedle, L. R., Goodwin-Downs, D., Souza Jr., J. & Cipponeri, A. (2020). The added value of sandplay therapy with emerging adults in an outdoor behavioral healthcare program. *Journal of Sandplay Therapy, 29*(1), 129–144.

Heiko, R. (2018). *A therapist's guide to mapping the girl heroine's journey in sandplay*. Rowman and Littlefield.

Kalff, D. M. (2020). *Sandplay: A psychotherapeutic approach to the psyche*. Analytical Psychology Press.

Papovich, C. (2019). *Trauma and children in foster care: A comprehensive overview*. CSP. Retrieved from https://www.csp.edu/publication/trauma-children-in-foster-care-a-comprehensive-overview/

Perry, B., & Dobson, C. L. (2013). The neurosequential model of therapeutics. In J. D. Ford & C. A. Courtois (Eds.), *Treating complex traumatic stress disorders in children and adolescents*. Guilford Press. https://doi.org/10.1017/s1352465814000095

Roesler, C. (2019). Sandplay therapy: An overview of theory, applications and evidence base. *The Arts in Psychotherapy, 64*, 84–94. https://doi.org/10.1016/j.aip.2019.04.001

Rogers-Mitchell, R., & Friedman, H. S. (2017). Archetypal themes in the sandplay process. *Journal of Sandplay Therapy, 26*(1), 8–10. https://doi.org/10.4324/9781003110002-7

Wiersma, J. K., Freedle, L. R., McRoberts, R., & Solberg, K. B. (2022). A meta-analysis of sandplay therapy outcomes. *International Journal of Play Therapy, 31*(4), 197–215. https://doi.org/10.1037/pla0000180

CHAPTER 17

A PSYCHODYNAMIC APPROACH TO TREATMENT PLANNING

Geoff Goodman

INTRODUCTION

Child Psychodynamic Therapy (CPDT) has existed at least since Hermine Hug-Hellmuth (1921), Melanie Klein (1923), and Anna Freud (1928) first began using children's play as an entrée into their internal worlds for therapeutic purposes. Almost 100 years later, the treatment first used by these psychoanalytic pioneers has changed, along with the entire field of psychodynamic therapy (PDT), but for many working in the field of child mental health, there is relatively little understanding of contemporary psychodynamic developments. While there is far less research evaluating the effectiveness of CPDT than psychodynamic therapy with adults or other forms of child treatment such as CBT, a number of narrative reviews of the evidence have now been published (e.g., Fonagy et al., 2015; Midgley & Kennedy, 2011; Palmer et al., 2013; Midgley et al., 2017, 2021), demonstrating good preliminary evidence for the value of CPDT. In the only meta-analysis to date (Abbass et al., 2013), short-term CPDT was found to be effective for a wide range of psychiatric diagnoses, including anxiety, emerging borderline personality disorder, depression, eating disorders, and mixed disorders. Short-term CPDT was also associated with persistent changes after termination, leading these authors to conclude that "certain blocks to personal and psychological development are positively affected by these interventions" (p. 873).

According to Goodman et al. (2016), the essential ingredients of CPDT include emphasizing the therapist's sensitivity to the child's feelings, tolerating strong affects or impulses, interpreting warded-off, unconscious wishes or feelings, and making links between the child's feelings and experience, and pointing out recurrent themes in the child's experience or conduct. The CPDT therapist also pays attention to the ways in which the child uses the therapeutic relationship to regulate his or her arousal and negative emotions and then uses a series of techniques to disrupt this pattern of affect regulation.

ATTACHMENT AND PATTERNS OF AFFECT REGULATION

Ainsworth (1979) described three patterns of attachment that can be observed as early as 12 months. Goodman (2010) argued that these three attachment patterns are directly related to three corresponding patterns of affect regulation discussed in the attachment literature. The secure (B) attachment pattern is associated with a balanced pattern of affect regulation. On the other hand, the anxious-resistant (C) attachment pattern corresponds to a hyperactivating pattern of affect regulation, while the anxious-avoidant (A) attachment pattern corresponds to a deactivating pattern of affect regulation (Kobak & Sceery, 1988; Main, 1990). Nonorganic encopresis represents a child's maladaptive strategy to deactivate arousal and disavow negative emotions. Due to the noxious smell of feces and the unsanitary mess,

DOI: 10.4324/9781003334231-19

nonorganic encopresis serves to push away chronically disappointing caregivers and others and isolate oneself from the vulnerability associated with this disappointment, rejection, and potential abandonment. Nonorganic encopresis is a conspicuously effective way of announcing to the world, "I'm now in charge of rejection!" The deactivating pattern of affect regulation creates a general vulnerability (Rutter, 1985, 1987) that combines with other risk factors in the development of nonorganic encopresis.

To treat encopresis, the CPDT model would address the underlying vulnerability created by the deactivating pattern of affect regulation. The therapist accomplishes this treatment goal by (1) using his or her relationship with the child to modify the deactivating pattern and (2) articulating the child's mind, emphasizing the child's affect, to establish mental closeness. The child would begin to use the therapist to facilitate affect regulation and consequently diminish the use of his or her symptoms for this purpose. Because of deficits in symbolic function associated with nonoptimal patterns of affect regulation, a contemporary CPDT model would diminish the role of interpretation (Cohen & Solnit, 1993; Lewis et al., 2000; Rosegrant, 2001) and accentuate the role of the therapeutic relationship in healing these affect-regulatory processes.

ROLE OF THERAPIST

In the following case scenario, I observed progress with an encopretic child only after I prioritized my relationship with him and made myself available as an affective container and regulator rather than an interpreter of intrapsychic conflict. I persisted in making an emotional connection with him—to give him a taste of a genuine, reciprocal relationship. Like a baseball player waiting for the perfect moment to steal a second base when the pitcher is not paying attention, I tolerated seemingly endless sadomasochistic interactions, waiting out my opportunity to make authentic contact while going unnoticed. This process consisted of pursuing emotional contact in the face of devaluation, rejection, and withdrawal, often using humor to "mark" these affective expressions. Humor permitted me to show my patient that (1) I understand what you are feeling (connection), and (2) I can symbolize your feeling in a playful manner even though I am not personally experiencing the same feeling (separation). Affects then become mentalized, represented verbally in the minds of both therapist and patient.

Keeping the child firmly in mind through "retaining mental closeness" (Bateman & Fonagy, 2004a, p. 44) facilitated this child's shift away from relying on encopresis for affect regulation toward relying on me, and later, his parents and peers, for this purpose. This child no longer felt compelled to so rigidly control the anxiety associated with separation and loss through his encopretic symptoms of retention and release. The play process took place in a potential space where our play overlapped (Winnicott, 1968), offering a pathway to explore relationships one step removed from reality (Mayes & Cohen, 1993) by testing out new ways of relating to me and regulating affect through me and by forming new expectations of affective responses from me. According to Bateman and Fonagy (2004b), the play process enables "feelings and thoughts, wishes and beliefs [to] be experienced by the child as significant and respected on the one hand, but on the other as not being of the same order as physical reality" (p. 84). This process naturally facilitates symbolic functioning, where words can encode unnamed affects and thus provide affective containment.

CASE SCENARIO

Dennis was a 5-year-old boy referred to me for outpatient psychotherapy by his parents. In the initial consultation, Dennis's parents expressed exasperation at their only child's stubbornness, expressed in his use of pull-ups for defecation instead of a toilet. They feared that Dennis's toilet-training refusal would interfere with his self-esteem as he was beginning kindergarten in the fall. At the time of referral, Dennis attended preschool for a full day, five days per week. Prior to this placement, Dennis had attended a different pre-school for a full day, five days per week, since age 2. His mother shared this information with me nondefensively, never having considered the possibility that a very young child might need more physical and emotional proximity to his secure base. I said nothing about this arrangement because both parents had already shared with me their need to work full-time. In the course of treatment, I also learned that the parents did not have relatives nearby, such as grandparents (i.e., secondary attachment figures) with whom they could leave Dennis while at work.

Dennis's parents reported that he had never been toilet-trained. At the time of the initial consultation, Dennis had used a toilet "a handful of times," according to his mother. His parents reported that they had attempted toilet training since Dennis was three by reward-ing Dennis for using a toilet with candy or toys, which had only a temporary impact on his behavior. Out of exasperation, Dennis's father sometimes used threats to get him to conform to their expectations of using a toilet, for example, "I'm going to put you down the drain." He also admitted to kicking Dennis in the buttocks after some accidents.

On the other hand, Dennis's mother sometimes behaved in ways that allowed him to receive gratification from the encopresis. At the time of the initial consultation, Dennis's mother was still cleaning up his accidents, wiping him, and putting new pull-ups on him. His parents' description of this routine strongly suggested that Dennis enjoyed playing the role of the baby with his mother, who readily shared her exasperation with me, even with Dennis in the office. His parents also reported other symptoms suggestive of oppositional behavior and a need for control, such as refusal of food presented to him at the dinner table, resistance to getting dressed in the morning, and resistance to getting ready for bed. Dennis also had an obsession with toy monster trucks, monster truck rallies (which he attended with his father), and monster truck video games. What was originally a father-son activity evolved into a devotion far exceeding the father's interest. Dennis stated that he wanted to be a monster truck driver when he grew up.

Case Formulation and Diagnosis

The foregoing history indicated a diagnosis of nonorganic encopresis (F98.1; World Health Organization, 2019). I understand Dennis's disorder, at the core, as an anxious-avoidant attach-ment to his caregivers that generalized to a mode of relating to his internal and external world, affecting both narcissistic and relational realms, primarily at anal levels and beyond. He essen-tially experienced himself as inadequate to live outside of his defensive hiding place, and he was deficient in experiencing the affects and strivings normally associated with preadolescent development (e.g., aspiring to be attractive, relating on a level of mutuality, contemplating an interpersonally directed sexuality). On the positive side, underlying his defenses, Dennis strongly yearned for human connection. Although greatly obscured by his sadomasochistic façade, he was deeply attached to his parents and became increasingly so to me.

This anxious-avoidant attachment was formed when Dennis's mother was experiencing unbearable tension at her workplace, which might have distracted her from being an emotionally present mother. It is not known whether Dennis's parents were rejecting of him during his infancy, but there is ample evidence that they were rejecting him during his toilet training by age 3. Dennis had been separated from his parents for 40 hours per week at a childcare center since age 2. Bowlby (1980) theorized that internal working models of parent-child relationships become increasingly resistant to change. Dennis might have been securely attached during infancy; however, coinciding with the difficulties he experienced with toilet training, his parents' attitudes toward him became rejecting, which in turn stimulated defensive processes compatible with an anxious-avoidant attachment pattern—isolation of affect (i.e., compartmentalization of one's own emotional responses), omnipotent control (i.e., the belief that one has unlimited power to make others fulfill one's needs), narcissistic withdrawal (i.e., investing one's emotional resources exclusively in oneself), undoing (i.e., behaving in ways to magically undo a destructive wish), devaluation (i.e., putting down someone else), and denial (i.e., ignoring all evidence that disconfirms one's wishes). Prototypes of these defensive processes can be observed as early as 12 months in the Strange Situation procedure (Ainsworth, 1979), in which the infant snubs the mother and pretends she is not in the room after a brief separation, as if to be saying, "I don't need you; in fact, I am dismissing you from my mind."

Causality was probably bidirectional: Dennis's toilet-training difficulties both stimulated and were stimulated by rejecting parental behaviors. The fact that Dennis's parents left him in full-time childcare at such an early age, however, might provide clues about the ultimate direction of causality. Belsky et al. (2007) suggested that the effects of early childcare can be both profound and long-lasting; however, parents who choose such childcare arrangements might have pre-existing characteristics (e.g., dismissing attachment patterns) that could also predispose their children to later struggles with emotional intimacy.

Regardless of the direction of causality or the developmental period when Dennis became anxious-avoidant with respect to his relationship with his parents (i.e., infancy vs. toddlerhood), the transference (i.e., feelings about parents transferred onto the therapist) strongly suggested this same attachment pattern. Dennis spent entire sessions trying to push me away through various means such as flatulating, cheating in competitive games, devaluing me, not answering questions, adopting a know-it-all attitude, or simply denying that I had any impact on him. In some sessions, he chose to play video games that completely excluded me. Dennis once intentionally threw a ball at my face and hit me in the eye. When I pointed out that he had hurt my eye, he started making clucking noises that indicated that he thought I had stopped playing because I am a chicken—afraid of getting hurt. I felt not only angry but also too stunned to say anything other than to stop the play. Perhaps I was afraid of expressing my own anger—no matter how justified it might have been as a self-protective response. Of the three channels of patient communication (Clarkin et al., 2006)—verbal, nonverbal, and countertransference—the channel that Dennis most skillfully used with me was countertransference. Despite this knowledge, feelings of helplessness led me at various points in the treatment to wonder whether CPDT was the appropriate treatment model. Self-reflection, however, always helped me to analyze these moments of countertransference and to recognize them for what they were: self-protective attempts by Dennis to push me away and thus diminish his feelings of vulnerability. Disdain was perfectly suited to accomplish this self-protective goal. In those moments when Dennis was feeling disdainful of me, sometimes it was good enough simply to act as a container rather than a retaliator.

Retaliation would have only gratified his need for engagement through control without the dreaded experience of any accompanying feelings of vulnerability elicited by the risk of loss of control and, by extension, risk of loss of me.

On the other hand, Dennis was extremely protective of our time together. Dennis's father, who dropped him off on Friday evenings for session, often liked to talk to me about his job, his weekend plans, and Dennis's recent challenges. While chatting (which lasted up to 10 minutes), Dennis often scolded his father for taking up his therapy time. His father then usually made a self-deprecating joke and left. If I was 2 minutes late for the session, Dennis told me I was 2 minutes late. He denied the meaning of this behavior, but it was obvious that Dennis valued the time that we spent together and was willing to assert himself to protect it. This behavior suggests that I had become important to Dennis in spite of the anxious-avoidant defensive processes that he typically employed to protect himself against getting emotionally close to others and allowing others to become important to him.

As one might expect, given the transference parameters just outlined, my counter-transference reactions (i.e., feelings stimulated by the patient's attitudes and behaviors) were consistent with a therapist who was perpetually assigned a masochistic role to play: I felt helpless, disillusioned, ineffectual, frustrated, humiliated, dismissed, marginalized, and invisible. Typically, I did not feel all these feelings in the same session, but invariably, I felt at least one of these feelings in every session. My countertransference reactions were notable because, unlike many of my other therapeutic relationships, I knew exactly what I felt in a session with Dennis. There was no ambiguity. Despite my knowledge of the origins of Dennis's psychopathology, I still found my responses to these countertransference reactions challenging.

PLAN FOR TREATMENT

1) Working with Dennis in once-per-week individual psychodynamic therapy to allow him to express any feelings that might motivate his reluctance to use a toilet.
   a) Using the therapist's relationship with Dennis to modify the deactivating pattern and,
   b) articulating Dennis's mind, emphasizing his affects, to establish mental closeness.
2) Working collaterally with Dennis's parents about twice monthly to agree on a uniform behavioral approach to Dennis's difficulties.
   a) Emphasizing the parents' feelings stimulated by Dennis's behavior, and
   b) using the parents' feelings as clues to decipher what Dennis might be communicating and why he might be communicating that message.

Setting Goals and Establishing Measurable Objectives

Psychodynamic therapists allow the child and parents to set their own goals and establish measurable objectives; the parents' and especially the child's reports of satisfaction with the treatment are the primary signposts of progress in these treatments. Following the initial referral, Dennis's parents had made amazing progress in adjusting their behavioral approach to Dennis's toileting difficulties. His father stopped making threats (goal #1), while his mother stopped cleaning Dennis after accidents, instead getting him to clean up after himself (goal #2). Dennis began to express angry feelings in therapy sessions, which coincided with his increased use of the toilet (goal #3). During the treatment, Dennis experienced some successes while sitting on the toilet and showed pride in these successes. Nevertheless, Dennis still experienced accidents, which prompted his parents to welcome the prospect of a more intensive, relationship-focused treatment.

Adjusting the Initial Treatment Plan

Because the parents' and child's objectives for treatment were only partially fulfilled (goal #3), the parents, child, and I agreed on revising the treatment plan. Thus, I increased the treatment frequency to four times per week at age 10[9] [10]. The parents were enthusiastic about Dennis's beginning a more intensive treatment. I recommended this increased frequency because of Dennis's high intellectual functioning: I believed he would eventually tolerate my attempts at symbolizing his mental contents, such as monster trucks, which I could use to represent internal feeling states. I hoped that this work would eventually cultivate Dennis's own capacity to symbolize (i.e., verbalize) his feelings and reduce his need to act out his feelings by having accidents.

At the onset of this more intensive treatment, Dennis used the defensive processes of isolation of affect and omnipotent control to exert the maximum degree of control over his internal and external world. Consistent with a deactivating pattern of affect regulation, Dennis was able to put his feelings into a compartment and leave them there for long periods of time, which gave him an illusory feeling of control. He also behaved as though he were more powerful than I and could therefore order me around. For example, I had to hold Dennis's toy monster trucks in a particular way; disobedience resulted in withdrawal and complete emotional unavailability. He seemed to use encopresis as a mode of distancing himself from others and forcing others to distance themselves from him when he or they were getting too emotionally close and therefore making him feel too emotionally vulnerable.

Paradoxically, these distancing strategies also maintained emotional involvement, even though the involvement was antagonistic. Dennis learned that fecal smells are an effective means of removing others from one's proximity while keeping him emotionally present in their minds as an antagonistic figure. I noticed Dennis's needs for emotional distance and invincibility coexisting with his needs for emotional closeness and camaraderie with me. Getting too close to me emotionally put Dennis at risk of getting rejected or abandoned by me. These are some of the most painful feelings experienced by human beings. I surmise that Dennis experienced these feelings every morning before his parents dropped him off for a full day of childcare at age 2, during his parents' initial attempts at toilet training.

Termination Process

In CPDT, the therapist continues treating the patient until the parents and child both agree that they feel satisfied with the progress the child has made. I inform the parents and child that they are always welcome to return if old issues flare up or new issues manifest themselves. In the case of Dennis and his parents, I knew that I could discontinue the treatment after receiving the following e-mail message from Dennis's mother: "From my point of view, [Dennis's] personality and attitude have changed. We see he has more empathy, is more appreciative, and is more verbal. Overall, he seems much happier. This is great progress.

Thank you." Although Dennis still occasionally had accidents, he was on his way to becoming a separate yet connected preadolescent who was about to face a series of new challenges presented by adolescence. CPDT gave him a foundation upon which he could meet those challenges.

CONCLUSIONS

In this chapter, I discussed the essential ingredients of CPDT, which include emphasizing the therapist's sensitivity to the child's feelings, tolerating strong affects or impulses, interpreting warded-off, unconscious wishes or feelings, making links between the child's feelings and experiences, and pointing out recurrent themes in the child's experience or conduct. I presented the fictional case of Dennis, a 5-year-old boy diagnosed with primary encopresis, to demonstrate how I formulated a treatment plan to help (1) Dennis with this symptom and his underlying anxious-avoidant attachment strategy of distancing from others and (2) his father's punitive responses and his mother's infantilizing responses to Dennis's symptom. I formulated three treatment goals, originating with the child and parents: (1) helping the father to stop making threats, (2) helping the mother to stop cleaning Dennis after accidents, and (3) helping Dennis to express angry feelings in therapy sessions, which would coincide with increased use of the toilet. Because goal #3 was only partially fulfilled, I made an adjustment to the initial treatment plan and increased the treatment frequency. This adjustment allowed for a more thorough fulfillment of goal #3 and an opening up of Dennis's relationships so that he no longer had to rely on distancing strategies to regulate his underlying painful affects. Dennis is now prepared to confront a new set of challenges waiting for him during adolescence.

Key Takeaways

- ♡ CPDT was found to be effective for a wide range of psychiatric diagnoses, including anxiety, emerging borderline personality disorder, depression, eating disorders, and mixed disorders.
- ♡ The CPDT therapist also pays attention to the ways in which the child uses the therapeutic relationship to regulate his or her arousal and negative emotions.
- ♡ Three patterns of attachment are directly related to three corresponding patterns of affect regulation discussed in the attachment literature.
- ♡ In CPDT, the child will use the therapist to facilitate affect regulation and consequently diminish the use of his or her symptoms for this purpose.
- ♡ The play process naturally facilitates symbolic functioning, where words can encode unnamed affects and thus provide affective containment.
- ♡ Psychodynamic therapists allow the child and parents to set their own goals and establish measurable objectives.
- ♡ In CPDT, the therapist continues treating the patient until the parents and child both agree that they feel satisfied with the progress the child has made.
- ♡ Essential ingredients to CPDT are emphasizing the therapist's sensitivity to the child's feelings, tolerating strong affects or impulses, interpreting warded-off, unconscious wishes or feelings, making links between the child's feelings and experiences, and pointing out recurrent themes in the child's experience or conduct.

REFERENCES

Abbass, A. A., Rabung, S., Leichsenring, F., Refseth, J. S., & Midgley, N. (2013). Psychodynamic psychotherapy for children and adolescents: A meta-analysis of short-term psychodynamic models. *Journal of the American Academy of Child and Adolescent Psychiatry, 52*, 863–875. https://doi.org/10.1016/j.jaac.2013.05.014

Ainsworth, M. D. S. (1979). Infant-mother attachment. *American Psychologist, 34*, 932–937. https://doi.org/10.1037/0003-066x.34.10.932

Bateman, A. W., & Fonagy, P. (2004a). Mentalization-based treatment of BPD. *Journal of Personality Disorders, 18*, 36–51.https://doi.org/10.1521/pedi.18.1.36.32772

Bateman, A. W., & Fonagy, P. (2004b). *Psychotherapy for borderline personality disorder: Mentalization-based treatment.* Oxford University Press. https://doi.org/10.1093/med:psych/9780198527664.003.0003

Belsky, J., Burchinal, M., McCartney, K., Vandell, D. L., Clarke-Stewart, K. A., & Owen, M. T. (2007). Are there long-term effects of early child care? *Child Development, 78*, 681–701.https://doi.org/10.1111/j.1467-8624.2007.01021.x

Bowlby, J. (1980). *Attachment and loss: Vol. 3. Loss, sadness and depression.* Basic Books.

Clarkin, J. F., Yeomans, F. E., & Kernberg, O. F. (2006). *Psychotherapy for borderline personality: Focusing on object relations.* American Psychiatric Publishing. https://doi.org/10.1176/ajp.2006.163.5.944

Cohen, P. M., & Solnit, A. J. (1993). Play and therapeutic action. *Psychoanalytic Study of the Child, 48*, 49–63. https://doi.org/10.1080/00797308.1993.11822378

Fonagy, P., Cottrell, D., Phillips, J., Bevington, D., Glaser, D., & Allison, E. (2015). *What works for whom? A critical review of treatments for children and adolescents* (2nd ed.). Guilford Press.

Freud, A. (1974). The theory of child analysis. In: *The Writings of Anna Freud, Vol. 1* (pp. 162–175). International Universities Press. (Original work published 1929)

Goodman, G. (2010). *Therapeutic attachment relationships: Interaction structures and the processes of therapeutic change.* Jason Aronson.

Goodman, G., Midgley, N., & Schneider, C. (2016). Expert clinicians' prototypes of an ideal child treatment in psychodynamic and cognitive-behavioral therapy: Is mentalization seen as a common process factor? *Psychotherapy Research, 26*, 590–601.

Hug-Hellmuth, H. V. (1921). On the technique of child analysis. *International Journal of Psycho-Analysis, 2*, 287–305.

Klein, M. (1923). The development of a child. *International Journal of Psycho-Analysis, 4*, 419–474.

Kobak, R. R., & Sceery, A. (1988). Attachment in late adolescence: Working models, affect regulation, and representations of self and others. *Child Development, 59*, 135–146.

Lewis, T., Amini, F., & Lannon, R. (2000). *A general theory of love.* Random House.

Main, M. (1990). Cross-cultural studies of attachment organization: Recent studies, changing methodologies, and the concept of conditional strategies. *Human Development, 33*, 48–61.

Mayes, L. C., & Cohen, D. J. (1993). Playing and therapeutic action in child analysis. *International Journal of Psycho-Analysis, 74*, 1235–1244.

Midgley, N., & Kennedy, E. (2011). Psychodynamic psychotherapy for children and adolescents: A critical review of the evidence base. *Journal of Child Psychotherapy, 37*, 232–260.

Midgley, N., O'Keefe, S., French, L. and Kennedy, E. (2017). Psychodynamic psychotherapy for children and adolescents: An updated narrative review of the evidence base. *Journal of Child Psychotherapy, 43*, 307–329.

Midgley, N., Mortimer, R., Cirasola, A., Batra, P., & Kennedy, E. (2021). The evidence-base for psychodynamic psychotherapy with children and adolescents: A narrative synthesis. *Frontiers in Psychology, 12*, 1–18.

Palmer, R., Nascimento, L. N., & Fonagy, P. (2013). The state of the evidence base for psychodynamic psychotherapy for children and adolescents. *Child and Adolescent Psychiatric Clinics of North America, 22*, 149–214.

Rosegrant, J. (2001). The psychoanalytic play state. *Journal of Clinical Psychoanalysis, 10*, 323–343.

Rutter, M. (1985). Resilience in the face of adversity: Protective factors and resistance to psychiatric disorders. *British Journal of Psychiatry, 147*, 598–611.

Rutter, M. (1987). Psychosocial resilience and protective mechanisms. *American Journal of Orthopsychiatry, 57,* 316–331.

Winnicott, D. W. (1968). Playing: Its theoretical status in the clinical situation. *International Journal of Psycho-Analysis, 49,* 591–599.

World Health Organization (WHO). (2019). *International statistical classification of diseases and related health problems* (10th ed.). Retrieved from https://icd.who.int/

CHAPTER 18

A NEUROBIOLOGICAL RELATIONAL APPROACH TO THERAPY PLANNING

Rita Grayson

INTRODUCTION

Relational neuroscience is all about how we are interconnected in remarkable ongoing ways. It is about how we are constantly shaping one another's neural firing patterns which are the wellspring of our thoughts and beliefs, feelings, bodily sensations, and tendencies in relationships. This interpersonal shaping goes on through the action of our resonance circuits and remains mostly below conscious awareness. For example, we now know that when we are in the presence of someone who feels trustworthy to us, the amygdala in both people is calmed without *doing* anything. Just being present with each other works this miracle. Neuroscience has also shown us that our autonomic nervous systems (ANS) are either in co-regulation or co-dysregulation as our systems resonate with each other. These are two small discoveries of relational neuroscience from the many ways we are intertwined. To exist in this world is to be constantly touched in every relationship, with other people, with our pets, with nature, with the cultural surround.

When we are very young, our neural circuits are particularly and profoundly responsive to how we are met. Through these relational experiences, we develop embodied expectations about who we are, how relationships will be for us, and how safe or scary this world is. We now know these expectations linger within us as the perceptual lens through which we see the world. Both the children and their parents who come to us carry these patterns in the struggles they are having now.

When we begin to see the world through the lens of these understandings, we can make sense of what has hurt the people who come to us and how we offer help to them. As we will see, the foundation we can offer is meeting each of them with nonjudgmental presence and without agenda, as much as humanly possible. Because of the safety that arises from this kind of receptivity, the innate healing wisdom that resides in each of us will emerge in our little ones and their parents. We hold the space. Their inner impulse toward healing integration of whatever traumas they carry guides our next steps. For many of us, this is quite different from what we have learned. This chapter will take you into a counseling room where these understandings guide our practice.

CASE SCENARIO

Initial Intake

I welcomed Stan and Felicia into my office and learned they were seeking help for their 9-year-old daughter, Janelle. They described Janelle as independent and strong-willed, stating she had always been this way. She had tantrums when things didn't go her way, first

DOI: 10.4324/9781003334231-20

getting very angry, and then collapsing into despair, saying things like "You hate me" and "You wish I was never born." Janelle had a younger brother, 7-year-old Nolan, who had an easy-going temperament. Continuing to gather family history, I learned Janelle was a planned pregnancy, easy delivery, and had no significant medical issues. Stan and Felicia had been married for 14 years and described their union as "happy" and their family as "loving." They both had stable careers and a social support system that included extended family and members of their church. Janelle was currently in fourth grade and was a competent student with no disruptive behaviors at school. She did experience social difficulties because of her inflexibility.

Once I heard the parents' concerns and gathered some basic history, I described my assessment process. I would meet with Janelle for three play therapy sessions, which would help me get to know her and establish a safe and fun therapeutic alliance. After those sessions, Stan, Felicia, and I would meet to discuss how we could work together to help Janelle, and set a course for her treatment. I let them know that our process will include parent sessions, separate from Janelle's. To promote safety, I met with parents separately from their child. I wanted parents to speak freely about their struggles without concern for what their child might hear.

Case Conceptualization

The relational neuroscience approach seeks to understand Janelle's inner world and her behavior. Janelle's challenges were familiar, having encountered them in my small clients many times over the years. I learned that although the symptoms may be similar, the causes may not be. Based on what relational neuroscience had taught me, Janelle's behavior made sense even though I may not have understood the reasons yet. I trusted that Janelle was not melting down to manipulate others into giving her what she wanted. She was melting down because not getting what she wanted was touching some unhealed pain and fear. Her behavior was adaptively protecting her from the full force of reexperiencing the initial wounding.

Assessment Process

Assessment with a neurobiological approach was making room for her inner world to speak to me. Although we wouldn't set a treatment plan until after Janelle's first three play therapy sessions, her therapy began the moment we met. Preparing to welcome Janelle, I kept in mind three key points guided by relational neuroscience. The first was to offer an invitation of safety into my office and into a relationship with me (Badenoch, 2018b). The second was to invite embodied experiences because the root causes of Janelle's difficulties may be outside her conscious awareness. Non-directive play therapy offered just such an invitation (Grayson & Fraser, 2022). The third was to prepare my inner world to receive Janelle (Badenoch, 2018a). I had already met Janelle through her parents' eyes, but it was important for me to set that aside as much as possible and be open to what would unfold in our time together. Recalling the qualities of attunement: presence, contact, reflection, responsiveness, and delight (Badenoch 2018c), I anticipated all the ways this child would delight me.

Stan brought Janelle to her first appointment and introduced us in the waiting room. I accompanied her to my playroom and explained that this is her time to explore and play with whatever she feels drawn to. In all three of her assessment sessions, Janelle chose the sandtray. Without saying a word, her choice told me that her inner world was ready to guide her on a path to healing and she was inviting me on that journey (Badenoch, 2018a).

Session #1

Janelle spent a good bit of time exploring the sandtray collection and chose the "beings" for her sandtray world. She chose princesses and princes, a castle, trees, a sarcophagus, and some gravestones. She placed them in the tray, moved and adjusted them along the way, signaling to me she was feeling her way through the process and finding the positions and relationships among the beings that felt settled in her body. After a while, she exhaled, relaxed her shoulders, and found my eyes. "It looks like you have created a world just the way you want it," I comment. Janelle nodded. "Can we take a look together and wonder about who is here and what it is like to be in this world?" Janelle nodded again and, together, we gazed at her creation. I invited her to tell the story of this world and she let me know that there are princes and princesses who lived together in the castle. There was a princess in the graveyard who was bad and couldn't figure out how to be good. No one wanted to play with her on the royal playground, so she snuck away to the evil forest and came across a spooky graveyard. As she told the story, Janelle used the bad princess figure to scratch at the sand and uncover the mummy she buried underneath a gravestone. She then opened the sarcophagus and laid the mummy inside.

Session #2

Janelle announced her intention to create a Halloween tray. She gathered gravestones, mummies, skeletons, the sarcophagus, bats, spiders, and spooky trees, and placed them in the tray. She also chose a peaceful-looking house and declared it haunted. Ordinary-looking people were added and identified as the mom, dad, son, and daughter. She told the story of the girl begging her mom to take her into the haunted forest. "No, no, no!" declares the mom. The girl snuck off when her parents weren't looking and made her way to the graveyard. Once there, she dug up all the graves. Janelle spent the rest of her session burying and unburying the skeletons and mummies she had placed in the graves.

Session #3

Janelle bounced into my playroom with a big smile on her face and announced that today we would do something different. "I am going to hide things in the sandtray and you have to find them. Turn around and don't peek!" I felt my system settle as my smile broadened. This play is very familiar to me, and I sensed that, after two fairly dark and heavy trays, Janelle was ready to explore our relationship. Would she make it easy or hard to find the ones she buries? I heard her moving around the shelves and the sandtray as I sat with my back to her and my eyes closed. "Ready!" she announced. I turned around and saw several mounds in the sandtray. Was she making it easy for me to find her hidden treasures or was she being tricky? I looked at her beaming face for clues and slowly circled my hand above the tray, noticing her response. When she seemed about to burst, I plunged my hand into the tray and came up with a prize! She was clearly delighted and so was I. We continued to play hide-and-seek in the sandtray, taking turns hiding and seeking. Burying and unbury-ing was still happening, but now we were doing it together.

Identifying Problem(s) and Diagnosis

Relational neuroscience invites us to look for the implicit roots beneath the protective adaptations. As I prepared for my meeting with Stan and Felicia, two qualities of Janelle's play stood out. First was the death theme accompanied by burying and unburying. Sec-ond was the hide-and-seek play, which I often encountered when children had significant attachment wounding. Given her history, I had difficulty connecting Janelle's play with her lived experience. My understanding of relational neuroscience told me the underlying cause could be encoded implicitly, before Janelle's brain was developed enough to create explicit memories (Badenoch, 2011), or it could be epigenetically passed down from previ-ous generations (Badenoch, 2018a). I decided to share my questions with Stan and Felicia in case there was some history I had missed. Having an explanation for Janelle's difficulties would settle us and help us feel more confident in our approach to helping her, but it was not necessary. We could develop an effective pathway for therapy even if we never under-stood the root cause of the difficulty.

We knew Janelle struggled with autonomic nervous system (ANS) regulation, and her therapy would center around increasing her sense of interpersonal safety. There was no diagnosis in the DSM-5 for ANS dysregulation, but because the behavioral struggles were happening with her parents and not at school, I would talk with Stan and Felicia about assigning the diagnosis of "parent-biological child conflict."

Stan and Felicia arrived in my office eager to hear my thoughts. I told them I had some more questions but assured them I also had strategies in mind that would help Janelle. Shar-ing my observations about her graveyard and hide-and-seek play, I wondered aloud about Janelle's experiences with death and learned another layer of her story.

When Felicia became pregnant, she and her mom were so excited! Felicia's grand-mother had been a pivotal person throughout her own childhood, and she anticipated how her mom would step into that role for Janelle. Tragically, a few months into the pregnancy, Felicia's mother was diagnosed with an aggressive form of cancer. The eager anticipation of Janelle's arrival was pushed aside in favor of medical appointments and grueling treatment that required Felicia to become her mother's primary caregiver. It was too painful for Felicia to imagine bringing Janelle into the world without her moth-er's support, so to cope, she virtually ignored her pregnancy except for the required prenatal appointments. Felicia's mother did not live to meet her new granddaughter and Felicia plunged into deep grief. Her recollection of Janelle's arrival is colored by the pain of her loss. Every time Felicia encountered the challenge of new motherhood, she missed her mom even more. The first weeks were rough, but gradually, as Janelle began to smile and interact with Felicia, her heart opened to this new little one and her grief gave way to the love she felt for her baby daughter.

Stan took Felicia's hand and, with sadness in his eyes, talked about how hard this time was for them as a couple. His job required him to travel a lot, and he hated leaving his wife and baby daughter. He tried to make up for his absence by taking over with Janelle when he was home, giving Felicia time to rest and recover. We all agreed that life had handed this new family an enormous challenge which they navigated as well as they possibly could.

Stan and Felicia's story was difficult to hear but provided a possible implicit root for Janelle's meltdowns. My challenge, at this moment, was to communicate this explanation without inviting shame into the room. This was such tricky territory when working with parents. They may have already felt some degree of inadequacy because their child was having trouble. It was essential that Stan and Felicia felt safe with me because we would need to work together to help Janelle. Feeling judged is the opposite of feeling safe and I needed Stan and Felicia to know that I was joining with them in their suffering, not judging their capacities as parents.

I proceeded carefully to unravel the underlying mystery of Janelle's graveyard and hide-and-seek play, checking in with Stan and Felicia often, allowing them time to process what I was saying. Together, we imagined the experience of burying something followed by digging it up. I asked them what they thought that experience might be like for the one being buried and the one doing the burying. Stan says it may feel like the one being buried is seen when it is dug up and pushed away when it is buried. Felicia recalled her period of grieving when she coped with her grief by putting away items that reminded her of her mother, taking them out briefly when she felt strong enough to feel her loss. "I think burying and unburying is like that," she told us. I commented on her wisdom, came up with a strategy to keep her from being swept away by grief, and allowed her to care for Janelle. I explained that Janelle's system likely embedded implicit memories of both being seen and being set aside.

I believed it would help Stan and Felicia to learn a little about relational neuroscience, so I asked them if we could spend some time talking about the autonomic nervous system, implicit memory, how traumatic experiences could influence behavior, and how trauma heals. These neurobiological processes would guide our formulation of a plan to help Janelle.

We started with the autonomic nervous system, and I explained that our ANS is designed to support survival. It was constantly scanning the environment, both external and internal, for danger and safety. This process happens at lightning speed below conscious awareness. Stephen Porges had given us the word "neuroception" to distinguish this from consciously feeling safe or not safe. If a threat is neuroceived, the ANS will shift into a fight or flight strategy to keep us safe. If the threat we neuroceive makes us feel helpless, we interpret this as life-threatening, and we shift into a collapse state, akin to "playing possum" (Porges, 2004). Because Janelle got angry when things don't go her way, I knew her ANS has neuroceived a threat. When she eventually collapses, I know she has moved into a felt sense of hopelessness. Given that there was no current danger in the external environment, I could assume her ANS was responding to a shift in her internal state. But what could that be?

To answer that question, we would need to understand implicit memory. Our brains and bodies constantly encode implicit memories, which hold the bodily sensations, behavioral impulses, emotions, perceptions, and sensory fragments experienced when the memory is created. There is no time stamp which means when an implicit memory awakens, we have no sense that we are recalling something from the past (Siegel, 2020). For Janelle, it was possible that not getting what she wanted touched the experience of losing connection with her parents in her infancy. If so, it likely brought with it the bodily-held distress of her internalized little one. Her ANS adaptively responds to the arising distress with a neuroception of threat and initiates a fight or flight response. When fighting wouldn't get her what she needed, her system dropped into a collapsed state as she felt hopeless about regaining relational connection. She puts this into words when she says she is not loved or wanted, probably reflecting the sense of despair she felt when Felicia was too absorbed in care for her mother and then too grief-stricken to attend to her.

There was good news in all of this for Stan and Felicia. When implicit memories open, they become available for healing via a disconfirming experience—what was needed but not available at the time of the difficulty (Ecker et al., 2012). To help explain this concept, we review Janelle's sandtrays for clues about what may have been happening in her brain and body as she played. We had a sense that her burying and unburying may reflect early experiences of connection and disconnection, bringing us closer to the neural nets holding that pain and fear. The safety and connection Janelle experienced in my playroom encoded within the initial abandonment wound, beginning to change her sense of being alone. The next time we were together and the implicit memory opened, it brought with it both experiences—the early abandonment and the connection. Every time reparative experiences such as these were encoded, the pain and fear of the original trauma is soothed. If Stan, Felicia, and I could repeatedly offer Janelle safety and connection when her sense of abandonment arises, Janelle would become better able to orient to the present and less likely to be swept away by her implicit past. This was the foundation of our therapy plan.

Setting Goals

With relational neuroscience we work to create a vision for when things are better. The therapy result Stan and Felicia were hoping for was clear: reduce the intensity and frequency of Janelle's tantrums. In terms of relational neuroscience, we focused on the underlying cause of the meltdowns, namely her implicitly encoded relational trauma and its effect on her ANS. We wanted to offer her an abundance of steadfast connection to soothe the original disconnection wounds. Working together, we formulated the following goal:

Increase Janelle's sense of interpersonal safety through repairing the implicit wounds from her early life, leading to a greater capacity to maintain relational connection when disappointed.

Establishing Measurable *(but not linear)* Objectives

A core value of relational neuroscience is allowing the inner wisdom of the client to guide the direction and pacing of the healing (Badenoch, 2018a). Rather than hold tightly to an agenda, we remain flexible, responding to what unfolds from moment to moment in sessions. At the same time, it is settling to have some sense of direction for the work. With the understanding that we can modify them at any time, Stan, Felicia, and I developed the following objectives:

- Decrease the number of Janelle's tantrums to no more than two per month, measured via parent report, without expecting that this will happen in a linear way. What can appear to be backsliding is actually more trauma coming to the surface which can require additional protective adaptation for a bit.
- Improve Janelle's peer relationships, evidenced by fewer times an adult intervenes, measured via parent and teacher report.

We also identified some steps we could take to help us achieve these overarching objectives.

- Establish a safe and collaborative relationship with Janelle and her parents, measured via parent feedback and observation of an increasing range of emotional expression in Janelle's play.
- Increase experiences of attunement and security for Janelle through play therapy and parent coaching, measured via therapist and parent report.
- Increase the parents' capacity to maintain the connection with Janelle when she experiences distress, measured via parent report.

Planning Theoretically-Based *(and scientifically-grounded)* Interventions *(supports for healing)*

Janelle's earliest experiences, before and after her birth, were colored by the comings and goings of her primary caregivers—Felicia succumbing to waves of grief and Stan's travel schedule. The implicit memories of this painful and frightening time awoke when she felt unseen, particularly when she was being denied something she wanted. Her ANS neuroceives a threat in her internal environment and adaptively shifted to survival strategies of the fight followed by collapse. Thanks to neuroplasticity (Doidge, 2007), implicit memories that are awake in body and mind are also available for modification through a disconfirming experience. In Janelle's case, what was needed and not consistently available in her infancy was a reliable connection with her parents. When these early implicit memories awaken, present-day experiences of welcoming, nonjudgmental connection can decrease her sense of abandonment. Since her anger and collapse make sense, we could receive them without needing to fix them. With repetition, it is possible that these modified implicit memories would hold more of a sense of connection and less of abandonment, allowing Janelle to respond to what was happening in the present with less influence from her painful past. Each time she was met, her ANS would experience co-regulation and those neural pathways would be strengthened.

Janelle's therapy included two approaches. I would see her for play therapy, and I would work directly with Stan and Felicia, helping them respond to Janelle's meltdowns a bit differently than before. As we saw in Janelle's use of the sandtray, play therapy invited implicitly held traumatic memories to open within the safe container of the play and our relationship (Grayson & Fraser, 2022). My attuned presence and responsiveness to Janelle as she played offers disconfirmation of her sense of early abandonment.

The work with Stan and Felicia centered on helping them maintain connection with Janelle even when she was melting down. In each of our parent sessions, we explored possible ways they could stay calm and let Janelle know they understood what she wanted even if they couldn't give it to her. We experimented with different approaches and refined or revised them along the way. Given that Stan and Felicia have different temperaments, we customized strategies. There was no one-size-fits-all approach to parenting, and I wanted to help each parent find the way of responding that works best for them.

Collaborating

Relational neuroscience puts collaboration at the core of healing work. Given what we know about mirror neurons and resonance circuits, through which we take in the intentions, emotional and bodily states of one another (Iacoboni, 2009), the word "collaboration" seems somewhat inadequate. When we collaborate, we work *with* someone to achieve a result. In therapy, we are *joining* one another to create a third entity I call the "we." It is in this "we" where the journey with our clients unfolds, co-suffering the difficulties and co-celebrating the triumphs. I liken this to whitewater rafting. River guides do not stand on the shore yelling instructions about how to navigate upcoming rapids. They are in the boat, experiencing the rapids alongside the passengers, offering their wisdom about how the river runs and their guidance for a successful trip.

When working with children, we sometimes underestimate the importance of joining with the parents. Children come and go in therapy according to the parents' wishes. In my work with Janelle, it is critically important for Stan and Felicia to feel my care and support. Social baseline theory (Beckes & Coan, 2011) tells us that when we have a felt sense of accompaniment, difficult and painful experiences become easier. For Stan and Felicia, sensing my presence "in the boat" not only made their work easier but also reduced the likelihood of Janelle's therapy ending prematurely.

Tracking Progress

Within relational neuroscience we follow the waves of implicit emergence followed by waves of behavioral change. To understand the role of progress tracking in relational neuroscience, it helps to understand differences in the ways our left and right hemispheres work. Therapy, a relational, right-brain process, is fluid in nature and asks us to set aside treatment goals and objectives in favor of what is unfolding moment-to-moment (Schore, 2019). This can be unsettling, particularly when we must rationalize our approach and document progress. The left hemisphere is very good at picking things apart and analyzing them (McGilchrist, 2009), an essential element of progress tracking. Knowing our work in therapy is effective builds trust that, when we are with our people, we can trust their inner wisdom to guide the work. If we lose confidence, we may be tempted take control, allowing treatment goals and objectives to direct the work. If this happens, therapy becomes more of a "doing to" and less of a "being with" experience for our people. Periodic progress tracking supports our sense that what we are doing is helping, grounding therapy in the right hemisphere.

The parent sessions with Stan and Felicia offer an opportunity to see how Janelle was progressing. We began them by answering the following questions:

- Is Janelle happy to come to her sessions?
- How many tantrums since our last session?
- How are things going with friends?

After that brief check-in, we guide our parenting work with:

- Do you feel seen, heard, and supported in our work together?
- What, if anything, feels better?
- What remains challenging?

Over time, answers to these questions along with shifts in Janelle's play would allow us to measure progress or prompt us to modify our treatment approach.

Termination Process Strategies

In the world of relational neuroscience, there is no such thing as graduation (a term I prefer over termination). As we journey with our clients, they internalize us and we internalize them. We become members of one another's inner community (Badenoch, 2018a). In this way, we continue to be a resource for our people long after the last therapy session (Shedler, 2010). The termination process is actually transitioning to inner support.

Because Stan, Felicia, and I constantly checked in with one another about Janelle's progress, there would naturally come a time when we agree our work is done for now. We would discuss how to include Janelle in the ending, often deciding on a few more sessions to ease the transition. Although I did not hold an agenda for these final sessions, trusting Janelle's inner wisdom to guide our time together, I did keep her healing steps in mind, looking for opportunities to remind her of how hard she worked and how far she has come. I make sure to let Janelle know that, even though our sessions are ending, our relationship continues to live on in our hearts and minds. Neurobiologically, I will always be with her.

In my professional training, I was taught "Once a client, always a client." We now have a neurobiological basis for this stance. We are far from perfect, but if we do our work well enough, our clients will internalize us just the way they need us to be. It is critical to protect this perception, as it is a resource to support them for years to come. This reality was reinforced when I met a young woman, I will call Maggie. She had done deep healing work with a therapist she came to love and respect. When their work was done, her therapist declared, "I am always a phone call away if you need me." A few years later, Maggie experienced some difficulty and reached out, asking for a single session. She wanted to hear her therapist's voice, which would open implicit memories of the rich work they had done and provide the felt sense of accompaniment Maggie needed. Her therapist was busy, and instead of offering her voice, she responded via text that she was not available. This misstep landed as a betrayal in Maggie's system, tainting all the work they had done together. With tears in her eyes, Maggie said, "She lied about always being there for me. What else did she lie about? I can't trust anything she ever said." Now, every time Maggie recalls some helpful interaction, it is overshadowed by her experience of being abandoned by her therapist. Maggie's story is a compelling reminder of how important we are to the people we serve long after their therapy ends. Ideally, we would always allow room in our schedules to welcome people back when they need us, but that is not always possible. From the perspective of relational neuroscience, everyone we have ever worked with is, implicitly, a current client and needs to be treated accordingly. Should Stan, Felicia or Janelle reach out to me at some point in the future, I would do my best to resume working with them. If that was not possible, I would take time to speak with them, listen deeply to their updated story, and facilitate a new connection with a colleague who can help (see Appendix B.7 for Sample Treatment Plan).

CONCLUSION

The field of relational neuroscience offers a scientific basis for our work. Grounded in an understanding of how we get hurt and how we heal, it supports an embodied relational approach in which our primary role as therapist is to offer sufficient safety so that the neural nets holding past wounds can open and become available for modification. This approach shifts the focus of therapy away from directing what happens in session in favor of offering presence and possible pathways (interventions) that we believe may be helpful. We trust the inherent healing drive within our people to choose the path that is best for them. In our assessment process, we look to the origin of the difficulty encoded within the brain and body, with an understanding that we may never know exactly why things are the way they are. We trust in the power of relationships to soothe past hurts and build resilience as our people internalize our care, creating an ongoing resource they will take with them long after therapy ends.

Key Takeaways

- Relational neuroscience is all about how we are interconnected in remarkable ongoing ways. This interpersonal shaping goes on through the action of our resonance circuits and remains mostly below conscious awareness.
- Neuroscience has also shown us that our autonomic nervous systems (ANS) are either in co-regulation or co-dysregulation as our systems resonate with each other.
- Three patterns of attachment are directly related to three corresponding patterns of affect regulation discussed in the attachment literature.
- Through relational experiences, people develop embodied expectations about who they are, how relationships will be, and how safe or scary this world is.
- The safety that arises from receptivity in relationship invites the innate healing wisdom that resides in every child and parent.
- Assessment with a neurobiological approach makes room for a child's inner world to speak to the therapist.
- Relational neuroscience invites us to look for the implicit roots beneath the protective adaptations.
- Goal setting in relational neuroscience is more of creating a vision for when things are better.
- A core value of relational neuroscience is allowing the inner wisdom of the client to guide the direction and pacing of the healing.
- Within relational neuroscience we follow the waves of implicit emergence followed by waves of behavioral change.

REFERENCES

Badenoch, B. (2011). *The brain-savvy therapist's workbook: A companion to being a brain-wise therapist.* Norton.

Badenoch, B. (2018a). *The heart of trauma: Healing the embodied brain in the context of relationships.* Norton. https://doi.org/10.1037/e557632012-001

Badenoch, B. (2018b). Safety is the treatment. In S. Porges et al. (Eds.), *Clinical applications of polyvagal theory: The emergence of polyvagal-informed therapies.* Norton.

Badenoch, B. (2018c). Trauma and the embodied brain: A heart based training in relational neuroscience for healing trauma [Webinar]. Sounds True. Retrieved from https://leading-edge-of-psychotherapy-sfm.soundstrue.com/bonnie-badenoch/?sq=1

Beckes, L., & Coan, J. A. (2011). Social baseline theory: The role of social proximity in emotion and economy of action. *Social and Personality Psychology Compass, 5*(12), 976–988. DOI:10.1111/j.1751-9004.2011.00400.x

Doidge, N. (2007). *The brain that changes itself: Stories of personal triumph from the frontiers of brain science.* Penguin. https://doi.org/10.1037/e723792007-017

Ecker, B., Ticic, R., & Hulley, L. (2012). *Unlocking the emotional brain: Eliminating symptoms at their root using memory reconsolidation.* Routledge.https://doi.org/10.4324/9780203804377

Grayson, R., & Fraser, T. (2022). *The embodied brain and sandtray therapy: Stories of healing and transformation.* Routledge. https://doi.org/10.4324/9781003055808

Iacoboni, M. (2009). *Mirroring people: The science of empathy and how we connect with others* (1st ed.). Picador. https://doi.org/10.1891/1946-6560.4.2.287

McGilchrist, I. (2009). *The master and his emissary: The divided brain and the making of the Western world.* Yale University Press.

Porges, S. W. (2004). Neuroception: A subconscious system for detecting threats and safety. *Zero to Three (j), 24*(5), 19–24.

Schore, A. N. (2019). *Right brain* psychotherapy (Norton Series on Interpersonal Neurobiology). Norton.

Shedler, J. (2010). The efficacy of psychodynamic psychotherapy. *American Psychologist, 65*(2), 98–109. DOI:10.1037/a0018378

Siegel, D. J. (2020). *The developing mind: How relationships and the brain interact to shape who we are* (3rd ed.). Guilford.

CHAPTER 19

A SYNERGETIC PLAY THERAPY®
APPROACH TO TREATMENT PLANNING

Lisa Dion and Judith Norman

INTRODUCTION

Synergetic Play Therapy® (SPT), developed in 2008, is a research-informed model of play therapy combining the therapeutic powers of play with nervous system regulation, interpersonal neurobiology, physics, attachment, mindfulness, and therapist authenticity (Dion, 2018). Physicist Buckminster Fuller coined the term *Synergetics* referring to the study of systems in transformation, emphasizing total system behavior that cannot be predicted by the behavior of any isolated components (Synergetics, 2022). SPT recognizes that the word itself is also reflective of what is happening in the playroom and how integration and healing occur. A union of states occurs as the SPT therapist attunes to their own internal states and then attunes to the child's internal states. In this union, a synergy forms, allowing for co-regulation to emerge. During this "synergy of systems," therapist and child enter something akin to a "synergetic field" where right-hemisphere-to-right hemisphere communication emerges.

In SPT, the most important role of the therapist is that of the external regulator. Children need to be held in the therapist's ventral embrace, allowing them to go deeper into their feelings and move toward their challenges (Badenoch, 2017; Kestly, 2016). This process of re-experiencing the dysregulation of traumatic experiences in tolerable doses, while simultaneously mindfully connecting to themselves facilitates trauma integration and transformation. As children move toward their challenging internal thoughts, feelings, and sensations, new neural connections can be created and eventually initiate new neural organization (Edelman, 1987; Tyson, 2002; Dion & Gray, 2014).

CASE PRESENTATION

Lara, mother of 4-year-old Becky, called the A Synergetic Play Therapy® Institute in distress, reporting that her daughter was out of control and that she needed help. For the past two years, Becky's behaviors had been escalating. What started as temper tantrums and angry outbursts had turned into attempts to physically hurt her younger 2-year-old sister and her mother, including, on a recent occasion threatening to smash a flower vase on top of her sister's head.

When the behaviors first began, support was sought out through their family doctor, who suggested that her behavior was age appropriate and encouraged more traditional discipline to manage the temper tantrums. As the behaviors continued to intensify, a decision was made by Lara and Ben, Becky's father, to seek additional support from a behavior specialist. The behavior specialist offered parenting support using a behavior modification lens. They were taught how to use time outs, ignore the behavior, and how to use a rewards system to

DOI: 10.4324/9781003334231-21

manage the behaviors. Becky's parents reported that these strategies did not work and escalated the behaviors further. Her parents continued to seek out ways to support Becky's choice to meet with a psychiatrist. The psychiatrist suggested medication to manage her behaviors, as well as a diagnosis of early-onset Oppositional Defiant Disorder tendencies.

Initial Intake

The SPT therapist approaches the initial intake from a relational framework, recognizing that caregivers are likely to be in their own states of nervous system activation as they begin the play therapy process. Becoming an external regulator for the caregiver is just as important as becoming an external regulator for the child in treatment. With this in mind, the therapist attunes to their own internal states, as well as the caregiver's internal states, thus allowing the caregiver to borrow the therapist's regulatory capacity. In doing so, the therapist supports a sense of safety and connection while also helping the caregiver be able to regulate their own activation in order to be able to talk about the child and the treatment. Traditionally, the intake process occurs without the child present so that the caregiver can speak openly about the concerns, and treatment can be discussed. Recognizing that in some situations, such as in agency settings, the child is required to be a part of the intake process, the therapist works to adapt the intake process while keeping a relational framework in mind.

The therapist also understands that when a caregiver is in their own activation, tracking time, details, and retaining information becomes more challenging. As such, the therapist helps organize the time for the caregiver by suggesting a possibility for how the time could be spent. As an example for a 50-minute intake session: during the first 20 minutes, the caregiver shares their concerns and what they would love to see as a result of treatment, the next 20 minutes, the therapist shares how SPT can help, what to expect in the treatment process and establishes treatment goals and the last 10 minutes is spent discussing the caregiver's involvement and answering any remaining questions Other items such as visual aids and experiential exercises are also used to support the caregiver's understanding of the process. In SPT, the relationship is always the most important part of the intake process, superseding information gathering as obtaining information can occur later in treatment and is ongoing. To further support this, the therapist typically asks the caregivers to fill out the clinical paperwork ahead of time. Included in the paperwork is a thorough questionnaire focused on significant life events and the child's cognitive, social, physical, and emotional development spanning from pregnancy until the current day.

Lara and Ben both participated in the initial intake without their daughters present. Lara's dysregulation and overwhelm were immediately visible, while Ben's dysregulation was more contained. While being co-regulated by the therapist, they were both invited to share their experiences, concerns and hopes for Becky in treatment. The therapist then explained what SPT is and drew an image of the Therapeutic Stages of SPT (explained in the Tracking progress section) as a way to help them understand the process of treatment. Goals, the timing of treatment, and parental involvement were also discussed.

Case Conceptualization

The conceptualization of the case begins at the first point of contact with the caregiver and continues throughout the treatment process. As the therapist begins to conceptualize what is happening, the therapist becomes curious about the child's history, physical and emotional development, and the child's unique profile, as well as other factors influencing the child, such as dynamics within the child's significant relationships, family dynamics, social and cultural influences. This information is gathered through the child questionnaire and through discussions in the intake with the caregiver.

As Lara and Ben discussed their concerns for Becky and the struggles they had been experiencing, the therapist listened for information related to parent/child dynamics, marital dynamics, sibling dynamics, and other significant relationship dynamics. Lara shared that she and her other daughter had become the main targets of Becky's rage. Ben expressed concern for Becky's behaviors and often felt helpless in knowing how to support his family. Lara discussed the pressure and shame she feels that her daughter behaves this way, worried about what other people think, especially her own mother. She also expressed a deep sadness as she reflected that she and Becky were once incredibly close before her other daughter was born. Other than the birth of her younger sister, no other major life changes were reported.

The primary questions and curiosities the therapist had as this information was shared were (1) Becky's perception about what happened when her sister was born, (2) Lara's internalized pressure and concern about what others think about her parenting, especially her mother, (3) the relationship disruption between Lara and Becky that occurred when her younger sister was born and has continued to occur since, (4) Ben's experience of helplessness.

Identifying Problem(s) and Diagnosis

From an SPT lens, children's symptoms are understood as symptoms of dysregulated states of the nervous system. Therefore, SPT treatment is focused on helping the child re-pattern the activation in their autonomic nervous system while integrating their perceptions of the challenging events in their life. When a child does come to therapy with a diagnosis, this information is considered in the overall conceptualization of the child and the family system and how best to offer treatment.

SPT recognizes that whatever the child's symptoms are, they are related to the conscious and unconscious perceptions the child is having or has had regarding their life experiences. As such, no behavior is viewed as dysfunctional but rather as an important part of the innate wisdom inside of the child. The child's behaviors, through the lens of nervous system activation, allow the therapist to recognize that the child is attempting to communicate how they are managing the thoughts, feelings, and sensations they are currently experiencing inside.

At the time treatment began, Becky was displaying symptoms such as being easily agitated and irritated, not sleeping well, hyperactive, impulsive, and acting out aggressively which led the psychiatrist to consider a diagnosis of early on-set Oppositional Defiant Disorder tendencies. The SPT therapist immediately understood that Becky was in a high state of sympathetic arousal, which meant that her ability to regulate her thoughts, feelings, and sensations was limited. Helping re-pattern her arousal state along with helping her process her feelings was of primary importance in treatment.

Setting Goals and Establishing Measurable Objectives

The purpose of goals from an SPT lens is twofold. First, they are essential for offering the therapist a way to view and track progress, and second, the therapist can use this information to help the caregivers understand the progress that is being made in therapy.

When establishing treatment goals, the goals must:

- Be developmentally appropriate.
- Consist of a way to measure progress. .
- Use "increase" and "decrease" instead of "all" or "none" language.

During the intake, Lara proposed the following goal, "Becky will stop getting so angry and hurting and threatening others." Using an SPT lens, the goal reconceptualized became, "Becky will increase how often she expresses her anger through words or non-aggressive actions. Becky will decrease the number of times she physically lashes out at her sister and mother." Given her developmental age and skill level, expecting Becky to never get angry or physically aggressive with others wasn't developmentally appropriate or realistic. The goal that was used was more in line with what Becky was capable of and provided a way to measure progress without using "all" or "none" language.

Assessment Process and Planning Theoretically Based Interventions

SPT does not have a formal assessment process to determine the best course of treatment. Instead, the SPT therapist takes everything learned in the intake process and paperwork to get curious about how to go about the therapy in a way that is best suited for the child, the child's family, and the goals for therapy. Three important considerations are made: (1) Will the caregiver be in the room for the treatment? (2) What treatment time frame would be most supportive to this child and family? and 3) Is a directive or non-directive approach most useful to start? Although these are assessed during the intake to get treatment started, each of these is also ongoing, allowing for adaptation at any time in treatment.

Caregiver in the Room

SPT does a combination of having a caregiver be in the playroom and working with the caregiver separately based on what is needed for treatment. In thinking through whether or not to have a caregiver be a part of a session, the therapist considers the caregiver's trauma history, ability to be an external regulator in the session, and whether or not the caregiver is willing to be in the session.

If it is determined in the intake that the child's anxiety or overwhelm is such that the child needs the support of the caregiver to be able to enter the therapy room, the therapist will invite the caregiver to join the first session to help be the child's external regulator. In this case, creating a neuroception of safety is the treatment goal for the first session. If the caregiver will join beyond the initial session or at another time during the process, the therapist will meet with the caregiver to do a "Training Session," offering the caregiver skills and an understanding of what to expect in the session or ongoing sessions. Whatever the decision, working with the caregivers regularly is an important part of the treatment approach.

Treatment Time

As the way treatment is approached is unique to each client and family, so is the timeframe for treatment. The therapist is flexible and adaptive to meet the needs of the child and family as well as what is required to meet the treatment goals.

Directive, Non-directive, or Both

SPT is a model of play therapy that includes both non-directive and directive interventions. Most SPT therapy begins using a non-directive approach, with the therapist following the child's lead, allowing an emergent process to unfold. However, if determined that a directive approach is needed, the SPT therapist will either weave it into the session or facilitate a directive session altogether. Whether non-directive or directive, the therapist uses attunement and authenticity to move towards and through the dysregulation that is ebbing and flowing in order to co-regulate the child. This process rewires neural connections as new neural templates are created. It also repatterns the nervous system, allowing movement between dysregulated states where there are limited options and choices for behavior to regulated states where options and choices exist.

In Becky's case, due to the crisis nature of the situation, it was determined that a more intensive treatment would be useful. It was decided that Becky would be seen individually for ten 50-minute sessions, roughly once a day for two weeks. A non-directive approach would also be used to start to allow Becky's process to unfold organically. It was also decided that Lara would not be a part of the sessions initially but would meet for parenting support during the course of therapy. At the end of the two weeks, the timing and intensity would be re-evaluated. At any point, if it was too much for Becky or the family, the therapy would be adjusted.

Collaborating and Including Client and Caregivers in Treatment Planning

The caregivers are involved in treatment planning and progress tracking every step of the way as the direction of treatment is continuously assessed and adjusted. This emergent process allows the SPT therapist to adapt to shifts in the child's life and family system while moving in and out of approaches that include having the caregiver in the room or not and are directive, non-directive, or a combination of the two.

During the intake process, it became evident that Lara was carrying internalized pressure and concern about what others think about her parenting, especially her mother, as well as deep sadness about the relationship disruption that occurred when Becky's younger sister was born. Although Ben also needed support, it was determined that Lara needed help first and would be the focus during the two-week intensive treatment process. Since Lara was often the target of Becky's attacks, it was important for Lara and Becky to each have their own separate sessions (at least initially) as they each processed their thoughts and feelings. This also allowed the therapist an opportunity to educate Lara on her role as Becky's external regulator and to explore what was in the way of her ability to co-regulate Becky when things become difficult. It was decided that Lara and the therapist would speak on the phone for 15 minutes at the end of each day and that Lara would meet with the therapist individually four times for a full parenting session over the course of the two weeks.

Tracking progress

Once therapy begins, SPT uses three primary processes to help track progress: (1) The A Synergetic Play Therapy® Therapeutic Stages, (2) The SPT Process of Change, and (3) Identifying the child's starting points in treatment.

The Therapeutic Stages in SPT

The child progresses through a series of stages, beginning with the Orientation phase and ending in Termination. The Orientation phase includes the child determining if their relationship with the therapist will allow them both to be fully authentic. The majority of the time, the child is in the Working Stage as they learn how to move towards their uncomfortable thoughts, feelings, and sensations. The SPT therapist becomes the External Regulator co-regulating the child towards their inner intensity supporting the re-patterning of the child's nervous system activation and integration of the perceptions of the challenging events in their life. As integration and re-patterning occur, the child begins to demonstrate more moments of connecting to themselves, thus increasing their ability to self-regulate. These moments are defined as empowerment. Once the child is in the empowerment stage, defined by a shift in play and patterns indicating the child's ability to stay connected to themselves for longer periods of time, the child will either continue to move toward the Termination or will go back to the Working Stage to process another challenge. During the termination phase, the focus is on strengthening and myelinating the newly formed neural pathways as well as creating closure for the therapy.

Orientation Phase

Becky quickly moved through the Orientation phase as she said hello to the therapist, oriented to the playroom, and jumped right into her play.

Working Phase

Becky quickly revealed the dysregulation she was experiencing inside, along with some of the perceptions that were influencing her behaviors. Through her play and interactions with the therapist, she helped the therapist understand that she felt hyper-vigilant and on edge, always wondering if she was going to get in trouble while simultaneously sensitive to perceived incongruencies in her environment. She also felt sad about the disconnect with her mother and a longing to be with her, but not knowing how. Becky's play also demonstrated a very young emotional age.

Working with Caregiver

During the parenting sessions, Lara shared that her distress regarding her daughter's challenges was compounded by her own perceived failings as a parent. She had lost her ability to trust her own intuition regarding parenting Becky as she subjugated her own beliefs to those of "experts" and her mother. She recounted knowing the advice she was receiving did not resonate with her beliefs but felt unable to speak out on behalf of her daughter. This left

Lara feeling powerless and questioning her own abilities as a parent. The therapist worked with Lara to trust herself again while also teaching her about co-regulation and emotional congruence. Lara was also asked to participate in various "homework" activities designed to help Lara attune and reconnect with Becky. The goal was to help Lara become a more congruent and predictable parent so that Becky's activation could begin to settle and they could heal the disruption that occurred when her younger sister was born.

Empowerment Phase

During the second week of therapy, Becky began to show greater and greater signs of self-regulation, as well as a shift in her play towards more mastery and age-appropriate play. Lara reported that her aggressive behaviors had decreased and that she was more relaxed and open toward her sister and towards her. Lara reported an increase in trusting herself and her ability to emotionally attune to Becky.

Termination Phase

As the intensive timeframe drew to an end, the therapist recognized that both Becky and Lara were ready for termination as they had both met their goals. As such, the therapist met with Ben and Lara and reviewed the progress made and suggested a follow-up conversation in two weeks to see if further therapy was needed. Lara canceled the conversation, stating that everything was going so well and that she and Becky were back to being connected again.

In addition to the Therapeutic Stages in SPT, the SPT Process of Change is a way for the therapist to conceptualize how change occurs, beginning with recognizing that the child must first explore their thoughts, feelings, and body sensations the way that they are. The child is then able to explore alternative behaviors, responses, and understandings resulting in the final step, which is the child's ability to respond differently, understand situations differently, and ultimately demonstrate a re-patterning of their activation.

Identifying the child's Starting Points is another tool used for tracking progress. Each time a child begins a journey through the SPT Therapeutic Stages, the therapist identifies the "starting points," which include key elements of the play and the child's state of dysregulation. What the play and patterns will likely look like once integrated and attachment to self is more easily accessible are then identified and used to help the therapist identify the progress being made.

CONCLUSION

SPT utilizes the therapeutic powers of play along with nervous system regulation, interpersonal neurobiology, physics, attachment, mindfulness, and therapist authenticity in its approach to treatment planning. As a child moves through the process of re-experiencing the dysregulation of traumatic experiences in tolerable doses, while simultaneously mindfully connecting to themselves, facilitating trauma integration and transformation, healing occurs. The process of treatment planning begins with the essential authentic presence of the therapist and the experience for the client of being fully seen and held. Progress in SPT is traced through four therapeutic stages of therapy, during which the therapist continues to act as the external regulator, authentically connected and attuned to the child and caregiver(s).

Key Takeaways

✡ A union of states occurs as the SPT therapist attunes to their own internal states and then attunes to the internal states of the child. In this union, a synergy forms, allowing for co-regulation to emerge.

✡ In SPT, the most important role of the therapist is that of the external regulator.

✡ The process of re-experiencing dysregulation of traumatic experiences in tolerable doses, while simultaneously mindfully connecting to themselves facilitates trauma integration and transformation.

✡ Becoming an external regulator for the caregiver is just as important as becoming an external regulator for the child in treatment.

✡ SPT treatment is focused on helping the child re-pattern the activation in their autonomic nervous system while integrating their perceptions of the challenging events in their life.

✡ When establishing treatment goals, the goals must be developmentally appropriate, consist of a way to measure progress and use "increase" and "decrease" instead of all or none language.

✡ The SPT therapist takes everything learned in the intake process and paperwork to get curious about how to go about the therapy in a way that is best suited for the child, the child's family, and the goals for therapy.

✡ Once therapy begins, SPT uses three primary processes to help track progress: 1. The Synergetic Play Therapy Therapeutic Stages, 2. The SPT Process of Change, and 3. Identifying the child's starting points in treatment.

✡ Once play patterns are integrated and attachment to self is more easily accessible, the therapist can identify progress in therapy.

REFERENCES

Badenoch, B. (2017). *The heart of trauma*. Norton.

Dion, L. (2018). *Aggression in play therapy: A neurobiological approach for integrating intensity*. Norton.

Dion, L., & Gray, K. (2014). Impact of therapist authentic expression on emotional tolerance in A Synergetic Play Therapy®. *International Journal of Play Therapy, 23*, 55–67. https://psycnet.apa.org/doi/10.1037/a0035495

Edelman, G. M. (1987). *Neural Darwinism*. Basic Books.

Kestly, T. (2016). Presence and play: Why mindfulness matters. *International Journal of Play Therapy, 1*, 14–23. https://psycnet.apa.org/doi/10.1037/pla0000019

Synergetics. (2022). In Wikipedia. Retrieved from https://en.wikipedia.org/wiki/Synergetics_(Fuller)

Tyson, P. (2002). The challenges of psychoanalytic developmental theory. *Journal of the American Psychoanalytic Association, 50*(1), 19–52. https://doi.org/10.1177/00030651020500011301

CHAPTER 20

TREATMENT PLANNING IN TRAUMAPLAY™: STORYKEEPING FOR THE FAMILY SYSTEM

Paris Goodyear-Brown

INTRODUCTION

TraumaPlay™ is an attachment-grounded, evidence-informed, flexibly sequential play therapy model for treating trauma with children and their caring adults. TraumaPlay™ therapists seek to understand the neurobiology of play, the neurobiology of trauma, and the power of one to heal the other. Each of the seven key components and goals within represents treatment goals empirically supported and considered to be best practices within the field of child trauma. The components provide a treatment planning scaffold on which a variety of clinically sound, play-based interventions can rest (see Figure 20.1).

Our supervisors have found that whether you have been doing clinical work for 2 years or 22 years, one of the core clinical questions remains: When do you trust the process of an approach that follows the child's lead, and when do you make more structured invitations that follow the child's need? Sometimes this need is a silent ask for more active alignment with children out of a stuck place in the therapeutic process.

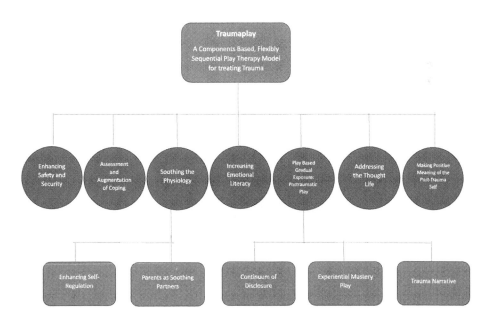

Figure 20.1 A Components Based, Flexibly Sequential, Play Therapy Model for Treating Trauma (Goodyear-Brown, P., 2021)

DOI: 10.4324/9781003334231-22

CO-REGULATION PRECEDES SELF-REGULATION

In TraumaPlay™ treatment planning, co-regulation always precedes self-regulation in a child's development (Schore & Schore, 2008; Siegel, 2001; Goodyear-Brown, 2022). Clinicians have long wrestled with which goal should be addressed first: attachment enhancement or trauma processing when children have experienced trauma. The TraumaPlay™ answer is to prioritize the child's relationship with the co-regulating caregiver above trauma reprocessing so that as the scary content (often called the *hard thing*) is processed, the child's big feelings and/or big behaviors can be more easily held by their primary caregiver.

Careful history-taking will show whether or not the child receiving services have had the thousands of repetitions of nurturing response to the child's needs to move from being wholly soothed by *the other* to being able to self-soothe. When attachment trauma is identified, a family systems lens must be used in treatment planning, and equipping parents to become soothing partners needs to be an elevated priority. The earlier in development a trauma occurs, the more important the goal of supporting co-regulating caregivers becomes (Goodyear-Brown, 2021). In the Adverse Childhood Experiences studies (Felitti et al., 1998), the identified adversities all have one profound thing in common: they all severely limit the availability of an attuned, available caregiver, one who can provide the reciprocity needed for a child to experience a neuroception of safety (Porges, 2011).

TraumaPlay™ practitioners explore the dynamics in a child's history or current relationship patterns that limit the felt sense of safety a child might have or that actively contribute to a felt sense of danger or threat, and then work to operationalize the felt sense of safety. Case conceptualization results in prioritizing attachment enhancement and co-regulation goals prior to diving deep into trauma narrative work. Establishing a felt sense of safety involves the therapist working, at all times in treatment, to embody three therapeutic roles: Safe Boss, Nurturer, and Storykeeper, giving the parents titrated doses of the relational interaction patterns we hope they will eventually give to their children. The Triune Brain graphic is introduced early in treatment planning to help caregivers organize treatment in a hierarchical way, informed by psychoeducation about bottom-up brain development (see Figure 20.2).

Additionally, the therapist embodies the triad of roles that align with the bottom-up brain development needs of our traumatized clients (Barfield et al., 2012; Perry & Hambrick, 2008). We simplify the language of neural hierarchy by pairing the brain stem with the work of regulation, the limbic brain with the work of connection, and the neocortex with the work of thinking, learning, or storying. The brain stem is asking *Am I safe?* So the TraumaPlay™ therapist moves into the role of *Safe Boss*. The limbic brain is asking *Am I loved?* So the therapist moves into the role of *Nurturer*. If these first two questions are answered in the affirmative, the thinking brain can ask *What can I learn from this?* The therapist moves into the role of *Storykeeper* to help make a coherent narrative of the child's trauma (see Figure 20.3). Part of the work of Storykeeping involves helping the child make sense of their current big behavior(s) by threading the needle of understanding all the way back to their earliest experiences.

There are times when it is a parent's big behaviors that exacerbate the felt sense of danger in the system. In these moments, the therapist becomes Storykeeper for the parent, inviting them with curiosity and compassion to reflect, and trace this current big behavior all the way back to their earliest origins, helping them to understand their own negative activation in relation to the child's actions. In many cases, this requires a referral of the parent for their own trauma work, while sometimes the TraumaPlay™ therapist can help both parent and child to have a shared sense of safety.

THE TRIUNE BRAIN

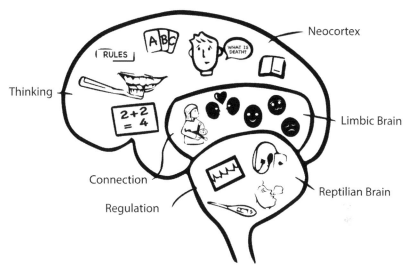

Figure 20.2 Regulation, Connection and Thinking (Goodyear-Brown, P., 2021)

Embodying the Relational Answers to Core Neurodevelopmental Questions

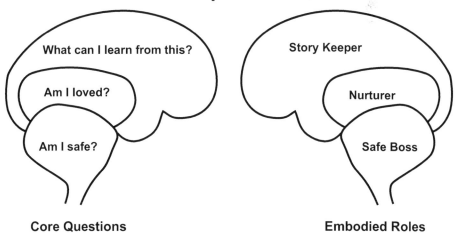

Figure 20.3 Embodying Relational Answers to Neurodevelopmental Questions (Goodyear-Brown, P., 2021)

On one level, treatment planning in TraumaPlay™ involves moving fluidly in and out of the triad of therapist roles: Safe Boss, Nurturer, and Storykeeper, as we follow the child's needs all along the way. Our hope for caregivers of traumatized children to eventually embody these three roles may require goals related to parental involvement in therapy. For a fully nuanced explication of the parent work, his author would refer you to *Parents as Partners in Child Therapy: A Clinician's Guide* (Goodyear-Brown, 2021).

The generalized components for supporting caregivers include the following:

- Psychoeducation to shift parental paradigms, especially in relation to big behaviors (Goodyear-Brown, 2022).
- Enhancing parental play skills for building attunement.
- Enhancing co-regulation skills for the parent, offering co-regulation strategies codified in the SOOTHE acronym (see Figure 20.5).
- Following the child's need in discipline.
- Offering in-vivo delighting-in experiences, as traumatized clients need more titrated doses of delight and nurture from their parents.
- Managing parental activation by building reflective capacity for the parent through prompts in play, sand, or expressive arts.
- Creating coherent narratives within the family system (see Figure 1.4 below).

Components of Parents as Partners

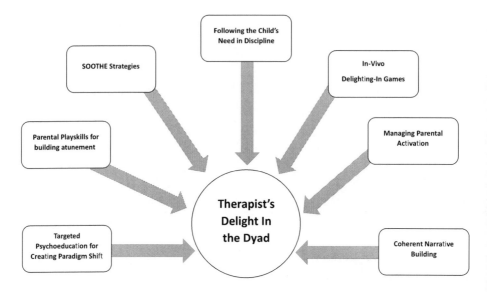

Figure 20.4 Components of Parents as Partners Treatment Planning (Goodyear-Brown, P. 2021)

One component of treatment that benefits most parents is the codified set of SOOTHE strategies. During our dyadic assessments, one or more of the SOOTHE strategies may be needed. The SOOTHE strategies may be taught all at once for parents who feel soothed by more knowledge. Other parents learn best if one strategy is offered at a time with extensive supported practice prior to moving on to the next skill. A tracking tool is offered to parents that help document their use of the strategies and helps the clinician better support the parent's skill acquisition (see Figure 20.5).

When parents enter treatment, they are often focused, understandably, on decreasing or extinguishing negative behaviors. We begin to shift the parent's paradigm, starting with the intake session, by refocusing the language of treatment planning around what we want to see grow or deepen, as opposed to what we want to see decrease. We begin by comparing the brain's experience-dependent shaping process (Greenough et al., 2002; Hebb, 1949; Perry, 2001; Sale, 2018) to the shaping of a path in a field of tall grass. When you walk over the grass once, it bounces back. After you have walked over it again and again and again, you lay down new pathways. We compare the pathways in the grass to the neurophysiological pathways (and the resulting behavioral changes) that we want to see created or deepened. We offer a Neural Pathways handout (see Figure 20.6) to the parent and ask them the following questions: *Looking at the top pathway in the brain, can you identify behavior that your child now does all on their own but you used to have to remind them to do over and over again?*

The parent might name flushing the toilet as the behavior. The therapist or parent would then write this behavior into the well-worn top pathway on the handout. *Looking at the*

S	O	O	T	H	E
Soft tone of Voice	Organize	Offer	Touch	Hear	End
Day:___ Event:	Day:___ Event:	Day:___ Event:	Day:___ Event:	Day:___ Event:	Day:___ Event:
How helpful?___	How helpful?___	How helpful?___	How helpful?___	How helpful?___	How helpful?___
Day:___ Event:	Day:___ Event:	Day:___ Event:	Day:___ Event:	Day:___ Event:	Day:___ Event:
How helpful?___	How helpful?___	How helpful?___	How helpful?___	How helpful?___	How helpful?___
Day:___ Event:	Day:___ Event:	Day:___ Event:	Day:___ Event:	Day:___ Event:	Day:___ Event:
How helpful?___	How helpful?___	How helpful?___	How helpful?___	How helpful?___	How helpful?___

**Please record three moments in the course of a week in with you used a SOOTHE strategy to calm your foster child. Write a few words that will help you remember the event and how the child responded to our intervention. Write in a number by "How helpful" according to the following scale: 1=Not at all helpful 2=A litle bit helpful, 3=Somewhat helpful, 4= very helpful 5=extremely helpful

Figure 20.5 SOOTHE Homework Tool for Parents (Goodyear-Brown, P. 2021)

Neural Pathways

Write in the most worn path a behavior that your child has already mastered.
Then identify one that he is still working on, and one that you will need to
intentionally practice to lay down new or deeper neural pathways.

Figure 20.6 Laying Down the Neural Wiring (Goodyear-Brown, P. 2021)

middle pathway, can you identify a behavior that your child is able to complete on their own at least 50%
of the time … the rest of the time, you still give reminders? The parent might name the child's teeth
brushing. The therapist or parent writes this behavior into the less worn pathway in the middle of the handout. *Looking at the bottom pathway, can you identify a behavior that still really requires*
you to be right beside your child, offering your Safe Boss presence as a help, for them to be able to complete the
behavior? The therapist or parent then writes this behavior into the bottom pathway. What
the parent reports here will become part of the treatment plan (see Figure 20.6). The rest of
the chapter will follow the clinical work of Lizzy's family from the intake session through to the
final session, illustrating how treatment planning is a fluid, co-created process that evolves
over the course of treatment, always anchored by the core components of TraumaPlay™.

CASE SCENARIO

Intake

Lizzy, a transracially adopted tweener, had lived in an orphanage setting in Africa for the
first 11 years of her life and had only been in the home of her adoptive family for 6 months
when Miranda, her adoptive mother, sought out therapy. Miranda's stated goal for Lizzy's
therapy was "for Lizzy to stop lying." Miranda was disgusted with Lizzy's pattern of lying
and repeated the phrase, "You can't trust anything that comes out of her mouth" more
than once in the first half hour of our meeting. I moved into the role of Nurturer, holding
Mom's intense feelings and judgments about Lizzy without censure. Shifting into the role

of Storykeeper I acknowledged with compassion how yucky it feels as a mom to have moments when you truly dislike your child. Miranda, who had been speaking in clipped, angry tones, suddenly became tearful and we were able to gently touch the underlying shame she feels at having such negative activation with her daughter. Now that mom had felt the power of compassion, I shifted into the Storykeeper role for Lizzy and worked with mom to help her understand the enormity of risk it would take for Lizzy to tell the truth and the trust that would need to be established in mom's responses each time she took this risk. We replaced the language *Lizzy will stop telling lies,* with *Lizzy will risk trusting her mom enough, to tell the truth.* I helped mom practice leaning into her daughter when a lie had been told, saying, "I see that it was too hard for you to tell me the truth right away, but I am right here and safe enough for you to risk it now. Can you take that risk?"

The premise of our approach to the biopsychosocial interview is steeped in our definition of Storykeeping as helping the family to thread the needle back from the child's current big behaviors to their earliest experiences. This tool captures the relevant information succinctly and can be used in case of conceptualization and in planning which pieces of parent psychoeducation will be most important for creating therapeutic paradigm shifts (see Figure 20.7).

Treatment planning begins with a thorough assessment. Parents come to treatment anxious for answers, but when clinicians are pressured by the urgency of the perceived demand, there is a risk of providing treatment that is not contextually grounded. When the presenting problem is not grounded in a systems framework, the treatment may be incoherent or limited. Therefore, you will hear TraumaPlay™ supervisors frequently say, "Let's slow it down a little." The assessment phase of TraumaPlay™ begins with an intake with the parent(s) only in order to become Storykeeper for the adult without potentially colluding with the parent's story about the child's badness in front of the child.

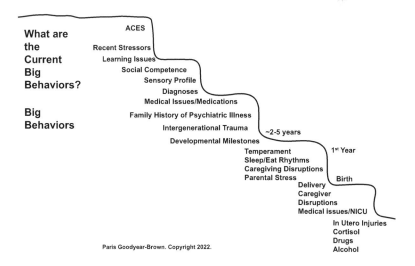

Figure 20.7 A TraumaPlay Storykeeping Template (Goodyear-Brown, P. 2021)

I asked Miranda to tell me the story of how Lizzy got to the orphanage. Impoverished and ill with several other children, Lizzy's mother left her at the orphanage when she was 2 months old. I wondered aloud with Miranda what it was like for Lizzy in utero, and together we shaped an understanding of poverty and food insecurity even from her earliest moments of life. I wondered with Miranda about the crowded conditions of the orphanage as Lizzy grew where babies' needs were only met intermittently with no attuned serve and return caregiver. I wondered out loud if Lizzy ever had to fight for food or sneak it and then lie about it. As I painted a picture, Miranda recalled a nugget that Lizzy had risked sharing with mom already-that if she hadn't done her assigned chores; she didn't get dessert, so Lizzy would work to control the narrative if a chore was missed. Lizzy developed the core belief that *I must control everything at all costs, of I will die.* I helped Miranda re-open her compassion well for her new daughter and embrace the thousands of repetitions of attuned care that would be needed to shift this belief.

A Dyadic Assessment

The next two sessions after the intake appointment are Nurture House Dyadic Assessments (NHDAs). These are structured playtimes between each parent and their child. The therapist orients the dyad to the space and begins embodying the three roles of Safe Boss, Nurturer, and Storykeeper for each dyad while observing the interactions from the corner of the room. The assessment begins by noting how the dyad presents in the waiting room (Are they sitting together or separately? Are they engaged in a joint activity or separate? Does the child seek proximity to the parent when the therapist enters). The dyad is ushered into a treatment room and first invited to engage in 5 minutes of child-led playtime, followed by five minutes of parent-led playtime, followed by a couple of minutes of parent-directed clean-up time. This part of the assessment is based on the DPIC from Parent-Child Interaction Therapy (PCIT) (Nelson & Olsen, 2018). It may include clinicians coding particular parent behaviors such as reflections, commands, descriptions of the child's play, number of questions asked by the parent, critical statements, nurturing touches, etc. These playtimes are followed by a series of tasks on cards, many of which are pulled from the Marshak Interaction Method (MIM) (Booth, 2020).

When I went into the lobby to meet Lizzy for the first time and greet Miranda, I noted that Miranda was sitting in a chair typing on her phone. Lizzy was sitting on the opposite side of the room with an iPad using a coloring app. When I walked in Miranda stood up and signaled for her daughter to come over to us with a sharp tone when Lizzy did not respond immediately. Once in the playroom, Lizzy explored the sandtray miniatures during the first five minutes while Mom asked her questions about each item Lizzy picked up. Lizzy excelled at the high structure tasks like building a block structure but seemed to freeze and become disorganized during the nurture tasks. She refused to let her mother feed her, shaking her head shyly and holding the bag of chips herself. Miranda seemed relieved to give over control of the snack and did not ask to be fed in return.

Individual Play-Based Assessment

After the dyadic sessions, the clinician meets with the client individually and completes play-based assessments of the client's current emotional literacy (often using the Color-Your-Heart, Goodyear-Brown 2002), the client's current coping repertoire (often using the Coping Tree, Goodyear-Brown, 2022), and the client's perceptions of their family dynamics (often using the Family Play Genostory, Goodyear-Brown, 2009) and the presenting problem.

When I normalized the behavior with Lizzy saying I have worked with lots of kids who found lying the way to get certain needs met in their orphanage, Lizzy looked relieved and explained that she had sometimes lied to avoid punishment or lied for other kids to save them from being punished or because they would give her their dessert or let her have their allotted screen time if she took their punishment for them. She explained that when a child was caught in a lie in the orphanage, the "auntie" would whip their hands with a switch until they bled, so she learned to lie convincingly. When these survival factors are understood, her lying can be reshaped as a marvelously adaptive coping behavior … but perhaps one that she no longer needs, at least not all the time or with everyone.

Mapping Progress

The clinician synthesizes all of the assessment data and offers observations and thoughts regarding treatment components during a parent-only feedback session, during which parents are invited into a collaborative treatment planning process while shifting parenting paradigms when needed. There is no quick fix for complex trauma. Caregivers can feel like a child taking one step forward and three steps backward. Treatment goals need to be measured with baby steps and framed as *relational risks of trust*. The dynamic between Lizzy and her mother began to shift, baby step by baby step.

One of our TraumaPlay™ mantras is *following the child's need*, both within a specific session and throughout the course of treatment. We want to enter the playroom with a clear case conceptualization and treatment plan but also simply be with a child, parent, or dyad in session. To this end, the TraumaPlay™ Mapping Tool is offered in TraumaPlay™ supervision (see Figure 20.8).

Using the graphic to represent a pinball machine, we can see the dynamic nature of the process. If the pinball represents the client in therapy, as the knob is pulled back, the client, therapist, and caregivers are jettisoned to the top of the pinball machine, joining and enhancing safety and security. After a period of time, the pinball is likely to move towards coping or soothing the physiology and, after spending time in these dimensions, will probably move down towards trauma narrative work. Even when much work has been done to enhance safety and security, a child might get into trauma narrative work and have some dissociation or overwhelm and need to bounce back up into soothing the physiology again. When a clinician is feeling stuck with a client, we will offer the mapping tool. We ask the clinician to label each part of the pinball machine with the number of sessions that have been spent in pursuit of each treatment goal and then we look for the ones that may need additional intervention. One pattern we have noticed is the neglect of parents as soothing partners. Often this is a component of treatment that needs more attention.

I decided to offer a rhythm of individual sessions with the client, followed by dyadic sessions with Mom and Lizzy. We played Delighting-In Games (Goodyear-Brown, 2021, 2022) with novelty being very important in supporting Lizzy's risk-taking with her mother. Lizzy and her mom created artistic renderings that they called Truth Trophies, as mom identified one time in each session when Lizzy had risked telling the truth the week before. They engaged in the Mood Manicure together (to enhance shared emotional narratives) (Goodyear-Brown, 2002, 2022). They played many hot-and-cold hide-and-seek games with hidden objects to help in their nonverbal attunement to one another. Eventually, they created a Timeline Garden together (Goodyear-Brown, 2022) that chronicled Lizzy's most joyful memories (the flowers above ground) and her hard things (represented by rocks and stones below ground), and most messy memories (represented by mud puddles). Twenty-eight sessions into treatment we began addressing Lizzy's thought life (she had turned 12 by then).

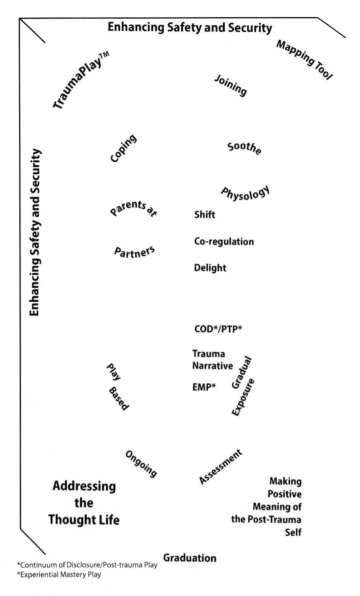

Figure 20.8 TraumaPlay Mapping Tool (Goodyear-Brown, P. 2021)

We named the messiness of adoption and the complexity of learning to trust again, and she drew a picture depicting her fear of being sent back to the orphanage if she lied. We enacted a commitment ceremony that involved a sandtray and candles. Mom and daughter painted each other's hands and pressed their hands to paper in a pattern to create a beautiful butterfly. After the painting is complete, I often ask, *What would you like to title this painting?* Mom, who months ago would have begun giving possible titles, simply looked at her daughter and waited. After several moments, Lizzy shyly said, "Family." All of our eyes focused on the paper (relieving Lizzy from the intensity of direct eye contact) as I wrote the word Family.

Termination and Closure of Therapy

Miranda and Lizzy took the painting home and eventually framed it. It is a core value embedded in the termination phase of TraumaPlay™ that we make a meaningful goodbye, especially for children like Lizzy, who have abrupt departures or felt abandoned from family members. Miranda and Lizzy had four sessions to create Treatment TakeAways (Goodyear-Brown, 2022), create keepsakes for each other, reflect on and narrate their journey through treatment in the sandtray, and celebrate with special food and a graduation ceremony. They returned at intervals in Lizzy's remaining years at home to work through new stuck places, but the feelings of being stuck were less and less related to the hard things and most frequently related to the belief that no matter what circumstances they faced, Miranda and Lizzy would stick together through them.

CONCLUSION

TraumaPlay™, has an umbrella framework of evidence-informed treatment goals and specific therapy planning tools that contribute to co-creating brain-based language used with children and caregivers. There are a variety of tools to help the therapist understand and document the child's trauma history through the Storykeeping lens, supporting parents in practicing co-regulation strategies and keeping them involved throughout the therapeutic process. The treatment planning process illustrated in the case example shows how TraumaPlay™ is implemented using the tools and terminology needed for effective treatment planning and implementation to promote healing and growth for children and families.

Key Takeaways

- ♥ The components of TraumaPlay™ provide a treatment planning scaffold on which a variety of clinically sound, play-based interventions can rest.
- ♥ In TraumaPlay™ treatment planning, co-regulation always precedes self-regulation in a child's development.
- ♥ TraumaPlay™ prioritizes the child's relationship with the co-regulating caregiver above trauma reprocessing so that as the scary content is processed, the child's emotions and behaviors can be more easily held by their primary caregiver.
- ♥ TraumaPlay™ practitioners explore the dynamics in a child's history or current relationship patterns that limit the felt sense of safety a child might have.
- ♥ The therapist embodies three therapeutic roles: Safe Boss, Nurturer, and Storykeeper, which the therapist must fluidly move in and out of as needed in treatment planning.
- ♥ The biopsychosocial interview is steeped in the definition of Storykeeping as helping the family thread the needle back from the child's current big behaviors to their earliest experiences.
- ♥ The therapist has a clear case conceptualization and treatment plan but also simply practices being with a child, parent, or dyad in session.
- ♥ TraumaPlay™ is implemented using the tools and terminology needed for effective treatment planning and implementation to promote healing and growth for children and families.

REFERENCES

Barfield, S., Dobson, C., Gaskill, R., & Perry, B. D. (2012). Neurosequential model of therapeutics in a therapeutic preschool: Implications for work with children with complex neuropsychiatric problems. *International Journal of Play Therapy, 21*(1), 30. https://psycnet.apa.org/doi/10.1037/a0025955

Booth, P. (2020). *Theraplay®—Theory, applications and implementation.* Jessica Kingsley.

Felitti, V. J., Anda, R. F., Nordenberg, D., & Williamson, D. F. (1998). Adverse childhood experiences and health outcomes in adults: The Ace study. *Journal of Family and Consumer Sciences, 90*(3), 31. https://psycnet.apa.org/doi/10.1037/t26957-000

Goodyear-Brown, P. (2002). *Digging for buried treasure: 52 prop-based play therapy interventions for treating the problems of childhood.* Sundog.

Goodyear-Brown, P. (2009). *Play therapy with traumatized children: A prescriptive approach.* Wiley.

Goodyear-Brown, P. (2019a). *Trauma and play therapy: Helping children heal.* Routledge. https://doi.org/10.4324/9781351216869

Goodyear-Brown, P. (2019b). Play therapy for children with attachment disruptions. *Prescriptive play therapy: Tailoring interventions for specific childhood problems* (pp. 231). Guilford.

Goodyear-Brown, P. (2021). *Parents as partners in child therapy: A clinician's guide.* Guilford Press.

Goodyear-Brown, P. (2022). *Big behaviors in small containers: 131 trauma-informed play therapy interventions for disorders of dysregulation.* PESI.

Greenough, W. T., Black, J. E., & Wallace, C. S. (2002). *Experience and brain development.* Blackwell. https://doi.org/10.1002/9780470753507.ch11

Hebb, D. O. (1949). The first stage of perception: Growth of the assembly. *The Organization of Behavior, 4,* 60–78. https://doi.org/10.7551/mitpress/4943.003.0006

Nelson, M. M., & Olsen, B. (2018). Dyadic parent–child interaction coding system (DPICS): An adaptable measure of parent and child behavior during dyadic interactions. *Handbook of parent-child interaction therapy* (pp. 285–302). Springer. https://doi.org/10.1007/978-3-319-97698-3_18

Perry, B. D. (2001). The neuroarcheology of childhood treatment: The neurodevelopmental costs of adverse childhood events. In K. Franey, R. Geffner, & R. Falconer (Eds.), *The cost of maltreatment: Who pays? We all do.* Family Violence and Sexual Assault Institute.

Perry, B. D., & Hambrick, E. P. (2008). The neurosequential model of therapeutics. *Reclaiming Children and Youth, 17*(3), 38–43.

Porges, S. W. (2011). *The polyvagal theory: Neurophysiological foundations of emotions, attachment, communication, and self-regulation (Norton Series on Interpersonal Neurobiology).* Norton.

Sale, A. (2018). A systematic look at environmental modulation and its impact in brain development. *Trends in neurosciences, 41*(1), 4–17. https://doi.org/10.1016/j.tins.2017.10.004

Schore, J. R., & Schore, A. N. (2008). Modern attachment theory: The central role of affect regulation in development and treatment. *Clinical social work journal, 36*(1), 9–20. https://doi.org/10.1007/s10615-007-0111-7

Siegel, D. J. (2001). Toward an interpersonal neurobiology of the developing mind: Attachment relationships,"mindsight," and neural integration. *Infant Mental Health Journal, 22*(1–2), 67–94. https://doi.org/10.1002/1097-0355(200101/04)22:1%3C67::AID-IMHJ3%3E3.0.CO;2-G

PART 3

SPECIAL POPULATIONS AND CONSIDERATIONS WITH TREATMENT PLANNING

CHAPTER 21

THERAPY PLANNING FOR SEXUALLY ABUSED CHILDREN AND ADOLESCENTS

Sueann Kenney-Noziska

INTRODUCTION

Childhood sexual abuse (CSA) is a worldwide social epidemic. According to the Centers for Disease Control (CDC), it impacts approximately 1 in 4 girls and 1 in 13 boys in the United States (2022). Although CSA can be perpetrated in intra- and extra-familial contexts, 91% of CSA is committed by someone known and trusted by the child and the child's family (CDC, 2022). The interpersonal betrayal inherent in CSA confuses victims and complicates treatment (Kenney-Noziska, 2019).

The short- and long-term adverse outcomes of CSA are well documented. CSA has been associated with anxiety, depression, posttraumatic stress, substance abuse problems, grief, and sexual revictimization (Hanson & Wallis, 2018). Additionally, functional and anatomical alterations in the brain result from trauma (Carletto et al., 2021). This is more pronounced and severe when interpersonal CSA is chronic. Expressive interventions such as play therapy, art therapy, and sandtray help access and process sensorily stored traumatic memories in a nonverbal, developmentally sensitive, trauma-informed manner.

ASSESSMENT FOR TREATMENT OF CHILDHOOD SEXUAL ABUSE

Best practice for assessing and treating trauma includes employing valid and reliable measures of PTSD and other common problems (Smith et al., 2019). Although informal play assessments are also necessary, a standardized, formal measure must be utilized. Assessment measures are available from various sources, including the National Child Traumatic Stress Network (NCTSN), the National Center for PTSD, Western Psychological Services (WPS), and Psychological Assessment Resources (PAR).

A common standardized assessment measure for cases of childhood abuse and trauma is the Trauma Symptom Checklist for Children (TSCC) and Trauma Symptom Checklist for Young Children (TSCYC) (Briere, 1996). The TSCC, completed by the client, is a broadband, standardized measure of acute and chronic posttraumatic symptomatology for children and youth ages 8–17. The TSCYC, completed by caregivers, is for children and youth ages 3–12 and measures posttraumatic stress and related psychological symptomatology. The TSCC and TSCYC include two validity scales that explore under-responding and over-responding, common test-taking pitfalls, and eight critical items. It also contains eight clinical scales (Anxiety, Depression, Anger/

DOI: 10.4324/9781003334231-24

Aggression, Posttraumatic Stress-Intrusion, Posttraumatic Stress-Avoidance, Posttraumatic Stress-Arousal, Dissociation, and Sexual Concerns) and an overall posttraumatic stress summary scale.

Additionally, multiple play therapy and expressive assessment approaches can be used with victims of CSA. Examples include the Extended Play-Based Developmental Assessment (EPBDA) (Gil, 2010), the Kinetic Family Drawing (KFD) (Burns & Kaufman, 1987), the House-Tree-Person Test (H-T-P) (Buck, 1948), the Lowenfeld World Technique (Lowenfeld, n.d.), and the Puppet Sentence Completion Task (Knell & Beck, 2000). Of course, none of these assessment tools are diagnostic or forensic. Nevertheless, they serve as valuable snapshots of a child's or adolescent's inner worldview and inform play and expressive approaches to trauma treatment.

THERAPY PLANNING FOR CHILDHOOD SEXUAL ABUSE

The evidence-based movement has provided clinicians with a better understanding of how to focus therapy for victims of CSA. Current best practices include a trauma-informed, trauma-focused approach whereby interventions are selected to focus on specific treatment needs (Fitzgerald & Berliner, 2018). Areas of overlap in evidence-based protocols are referred to as core components of trauma treatment and include the following intervention objectives per the National Child Traumatic Stress Network (NCTSN, 2023): (a) assessment and engagement; (b) psychoeducation about trauma reminders and loss reminders to strengthen coping skills; (c) psychoeducation about posttraumatic stress reactions and grief reactions to strengthen coping skills; (d) teaching emotional regulation skills to strengthen coping skills; (e) constructing a trauma narrative to reduce posttraumatic stress reactions; and (f) teaching safety skills to promote personal safety.

Family systems issues, disclosure and post-disclosure experiences, and social system factors will influence the therapy process. Multidisciplinary involvement (i.e., child protective services, the legal system) in cases of CSA is common and may shift the course of therapy. Additionally, cultural influences are essential considerations and should be defined broadly. According to Hays (2016), culture encompasses age, religion or spirituality, ethnicity, national origin, gender, socioeconomic status, and other influences (see Appendixes B.8 and C.5).

CONCLUSION

CSA, a prominent social and public health issue, is known for its deleterious short- and long-term impact. This includes adverse mental health, medical, social, and other functional outcomes. Play therapy and other expressive interventions can be utilized in a trauma-informed, focused manner to meet children's and adolescents' treatment needs developmentally and appropriately. Arguably, expressive approaches are holistic and are naturally geared at accessing and reprocessing traumatic and somatically stored memories. They can also be focused and directive to conform with components of evidence-based treatment protocols.

Key Takeaways

- The interpersonal betrayal inherent in CSA confuses victims and complicates treatment In TraumaPlay™ treatment planning, co-regulation always precedes self-regulation in a child's development.
- Expressive interventions such as play therapy, art therapy, and sandtray help access and process sensorily stored traumatic memories in a nonverbal, developmentally sensitive, trauma-informed manner.
- Although informal play assessments are necessary with CSA, a standardized, formal measure must be utilized.The therapist embodies three therapeutic roles: Safe Boss, Nurturer, and Storykeeper, which the therapist must fluidly move in and out of as needed in treatment planning.
- The biopsychosocial interview is steeped in the definition of Storykeeping as helping the family thread the needle back from the child's current big behaviors to their earliest experiences.
- The therapist has a clear case conceptualization and treatment plan but also simply practices being with a child, parent, or dyad in session.
- TraumaPlay™ is implemented using the tools and terminology needed for effective treatment planning and implementation to promote healing and growth for children and families.
- Core components of treating CSA are: 1. assessment and engagement, 2. psychoeducation about trauma reminders and loss reminders to strengthen coping skills, 3. psychoeducation about posttraumatic stress reactions and grief reactions to strengthen coping skills, 4. teaching emotional regulation skills to strengthen coping skills, 5. constructing a trauma narrative to reduce posttraumatic stress reactions, and 6. teaching safety skills to promote personal safety.

REFERENCES

Briere, J. (1996). *Trauma symptom checklist for children (TSCC)*, professional manual. Psychological Assessment Resources. https://doi.org/10.1037/10267-003

Buck, J. N. (1948). The H-T-P test. *Journal of Clinical Psychology, 4*(2) 151–159. https://doi.org/10.1002/1097-4679(194804)4:2%3C151::aid-jclp2270040203%3E3.0.co;2-o

Burns, R. C., & Kaufman, S. H. (1987). *Kinetic family drawings: An introduction to understanding children through kinetic drawings.* Brunner/Mazel. https://doi.org/10.1192/bjp.118.545.480

Carletto, S., Panero, M., Cavallo, M., & Pagani, M. (2021). Neurobiology of posttraumatic stress disorder. In R. A. J.O. Dierckx, A. Otte, E. F. J. de Vries, & A. van Waarde (Eds.), *PET and SPECT in psychiatry* (pp. 411–435). Springer.https://doi.org/10.1007/978-3-030-57231-0_11

Centers for Disease Control (CDC). (2022, April 6). *Fast facts: Preventing child sexual abuse.* Retrieved from https://www.cdc.gov/violenceprevention/childsexualabuse/fastfact.html

Fitzgerald, M. M., & Berliner, L. (2018). Mental health intervention in child maltreatment. In J. B. Klika, and J. R. Conte (Eds.), *The APSAC handbook on children maltreatment* (4th ed., pp. 200–215). Sage. https://journals.sagepub.com/doi/10.1177/1077559514567943

Gil, E. (2010). *Extended play-based developmental assessment.* Self-Esteem Shop.

Hanson, R. F., & Wallis, E. (2018). Treating victims of child sexual abuse. *American Journal of Psychiatry, 175*(11), 1064–1070. https://doi.org/10.1176/appi.ajp.2018.18050578

Hays, P. A. (2016). *Addressing cultural complexities in practice: Assessment, diagnosis, and therapy* (3rd ed.). American Psychological Association. https://psycnet.apa.org/doi/10.1037/14801-000

Kenney-Noziska, S. (2019). Therapeutic games for sexually abused children. In C. E. Schaefer & J. Stone (Eds.), *Game Play* (3rd ed., pp. 239–254). Wiley.

Knell, S., & Beck, K. W. (2000). Puppet sentence completion task. In K. T. Gitlin-Wiener, K. Sandgrund, & C. Schaefer (Eds.), *Play diagnosis and assessment* (pp. 704–721). Wiley. https://www.taylorfrancis.com/chapters/edit/10.4324/9781315181349-5/puppet-sentence-completion-task-psct-susan-knell

National Child Traumatic Stress Network (NCTSN). (2023). Core components of trauma-informed interventions. Retrieved January 4, 2023, from: http://www.nctsn.org/resources/topics/treatments-that-work/promising-practices

Smith, P., Dalgleish, T., & Meiser-Stedman, R. (2019). Practitioner review: Posttraumatic stress disorder and its treatment in children and adolescents. *Journal of Child Psychology and Psychiatry*, *60*(5), 500–515. 500–515. https://acamh.onlinelibrary.wiley.com/doi/10.1111/jcpp.12983

CHAPTER 22

THERAPY PLANNING WITH EMDR® AND PLAY THERAPY

Ann Beckley-Forest and Rhonda Johnson

Eye Movement Desensitization and Reprocessing (EMDR®) is an evidence-based psychotherapy approach designed for the treatment of posttraumatic stress and is now used widely with both children and adults to provide relief from the trauma symptoms which disrupt healthy emotional development and well-being. Francine Shapiro, the originator of EMDR®, used an Adaptive Information Processing (AIP) model to conceptualize both the healthy process by which humans learn from their experiences in order to grow and the maladaptive disruptions to this process caused by our efforts to cope with traumatic and threatening experiences.

The EMDR® phases are designed to prepare the client to retrieve and face the memories of such experiences and re-establish the healthy flow of affective, somatic, and cognitive information along channels that allow the person to heal and move forward. (Shapiro, 2017). Efficacy of EMDR® with children is well-established in the literature (DeRoos et al., 2011; Fleming, 2012; Moreno-Alcazar et al., 2017) always with a nod to the need for developmentally-sensitive adaptation and the challenges of working in more complex trauma cases (Gomez, 2013). EMDR® should only be used by a fully trained EMDR® therapist.

AIP thinking integrates well with play therapy models which expand the understanding of how children learn through experimentation. In order for EMDR® to be effective in helping the child to remove blocks and allow adaptive information to reach the traumatic memory network, we have to be able to reach and activate the memory and its related associations. A robust application of the therapeutic powers of play (Schaefer and Drewes, 2014) can create a safe haven in the play therapy relationship, increase emotional regulation and grounding through the incorporation of prescriptive play activities (Kestly, 2016) and develop the child's ability to gradually approach disturbing material through play and metaphor (Parker et al., 2021; Ryan and & Edge, 2012). All of these elements are essential considerations in the integration of EMDR® into a play therapy approach (Beckley-Forest, 2020; Marks, 2017).

A play-therapy-supported EMDR® approach for treating trauma is essentially a flexible approach that incorporates the eight phases of EMDR® into four main treatment goals.

- **Stabilization** and establishment of here-and-now physical and emotional safety.
- **Preparation** for exposure work, especially to include playful grounding and regulation, play therapy as projective space, containment strategies, and access to positive affect.
- **Gradual exposure** to traumatic memories and themes to promote "digestion" and integration of sensory material and more adaptive beliefs about the self. We engage in this digestion while involving the child in bilateral or dual attention stimulation (BLS/DAS) which expands this integrative capacity and is an essential part

DOI: 10.4324/9781003334231-25

of the EMDR® process. Careful attention to metaphors and themes in the play which touch on traumatic material serves as the bridge to trauma narrative work grounded in play and expressive modalities. The therapist can then become more directive in leading the child toward gradual exposure to trauma memories, providing a congruent setting for the processing phases of EMDR®.

- **Reevaluation** on an ongoing basis of how the processing of the memories is affecting the present functioning and future goals for the child.

TREATMENT PLANNING FOR USE OF EMDR® AND PLAY THERAPY

Goals, objectives, and interventions are selected in line with an EMDR® approach to providing play therapy for children and families.

Goal #1: Establishment of physical and emotional safety.

Objective 1: The child will demonstrate comfort with the play therapy setting as evidenced by initiating a play activity or story at least once in the session over three sessions.

Intervention: child-centered play time, with the therapist in a neutral, tracking, and supportive role.

Objective 2: The child will initiate two self-soothing strategies in and out of the play therapy setting.

Intervention: Deep breathing by pretending to blow bubbles used in sessions, riding his bike outside if accessible, or imagining his calm, safe place created in the sand tray.

Objective 3: The child's parents will demonstrate an expanded repertoire of positive parenting strategies to help the child de-escalate as evidenced by self-reported success at avoiding shame and authoritarian discipline strategies 75% of the time.

Intervention: Parent coaching sessions, scheduled time for family fun without an agenda or discipline.

Goal #2: Increased capacity for emotional regulation.

Objective 1: Identify two emotions contributing to negative beliefs and to understand parts of self.

Intervention: Recognize emotions both positive and negative through the use of emotion memory card game and identifying emotions on children's faces.

Intervention: Use of ALLMEE doll© or similar tool with emotional parts, modeling how his angry part doesn't have to be in charge for the child to feel safe when his competence is threatened.

Objective 2: Child will practice regulation by recognizing sensations in the play therapy setting.

Intervention: Use of wand or toy magnifying glass to teach him to recognize sensations when practicing very fast, medium, and then very slow regulation with toys and activities including—a slinky, hopping back and forth, throwing a ball, and riding his bike.

Goal #3: Decreased reactivity to trauma-related triggers.

Objective1: Child will have two decreased symptoms and behaviors following processing of trauma material.

Intervention: Processing present triggers and past trauma material with bilateral stimulation using play therapy-supported EMDR® protocol.

Objective 2: Child will actively participate in processing trauma-related material to a lower distress level.

Intervention: EMDR® storytelling protocol for reprocessing targeted attachment experiences by bridging from posttraumatic play with baby animals and including Rodney's adoptive parents in the storytelling process.

Goal #4: Acceptance of personal narrative and consistent improvements in current functioning and readiness for future growth.

Objective 1: Child will exhibit pride and joy in his strengths and competencies

Intervention: child-centered play themes around mastery and empowerment.

Objective 2: Child will seek comfort from a support figure when experiencing distressing emotions.

Intervention: Reevaluation of trauma target reactivity with parents using Popcorn Night handout (Monaco, 2020).

Objective 3: Child can imagine a future template with a positive ending.

Intervention: EMDR® FUTURE template: Imagining himself responding positively to a challenging situation with the belief "I can handle it" while engaging in BLS with light-up drumsticks.

CONCLUSION

The research literature supports the efficacy of EMDR® adapted to the developmental needs of children for treating and bringing relief for posttraumatic stress. The combination of EMDR® and play therapy is appropriate for therapists fully trained in both EMDR® and play therapy.

Key Takeaways

- ☿ EMDR is designed for the treatment of post-traumatic stress and is now used widely with both children and adults to provide relief from the trauma symptoms that disrupt healthy emotional development and well-being.
- ☿ EMDR should only be used by a fully trained EMDR therapist.
- ☿ Use of the Powers of Play can create a safe haven in the play therapy relationship, increase emotional regulation and grounding through the incorporation of prescriptive play activities.
- ☿ There are eight phases of EMDR which lead to the four goals: Stabilization, Preparation, Gradual Exposure, and Reevaluation.

REFERENCES

Beckley-Forest, A. (2020). Using both EMDR® and prescriptive play therapy in adaptive information processing: A rationale and essential considerations for integration In A. Beckley-Forest & A. Monaco (Eds.), *EMDR® with children in the play therapy room: An integrated approach.* Springer. 500–515. https://acamh.onlinelibrary.wiley.com/doi/10.1111/jcpp.12983

DeRoos, C., Greenwald, R., den Hollander-Gijsm, M., Noorthoorn, E., van Buuren, S., & de Jongh, A. (2011). A randomized comparison of cognitive behavioral therapy (CBT) and eye movement desensitization and reprocessing in disaster-exposed children. *European Journal of Psychotraumatology, 2,* 5694–5704. https://doi.org/10.3402/ejpt.v2i0.5694

Fleming, J. (2012). The effectiveness of eye movement desensitization and reprocessing in the treatment of traumatized children and youth. *Journal of EMDR® Practice and Research, 6*(1). http://dx.doi.org/10.1891/1933-3196.6.1.16

Gomez, A. (2013) *EMDR® therapy and adjunct approaches with children.* Springer https://doi.org/10.1891/9780826106988

Kestly, T. A. (2016). Presence and play: Why mindfulness matters. *International Journal of Play Therapy, 25*(1), 14–23. https://doi.org/10.1037/pla0000019

Marks, R. P. (2017). When play therapy is not enough: Using eye movement desensitization and reprocessing/bilateral stimulation in combination with play therapy for the child with complex trauma. In A. Hendry & J. Hasler (Eds.), *Creative therapies for complex trauma: Helping children and families in foster care, kinship care or adoption* (pp. 164–180). Jessica Kingsley.

Monaco, A. (2020) Popcorn night: Effectively managing closure phase and reevaluation with parents. In A. Beckley-Forest & A. Monaco (Eds.) *EMDR® with children in the play therapy room: An integrated approach* (pp. 413–426). Springer. https://doi.org/10.1891/9780826106988

Moreno-Alcazar, A., Treen, D., Valiente-Gomez, A., Sio-Erlos, A., Perez, V., Amann, B. L. & Radua, J. (2017). Efficacy of eye movement desensitization and reprocessing in children and adolescents with post-traumatic stress disorder: A meta-analysis of randomized controlled trials. *Frontiers in Psychology, 8*(1750), 1–10. DOI: 10.3389/fpsyg.2017.01750

Parker, M. M., Hergenrather, K., Smelser, Q., & Kelly, C. T. (2021). Exploring child-centered play therapy and trauma: A systematic review of literature. *International Journal of Play Therapy, 30*(1), 2–13. https://doi.org/10.1037/pla0000136

Ryan, V., & Edge, A. (2012). The role of play themes in non-directive play therapy. *Clinical child psychology and psychiatry, 17*(3), 354–369. https://doi.org/10.1891/9780826106988

Schaefer, C. E. & Drewes, A. A. (2014). *Therapeutic powers of play: 20 core agents of change* (2nd ed.). Wiley.

Shapiro, F. (2017). *Eye movement desensitization and reprocessing (EMDR®) therapy: Basic principles, protocols, and procedures.* Guilford.https://doi.org/10.1002/anxi.3070020302

CHAPTER 23

PSYCHOTHERAPY TREATMENT
PLANNING WITH CHILDREN IN CRISIS

Claudio Mochi and Isabella Cassina

INTRODUCTION

Crisis and critical contexts are characterized by the presence of highly challenging and threatening circumstances that have the potential to overwhelm the individual's coping skills and make the situation intolerable. Events such as natural and human-made disasters can trigger psychological suffering and pos-traumatic reactions in both children and adults. Nevertheless, "there is no immediate and causal relationship between a specific event and individual reactions" (McFarlane and De Girolamo cited in VanFleet and Mochi, 2015, p. 170). This is because factors like the nature of the crisis, how it is perceived by the person, the characteristics of the latter, and those of its environment come into play.

Each critical context is objectively and subjectively different. A critical event often triggers a multitude of additional stressors that linger over time. Some contexts are characterized by the presence of multiple stressors that tend to accumulate, making the environment increasingly dense with challenges. Additionally, even if exposure to critical circumstances is time-limited, the reactions generated are unlikely to be able to be addressed by short-term interventions.

These circumstances are conveyed with the Avalanche Metaphor (Cassina, 2023), originally developed to illustrate the growing, devastating, and lasting impact of forced migration on children and families. The metaphor applies to critical contexts in general and emphasizes how the end of a natural disaster or conflict does not coincide with the end of psychosocial difficulties for individuals. Supporting the community in recovering from complex psychosocial conditions requires an effort from the entire support system, which has often experienced severe damage.

CONCEPTUALIZING TREATMENT FROM
A PROCESS-ORIENTED PERSPECTIVE

Unlike highly structured programs, process-oriented interventions allow adherence to the multiplicity of necessities by ensuring attunement, consistency, and predictability. In fact, this type of approach implies a chain of actions and different phases that facilitate the understanding of needs, the enhancement of local resources, and the involvement of the support system. Rather than identifying an emergency protocol and standardized activities, it is preferable to take the appropriate time to co-create customized and interrelated actions. Some researchers (Bonanno et al., 2010; Masten and Narayan, 2012) argue that specialized interventions conducted too quickly are often counterproductive. Porges (2017, p. 24) points out that for "any treatments to

DOI: 10.4324/9781003334231-26

be effective and efficient it is necessary to keep the autonomic nervous system out of a state of defense" offering safe spaces and time to build connection and engagement.

In critical contexts, specialized interventions such as play and expressive therapies are part of a larger program. The approach "Coping with the present while building for the future" (CPBF) (Cassina and Mochi, 2023) offers useful references in developing a treatment plan. Here is a selection:

- *Multilayered intervention*: crisis interventions involve "a progression of actions that starts from the less specialized activities addressed to the larger population, to the most refined forms of treatment addressed to smaller groups" (Cassina & Mochi, 2023).

  op. cit.: 15). The process should be articulated to (1) meet the primary needs of the community, (2) promote a sense of safety and motivate involvement, (3) strengthen individual capacities (empowerment), and finally (4) develop specialized therapeutic treatments.

- *Grounding phase*: the implementation of advanced therapeutic activities (up to the treatment of trauma in an individual modality where necessary) is based on the effective implementation of preparatory activities that enable the development of a broad knowledge of local needs and culture, a sense of safety, and trusting relationships.

- *Pattern need-goal-activity (N-G-A)* (Cassina and Mochi, 2023): crisis interventions are shaped following a pattern that involves a constant needs assessment on which goals are defined and activities developed. Regular monitoring of the context makes it possible to identify emerging needs, define increasingly specific goals and develop new activities. The pattern N-G-A repeats itself over time.

- *Involvement of the support system*: it is advisable to include caregivers (and other significant adults in children's lives) in crisis interventions in order to provide children with the highest number of supportive interactions even outside the playroom (intended as the therapy space). Including caregivers is as essential as it requires gradualness and attention as they themselves are subjected to circumstances of extreme stress and potentially traumatized.

"In a process-oriented approach to treatment, case formulation is an ongoing process" (Elliott and Greenberg, 2016, p. 6) that is certainly enriched by therapeutic experiences inside the playroom but also by grounding work and increased knowledge of the context. In the CPBF approach, the gathering of information about the presenting problem(s) and needs takes place constantly allowing for the articulation of progressively specific supportive and therapeutic proposals as indicated by the N-G-A pattern. Within this development of knowledge, some of the most influential aspects to consider are: children's pretend play ability and regulatory skills, involvement of the caregivers in the therapeutic process, and the opportunities of the whole support system to offer co-regulatory experiences outside the playroom.

CONCLUSION

Times of crisis when working with children and families require special consideration to the context of the current events, resources, support systems, and any other relevant factors. Recovery from crisis-related psychosocial conditions requires effort from the child's entire support system even though those support systems may also be suffering due to the crisis at hand. Specifically structured programs that lend to process-oriented interventions help the therapist to meet the psychological needs of the child by ensuring attunement, consistency, and predictability.

Key Takeaways

♡ A critical event often triggers a multitude of additional stressors that linger over time. Some contexts are characterized by the presence of multiple stressors that tend to accumulate, making the environment increasingly dense with challenges.

♡ Unlike highly structured programs, process-oriented interventions allow adherence to the multiplicity of necessities by ensuring attunement, consistency, and predictability.

♡ In critical contexts, specialized interventions such as play and expressive therapies are part of a larger program.

♡ In the CPBF approach, the gathering of information about the presenting problem(s) and needs takes place constantly, allowing for the articulation of progressively specific supportive and therapeutic proposals.

REFERENCES

Bonanno, G. A., Brewin, C. R., Kaniasty, K., & Greca, A. M. L. (2010). Weighing the costs of disaster: Consequences, risks, and resilience in individuals, families, and communities'. *Psychological science in the public interest, 11*(1), 1–49. https://journals.sagepub.com/doi/10.1177/1529100610387086

Cassina, I. (2023). Recovering lost playtime. Principles and intervention modalities to address the psychosocial wellbeing of asylum seekers and refugee children. In I. Cassina, C., Mochi, & K., Stagnitti (Eds.), *Play therapy and expressive arts in a complex and dynamic world: Opportunities and challenges inside and outside the playroom* (pp. 50–68) Routledge. https://www.taylorfrancis.com/chapters/edit/10.4324/9781003252375-4/recovering-

Cassina, I., & Mochi, C. (2023). Applying the therapeutic power of play and expressive arts in contemporary crisis work. A process-oriented approach. In I. Cassina, C. Mochi, & K. Stagnitti (Eds.), *Play therapy and expressive arts in a complex and dynamic world: Opportunities and challenges inside and outside the playroom* (pp. 6–27). Routledge.https://www.taylorfrancis.com/chapters/edit/10.4324/9781003252375-4/recovering-

Elliott, R., & Greenberg, L. S. (2016). Humanistic-experiential psychotherapy in practice: Emotion-focused therapy. In A. J. Consoli, L. E. Beutler, & B. Bongar (Eds.) https://psycnet.apa.org/doi/10.1037/10439-009 , *Comprehensive textbook of psychotherapy: Theory and practice* (2nd ed., pp. 106 –120). Oxford University Press. https://psycnet.apa.org/doi/10.1037/10439-009

Masten, A. S., & Narayan, A. J. (2012). Child development in the context of disaster, war, and terrorism: Pathways of risk and resilience. *Annual review of psychology, 63*, 227–257. https://www.taylorfrancis.com/chapters/edit/10.4324/9781003252375-4/recovering-

Porges, S. W. (2017). *The pocket guide to the polyvagal theory: The transformative power of feeling safe.* Norton.

VanFleet, R., & Mochi, C. (2015). Enhancing resilience in play therapy with child and family survivors of mass trauma. In D. Crenshaw, R. Brooks, & S., Goldstein (Eds.), *Enhancing resilience in play therapy* (pp. 168–193). Guilford.

CHAPTER 24

A NEURODIVERSITY-AFFIRMING APPROACH TO THERAPY PLANNING

Robert Jason Grant

INTRODUCTION TO NEURODIVERSITY

The term neurodiversity appeared publicly in 1998 when journalist Harvey Blume published an article in the *Atlantic* stating that neurodiversity may be every bit as crucial for the human race as biodiversity is for life in general (Blume, 1998). Who can say what form of wiring will prove best at any given moment (Armstrong, 2015)? Judy Singer, an Australian sociologist, is widely credited with coining the term neurodiversity. It is reported that Singer and Blume corresponded about the topic and Singer wrote about neurodiversity in her thesis in 1998. It was in 1999 that she furthered her work in neurodiversity while writing a chapter "Why Can't You be Normal for Once in Your Life?" based on her thesis which was published in the UK. Since its origins, the term has grown immensely with additional understanding and research support (Singer, 2017).

Neurodiversity is the diversity of human neurotypes (Kras, 2009; Armstrong, 2010; den Houting, 2019; Chapman, 2021). There exists diversity in the way the brain operates and navigates across humans. Thus, neurodiversity affirming is the act of valuing neurodiversity and affirming a child's neurotype. Neurodiversity affirming is a commitment to putting forth relationships, interactions, processes, and approaches that value and uplift the child's neurotype, in the case of neurodivergent children, respecting their neurodivergence (Grant, 2022).

Walker (2021, pp. 34–41) defined several key terms related to neurodiversity, highlighting their meanings and proper usage:

Neurodiversity: the diversity of human minds, the infinite variation in neurocognitive functioning within our species. It is a biological fact. It's not an approach, a belief, or a political position.

Neurodiversity paradigm: a specific perspective on neurodiversity that involves the following fundamental principles:

1. Neurodiversity is a natural and valuable form of human diversity.
2. The idea that there is one "normal" or "healthy" type of brain or mind, or one "right" style of neurocognitive functioning, is a culturally constructed fiction.
3. The social dynamics that manifest in regard to neurodiversity are similar to the social dynamics that manifest in other forms of human diversity (e.g., diversity of ethnicity, gender, or culture).

Neurodiversity movement: a social justice movement that seeks civil rights, equality, respect, and full societal inclusion for the neurodivergent.

Neurodivergent: having a mind that functions in ways that diverge significantly from the dominant societal standards of "normal." This is often connected to a diagnosis such as autistic,

DOI: 10.4324/9781003334231-27

ADHD, sensory different, etc. but a person does not have to have a diagnosis to be neurodivergent. Being neurodivergent is thought of as an identity, not something to be fixed or cured.

Neurotypical: having a style of neurocognitive functioning that falls within the dominant societal standards of "normal." Neurotypical is a social construct not a type of neurology.

SPECIAL CONSIDERATIONS FOR THERAPY PLANNING WITH NEURODIVERGENT CHILDREN

Neurodiversity affirming is an action. It is a set of processes that collate from neurodiversity-informed understanding (Grant, 2021; Dallman et al., 2022; Dwyer, 2022). The neurodiversity-affirming child therapist has a thorough understanding of neurodiversity which includes the movement and paradigm, ableism, the medical and social models of disability, and the history of non-affirming/ableist therapy approaches initiated with neurodivergent children. It is this knowledge that translates into affirming awareness and approaches in therapy practice.

A neurodiversity-affirming approach should be implemented in therapy involving neurodivergent children. Grant (2023) outlined tenets of a neurodiversity-informed and affirming approach in AutPlay® Therapy:

1. Recognize that neurodiversity means there is no such thing as a normal brain. Variation in neurology is natural, and none is more right or wrong than another.

2. Understand that neurodivergent children (autistic, sensory differences, ADHD, etc.) are not in play therapy because they are neurodivergent. They are in therapy because they have needs such as anxiety, regulation challenges, trauma issues, social needs, parent/child relationship issues, etc. Being informed and aware of the neurodivergent child may require different methods of implementing play therapy to match the child's neurotype. Navigation should come from the perspective, "I'm not going to work with you on changing who you are. I'm going to work with you on how to help you get what you want or need."

3. Honor the child's play preferences and special interests. All neurodivergent children play and there are multiple types and ways to play. Each child's play preferences should be respected and neurodivergent children should not be forced to play a specific way.

4. Encourage children's voices to be heard and valued in deciding on processes, needs, and goals. Children should have a say in what needs they want to address.

5. Avoid play interventions that promote masking and camouflaging. Instead, focus on strengths and help children recognize what they already do well; help them utilize their strengths to address their needs.

6. Recognize that different is okay, different is not bad, wrong, or a problem, navigating differently is supported. The focus is never on trying to change a neurodivergent child to "look" like a neurotypical standard.

7. Value relationship development as a core process in AutPlay® Therapy. Therapeutic relationship is key to working with neurodivergent children and their families and should begin with first contact and continue until termination.

8. Understand that play is the natural language of children. The therapeutic powers of play are a grounding principle in AutPlay® Therapy. Play is the change agent and not the way to get to a change agent. Play is not withheld or used as a reward to gain compliance.

9. Recognize the play therapy process may involve addressing self-worth, understanding identity, the social model of disability, the double empathy problem, and self-advocacy development.

10. Conceptualize that the play therapy process may involve non-directive methods, directive methods, or an integrative or prescriptive approach. The therapy approach and process should be individualized to the unique neurotype of each child, understanding their spectrum of presentation.

CONCLUSION

Neurodivergent children possess a unique identity. In the past, mental health services have not valued this identity and, instead, have focused on aiming to direct neurodivergent children toward practicing neurotypical behaviors. Commitment to being a neurodiversity-affirming child therapist requires a thorough understanding of the concept of neurodiversity and how ableism and the medical and social models of disability can and have caused harm historically to neurodivergent children. With this knowledge, therapists can consciously shift into affirming awareness and approaches in the process of case conceptualizing and therapy planning.

Key Takeaways

♡ Neurodiversity affirming is the act of valuing neurodiversity and affirming a child's neurotype.

♡ Neurodiversity affirming is a commitment to putting forth relationships, interactions, processes, and approaches that value and uplift the child's neurotype, in the case of neurodivergent children, respecting their neurodivergence.

♡ The neurodiversity-affirming child therapist has a thorough understanding of neurodiversity which includes the movement and paradigm, ableism, the medical and social models of disability, and the history of non-affirming/ableist therapy approaches initiated with neurodivergent children.

♡ Neurodivergent children are not in play therapy because they are neurodivergent. They are in therapy because they have needs such as anxiety, regulation challenges, trauma issues, social needs, parent/child relationship issues, etc.

♡ Each child's play preferences should be respected and neurodivergent children should not be forced to play a specific way.

REFERENCES

Armstrong, T. (2010). *Neurodiversity: Discovering the extraordinary gifts of autism, ADHD, dyslexia, and other brain differences.* Da Capo.

Armstrong, T. (2015). The myth of the normal brain: Embracing neurodiversity. *AMA Journal of Ethics, 17*(4), 348–352. DOI:10.1001/journalofethics.2015.17.4.msoc1-1504

Blume, H. (1998), August 15). *Neurodiversity*. The Atlantic. Retrieved March 19, 2023, from https://www.theatlantic.com/magazine/archive/1998/09/neurodiversity/305909/?utm_source=copy-link&utm_medium=social&utm_campaign=share

Chapman R. (2021). Neurodiversity and the social ecology of mental functions. *Perspectives on Psychological Science, 16*(6), 1360–1372. DOI:10.1177/1745691620959833

Dallman, A. R., Williams, K. L., & Villa, L. (2022). Neurodiversity-affirming practices are a moral imperative for occupational therapy. *The Open Journal of Occupational Therapy, 10*(2), 1–9. DOI.org/10.15453/2168-6408.1937

den Houting, J. (2019). Neurodiversity: an insider's perspective. *Autism, 23,* 271–273. DOI:10.1177/1362361318820762

Dwyer, P. (2022). The neurodiversity approach(es): What are they and what do they mean for researchers? *Human Development, 66,* 73–92. DOI:10.1159/000523723

Grant, R. J. (2021). *Understanding autism: A neurodiversity affirming guidebook for children and teens.* AutPlay® Publishing.

Grant, R. J. (2022). *Understanding sensory differences: A neurodiversity affirming guidebook for children and teens.* AutPlay® Publishing.

Grant, R. J. (2023). *The AutPlay® therapy handbook: Integrative family play therapy with neurodivergent children.* Routledge.

Kras, J. F. (2009). The "ransom notes" affair: when the neurodiversity movement came of age. *Disability Studies Quarterly, 30,* 1065. DOI:10.18061/dsq.v30i1.1065

Singer, J. (2017). *Neurodiversity: The birth of an idea.* Kindle.

Walker, N. (2021). *Neuroqueer heresies: Notes on the neurodiversity paradigm, autistic empowerment, and post normal possibilities.* Autonomous Press. https://doi.org/10.1080/02604027.2022.2094194

CHAPTER 25

TREATMENT PLANNING WITH CHILDREN DURING HIGH-CONFLICT DIVORCE

Lynn Louise Wonders

INTRODUCTION

A certain degree of conflict between parents going through a divorce is normal. Different levels of conflict intensity fall somewhere on a continuum (Wonders, 2019) but true *high conflict* between parents is rare and can be damaging to the emotional and mental well-being of children. The literature indicates that when a child witnesses high levels of intensely hostile dynamics between parents, there is a reliable predictability that the child will develop various mental and emotional problems, including anxiety and depression (O'Hara et al.; Wonders, 2019). High-conflict divorce has been shown to contribute to a high risk of trauma in children (Van der Wal et al., 2019). There is often personality pathology present with parents who are tangled in these intractable and destructive dynamics (Greenham & Childress, 2022). Suppose a therapist is aware of these dynamics. In that case, it is advisable to structure the therapeutic process and the therapist's relationships with the parents and with the child to avoid having the parents' conflict pollute the therapeutic process.

INTAKE AND INTERACTIONS WITH CAREGIVERS

Meeting parents, as in any initial intake, is a time for rapport-building and conducting the biopsychosocial intake of information; but the initial intake session is also a time to orient parents to the purpose and structure of therapy and set forth clear policies and protocols (Wonders, 2019). When parents are embroiled in high conflict, their executive functioning is often eclipsed by overactive limbic brain activity, often expressed as rage toward one another. With this in mind, the therapist must be mindful of the pace and manner in which this initial session is conducted.

It is often best to meet with parents in separate intake sessions or over telehealth if both parents attend the session. This will help to mitigate their conflict from escalating and derailing a single intake session. The therapist will need to set parameters for the session(s) as a time to gather background information about the child and family, not a time to focus on details of the parents' conflict. In the first session, the therapist will need to establish the therapist's role there to support the child, not an evaluator of custody nor a mediator for the parents' conflict. Equally important, the therapist needs to make clear that a non-bias position will be observed, with both parents receiving identical updates on the child's progress and equal access to the therapist for questions about the child's progress in therapy. Referrals may be provided for parents to seek individual counseling support and maybe co-parenting counseling outside of the child's therapy (Wonders, 2019).

In most other clinical cases, it would be important to involve caregivers as partners working toward the best interest of the child's healing and growth. In high-conflict divorce

DOI: 10.4324/9781003334231-28

cases, this may not be possible due to parents' inability to focus on what is best for their child. Suppose parents attempt to triangulate the therapist and inject their conflict into the child's therapy. In that case, it may be necessary to reduce the amount of contact with parents to minimal updates and opportunities to answer questions about the child's therapy progress. Supporting children through their parents' high-conflict divorce often calls for the therapist to create an oasis in the playroom for the child to have a break from the ongoing high levels of tension, fighting, and conflict at home (Wonders, 2019). That oasis will typically mean avoiding having parents present in the therapy room.

It is of utmost importance that the parents be invited and encouraged to see the value in bringing the child to therapy without interruption to the regularly scheduled sessions so that the child can have a chance to work through all the mixed emotions and stress children of divorce commonly experience. The parents will likely need ongoing reminders that the focus of therapy is what the child needs rather than their conflict with one another.

GOALS

Typically, goals for a child whose parents are experiencing a high-conflict divorce will be focused on:

1) The child's developed clarity and ability to identify their own thoughts and feelings separate from the thoughts and feelings of their parents.

2) The child's ability to feel safe, knowing there are safe people and safe places with which to connect outside of the high conflict of their home life.

3) The child's ability to experience nervous system regulation in session and then to achieve self-regulation success outside of session using soothing skills.

4) The child's development of respectful assertiveness skills about their rights as a child of divorce. The latter goal will be rooted in a psychoeducation intervention the therapist will implement with the parents first and later with the child (Wonders, 2019, pp. 80–82):

OBJECTIVES

Objectives are established to measure progress toward the goals set for therapy.
Examples:

Objective 1: Child client will successfully identify and sort parents' vs. child's thoughts using the *Thought Sorting Buckets* intervention by the tenth week of therapy.

Objective 2: Child client will indicate four "safe people and places" through a sandtray intervention by the twelfth week of therapy.

Objective 3: Child will demonstrate a ready ability to practice soothing skills with therapist in session by the sixth week in therapy and will report the use of a self-soothing kit outside of session by eighth week in therapy.

Objective 4: Child will comfortably refer to the child's bill of rights when parents are divorcing and report in therapy two opportunities to practice what the child had with parents outside of therapy by the fifteenth week in therapy.

INTERVENTIONS

In the beginning of therapy with a child whose parents are embroiled in high levels of conflict, it is often advisable for the clinician to remain child centered to establish a therapeutic environment that is more relaxed and permissive, allowing the child to explore and express whatever it is they need in their own time. A child-centered approach can provide the child with an opportunity to experience the therapist as one adult in their life who is solely focused on them, their feelings, and their expressions with great attention, as this is often missing from the child's lived experience when parents are having high levels of conflict and the family is going through such a stressful time. As the child becomes more comfortable with the therapist in the playroom, the therapist can shift to more facilitative interventions that may support the goals of therapy listed above. One intervention that can be implemented with the parents and the child is the Child's Bill of Rights When There is a Divorce (Wonders, 2019). This can help guide the parents' behavioral choices and support the child in differentiating their own thoughts and feelings from those of their parents' while offering the child an opportunity to be empowered to express with respect what they need from their parents (Wonders, 2019).

As a child of divorced or divorcing parents, you have a right to. . .

1. Love both of your parents and be loved by both of your parents without feeling guilty. Your parents should both encourage you to love the other parent.
2. Be protected from your parents' anger with each other. Your parents may have a hard time getting along with each other, but that is not your problem to fix. You should not have to hear your parents fighting.
3. Be kept out of the middle of your parents' conflict. You should not be made to feel you need to pick sides, be a messenger for either of your parents or hear your parents complain about the other parent.
4. Never be asked to keep secrets from either of your parents. It's not right for a kid to be asked by a parent to keep a secret from the other parent.
5. Never to feel you have to choose one of your parents over the other. There is plenty of love to go all the way around!
6. Not feel responsible for either of your parents' feelings. They are grown-ups, and you're a kid! They need help and support from other grown-ups, not from you. It is not your job to take care of either of your parents.
7. Know well in advance about important changes that will affect your life; for example, when one of your parents is going to move or remarry. These big changes should never be a sudden surprise to you.
8. Reasonable financial support during your childhood and through your college years.
9. Feel your feelings, to express your feelings, and to have both parents listen to how you feel with respect for your feelings.
10. Be a kid. You are not an adult and should not be involved in adult issues (pp. 79–81).

DOCUMENTATION

As part of the treatment planning process, the therapist will maintain a thorough yet concise clinical record that documents all communications with parents, the goals, objectives, interventions, and progress in therapy. There is a delicate balance that is especially important when working with a child whose parents are involved in a high level of conflict. One reason is that either parent could request the record at any time, and the information in the record should not lead to a parent turning their anger toward the child. Additionally, high-conflict cases are most often involved with court litigation. The clinician should consider that anything said or written in the record will possibly be subpoenaed and, therefore, should contain accurate but sterile clinical language void of any hint of editorial opinion so as not to lend to the interpretation of bias toward either parent and to avoid causing harm to the child (Wonders, 2019). When documenting encounters with caregivers, the clinician must report only the facts and avoid any language that might result in an inflammatory response should parents read the record or an attorney interpret the language for the court to be weaponized.

Example

Language to avoid: *When Father and client arrived for therapy, Father forcefully entered the playroom. Father was irate with the therapist upon being requested to wait in the waiting room per policy so the child could have his therapy time, and Father violently slammed the playroom door upon exiting, alarming the child and knocking all of the toys off of the shelf.*

More Advisable Alternative Language: *Therapist greeted Father and child. Father entered the therapy room, asserting the need to speak with therapist alone. The therapist provided a reminder of the policy regarding parents scheduling parent consultation time separate from the child's therapy time and ensured Father he would be contacted after the session. Father appeared to experience an emotionally dysregulated response upon exiting the playroom.*

TERMINATION OF THERAPY

Due to the volatile nature of dynamics and emotionally driven decisions parents embroiled in high conflict often make, there is a high risk a child will be prematurely removed from therapy by an angry parent. For this reason, the therapist needs to set a policy from the beginning that at least one closure session will be required if the parents should decide to end the child's therapy prematurely. Additionally, the therapist will want to begin talking with the child about the end of therapy from the very beginning by adding an element of uncertainty about how many times the child will be able to come to the playroom so that the risk of a child feeling abandoned by the therapist should the parents suddenly stop bringing the child. Preparing for the end of therapy can begin in the first session with the child and every session after by giving the child an object to add to a collection of reminders of what they are gaining from therapy, such as a string and a clothespin after each session that holds a small piece of paper on which the child writes something they enjoyed or learned in session or a picture they draw during the session. The child can hang the string of clothes pins and papers in a closet or their bedroom or keep them in a box under their bed. The same can be done with smooth stones on which words of encouragement can be written or painted and taken home. This way, in case there is the premature termination of therapy, the child will have tangible reminders of their positive experiences in therapy.

CONCLUSION

When children witness their parents' high-conflict divorce, the process of conceptualizing what the child is experiencing and determining how to plan for the child's therapy requires consideration. Given the proclivity of emotional dysregulation parents frequently experience and the common occurrence of personality pathology in parents with intractable dynamics, the therapist needs to preserve the integrity of the child's therapeutic experience. Where in other cases, the parents' involvement in therapy is considered critically important; in these kinds of cases unguarded parent involvement can interfere with the therapist's ability to provide what the child most needs. Firm parameters should be established with clear policies and protocols from the first encounter with parents. The therapy is often the place of respite from the ongoing conflict and tension at home. Treatment planning with high-conflict divorce cases requires strategic, sensitive steps for creating a predictable structure that doesn't leave room for the otherwise inevitable spill-over of angry emotions parents frequently feel and express.

Key Takeaways

- ✡ When children's parents are embroiled in high conflict divorce, the therapist's case conceptualization and process of planning for therapy involves special consideration.
- ✡ High conflict divorce has been shown to contribute to a high risk of trauma in children.
- ✡ With high conflict divorce, it is advisable to structure the therapeutic process and the relationships with parents and the child to avoid having the parents' conflict pollute the therapeutic process.
- ✡ The therapist will need to establish their role of therapist there to support the child, not an evaluator of custody nor a mediator for the parents' conflict.
- ✡ The therapist needs to make clear that a non-biased position will be observed with both parents.
- ✡ Supporting children through their parents' high conflict divorce often calls for the therapist to create an oasis in the playroom.
- ✡ Typically, goals for a child whose parents are experiencing a high conflict divorce will be focused on helping the child to differentiate their own feelings/thoughts from those of their parents, experience emotional safety, nervous system regulation, and respectful assertiveness skills.

REFERENCES

Greenham, M. B., & Childress, C. A. (2022). *Dark personalities and induced delusional disorder, Part I: The research gap underlying a crisis in the family and domestic violence courts*. Author.

O'Hara, K. L., Sandler, I. N., Wolchik, S. A., & Tein, J. Y. (2019). Coping in context: The effects of long-term relations between interparental conflict and coping on the development of child psychopathology following parental divorce. *Development and Psychopathology, 31*(5), 1695–1713. https://doi.org/10.1017/s0954579419000981

Van der Wal, R. C., Finkenauer, C., & Visser, M. M. Reconciling mixed findings on children's adjustment following high-conflict divorce. *J Child Fam Stud, 28*, 468–478 (2019). https://doi.org/10.1007/s10826-018-1277-z

CHAPTER 26

TREATMENT PLANNING WITH LGBTQ+ (SOGIE) YOUTH AND FAMILIES

Kurt W. Oster

INTRODUCTION

As clinicians and practitioners of mental health and the healing arts specializing in working with children and families, treatment planning becomes a vital part of the therapeutic relationship, service delivery, and treatment process. In clinical practice, and based on the families' beliefs, sometimes mental health can be a taboo subject to address, speak about, or to seek help with. Furthermore, for lesbian, gay, bisexual, transgender, questioning, queer, intersexual, and asexual plus (LGBTQ+) youth *coming out* may be a fearful experience due to family values, beliefs, and cultural values. As such, there are continually growing concerns and challenges presented by politicians and groups arguing that gender-affirming and LGBTQ+-affirming care are not evidence-based or are "dangerous." This rhetoric poses significant challenges for mental health professionals when developing treatment plans.

To effectively treat our clients, we must look to evidence-based research as the governing principle of best practice. The field of practice with LGBTQ+ clients is both a new field and an old field. In contrast, matters of LGBTQ+ have been discussed in the overall academic body of scholarly literature and still need to be expanded. At the core of the research is a focus on the power of family as the primary focus on reducing risk factors and promoting the client's overall well-being. Meyer and Sikk (2016) explain the study of LGBTQ+ history that focuses on the struggles and strengths of cultural, social, and national narratives of a group considered to be nonnormative. An effectively written and developed treatment plan can help drive effective service delivery that is informed by evidence-based practice, provides linkage to resources, and lays out the treatment modalities to be best utilized.

As such, treatment planning for individuals who identify as members of the LGBTQ+ community, while rooted in best practices, should include and focus on critical aspects of the new and expansive approach of sexual orientation, gender identity, and expression (SOGIE). In addition, it is clinically relevant to note that an individual or family being part of the LGBTQ/ SOGIE community does not constitute a medical concern, and their SOGIE identity should not be medically pathologized during treatment. All-in-all, treatment planning for members of the SOGIE community should support the exploration of helping the client understand who they are and focus on developing the sense of "self."

THE DEVELOPMENT OF A NEW LANGUAGE: DEFINING SOGIE

To effectively and competently work with youth who identify with the LGBTQ+ Community, Johnson (2019) explains that proper terminology and clear and accessible language

DOI: 10.4324/9781003334231-29

becomes critical in building trust among individuals, families, and communities. When practitioners work to develop effective treatment plans to support LGBTQ+ youth, several vital aspects shall be considered. As per Johnson (2019), the term SOGIE is used broadly to describe all people by their overall sexual orientation, gender identity, and expression. According to American Psychological Association. (2012), the APA in 1975 adopted a resolution stating that,

> "Homosexuality per se implies no impairment in judgment, stability, reliability, or general social or vocational capabilities" and urging "all mental health professionals to take the lead in removing the stigma of mental illness that has long been associated with homosexual orientations."

Furthermore, the acronym and term SOGIE, Johnson (2019) explains, is utilized by the United Nations, which they created to honor the fluidity of the expanding identities of the LGBTQ+ community. Most recently, two National Association of Social Work (NASW) state chapters, including New York and Texas, have adopted the term in the names of the committee representing the LGBTQ+ community. Overall, one of the most pivotal aspects of treatment planning is the effective use of guiding clients through identifying their sexual orientation, gender identity, and/or expression.

MOVING TOWARD INTERSECTIONALITY AND INCLUSION

The idea around the original pathologizing of LGBTQ+ as a mental health disorder was captured by Russell and Fish (2016), who explained that before the 1970s, society saw that the DSM listed "homosexuality" as a "sociopathic personality disturbance." The Substance Abuse and Mental Health Services Administration (Abuse, 2015) noted that being a sexual or gender minority LGBTQ does not constitute a mental disorder; however, being associated with this minority has increased psychosocial issues and distress. Furthermore, the National Association of Social Work (2019) National Committee on Lesbian Gay, Bisexual, and Transgender Issues calls for removing other diagnoses tied to pathologizing LGBTQ+ as a mental health disorder noting these diagnoses to be harmful, misguiding, and stigmatizing. These disorders included Gender Identity Disorder, Gender Incongruence, Gender Dysphoria, Transvestic Fetishism, and Transvestic Disorder. (NASW, 2019). As mental health professionals, we must move away from this pathologizing of LGBTQ+ and become inclusive. Therefore, inclusiveness and the focus on the Crenshaw's Intersectionality model should be reflected in treatment planning (Crenshaw, 2017).

What mental health challenges do individuals and families of the SOGIE community face? As such, it is clinically relevant to note that Case Western Reserve University (2020) explain that *coming out* is a lifelong process, and that the journey occurs in many different ways and can affect individuals' mental health. Furthermore, Case Western Reserve University (2020) notes that coming out and living an open life are things you do not do once but multiple times over your lifetime. Canady (2022) argues that SOGIE youth are at high risk of mental health problems and suicide if they do not have the experience of coming out and owning their identity. Case Western Reserve University (2020) expands upon this, noting that coming out is a constant internal and external process met with pain, misunderstanding, and hardship. Therefore, when practitioners work with youth and families to develop treatment plans, the plans should focus on treating mental health issues, not orientation, identity, or expression.

Effective treatment planning becomes vital for several reasons. Research points to multiple risk factors affecting the SOGIE community's youth and their families. According to Project (2022), concerns for SOGIE youth include increased suicide ideation and attempts, anxiety, depression, and a lack of access to effective or fear of accessing mental health care. Furthermore, it becomes relevant to understand that ten critical areas are identified that influence these factors as the reasons for the lack of or fear of access to services among SOGIE youth.

Project (2022) explains these ten areas to include (1) fear of discussing mental health concerns; (2) concerns with obtaining parent/caregiver permission; (3) fear of not being taken seriously; (4) lack of affordability; (5) fear of care not working; (6) fear of being outed; (7) fear of their identity being misunderstood; (8) concerns with receiving virtual care at home; (9) lack of transportation options; and (10) Lack of parent/caregiver permission. Therefore, for mental health professionals and practitioners, when developing treatment plans for SOGIE youth, it becomes critical to understand what research points to as concerns and best practices. In the case of SOGIE youth, it becomes apparent that issues around self-worth, fear, lack of understanding or access to services, and a fear of not being believed or taken seriously are the overarching concerns influencing mental health treatment.

TREATMENT PLANNING TO PROMOTE THE AUTHENTIC SELF

As mental health professionals and practitioners, several factors must be considered when we develop treatment plans. The first of these will focus on the promotion and development of the authentic self. For youth, the struggle comes from discovering who they are. One robust method in this process is utilizing various tools such as the "Sexualitree" (Rayne and Killerman, n.d.), "Gender Bread Person" (Killerman, 2017), or the "Gender Unicorn" (Trans Student Educational Resource, 2015). Tools such as these help practitioners to be effective in helping SOGIE youth and families see the ways and experiences individuals may have around their sexuality, identity, and expression. Another factor that treatment plan practitioners should consider is the effective and proper use of language, preferred names, and pronouns. For example, Conover et al. (2021) note that we may look at a person and, based on appearance, may not know how they identify, and the authors go on to explain that pronouns help individuals feel seen and affirmed. In contrast, the improper use of pronouns can cause someone to be "misgendered or mispronounced," causing the individual to feel not seen, disrespected, or dysphoric (Conover et al., 2021).

Throughout, the literature remains focused on treating children and youth with respect and allowing them the right to have access to physical and emotional safety, quality care, and access to available and necessary resources. In the process of treatment planning with SOGIE youth, practitioners should work with individuals and families to address underlying and current traumas and promote safety, well-being, and acceptance. (Abuse, 2015). Serving SOGIE youth and their families and developing their treatment plans is like working with any other client. While the treatment planning process does not change, practitioners in mental health and the healing arts should adopt two critical models of practice to serve clients effectively.

MODELS OF PRACTICE IN TREATMENT PLANNING

Although various approaches exist in the treatment planning process for work with SOGIE youth and their families, practitioners should be familiar with the Gay Affirmative Practice (GAP) model (Crisp and McCave, 2007) and the American Psychological Association's 21 best-practice guidelines (2012) that govern how psychologists and other mental health professionals should practice as it relates to lesbian, gay, transexual and bisexual clients. For treatment planning to be effective, the GAP model promotes three main domains when working with clients of the SOGIE community. The first domain of the GAP model explores the person (client) in the environment and the context, which intersects various other environments. Second, the model, through the foundations of the social work practice, looks at the strengths perspective of self-determination of clients, a focus on health, rather than pathology, of the SOGIE identity, and consciousness-raising. The GAP model examines cultural competency in knowledge, attitudes, and skills (Crisp and McCave, 2007).

While the GAP model is one approach to effective treatment planning, a second approach is focused on the American Psychological Association's (2012) 21 guidelines broken into six key areas when working with LGBTQ clients. Not only do the guidelines provide a foundation to practice, but they also support the work of Crisp and McCave (2007). For practitioners to see successful therapy outcomes with SOGIE individuals and families, practitioners should build their cultural competency understanding of (1) attitudes towards homosexuality and bisexuality, SOGIE relationships and families; (2) issues of diversity for the SOGIE community; (3) economics and workplace issues within the SOGIE community; (4) education and training for professionals and, (5) continued research in the field.

CONCLUSION

All-in-all, treatment planning for SOGIE youth and families, while not different from the traditional process of treatment planning, becomes focused on the practitioner understanding what it is to observe affirming practice. The treatment planning process should and must focus on helping each SOGIE youth find their authentic self while working with families to develop understanding, promote an affirming environment, and allow for the growth of all parties. If done correctly, affirmative treatment planning can transform the lives of SOGIE individuals, including bringing them happiness, allowing them to feel a connection to the community, helping them learn about support, promoting self-love, building a positive growth mindset, and developing resilience. It becomes crucial to remember that conversion therapy and praying the gay away are not the answer to mental health services for SOGIE clients. Overall, the goal of a robust, transformative treatment plan that embraces who a SOGIE individual or family is should focus on building resilience, meeting individuals where they are, and building allyship within the family structure.

Key Takeaways

- ♀ For LGBTQ+ (SOGIE) youth coming out may be a fearful experience due to family values, beliefs, and cultural values. Coming out is a lifelong process, and the journey occurs in many different ways and can affect individuals' mental health.
- ♀ There is a new and expanding perspective called SOGIE which stands for sexual orientation, gender identity, and expression.
- ♀ Concerns for SOGIE youth include increased suicide ideation and attempts, anxiety, depression, and a lack of access to effective or fear of accessing mental health care.
- ♀ An effectively written and developed treatment plan can help drive effective service delivery that is informed by evidence-based practice, provides linkage to resources, and lays out the treatment modalities to be best utilized.
- ♀ Being part of the LGBTQ/ SOGIE community does not constitute a medical concern, and their SOGIE identity should not be medically pathologized during treatment.
- ♀ Therapists should be familiar with the Gay Affirmative Practice (GAP) model and the APA 21 best-practice guidelines that govern how psychologists and other mental health professionals should practice as it relates to LGBTQ+/SOGIE youth.

REFERENCES

Abuse, S. (2015). Mental health services administration, ending conversion therapy. Supporting and affirming LGBTQ youth. HHS publication no.(SMA) 15-4928. Substance Abuse and Mental Health Services Administration.

American Psychological Association. (2012). Guidelines for psychological practice with lesbian, gay and bisexual clients. *American Psychologist, 67*(1), 10–42 DOI:10.1037/a0024659

Canady, V. A. (2022). Trevor Project explores MH of multiracial LGBTQ youth. *Mental Health Weekly, 32*(33), 7–8. https://doi.org/10.1002/mhw.33346

Case Western Reserve University. (2020). "Coming out." Lesbian gay bisexual transgender center. Retrieved from https://case.edu/lgbt/workshops-and-training/safe-zone/coming-out

Conover, K. J., Matsuno, E., & Bettergarcia, J. (2021). Pronoun fact sheet [Fact sheet]. American Psychological Association, Division 44: The Society for the Psychology of Sexual Orientation and Gender Diversity. Retrieved from https://www.apadivisions.org/division-44/resources/pronouns-fact-sheet.pdf

Crenshaw, K. W. (2017). *On intersectionality: Essential writings.* The New Press.

Crisp, C., & McCave, E. L. (2007). Gay affirmative practice: A model for social work practice with gay, lesbian, and bisexual youth. *Child Adolescence Social Work Journal, 24,* 403–421 DOI:10.1007/s10560-007-0091-z

Johnson, K. (2019). SOGIE handbook. Sexual orientation, gender identity, and expression affirming approach and expansive practices. Health Research, Inc. Retrieved from https://onecirclefoundation.org/media/pdfs/SOGIE_Handbook.pdf

Killerman, S. (2017). The genderbread person. Retrieved from https://www.itspronoucedmetrosexual.org/genderbread-person/#usage

Meyer, L., & Sikk, H. (2016). Introduction to lesbian, gay, bisexual, transgender, and queer history (L.G.B.T.Q. history) in the United States. In M. E. Springgate (Ed.), *L.G.B.T.Q. America. A theme study of lesbian, gay, bisexual, transgender and queer history.* National Park Foundation. Retrieved from www.nps.gov/subjects/tellingallamericansstories/lgbtqthemestudy.htm

National Association of Social Workers. (2019). Gender identity disorder and the D.S.M. *National Association of Social Workers National Committee on Lesbian, Gay, Bisexual, and Transgender Issues (N.C.L.B.T.I.) Policy Statement.* Retrieved from https://www.socialworkers.org/Practice/LGBT/Gender-Identity-Disorder-and-the-DSM

Rayne, K., & Killerman, S. (n.d.). The sexualitree. Retrieved from www.sexualitree.org

Russell, S. T., & Fish, J. N. (2016). Mental health in lesbian, gay, bisexual, and transgender (L.G.B.T.) youth. *The Annual Review of Clinical Psychology*. 10.1146/annurev-clin-psy-021815-093153 https://doi.org/10.1146/annurev-clinpsy-021815-093153

Trans Student Educational Resources. (2015). The gender unicorn. Retrieved from http://www.transstudents.org/gender

RACE-BASED ASSESSMENT, DIAGNOSIS, AND TREATMENT PLANNING WITH BLACK CHILDREN AND FAMILIES

April Duncan

INTRODUCTION

Black children and adults experience high levels of race-based stress that directly impact their moods and behaviors, otherwise known as racial trauma. Racial trauma occurs when individuals experience daily interactions with racism, prejudice, and discrimination that contribute to symptoms mimicking posttraumatic stress disorder (PTSD) (Henderson et al., 2019). However, many clinicians overlook these stressors in their clinical assessment of Black children, which may result in incorrect diagnoses. Differential diagnosis can be difficult, as trauma often presents as anxiety, depression, and defiance. And because the behavior of Black children often does not fit the Eurocentric models of behavior, it places them at a higher risk for misdiagnosis and ineffective treatment. If practitioners are not using a racial trauma lens when they are assessing the behaviors of Black children, they are inadvertently causing harm and could be contributing to negative short- and long-term mental health outcomes.

Studies have found untreated racial trauma in Black children is correlated with an increased risk for anxiety, depression, PTSD, and suicide (Arshanapally et al., 2018; Assari et al., 2017; Pachter et al., 2018; Polanco-Roman et al., 2019; Walker et al., 2016). However, the lack of a racial trauma lens may lead to ineffective treatment that fails to address the root issue of the ongoing racial stress and trauma Black children experience throughout their lifetime. Therefore, it is imperative that mental health professionals develop this lens when treating Black children, including culturally appropriate screening tools, understanding important cultural factors, collaborations with caregivers, and prioritizing the therapeutic relationship.

ASSESSMENT WITH BLACK CHILDREN AND FAMILIES

To develop this lens, clinicians should employ an ecosystemic framework by considering all the environmental factors in the lives of Black children, especially race-based stressors. However, the most important thing is establishing a trusting, non-judgmental, and supportive relationship with Black children and their caregivers, which will require patience and empathy. Professionals should also develop an awareness of the signs of racial trauma, which include avoidance, hypervigilance, distress, intrusive thoughts, anxiety, and/or depression (Villiness, 2020). Additionally, clinicians should utilize race-based clinical assessments and observe play themes if using play therapy.

DOI: 10.4324/9781003334231-30

Table 27.1 Play Themes Associated with Racial Trauma

Play Theme	Description	Interpretation
Greif	Shown when the child has scenes of death or dying in their play	May be associated with a grief/bereavement event such as being involved in the child welfare system
Connection	Shown when a child is constantly seeking the attention of the therapist. They may say things like "watch this" or "look"	The child may be seeking a connection and/or stronger attachments
Self-esteem	Shown when the child is something they have accomplished in session	This may be a sign of low self-esteem/confidence in the child
Aggression	Shown when a child is engaging in a form or aggressive play like toy swords or toy guns	The child may be dealing with feelings of anger and/or frustration in dealing with racial stressors
Independent Play	Shown when a child plays independently and does not invite the therapist into the play	The child may not trust the therapist or may not feel comfortable in the therapeutic relationship yet
Fear	Shown when a child is afraid or avoids certain toys or areas of the playroom	May be the child's trauma response to racial stressor(s)
Anger	Shown when a child communicates anger themselves or between two characters in a role play	May be the child's emotional response to their racial stressor(s)
Mistrust	Shown when a child doesn't feel comfortable telling the therapist something	The child may not feel comfortable with the therapist, possible due to racial mistrust
Protection & Safety	Shown when a child uses toys to protect themselves or keep the therapist away (e.g. handcuffs)	May be the child's coping response to their racial stressor(s)
Chaos	Shown when the child creates a "mess" in the playroom	Can be the child's way of communicating the internal chaos they feel because of the racial stressor(s)

Clinical assessments that screen for race-based experiences should be included in intake paperwork. For example, the Philadelphia ACE Survey (Philadelphia ACE Project, 2021) and the Race-Related Events Scale (Waelde et al., 2010) gathers background information on racial trauma exposure in children. Assessments like the Race-Based Traumatic Symptom Scale (Carter et al., 2013) and the Trauma Symptoms of Discrimination Scale (Williams et al., 2018) can be used pre-and post-treatment to screen for the child's specific presentation (e.g., avoidance). Clinicians should also consider using play therapy as both a rapport-building and assessment tool when considering mental health diagnoses in Black children. This non-threatening approach allows children to express and explore their life situations at a pace that is comfortable for them, which is key when dealing with racial mistrust (Duncan, 2023). Additionally, play themes associated with racial trauma should be considered when conceptualizing the client's presenting issues. Play themes are descriptions of a child's play in play therapy sessions that communicate their emotions and/or needs (Ryan & Edge, 2012). This information, along with information collected from collateral contacts and the clients, can help paint the clearest picture to develop the most effective treatment goals.

Case Conceptualization

Black children are exposed to racial trauma as the result of living in a country where systemic and institutional racism results in higher rates of exclusionary discipline in school, more interactions with law enforcement, higher rates of juvenile incarceration, and disparities in the child-welfare system (Dunbar & Barth, 2007; Office for Civil Rights, 2021; Rovner, 2016). The racial stressors Black children experience should be considered when assessing for mental health conditions like major depressive disorder and generalized anxiety disorder. Studies have found that Black children experience an average of five acts of discrimination a day (English et al., 2020). In schools, Black students are three times more likely to be suspended and expelled, with disparities appearing early as Black preschoolers account for 44% of children with more than one out-of-school suspension (Office for Civil Rights, 2020). There is a direct correlation between exclusionary discipline and the juvenile system, with reports finding that children who are suspended or expelled are three times more likely to encounter the juvenile justice system the following year (Fabelo et al., 2011).

Another systemic factor to consider when working with Black children and families is their family composition. Approximately 30% of Black children have a family member who is currently or previously incarcerated (Ghandnoosh et al., 2021) and they also make up almost a quarter of the children in the child-welfare system (Child Welfare Information Gateway, 2021). This increases the likelihood that a clinician will be working with a child with an incarcerated caregiver and/or involved in the child-welfare system, which means their family and home environment may not look like the "traditional" model of families. This could also mean coordinating with a case worker or a family member/foster parent if the client is involved in the child-welfare system. Another factor to consider is community violence, as homicide is the leading cause of death for Black youth ages 15–24 (Merrick et al., 2019). All three of these stressors may trigger grief reactions that resemble depressive or anxious symptoms. This makes it even more important to screen for background information to provide additional context to the child's presenting problem.

Other things clinicians should assess for are the client's attitude towards themselves, anxiety and patterns of defense, sexual orientation, gender identity, immigration and level of acculturation (if the client is not born in America), family structure, attitudes about mental health, help-seeking behavioral patterns, racial/ethnic composition of the child's school, feelings towards teachers and staff, and any effects regarding current societal issues (i.e., racial protests) (Ho, 1992). It is important to remember that Black children and their caregivers may not feel comfortable answering certain questions in the intake appointment, so clinicians should give clients the option to skip questions they are uncomfortable answering and revisit them later in treatment once a therapeutic relationship has been established.

TREATMENT PLANNING WITH BLACK CHILDREN

Treatment goals for Black children will vary, but there are some central goals to address racial stress. Goals may focus on learning coping skills to manage stressors or anger management skills to manage feelings of anger and frustration. For Black children who have incarcerated family members and/or are involved in the child-welfare system, goals may be grief-related while also focusing on building healthy attachments in the absence of important caregivers. Black LGBTQ+ youth, who are at increased risk for bullying and suicide (Duncan, 2023), may have goals that focus on community resources to develop a healthy support system and manage any depressive and/or suicidal thoughts. Lastly, most Black children could benefit from goals that are centered on building self-esteem and empowerment, as they may deal with feelings of inferiority because of their race-based experiences.

Table 27.2 Treatment Goals for Racial Trauma

Goal focus	Goal #1	Goal #2
Anger	**Goal:** The child will decrease feelings of anger **Intervention:** The therapist will use an anger thermometer to assess the client's level of anger	**Goal:** The child will redirect anger to more appropriate outlets **Intervention:** The child will use a punching bag to externalize feelings of anger
Hypervigilance	**Goal:** The child will decrease hypervigilance towards police officers **Intervention:** The therapist will use exposure therapy to address hypervigilance	**Goal:** The child will have an increased sense of safety **Intervention:** The therapist will use sand tray therapy to help the client identity safe people
Grief	**Goal:** The child will grieve their lost in a healthy way **Intervention:** The child will participate in art therapy to create a memory of their loved one	**Goal:** The child will express their emotions around their loss **Intervention:** The child will participate in art activities to express feelings of grief
Anxiety	**Goal:** The child will verbalize a decrease in anxiety symptoms in relation to their identified stressor **Intervention:** The therapist will use clinical scales to monitor symptoms	**Goal:** The child will decrease negative thoughts around the identified stressor **Intervention:** The child will keep an anxiety log to track negative thoughts
Depression	**Goal:** The child will return to their normal level of activity prior to the stressor **Intervention:** The therapist will use CBT to identify the source of the client's depression	**Goal:** The child will decrease suicidal thoughts **Intervention:** The child will use participate in play therapy to learn healthy coping skills

TRACKING CLINICAL PROGRESS

There are several indicators of clinical progress in Black children and adolescents. First, if using play themes, there will be a change in duration and intensity in that specific theme. For example, if the child displays the grief theme during their sessions, the therapist will look for the frequency of that play to decrease. Another way to track progress in Black children is seeing an increase in disclosure and communication in sessions, which may signal a higher level of trust and an established therapeutic relationship. If using clinical assessments, caregivers (and the child, if possible) should complete the assessments prior to reviewing and changing treatment goals. The clinician will look for a decrease in the scores from the original screening, along with self-reports of improved behavior and well-being from the child and the adults in their lives.

The use of scaling questions will also be useful when assessing treatment progress. For example, the clinician may ask, "How would you rate your sadness before we started together? How would you rate your sadness now?" This can be equally impactful for caregivers who may struggle to see the improvement because the behavior is still present. Verbally rating behaviors pre-treatment versus where they are at the time of the discussion may also help the caregiver buy into the work being done by the therapist, which may strengthen the therapeutic relationship.

COLLABORATING WITH CAREGIVERS OF BLACK CHILDREN

The racial trauma lens should also extend to the caregivers of Black children. Personal and historical experiences with racial trauma may lead to a level of mistrust that may take Black children and the adults in their lives longer to develop a trusting relationship with their clinician. Black children are often told not to share information outside the home. To treat the child most effectively, clinicians will need their trust, which often comes from the approval of the caregivers. Therefore, clinicians should also make a concerted effort to develop trusting relationships with the child's caregivers. This can be achieved through parent consultations that can be held throughout the child's treatment, where both the clinician and caregivers can check on the child's progress and address any additional concerns. Clinicians may also use that time to provide psychoeducation to the caregivers on racial trauma and parenting tips to help their child manage racial stressors. If possible, the clinician should also consider family therapy, as the stressors experienced by the child may also be experienced by the family system. Additionally, consideration should be made regarding the family composition assessed in intake and any limitations in the caregiver's ability to participate in services (e.g., supervised visits).

TERMINATION WITH BLACK CHILDREN AND FAMILIES

Unfortunately, it is inevitable that Black children will continue to be exposed to racial stressors during and after treatment. Essentially, the goal is to help Black children function within dysfunctional systems and environments. Therefore, the long-term treatment goals are often more focused on helping Black children develop more effective coping skills to manage these stressors so they do not impede their mental health or disrupt their daily functioning. Successful termination will include goal attainment and a decrease in any trauma-related symptoms. Clinicians may also consider "once a client, always a client" by allowing clients who have ended treatment to return when needed without having to go on a waitlist. It will also be important to normalize their need to return to treatment if there are new or more intense stressors that arise. Another factor to consider is case management after termination, like referrals to group therapy, community resources for additional support, and even encouraging clients to become involved in social advocacy as a means of empowerment.

CONCLUSION

Mental health professionals are ethically bound to "do no harm". However, Black children are harmed when professionals neglect the parts of their stories they are afraid or ashamed to explore. Helping professionals must utilize a racial trauma lens when working with Black children and families to provide the most accurate diagnosis possible. In doing so, they can create more effective, trauma-informed courses of treatment that can adequately address the roots of the issues rather than placing a band-aid over their symptoms. As a result, clinicians may be better positioned to help empower Black children and caregivers to support their mental health needs in a world that will continually trigger them. That will include constant self-reflection to recognize and address any biases that may be present in clinical work with Black children and families. It includes looking in a mirror and taking accountability for anything that may be unintentionally contributing to the problem as opposed to the solution. It is to be human in recognizing faults, but exhibiting compassion in a way that allows professionals to take off their blinders and truly see the realities of Black children, then give voice to those realities by honoring how their circumstances may be impeding their functioning. That is what it truly means to be a helping professional.

Key Takeaways

- ♀ Racial trauma occurs when individuals experience daily interactions with racism, prejudice, and discrimination that contribute to symptoms mimicking posttraumatic stress disorder (PTSD).
- ♀ Because the behavior of Black children often does not fit the Eurocentric models of behavior, it places them at a higher risk for misdiagnosis and ineffective treatment.
- ♀ Therapists must use a racial trauma lens when assessing the behaviors of Black children, or they can inadvertently cause harm and contribute to negative short- and long-term mental health outcomes.
- ♀ Signs of racial trauma include avoidance, hypervigilance, distress, intrusive thoughts, anxiety and/or depression.
- ♀ Clinical assessments that screen for race-based experiences should be included in intake paperwork.
- ♀ It is important to remember Black children and their caregivers may not feel comfortable answering certain questions in the intake appointment and should be given the option to skip questions and revisit them later in treatment once a therapeutic relationship has been established.
- ♀ The racial trauma lens should also extend to the caregivers of Black children. Personal and historic experiences with racial trauma may lead to a level of mistrust that may take Black children and the adults in their lives longer to develop a trusting relationship with their clinician.

REFERENCES

Arshanapally, S., Werner, K., Sartor, C., & Bucholz, K. (2018). The association between racial discrimination and suicidality among African-American adolescents and young adults. *Archives of Suicide Research, 22*(4), 584–595. https://doi-org.libproxy1.usc.edu/10.1080/13811118.2017.1387207

Assari, S., Moazen-Zadeh, E., Caldwell, C., & Zimmerman, M. (2017). Racial discrimination during adolescence predicts mental health deterioration in adulthood: Gender differences among Blacks. *Frontiers in Public Health, 5,* 104. https://doi.org/10.3389/fpubh.2017.00104

Carter, R. T., Mazzula, S., Victoria, R., Vazquez, R., Hall, S., Smith, S., Sant-Barket, S., Forsyth, J., Bazelais, K., & Williams, B. (2013). *Race-based traumatic stress symptom scale (RBTSS)* [Database record]. PsycTESTS. https://dx.doi.org/10.1037/t19426-000

Child Welfare Information Gateway. (2021). Child welfare practice to address race disproportionality and disparity. https://www.childwelfare.gov/pubpdfs/racial_disproportionality.pdf

Duncan, A. (2023). *Black students matter: Play therapy to support Black students experiencing racial trauma.* Oxford Publishing.

Dunbar, K., & Barth, R.P. (2007). *Racial disproportionality, race disparity and other race-related finding in published works derived from the National Survey of Child and Adolescent Well-being.* Casey-CSSP Alliance for Racial Equity in Child Welfare. https://assets.aecf.org/m/resourcedoc/aecf-CFP-RacialDisproportionalityRaceDisparityAndOtherRaceRelatedFindingsInPublishedWorksDerivedFromTheNationalSurveyOfChildAndAdolescentWellBeing-2008.pdf

English, D., Lambert, S., Tynes, B., Bowleg, L., Zea, M., & Howard, L. (2020). Daily multidimensional racial discrimination among Black U.S. American adolescents. *Journal of Applied Developmental Psychology, 66,* 101068. https://doi.org/10.1016/j.appdev.2019.101068

Fabelo, T., Thompson, M. D., Plotkin, M., Carmichael, D., Marchbanks III, M. P. & Booth, E. A. (2011). *Breaking school's rules: A statewide study of how school discipline relates to students' success and juvenile justice involvement.* Council of State Governments Justice Center. https://csgjusticecenter.org/wp-content/uploads/2020/01/Breaking_Schools_Rules_Report_

Ghandnoosh, N., Stammen, E., & Muhitch, K. (2021). *Parents in prison.* The Sentencing Project. https://www.sentencingproject.org/app/uploads/2022/09/Parents-in-Prison.pdf

Henderson, D., Walker, L., Barnes, R., Lunsford, A., Edwards, C., & Clark, C. (2019). A framework for race-related trauma in the public education system and implications on health for Black youth. *Journal of School Health, 89*(11), 926–933. https://doi-org.libproxy1.usc.edu/10.1111/josh.12832

Ho, H. K. (1992). *Minority children and adolescents in therapy.* Sage.

Merrick, M. T., Ford, D. C., Ports, K. A., Guinn, A. S., Chen, J., Klevens, J., ... & Mercy, J. A. (2019). Vital signs: Estimated proportion of adult health problems attributable to adverse childhood experiences and implications for prevention—25 States, 2015–2017. *Morbidity and Mortality Weekly Report, 68*(44), 999.

Office for Civil Rights. (2020). *The use of restraint and seclusion on children with disabilities in k-12 schools.* U.S. Department of Education, 2017-2018 Civil Rights Data Collection (CRDC). https://www2.ed.gov/about/offices/list/ocr/docs/restraint-and-seclusion.pdf

Office for Civil Rights. (2021). *An overview of exclusionary discipline practices in public schools for the 2017–2018 school year.* U.S. Department of Education, 2017–2018 Civil Rights Data Collection (CRDC). https://ocrdata.ed.gov/assets/downloads/crdc-exclusionary-school-discipline.pdf

Pachter, L., Caldwell, C., Jackson, J., & Bernstein, B. (2018). Discrimination and mental health in a representative sample of African-American and Afro-Caribbean Youth. *Journal of Racial and Ethnic Health Disparities, 5*(4), 831–837. https://doi.org/10.1007/s40615-017-0428-z

Philadelphia ACE Project. (2021). Philadelphia ACE survey. https://www.philadelphiaaces.org/philadelphia-ace-survey

Polanco-Roman, L., Anglin, D., Miranda, R., & Jeglic, E. (2019). Racial/ethnic discrimination and suicidal ideation in emerging adults: The role of traumatic stress and depressive symptoms varies by gender, not race/ethnicity. *Journal of Youth and Adolescence, 48*(10), 2023–2037. https://doi.org/10.1007/s10964-019-01097-w

Rovner, J. (2016). *Racial disparities in youth commitments and arrests.* The Sentencing Project. https://www.sentencingproject.org/app/uploads/2022/08/Racial-Disparities-in-Youth-Incarceration-Persist.pdf

Ryan, V., & Edge, A. (2012). The role of play themes in non-directive play therapy. *Clinical child psychology and psychiatry, 17*(3), 354–369. https://doi.org/10.1177/1359104511414265

Villiness, Z. (2020). What to know about racial trauma. *Medical news today.* https://www.medical-newstoday.com/articles/racial-trauma#who-is-affected

Waelde, L., Pennington, D., Mahan, C., Mahan, R., Kabour, M., & Marquett, R. (2010). Psychometric properties of the race-related events scale. *Psychological Trauma, 2*(1), 4–11. https://doi.org/10.1037/a0019018

Walker, R., Francis, D., Brody, G., Simons, R., Cutrona, C., & Gibbons, F. (2016, May 3). A longitudinal study of racial discrimination and risk for death ideation in African American youth. *Suicide and Life-Threatening Behavior, 47*(1), 86–102. https://doi-org.libproxy1.usc.edu/10.1111/sltb.12251

Williams, M. T., Printz, D. M. B., & DeLapp, R. C. T. (2018). Assessing racial trauma with the Trauma Symptoms of Discrimination Scale. *Psychology of Violence, 8*(6), 735–747. https://doi.org/10.1037/vio000021

CHAPTER 28

MINDFULNESS IN TREATMENT PLANNING

Lynn Louise Wonders

INTRODUCTION

The purpose of practicing mindfulness is to increase connection to the present moment, which can easily be missed or overlooked when the brain is consumed by cognitive processes and emotional activity (West, 2016). As therapists, if we miss the present moment when with clients, we are missing vital information.

With the rise of mainstream attention to the practice of mindfulness, there have been significant research studies that have boosted the position that the effects of mindfulness practice have significant benefits for human functioning (Ganesan et al., 2022; Lynn & Basso, 2023; Ong et al., 2014; Quach et al., 2016; Zhou et al., 2023). Mental health professionals can practice mindfulness personally within the therapist's role and incorporate mindfulness-based techniques and skills into the psychotherapy treatment plan with children and their families.

MINDFULNESS PRACTICE

Mindfulness can be defined as the capacity to purposefully attend to an experience in the present moment with full awareness and acceptance. It is a concept found in many established practices such as yoga, breath work, meditation, and stress management programs (Van Dam et al., 2018). While mindfulness has roots in Buddhism, it has become a widely respected and proven secular practice for managing stress, particularly in the past few decades (Kabat-Zinn, 2011). One form of mindfulness practice called Mindfulness-based Stress Reduction (MBSR), first introduced by Jon Kabat-Zinn, includes a focused, mindfulness meditation practice, and this program led to positive changes to the brain, including increased gray matter and improved learning, memory, and emotion regulation (Brown et al., 2015; Hölzel et al., 2011; Lazar et al., 2005; Wonders, 2022). There have been many research studies following the benefits of mindfulness practice in school classrooms, and one such study followed a group of children who practiced a dynamic mindfulness practice in school, with results showing that the children experienced significant reductions in anxiety and depression symptoms (Frank et al., 2016; Wonders, 2022). A study by Skinner and Beers (2016) showed how elementary school teachers and their classes experienced benefits when teachers practiced mindfulness skills, with a greater ability to relate to their students and manage stress, with secondary results of improved learning measures and social connections for the children in those classrooms. Bergen-Cico et al. (2015) found that a group of middle school students who participated in a mindfulness program showed increased self-regulatory skills. Children who participated in mindfulness programs together experienced greater social cohesion (Meyer & Eklund, 2020; Beauchemin et al., 2008). Flook et al. (2010) wrote about a group of elementary school children who experienced improved executive functioning after participating in a mindfulness awareness program.

DOI: 10.4324/9781003334231-31

With so much research demonstrating mindfulness programs in school settings correlating with significant benefits for children and teachers, it follows that mental health professionals working with children and families can have seen benefits with child clients and their families when including mindfulness practices as part of the treatment plan. There are numerous ways to introduce mindfulness through play-based therapeutic interventions, and the Mindfulness-based Play Therapy™ approach provides therapists with a means to do just that.

MINDFULNESS-BASED PLAY THERAPY™

Mindfulness-based Play Therapy™ (MBPT) is an approach developed by Lynn Louise Wonders after 30 years of personal practice, teaching, and writing about mindfulness and over 20 years of implementing mindfulness-based interventions in therapy with children and families. MBPT is a neurobiologically informed, empirically supported, transtheoretical approach to providing mindfulness-based play therapy for children and families that synthesizes non-directive and directive theoretical orientations and approaches to therapy. It is rooted in the empirical evidence demonstrated by research studies and supports children who present in therapy with symptoms of anxiety, depression, and trauma. MBPT also supports those who identify as autistic, ADHDer, and neurodivergent. MBPT supports children's caregivers and family systems, as well.

MINDFULNESS IN THE INTAKE

Relational neurobiology says that relational attunement, presence, reflection, responsiveness, and delight create meaningful connection (Badenoch 2018; Grayson, 2023). A clinician can practice mindfulness by first taking time to come into the present moment before greeting the clients, connecting to self with the use of intentional focus, breathing, and grounding practices. The clinician can then be more fully present with the clients through active listening skills and attunement to caregivers and children in gathering contextual information about the child's and family's lived experiences. A delicate balance of mindful presence with information gathering is required to make and maintain attuned connections with clients to establish the beginnings of meaningful rapport, trust, and connection.

MINDFULNESS IN CASE CONCEPTUALIZATION

The practice of mindfulness encompasses ongoing expanding awareness while remaining connected to what is presented throughout the process of therapy. Through the process of conceptualizing a child's and family's reasons for coming to therapy, the mindful therapist attends to the client's past experiences in various systemic contexts (underlying and contributing factors) to weave together an understanding of what the client is presently experiencing (symptoms) and facing in the future potentially (risks and/or improvements). Once the initial case conceptualization is developed, the therapist can join with the child and family to develop a vision for a more desirable experience (goals) with mindful measures (objectives) and carefully selected methods for working in the direction of that more desirable experience (interventions).

MINDFULNESS-BASED INTERVENTIONS

In addition to the foundational effect of the clinician practicing mindfulness personally to enhance the quality of presence and connectedness to the clients and the therapeutic process, it is also beneficial to introduce play-based and expressive, exploratory activities for the client to experience that will provide experiential instruction as to the practice of mindfulness. Garrote-Caparós et al. (2022) have shown significantly positive outcomes when mindfulness-based interventions were introduced to clients in the psychotherapy process. MBPT teaches therapists specific play-based methods for introducing children to practices of engaging their breath, sensory exploration, and somatic awareness to see the benefits of increased focus, nervous system regulation, and deeper relationship connections in therapy and with family members, friends, and others.

MINDFULNESS-BASED THERAPY PLANNING

When the therapist is practicing mindfulness personally, it carries over into the therapist's work and can then support the authenticity of being with the client in planning for therapy. Attuning to the child and caregivers, the therapist invites the clients to share their wishes for what may result from coming to therapy. Together, collaboratively, goals are agreed upon, and the therapist determines which theoretically based interventions are the best fit for the goals set for therapy. Measurable objectives are decided upon together and are revisited as a way of checking in mindfully as to the progress of therapy. Ongoing attunement to the child and caregivers every step of the way supports the therapist in being flexible and capable of adjusting the plan as needed according to what the child and caregivers are reporting, with ample opportunity to share and discuss the process of therapy in a way that feels connected, authentic and therapeutically appropriate.

MINDFULNESS-BASED TERMINATION OF THERAPY

In MBPT, the therapist constantly attunes to the client's state of being. The process of bringing closure to the therapy process is done through specific and cautious means to avoid abrupt endings, and hold reverence for the therapeutic alliance. Mindfulness practices can serve as rituals observed to create continuity throughout the therapeutic journey establishing, reinforcing, and enhancing the therapeutic alliance and honoring the therapeutic process. Ongoing practices such as mindfully listening to the chime of a singing bowl or a bell at the end of sessions can be incorporated into closing out the therapy, symbolizing the lingering, positive effects of having experienced therapy together.

CONCLUSION

There is an abundance of research conducted over the past 30 years showing significant benefits of mindfulness practice. The burgeoning current research that bridges mindfulness and neurobiology demonstrates clear ties to why it is important for mental health professionals working with children and families to practice mindfulness personally to optimize their role as therapists and incorporate mindfulness-based activities, experiences, and psychoeducation for children and families. Combining what we know about the mental health effects of the autonomic nervous system's activation because of trauma with what the research shows about the positive effects of mindfulness practices, professionals can easily fold in mindfulness to any psychotherapy model or theoretical approach.

Key Takeaways

- ♡ Mindfulness can be defined as the capacity to purposefully attend to an experience in the present moment with full awareness and acceptance.
- ♡ There have been significant research studies that have boosted the position that the effects of mindfulness practice have significant benefits for human functioning.
- ♡ The benefits of mindfulness practice in school classrooms have been demonstrated in numerous research studies.
- ♡ The Mindfulness-based Play Therapy™ (MBPT) is designed to provide a combination of non-directive and directive play-based therapeutic experiences for child clients and their families rooted in evidence-based research about mindfulness-based practices.
- ♡ MBPT is a neurobiologically informed, empirically supported transtheoretical approach to providing mindfulness-based play therapy for children and families that synthesizes several play therapy and psychotherapy seminal theories.
- ♡ Combining what we know about the mental health effects of the autonomic nervous system's activation because of trauma with what evidence-based research shows about the positive effects of mindfulness practices, professionals can easily fold in mindfulness to any psychotherapy model or theoretical approach.

REFERENCES

Badenoch, B. (2018). Trauma and the embodied brain: A heart-based training in relational neuroscience for healing trauma [Webinar]. Sounds True. Retrieved from https://leading-edge-of-psychotherapy-sfm.soundstrue.com/bonnie-badenoch/?sq=1 https://doi.org/10.4324/9781315692364-2

Beauchemin, J., Hutchins, T. L., & Patterson, F. (2008). Mindfulness meditation may lessen anxiety, promote social skills, and improve academic performance among adolescents with learning disabilities. *Complementary Health Practice Review*, *13*(1), 34–45. https://doi.org/10.1177/1533210107311624

Bergen-Cico, D., Razza, R., & Timmins, A. (2015). Fostering self-regulation through curriculum infusion of mindful yoga: A pilot study of efficacy and feasibility. *Journal of Child and Family Studies, 24,* 3448–3461 (2015 https://doi.org/10.1007/s10826-015-0146-2

Brown, K. W., Creswell, J. D., & Ryan, R. M. (2015). *Handbook of mindfulness: Theory, research, and practice.* Guilford.

Flook, L., Smalley, S. L., Kitil, M. J., Galla, B. M., Kaiser-Greenland, S., Locke, J., Ishijima, E., & Kasari, C. (2010). Effects of mindful awareness practices on executive functions in elementary school children. *Journal of Applied School Psychology*, *26*(1), 70–95. https://doi.org/10.1080/15377900903379125

Frank, J. L., Kohler, K., Peal, A., & Bose, B. (2016). Effectiveness of a school-based yoga program on adolescent mental health and school performance: Findings from a randomized controlled trial. *Mindfulness*, *8*(3), 544–553. https://doi.org/10.1007/s12671-016-0628-3

Ganesan, S., Beyer, E., Moffat, B., Van Dam, N. T., Lorenzetti, V., & Zalesky, A. (2022). Focused attention meditation in healthy adults: A systematic review and meta-analysis of cross-sectional functional MRI studies. *Neuroscience & Biobehavioral Reviews, 141*, https://doi.org/10.1016/j.neubiorev.2022.104846

Garrote-Caparrós, E., Lecuona, Ó., Bellosta-Batalla, M., Moya-Albiol, L., & Cebolla, A. (2022). Efficacy of a mindfulness and compassion-based intervention in psychotherapists and their patients: Empathy, symptomatology, and mechanisms of change in a randomized controlled trial. *Psychotherapy*. Advance online publication. https://doi.org/10.1037/pst0000467

Grayson, R., (2023). A neurobiological relational approach to therapy planning in *Treatment planning for children and families: A guide for mental health professionals*,

Hölzel, B. K., Carmody, J., Vangel, M., Congleton, C., Yerramsetti, S. M., Gard, T., & Lazar, S. W. (2011). Mindfulness practice leads to increases in regional brain gray matter density. *Psychiatry research, 191*(1), 36–43. https://doi.org/10.1016/j.pscychresns.2010.08.006

Kabat-Zinn, J. (2011). Some reflections on the origins of MBSR, skillful means, and the trouble with maps. *Contemporary Buddhism, 12*, 281–306. https://doi.org/10.1080/14639947.2011.564844

Lazar, S. W., Kerr, C. E., Wasserman, R. H., Gray, J. R., Greve, D. N., Treadway, M. T., McGarvey, M., Quinn, B. T., Dusek, J. A., Benson, H., Rauch, S. L., Moore, C. I., & Fischl, B. (2005). Meditation experience is associated with increased cortical thickness. *Neuroreport, 16*(17), 1893–1897. https://doi.org/10.1097/01.wnr.0000186598.66243.19

Lynn, S., & Basso, J. C. (2023). Effects of a neuroscience-based mindfulness meditation program on psychological health: Pilot randomized controlled trial. *JMIR Formative Research, 7*(1), e40135. https://doi.org/10.2196/40135

Meyer, L., & Eklund, K. (2020). The impact of a mindfulness intervention on elementary classroom climate and student and teacher mindfulness: A pilot study. *Mindfulness, 11*, 991–1005. https://doi.org/10.1007/s12671-020-01317-6

Ong, J. C., Manber, R., Segal, Z., Xia, Y., Shapiro, S., & Wyatt, J. K. (2014). A randomized controlled trial of mindfulness meditation for chronic insomnia. *Sleep, 37*(9), 1553–1563. https://doi.org/10.5665/sleep.4010

Quach, D., Mano, K. E. J., & Alexander, K. (2016). A randomized controlled trial examining the effect of mindfulness meditation on working memory capacity in adolescents. *Journal of Adolescent Health, 58*(5), 489–496. https://doi.org/10.1016/j.jadohealth.2015.09.024

Skinner, E., & Beers, J. (2016). Mindfulness and teachers' coping in the classroom: A developmental model of teacher stress, coping, and everyday resilience. *Mindfulness in Behavioral Health*, 99–118. https://doi.org/10.1007/978-1-4939-3506-2_7

Van Dam, N. T., van Vugt, M. K., Vago, D. R., Schmalzl, L., Saron, C. D., Olendzki, A., Meissner, T., Lazar, S. W., Kerr, C. E., Gorchov, J., Fox, K. C. R., Field, B. A., Britton, W. B., Brefczynski-Lewis, J. A., & Meyer, D. E. (2018). Mind the hype: A critical evaluation and prescriptive agenda for research on mindfulness and meditation. *Perspectives on Psychological Science, 13*(1), 36–61. https://doi.org/10.1177/1745691617709589

West, M. A., & Batchelor, M. (2016). *The psychology of meditation: Research and practice*. Oxford University Press. https://doi.org/10.1093/med:psych/9780199688906.003.0002

Wonders, L. L., (2022). Mindfulness nature play therapy. In J. A. Courtney, J. L. Langley, L. L. Wonders, R. Heiko, & R. LaPiere (Eds.). (2022). *Nature-based play and expressive therapies: Interventions for working with children, teens, and families*. Routledge. https://doi.org/10.4324/9781003152767-13

Zhou, D., Kang, Y., Cosme, D., Jovanova, M., He, X., Mahadevan, A., Ahn, J., Stanoi, O., Brynildsen, J. K., Cooper, N., Cornblath, E. J., Parkes, L., Mucha, P. J., Ochsner, K. N., Lydon-Staley, D. M., Falk, E. B., & Bassett, D. S. (2023). Mindful attention promotes control of brain network dynamics for self-regulation and discontinues the past from the present. *Proceedings of the National Academy of Sciences, 120*(2), e2201074119. https://doi.org/10.1073/pnas.2201074119

CHAPTER 29

FAMILIES, CHILDREN, AND TECHNOLOGY IN TREATMENT PLANNING

*Mary Affee, Lynn Louise Wonders,
Courteney Matteson, and Julia Krebs*

INTRODUCTION

Screens and mobile devices are ubiquitous and very much a part of everyday life for large numbers of people around the world. While *the digital divide* was exacerbated during the COVID-19 pandemic, highlighting the inequity of access to the Internet for many people around the world (Blundell et al. 2020), one year after the first pandemic lockdown was enforced, the volume of Internet traffic increased by approximately 40%, which was much higher than what researchers anticipated for typical annual growth (Feldman et al., 2021). In another study, a 52% increase in screentime usage was recorded (Madigan et al., 2022).

Clinicians need to explore how a child's and family's technology use and habits may impact the mental health of clients. As part of a comprehensive assessment, it is important to recognize the potential impact technology may have on behavior, presenting concerns, moods, and relationships. Underscoring the importance of seeing children, teens, and family members as parts of a whole system, the consideration of how technology may impact interpersonal relationships within the family and behaviors is important for conceptualizing symptomology and treatment planning.

IMPACT OF TECHNOLOGY ON CHILDREN AND FAMILIES

Technology has become a tapestry that connects humans all over the world for better or worse. Parenting in a technology-centric world can be difficult and challenging. COVID-19 created both a positive and deleterious impact on our society's relationship with and reliance on technology (Prati & Mancini, 2021). One concern is the surmounting resistance and defiance observed among children and adolescents when asked to disconnect from their digital devices. Many parents and professionals are questioning the possible implications technology has played in reshaping behavior, moods, relationships, and mental health (Scott et al., 2017). Identity development may be shaped by the myopic social media phenomena (Kawamoto, 2021; Manago, 2015), and concern has grown about adolescent dependency on social media and correlating risky behaviors (Vannuci et al., 2020).

There was a rapidly growing body of research literature examining connections between high usage of screen time technology and the physical and mental health of children and adolescents (Lissak, 2018) *prior to* the COVID-19 pandemic, and now there is an even greater uptick in research studies published between 2020 and 2023 about the connections between problematic Internet usage and mental health. Lifestyle changes necessitated by the stay-at-home requirements of the COVID-19 pandemic of 2020–2021 resulted in significantly

DOI: 10.4324/9781003334231-32

increased levels of screen time (Eyimaya & Irmak, 2021; Drumheller & Fann, 2022). Madigan et al. (2022) conducted a meta-analysis that showed there was a 52% increase in screentime with the highest increase among children ages 12 to 18 years of age with handheld devices and personal computers as the most common sources. Excessive screen time usage during the pandemic yielded high levels of stress for parents and correlated behavioral problems in children (Shelleby et al., 2022). The sedentary nature associated with so much time spent in front of screens is affiliated with concerning negative health outcomes in adolescents (Musa et al., 2022). Excess screen time exposure has been associated with low self-esteem, mental and behavioral health problems, impaired learning, and an increased risk of early cognitive decline (Neophytou et al., 2019). Marsden et al. (2020) register concern about the rise in addictions during the pandemic, and screen addiction is a concern of many researchers (Lozano-Blasco et al., 2022; Meng et al., 2022).

According to family systems theory, a family is an interrelated unit, operating as a dynamic system within which one member's experiences affect other members of the family (Kerig, 2019; Whiteside et al., 2011). It is important to consider the individual mental health status of each family member within the context of family dynamics (Tooth et al., 2021). During the COVID-19 pandemic, there was both an increase in screen technology usage for families and an increased prevalence of stress, anxiety, and depression (de Miranda et al., 2020; Majumdar et al., 2020; Turna et al., 2021). The high levels of stress experienced by parents during the COVID-19 pandemic correlated with increased levels of problematic behavior in children (Shelleby et al., 2022). Adolescents reported a significant frequency of tension headaches during the COVID-19 pandemic significantly correlated with increased screen time, poor sleep habits, and anxiety (Wehbe et al., 2022). The relationship between excessive screen usage and mental health problems was significant among children ages 18 months to 12 years of age when measured with a problematic-screen-usage scale and other mental health scales (Anitha & Narasimthan, 2020). However, it's important not to jump to sweeping conclusions. The research only demonstrates associations, which means that increased screen time is not necessarily the cause of the problems (Richtel, 2021). Other variables such as socioeconomic status, the situational stress of living through a pandemic, and the stress many caregivers felt from having to parent during the day while working from home full-time must be considered. What concerns many researchers is that the excessive use of technology devices is not a healthy substitute for interpersonal connection and all the activities that contribute to good health and social, emotional, psychological, and physical development that includes physical play (Richtel, 2021). In some cases, parents reported that when their children exceeded recommended daily limits for screentime, they actually experienced improved mental health (Przybylski & Weinstein, 2019) so there is some variability in the research.

In early 2023, the American Psychological Association released the written testimony of Mitch Prinstein, Chief Science Officer, stating there is a prevalent and pervasive crisis in the state of mental health among children and adolescents, citing research findings regarding possible adverse effects of technology and social media (Protecting our children online, 2023). Further research is needed for a closer examination of the nature and quality of the online programs, applications, and content accessed by family members on their electronic devices. When assessing and conceptualizing presenting challenges and concerns in psychotherapy, it remains important for clinicians to gather information from caregivers and children about their relationship with technology and collaboratively set goals and objectives that may include changes in behaviors and habits.

According to the interrelatedness of dynamics in family systems theory (Broderick, 1995), any effects of excessive screen time on children's mental health would potentially affect the state of mind and resulting behaviors of caregivers and other members of the family as a system. For mental health professionals to assist families receiving psychotherapy support services, it will be important to examine the possible effects of screen time usage overall and differing kinds of screen activity to inform the family's therapy plan. Mental health professionals will ideally conduct clinical formulation that reflects on the context of the family members' dynamics and lived experience before developing a treatment plan (Tooth et al., 2021; Gazzillo et al., 2021).

Some mental health professionals may feel uncertain as to whether excessive time on digital technology in fact negatively impacts the mental health of children and families as the research conclusions are correlational (Davie, 2022). Until the research can provide more clarifying data, clinicians can rely on contextual information of the family's presentation and self-reports and consider the research that supports the importance of secure healthy attachments (Diamond et al., 2021) and encourage families to find ways for children, caregivers, and other family members to benefit from personal, face-to-face connections (Martino et al., 2015).

Dangerous Risks

There is a true risk of danger when children and adolescents have unsupervised access to the Internet including exposure to *the dark web* (Ferrara et al., 2021). Some children and teens are victims of cyberbullying, pedophilia, and exposure to pornography on the Internet. A recent study conducted (Dienlin and Johannes, 2020) found that 50% of 11–13-year-olds, 65% of 14–15-year-olds, and 78% of 16–17-year-olds have all reported seeing pornography. Of the children and teens that were sampled, 75% of their caregivers believed they had not been exposed to pornography when, in actuality, 53% of their children had in fact, viewed pornography.

Also worth noting is the vulnerability and potential addictive properties related to technology, gaming, and social media usage (Jin et al., 2021). The World Health Organization included *gaming disorder* in the International Classification of Diseases, described as a pattern of digital gaming or video gaming characterized by compulsive gaming, prioritized and taking precedence over other activities and interests regardless of negative consequences (World Health Organization, 2020). Research shows that regions in the brain are activated while engaged in digital gaming, similar to the use of other addictive substances producing dopamine, a chemical that our brain produces associated with pleasure and reward (Guan & Chen, 2023). These dopamine hits increase the likelihood and motivation to repeat these behaviors (Haynes, 2018), essentially describing the cycle of addictive behaviors. In addition to gaming addiction, the developing brains of children and adolescents will seek out social rewards, often resulting in excessive social media engagement. Teens are developmentally motivated to pursue connection and often do so through Internet avenues. Combining that natural motivation and easy and regular Internet access often eclipses their ability to make a safe and informed decision.

SUPPORTING AND GUIDING FAMILIES

Understanding the possibility that technology may impact interpersonal relationships, families, and mental health, forming a thorough assessment that includes a technology assessment can be paramount. When seeking information to inform the treatment planning process better, collaboration is key. Inviting caregivers into the process can begin with the following questions:

- Does the child/teen have control of their own screen use?
- Does the child/teen exhibit loss of interest in other activities?
- Does the child/teen have an obsessive need for technology use?
- Has your child/teen experienced emotional dysregulation, such as tech tantrums and/or aggressive behavior (verbally or physically), when screens are removed or not present?
- Do screens or technology cause any serious family conflicts?
- Have you seen increased anxiety, attention issues, or moodiness related to your child's/teen's use of technology?
- How do caregivers use technology?
- Have boundaries and rules with technology ever been discussed as a family?
- Does technology impact their mental health? (what feelings are associated?)
- Does technology impact family structure? (i.e., meal times, holidays)
- Does technology impact the family's ability to connect and engage in activities outside of the home?
- Does technology interfere with scheduled mealtimes, the ability to prepare healthy meals, make healthy choices, etc.?
- Does technology interrupt sleep?
- Does technology interrupt eating?
- Has the child/teen been exposed to pornography? If so, how was that handled?
- When was the child first exposed to technology?
- How has the relationship with technology developed?
- Was technology passively introduced or intentionally introduced?
- Did the client ever have boundaries related to technology?
- How many hours per day does your family spend engaged on an electronic device while in the presence of other family members, although not directly engaged with them?
- Do you or anyone in your family become defensive or secretive when people question you about your screen usage?
- Has your child/teen utilized used devices despite there being negative consequences to the use?

Recommendations for Improving Family Connections

When supporting families with healthy practices with technology among family members, clinicians may find sharing the following recommendations with caregivers a part of the collaborative therapy planning process.

1. Model healthy screen activity:

Caregivers may wish to examine their over-use and over-dependency on technology by evaluating how much time is spent on screens, how much time is spent in nature, and interacting face-to-face with friends, family, neighbors, and colleagues. If caregivers want to help children and teens step away from screens effectively, they must practice stepping away from screens. Caregivers should be prepared to model the changes they are asking of their children.

2. **Organize screen-free family time:**

   Encourage caregivers to observe family dinners regularly with a no-screens rulemaking face-to-face time with family members a priority. Encourage organizing family outings and leaving phones and tablets at home. Suggest family nature excursions to a local park, a hiking trail, a beach, or some other places in nature.

3. **Create screen-free zones in the home:**

   Caregivers and children can discuss and agree on certain areas of the home as screen-free zones preserving certain spaces for discussion, rest, playing board games, or other screen-free activities.

4. **Make a family screen contract:**

   Caregivers and children can meet and agree on family rules about the use of technology and create a contract everyone in the family signs.

5. **Creating a family vision board:**

   Engaging in this playful and creative family project, caregivers and children can collect old magazines and together select images and words that represent what they want collectively as a family for the family outside of the technology-related activity and affix images and words to a poster board that can be hung on a wall in the family room to remind each member of the family's hopes and goals.

6. **Engage in family digital detoxes:**

   Taking a break from all or most screen time as a family is a wonderful way to break any potential addiction cycles and to encourage face-to-face connections in the family.

7. **Create mindful intentionality around technology usage:**

   Support families in developing more conscious planning and follow through when using technology. An example is to use a tablet for homework use, to play a game with a time limit built in, or to engage in a video conference meeting.

8. **Play online games with children rather than forbidding them:**

   Encourage caregivers to have their children show and teach them how to play their favorite games and join in the games. This will help caregivers to understand better what their digital native children are doing and also will provide another opportunity for connection.

CONCLUSION

Technology has advanced our society in myriad ways, and there are countless advantages and benefits of living in a world with so many resources and avenues for learning, working, and connecting online. There are also many risks and costs of such all-pervasive availability of online access, especially for children and families. Often, the potential risk factors are overlooked in treatment planning with children, teens, and families. It is essential to explore the potential impact that technology has on behavior, mental health, and inter-personal connections for better and for worse. The areas that need to be continuously explored regarding technology impact our physical health and movement, exposure to sexual content, gaming, isolation behavior, and moods associated with social media, with a special focus on mental health symptomatology assessment pre- and post-technology engagement. Assessing children in therapeutic settings requires a thorough understanding of them in all contexts, including their relationships with technology and social media. Mental health providers should include caregivers in the treatment planning and inform them of the potential risks associated with technology and social media while assisting them with developing a family technology plan tailored to their family's needs.

Key Takeaways

- Clinicians need to explore how a child's and family's technology use and habits may impact the mental health of clients.
- Technology has become a tapestry that connects humans all over the world for better or worse.
- COVID-19 created both a positive and deleterious impact on our society's relationship with and reliance on technology.
- Excessive use of technology devices is not a healthy substitute for interpersonal connection and all the activities that contribute to good health, social, emotional, psychological, and physical development that includes physical play.
- The effects of excessive screen time on children's mental health would potentially affect the state of mind and resulting behaviors of caregivers and other members of the family as a system.
- Technology has advanced our society in myriad ways and there are countless advantages and benefits of living in a world with so many resources and avenues for learning, working, and connecting online. There are also many risks and costs of such all-pervasive availability of online access, especially for children and families.

REFERENCES

Anitha, G. F. S., & Narasimhan, U. (2020). Coronavirus disease 2019 and the inevitable increase in screen time among Indian children: Is going digital the way forward?. *Industrial Psychiatry Journal, 29*(1), 171. https://doi.org/10.4103/ipj.ipj_131_20

Blundell, R., Costa Dias, M., Joyce, R., & Xu, X. (2020). COVID-19 and inequalities. *Fiscal studies, 41*(2), 291–319. https://doi.org/10.1111/1475-5890.12232

Broderick, C. B. (1995). *Understanding family process: Basics of family systems theory.* Sage.

Davie, M. (2022). Screen time: How much is too much? *Paediatrics & Child Health, 32*(8), 307–310. https://doi.org/10.1016/j.paed.2022.05.005

de Miranda, D. M., da Silva Athanasio, B., Oliveira, A. C. S., & Simões-e-Silva, A. C. (2020). How is COVID-19 pandemic impacting mental health of children and adolescents?. *International Journal of Disaster Risk Reduction, 51*, 101845. https://doi.org/10.1016/j.ijdrr.2020.101845

Diamond, G., Diamond, G. M., & Levy, S. (2021). Attachment-based family therapy: Theory, clinical model, outcomes, and process research. *Journal of Affective Disorders, 294*, 286–295. https://doi.org/10.1016/j.jad.2021.07.005

Dienlin, T. and Johannes, N. (2020). The impact of digital technology use on adolescent well-being. *Dialogue in Clinical Neuroscience, 22*(2), 135–142. https://doi.org/10.31887/dcns.2020.22.2/tdienlin

Drumheller, K., & Fan, C.-W. (2022). Unprecedented times and uncertain connections: A systematic review examining sleep problems and screentime during the COVID-19 pandemic. *Sleep Epidemiology, 2*, 100029. https://doi.org/10.1016/j.sleepe.2022.100029

Eyimaya, A. O., & Irmak, A. Y. (2021). Relationship between parenting practices and children's screen time during the COVID-19 pandemic in Turkey. *Journal of Pediatric Nursing, 56*, 24–29. https://doi.org/10.1016/j.pedn.2020.10.002

Feldman, A., Gasser, O., Lichtblau, F., Pujol, E., Poese, I., Dietzel, C., ... & Smaragdakis, G. (2021). A year in lockdown: how the waves of COVID-19 impact internet traffic. *Communications of the ACM, 64*(7), 101–108. https://doi.org/10.1145/3465212

Ferrara, P., Franceschini, G., Corsello, G., Mestrovic, J., Giardino, I., Vural, M., ... & Pettoello-Mantovani, M. (2021). The dark side of the web—a risk for children and adolescents challenged by isolation during the novel coronavirus 2019 pandemic. *The Journal of Pediatrics, 228*, 324–325. https://doi.org/10.1016/j.jpeds.2020.10.008

Gazzillo, F., Dimaggio, G., & Curtis, J. T. (2021). Case formulation and treatment planning: How to take care of relationship and symptoms together. *Journal of Psychotherapy Integration, 31*(2), 115–128. https://doi.org/10.1037/int0000185

Guan, J., & Chen, T. (2023). Exploring addiction mechanism of different game types. *Journal of Education, Humanities and Social Sciences, 8*, 1490–1496. https://doi.org/10.54097/ehss.v8i.4509

Haynes, T. (2018). *Dopamine, smartphones and you: A battle for your time.* Harvard University Graduate School of Arts and Sciences.

Jin, Y., Qin, L., Zhang, H., & Zhang, R. (2021). Social factors associated with video game addiction among teenagers: School, family and peers. *2021 4th International Conference on Humanities Education and Social Sciences (ICHESS 2021)* (pp. 763–768). Atlantis. https://doi.org/10.2991/assehr.k.211220.131

Kawamoto, T. (2021). Online self-presentation and identity development: The moderating effect of neuroticism. *PsyCh Journal, 10*(5), 816–833. https://doi.org/10.1002/pchj.470

Kerig, P. K. (2019). Parenting and family systems. *Handbook of parenting, 3*–35. https://doi.org/10.4324/9780429433214-1

Lissak, G. (2018). Adverse physiological and psychological effects of screen time on children and adolescents: Literature review and case study. *Environmental Research, 164*, 149–157. https://doi.org/10.1016/j.envres.2018.01.015

Lozano-Blasco, R., Latorre-Martínez, M., & Cortés-Pascual, A. (2022). Screen addicts: A meta-analysis of internet addiction in adolescence. *Children and Youth Services Review, 135*, 106373. https://doi.org/10.1016/j.childyouth.2022.106373

Madigan, S., Eirich, R., Pador, P., McArthur, B. A., & Neville, R. D. (2022). Assessment of changes in child and adolescent screen time during the COVID-19 pandemic: A systematic review and meta-analysis. *JAMA pediatrics, 176*(12), 1188. https://doi.org/10.1001/jamapediatrics.2022.4116

Majumdar, P., Biswas, A., & Sahu, S. (2020). COVID-19 pandemic and lockdown: Cause of sleep disruption, depression, somatic pain, and increased screen exposure of office workers and students of India. *Chronobiology International, 37*(8), 1191–1200. https://doi.org/10.1080/07420528.2020.1786107

Manago, A. M. (2015). Identity development in the digital age: The case of social networking sites. In K. C. McLean & M. Syed (Eds.), *The Oxford handbook of identity development* (pp. 508–524). Oxford University Press. https://doi.org/10.1093/oxfordhb/9780199936564.013.031

Marsden, J., Darke, S., Hall, W., Hickman, M., Holmes, J., Humphreys, K., ... & West, R. (2020). Mitigating and learning from the impact of COVID-19 infection on addictive disorders. *Addiction, 115*(6), 1007. https://doi.org/10.1111/add.15080

Martino, J., Pegg, J., & Frates, E. P. (2015). The connection prescription: Using the power of social interactions and the deep desire for connectedness to empower health and wellness. *American Journal of Lifestyle Medicine, 11*(6), 466–475. https://doi.org/10.1177/1559827615608788

Meng, S. Q., Cheng, J. L., Li, Y. Y., Yang, X. Q., Zheng, J. W., Chang, X. W., ... & Shi, J. (2022). Global prevalence of digital addiction in general population: A systematic review and meta-analysis. *Clinical Psychology Review, 92*, 102128. https://doi.org/10.1016/j.cpr.2022.102128

Musa, S., Elyamani, R., & Dergaa, I. (2022). COVID-19 and screen-based sedentary behaviour: Systematic review of digital screen time and metabolic syndrome in adolescents. *PLOS One, 17*(3), e0265560. https://doi.org/10.1371/journal.pone.0265560

Neophytou, E., Manwell, L. A., & Eikelboom, R. (2019). Effects of excessive screen time on neurodevelopment, learning, memory, mental health, and neurodegeneration: A scoping review. *International Journal of Mental Health and Addiction, 19*(3), 724–744. https://doi.org/10.1007/s11469-019-00182-2

Prati, G., & Mancini, A. D. (2021). The psychological impact of COVID-19 pandemic lockdowns: A review and meta-analysis of longitudinal studies and natural experiments. *Psychological medicine, 51*(2), 201–211. https://doi.org/10.1017/s0033291721000015

Protecting our children online. 118th Cong. (2023). (testimony of Mark Prinstein, PhD, ABPP). https://www.apaservices.org/advocacy/news/testimony-prinstein-protecting-children-online.pdf

Przybylski, A. K., & Weinstein, N. (2019). Digital screen time limits and young children's psychological well-being: Evidence from a population-based study. *Child development, 90*(1), e56–e65. https://doi.org/10.1111/cdev.13007

Richtel, M. (2021). Children's screen time has soared in the pandemic, alarming parents and researchers. *The New York Times*, 17.

Scott, D. A., Valley, B., & Simecka, B. A. (2017). Mental health concerns in the digital age. *International Journal of Mental Health and Addiction, 15*, 604–613. https://doi.org/10.1007/s11469-016-9684-0

Shelleby, E. C., Pittman, L. D., Bridgett, D. J., Keane, J., Zolinski, S., & Caradec, J. (2022). Associations between local COVID-19 case rates, pandemic-related financial stress and parent and child functioning. *Journal of Family Psychology*.

Tooth, L. R., Moss, K. M., & Mishra, G. D. (2021). Screen time and child behaviour and health-related quality of life: Effect of family context. *Preventive Medicine, 153*, 106795. https://doi.org/10.1016/j.ypmed.2021.106795.

Turna, J., Zhang, J., Lamberti, N., Patterson, B., Simpson, W., Francisco, A. P., ... & Van Amerin-gen, M. (2021). Anxiety, depression and stress during the COVID-19 pandemic: Results from a cross-sectional survey. *Journal of Psychiatric Research, 137*, 96–103. https://doi.org/10.1016/j.jpsychires.2021.02.059

Vannuci, A., Simpson, E. G., Gagnon, S., & Ohannessian, C. M. (2020). Social media use and risky behaviors in adolescents: A meta-analysis. *Journal of Adolescence, 79*, 258–274. https://doi.org/10.1016/j.adolescence.2020.01.014

Wehbe, A. T., Costa, T. E., Abbas, S. A., Costa, J. E., Costa, G. E., & Wehbe, T. W. (2022). The effects of the COVID-19 confinement on screen time, headaches, stress and sleep disorders among adolescents: A cross sectional study. *Chronic Stress, 6*, 247054702210998. https://doi.org/10.1177/24705470221099836

Whiteside, M. F., Aronoff, C. E., & Ward, J. L. (2016). *How families work together*. Springer.

World Health Organization. (2020). Excessive screen use and gaming considerations during COVID19.

CHAPTER 30

TREATMENT PLANNING IN CLINICAL SUPERVISION

Eleah Hyatt

INTRODUCTION

Clinical supervision is a crucial aspect of counselor training and is a structured relationship that supports supervisees in attaining attitudes, skills, and knowledge needed to be a responsible and effective therapist (Morgan & Sprenkle, 2007). Lee and Nelson (2014) advise that "supervisory relationships must be respectful, competency-based and task-oriented" (p. 9) and that the relationship between the supervisee and supervisor must be one of "trust, openness, vulnerability and commitment to quality of training" (Lee & Nelson, 2014). Supervisees can openly reflect upon their experiences in relation to cognitive, metacognitive, and affective domains (Gordon et al., 2000) when they feel safe. Woven into the role of the supervisor is a delicate balancing act between counselor development and client welfare in addition to "encouraging compliance with relevant legal, ethical and professional standards for clinical practice" (ACA, 1988). Morgan and Sprenkle (2007) point out that it is the supervisor's responsibility to attend not only to the professional development and competencies of individual supervisees but also to the profession as a whole so that client care and ethical standards are upheld. To accomplish this role, supervisors often serve as gatekeepers, monitoring and contributing to "the safety and wellbeing of not only their trainees but also various institutions and the public" (Lee & Nelson, 2014).

THE TEACHING COMPONENT OF SUPERVISION

It is in the context of this unique relationship through which deep and individualized learning occurs. In the initial phases of clinical experience, supervisees must transition between interacting with clinical content in a traditional, theory-driven, teacher-dependent, pedagogical learning environment to interacting in a real-world setting. Reorientating supervisees around the necessity of becoming self-directed learners in the field by synthesizing knowledge in the context of daily problem-solving and professional practice versus receiving the knowledge in neatly packaged content areas (Pickens et al., 2012) is both a challenge and an opportunity for advanced growth and learning. "Supervision must be a safe place for learning" (Lee & Nelson, 2014), where supervisees feel welcome to explore theories, admit clinical support needs, and experiment with new techniques and methods of following their client's needs. This relationship context becomes a place where systemic interventions can be isomorphically experienced (Ungar, 2006), which enhances the development of a supervisees' internal guidance systemic and sparks the beginning of growth-oriented supervision and metacognitive skills.

As new counselors enter post-degree stages of practice, they must develop advanced skills, caseload management, and complex conceptualization of client needs (Budesa &

DOI: 10.4324/9781003334231-33

Minton, 2022). One of the privileges of being a supervisor is the opportunity to support a new clinician through the process of creating an internal guidance system around clinical practice and ethical care. The process of strengthening this internal guidance system is facilitated by walking the supervisee through the transition from *external guidance* to *shared guidance* and then to *internal guidance* (Gordon et al., 2000), which results in a fully self-regulated learner. Supervisors are tasked with the responsibility of teaching evidence-based principles of therapeutic change and the manners in which outcome measures can be used to enhance treatment progress in clinical work (Holt et al. 2015). Supervisees can be encouraged to expand their understanding of various theories, models, and philosophies of change through the intentional pursuit of postgraduate workshops and readings of evidenced based practice. This work can broaden their conceptualizing skills and help them develop a more integrated approach to therapy and a conceptual base.

ENSURING CLINICIAN COMPETENCY IN SUPERVISION

Ethically guided clinical supervision supports the development of competence in supervisees by expanding their capacity to organize and clarify the clinical picture, consider immediate and longer-term outcomes, and flexibly offer suitable interventions (Lee & Nelson, 2014). These metacognitive skills are developed through the "shared learning" aspect of a safe supervisory relationship where supervisees can learn to recognize their own thinking and learning strategies and organize their own knowledge base (Gordon et al., 2000). Developing a clinical treatment plan becomes the reflective framework through which these competency skills are illuminated as a clear conceptual map so that the focus of therapy can be formed. Regulating bodies such as the American Association for Marriage and Family Therapy recognize this component of counselor training in the third domain of the MFT Core Competencies, "Treatment Planning and Case Management," as an important aspect that improves the quality of services delivered by marriage and family therapists (AAMFT, 2004) in addition to the ACA Code of Ethics which identifies "Counseling Plans" as a facilitator of client growth and development (ACA, n.d).

Supervisors who practice from a developmental model of supervision will understand that "supervisees pass through many predictable, universal stages in their growth as clinicians, or in their supervisory relationships. Each stage is characterized by particular needs, conflicts, and tasks that the clinician must resolve to continue his or her growth" (Morgan & Sprenkle, 2007). This appreciation of developmental stages can be used to support the supervisor in making an important shift towards an andragogical training approach which actively involves the supervisee in constructing their own knowledge, making sense of the learning and applying what is learned (Chang, 2010) "premised on the assumption that students, not teachers are the locus of learning" (Pickens et al., 2012).

CONCLUSION

Clinicians in supervision should be prepared to articulate a reasonable, theory-based rationale for their ideas and actions (Lee & Nelson, 2014) throughout a client's clinical course of treatment, as captured in a carefully crafted treatment plan. The development of a supervisee's internal guidance system and improvement of case conceptualization skills is an important aspect of counselor training and is facilitated best in the context of an attuned and responsive supervisory relationship.

Key Takeaways

- ✧ The clinical supervisory relationship must be one built on trust and safety.
- ✧ It is the supervisor's responsibility to attend not only to the professional development and competencies of individual supervisees but also to the profession so that client care and ethical standards are upheld.
- ✧ Supervision is a place for learning and the supervisor has a responsibility to effectively teach in a way that supervisees can learn how to develop and work from a plan for treatment.
- ✧ Supervisees can be encouraged to expand their understanding of various theories, models, and philosophies of change.
- ✧ Metacognitive skills are developed through the 'shared learning' aspect of a safe supervisory relationship where supervisees can learn to recognize their own thinking and learning strategies and organize their own knowledge base.
- ✧ Developing a clinical treatment plan becomes the reflective framework through which competency skills are illuminated as a clear conceptual map so that the focus of therapy can be formed.

REFERENCES

AAMFT. (2004). AAMFT core competencies. Retrieved April 6, 2023, from AAMFT: https://www.aamft.org/Documents/COAMFTE/Accreditation%20Resources/MFT%20Core%20Competencies%20(December%202004).pdf

ACA code of Ethics—American Counseling Association. (n.d.). Retrieved April 11, 2023, from https://www.counseling.org/resources/aca-code-of-ethics.pdf

American Counseling Association, (1988). Ethical standards (3rd rev.). Journal of Counseling and Development, 67, 4–8. https://doi.org/10.1002/j.1556-6676.1988.tb02001.x

Budesa, Z., & Barrio Minton, C. A. (2022). Enhancing counselor education and supervision through deliberate practice. Teaching and Supervision in Counseling, 4(1), 5. https://doi.org/10.7290/tsc04k3n1

Chang, S. (2010). Applications of andragogy in multi-disciplined teaching and learning. Journal of Adult Education, 39(2), 25–35.

Gordon, J., Hazlett, C., Ten Cate, O., Mann, K., Kilminster, S., Prince, K.,& Newble, D. (2000). Strategic planning in medical education: Enhancing the learning environment for students in clinical settings. Medical Education, 34(10), 841–850. https://doi.org/10.1046/j.1365-2923.2000.00759.x

Holt, H., Beutler, L. E., Kimpara, S., Macias, S., Haug, N. A., Shiloff, N., & Stein, M. (2015). Evidence-based supervision: Tracking outcome and teaching principles of change in clinical supervision to bring science to integrative practice. Psychotherapy, 52(2), 185. https://doi.org/10.1037/a0038732

Lee, R. E., & Nelson, T. S. (2014). The contemporary relational supervisor (1st ed.). Routledge.

Morgan, M. M., & Sprenkle, D. H. (2007). Toward a common-factors approach to supervision. Journal of Marital and Family Therapy, 33(1), 1–17. https://doi.org/10.1111/j.1752-0606.2007.00001.x

Pickens, B. C., Lancaster, C., Schaefgen, B., James, R. K., & Constantine, D. (2012). Project based learning: enriching counselor education through real world learning. Article VISTAS, 1, 1–12.

Ungar, M. (2006). Practicing as a postmodern supervisor. Journal of Marital and Family Therapy, 32(1), 59–71.

APPENDIX A

Sample Assessment and Intake Forms

Example
Wonders-Affee Child Contextual Intake Assessment

Family

Jose, Brother, Single Mom in one house. Father lives out of state rarely visits. Big extended family all very close. Grandfather died alone of Covid in hospital.

Culture

Jose is first generation Mexican-American. Mom & Dad immigrated before Jose was born. Family gathers weekly. Part of their culture is to share a bed and co-sleep - their house is one bedroom.

School

Jose attends local elementary Title I school and is on free lunch program. Jose struggles academically and pandemic online school was very hard for him. Currently exhibiting school refusing behavior.

Technology

Prior to pandemic Jose played video games with friends in person 6 hours/week and played solo 10 hours/week. During pandemic Jose's usage quadrupled. Family tv time was only weekends before pandemic but 'all the time' during and since pandemic.

Religion/Spiritual

Jose and his family have always attended Sunday Mass at Catholic Church and used to attend regular parish activities weekly before pandemic. Since pandemic attendance has waned and Jose never wants to go.

Nature

Jose does not spend much time in nature as family lives in an urban setting and the nearest park is several blocks away. Mom doesn't feel it's safe for the kids to walk there alone and she is now working two jobs.

Physical/Medical

Jose was born premature at 32 weeks and was in ICU for three weeks. Jose had tubes in his ears at age 3. Jose suffers from eczema on his legs and arms.

Interests

Jose loves video games and soccer. He likes to watch wrestling matches on TV. Jose used to love to build with Legos.

Community

Many families in the neighborhood are very close and gathered weekly for potlucks before pandemic and are trying to do this again now. Church is a strong source of community for the family but Jose is refusing to attend either.

Mental/Emotional

Dad left the family and moved away and this left the mom and sons feeling sad and confused. Mom reports feeling anxious about money and worried about Jose. Jose is anxious and withdrawn.

2023 Created by Lynn Louise Wonders and Mary Affee.

Wonders-Affee
Domains of BioPsychoSocial Development

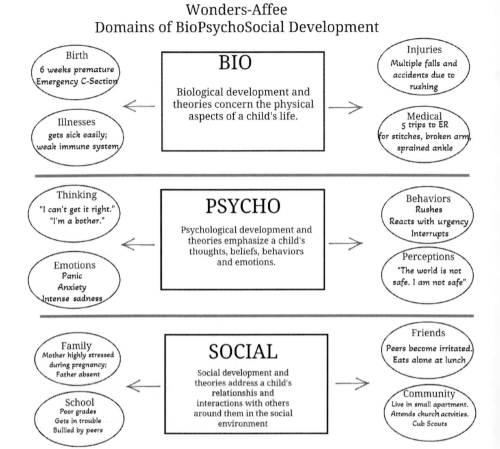

Birth
6 weeks premature
Emergency C-Section

Illnesses
gets sick easily;
weak immune system

BIO

Biological development and
theories concern the physical
aspects of a child's life.

Injuries
Multiple falls and
accidents due to
rushing

Medical
5 trips to ER
for stitches, broken arm,
sprained ankle

Thinking
"I can't get it right."
"I'm a bother."

Emotions
Panic
Anxiety
Intense sadness

PSYCHO

Psychological development and
theories emphasize a child's
thoughts, beliefs, behaviors
and emotions.

Behaviors
Rushes
Reacts with urgency
Interrupts

Perceptions
"The world is not
safe. I am not safe"

Family
Mother highly stressed
during pregnancy;
Father absent

School
Poor grades
Gets in trouble
Bullied by peers

SOCIAL

Social development and
theories address a child's
relationshis and
interactions with others
around them in the social
environment

Friends
Peers become irritated.
Eats alone at lunch

Community
Live in small apartment.
Attends church actvities.
Cub Scouts

2023 Created by Lynn Louise Wonders and Mary Affee.

Sample
Effects of Pandemic on Children & Families Assessment

How was your family affected by the COVID-19 pandemic? ⟶ Children had online school. I was out of work and had to get on unemployment. My father died alone from COVID in the hospital.

PRIOR to Pandmic

How were your child's and family's interactions with one another PRIOR to pandemic? ⟶ We had family together all the time, Sunday church and meal the whole family. We went back and forth to one another's homes all the time.

How were your child's and family's social interactions PRIOR to pandemic? ⟶ Jose played soccer with his friends and video games with friends. Our family gathered with other families for potlucks every Wednesday.

How were your child's and family's level of technology use PRIOR to pandemic? ⟶ Jose video games with friends, we watched tv together on weekends not during the week. We use cell phones to text and call mostly

How was your child's school experience PRIOR to pandemic? ⟶ Jose went to school regularly. He enjoyed seeing his friends but he struggled with academics.

How was your child's and family's moods and emotional wellbeing PRIOR to pandemic? ⟶ Mostly happy as a family. Jose was moody but not as unhappy as he is now.

DURING the Pandemic

How were your child's and family's interactions with one another DURING pandemic? ⟶ Our immediate family was all home together constantly. We couldn't get together with extended family during lockdown and it was hard.

How were your child's and family's social interactions DURING to pandemic? ⟶ He played video games over the computer with friends but he didn't see his friends. He got very lonely. We missed our family friends too.

What was your child's and family's level of technology DURING pandemic? ⟶ Tv was always on. Kids were on Zoom for school classes. Only way we could see friends and family was Facetime or Zoom.

How as your child's school experience DURING pandemic? ⟶ Online school - kids hated it especially Jose. They were bored and distracted - no one to help them if they didn't understand something.

How was your child's and family members' moods and emotional health DURING pandemic? ⟶ Very moody - we got on each other's nerves. Anxious, depressed all of us

Currently

How are your child and family's interactions now? ⟶ Still kind of strained because I think the pandemic kind of broke us as a family. Jose is very anxious, doesn't want to go to school. He isolates.

How are your child and family's social interactions now? ⟶ Jose has lost interest. He doesn't want to see his friends like before and he doesn't want to go to potluck or church.

What is your child's and family's use of technology now? ⟶ Probably too much. We all got used to it and it's hard to stop now.

How are your child and family's moods and emotions now? ⟶ Jose is anxious and seems depressed. The mood in the house is tense.

2023 Created by Lynn Louise Wonders & Mary Affee.

Sample Diagnosis Determination Tool

Observable Behavioral Symptoms
(Compare to DSM-5-TR Criteria)

Emotional outbursts at home__ at school ✓
Difficulty/inability of regulating emotions ✓__
Aggressive behavior toward others__
Difficulty focusing/attending __
Impulsivity__
Angry outbursts ✓
Incosolable sadness/crying__
Stealing or hiding food or other items__
Lying/Exaggerating__
Withdrawal/isolation ✓
Shutting down__ ✓
Refusing to talk ✓
Easily fatigued__
Restlessness__
Intrusive thoughts__

Sleep disturbance ✓
Trouble falling asleep__
Trouble staying asleep__
Trouble waking in a.m. ✓
Nightmares__
Night terrors ✓
Excessive/repeated habits daily__
Asking same question repeatedly__
Excessive counting__
Repeated use of curse words/rude gestures__
Blurting out inappropriate words__
Aversion/avoiding certain places/people__
Other:_____

_____

Behavioral Symptom Impact

Impairing interpersonal functioning: Severe ✓ Moderate__ Mild__ None__
Impairing family functioning: Severe__ Moderate ✓ Mild__ None__
Impairing social functioning: Severe__ Moderate__ Mild__ None__
Impairing educational functioning: Severe ✓ Moderate__ Mild__ None__
Impairing cultural functioning: Severe__ Moderate ✓ Mild__ None__
Impairing spiritual functioning: Severe__ Moderate ✓ Mild__ None__

Common DSM-5-TR Childhood Diagnoses

ADHD * Anorexia* Anxiety unspecified * Autism Spectrum Disorder* Binge-eating*
Bulimia * Dermatillomania * Encopresis* Enuresis* Generalized Anxiety Disorder *
Obessive Compulsive Disorder* PANS/PANDAS* Pervasive Development Disorder * Post
Traumtic Stress Disorder *✓ Separation Anxiety Disorder* Tics Disorders * Trichotillomania *

When did behaviors begin? some prior to pandemic but severely worsened during and after pandemic
_____
How frequent are the behaviors? Daily_____

2023 Created by Lynn Louise Wonders & Mary Affee.

Sample Treatment Plans

Example Plan For Therapy

Client Name: Jose Ruiz	DOB: 12/21/2016	Date of Intake: 02/28/2023	Date of Plan: 03/12/2023

Presentation

Presenting Challenges:
nighttime anxiety; school refusal

Diagnostic Impression:
300.00/F41.9; Unspecified Anxiety Disorder

Other: Child presents as very shy and withdrawn

Cultural Context:
Mexican-American, Catholic;
Co-sleeping - cultural norm

Family Context:
Parents recently divorced; father
moved out of state

Goals & Objectives

Goal #1: Reduce frequency, intensity, and duration of the anxiety symptoms so that daily functioning is not impaired.

Objective 1: Client will be able to identify and express feelings of anxiety by 04/15/2023

Objective 2: Client will use self-soothing skills when feeling anxious by 04/28/2023

Goal #2: Fall asleep and remain asleep without interruption until morning most nights.

Objective 1: Client will learn and practice sleep-time coping skills in session by 03/28/2023

Objective 2: Client will use sleep-time coping skills nightly by 04/15/2023

Goal#3: Attend school regularly

Objective 1: Client will attend half days of school by 04/01/2023

Objective 2: Client will use coping skills at school and complet a full day by 04/15/2023

Interventions

Model/Theories: CCPT; CBPT

Child-Led withTracking/Reflecting:✓ Bibliotherapy ✓ Puppet/Figures✓ Measure Scales__
Expressive/Creative: ✓ Sand Tray:✓ Water Play:__ CBPT Games ✓ Sensory Play__
PsychoEd:__ Family Tx:__ Parent Training/Consultation: ✓ School Consultation: ✓
Other:_____

Sample Goal Directed Treatment Plan Outline

Presenting Challenges and Concern:

Client is too anxious in social situations and at school to participate in events and class projects. (Social Phobia)

Presenting Potentials and Strengths:

Client is naturally artistic (drawing); Client loves to sing and dance at home

Goal 1 for Therapy:

Reduce anxiety symptoms so client can attend social events and participate in class projects

   Objective 1 for Goal 1:

   Client will attend a birthday party and stay for one hour by the end of April.

   Objective 2 for Goal 1:

   Client will use his artistic skills to create a unique book report and present to the class by the 15th of May

Interventions for Goal 1:

CCPT for rapport building; CBPT gradual exposure and confidencie building techniques

Goal 2 for Therapy:

Promote client's ability to connect and form meaningful social relationships.

   Objective 1 for Goal 2:

   Client will demonstrate skills for communicating socially with peers in group play therapy by end of July.

   Objective 2 for Goal 2:

   Caregivers will report client initiates invitation for one friend to sleep over by end of June.

Interventions for Goal 2:

Puppet based communication skills traiining; Sand tray with social prompts; group play therapy

Theoretical Orientation(s) and Models/Approaches:

Child Centered Play Thearpy; Cognitive Behavioral Play Therapy; Group Play Therapy

AutPlay Therapy Example Therapy Plan

Client Name: Ronan Lomas
DOB: 0/00/00
Date of Plan: 0/00/00

Parent/Guardian Name: Tammy and John Lomas
Provider Name: Robert Jason Grant Ed.D
Location of Service: Office
Diagnosis/Presenting Needs: Previous psychological evaluation diagnosis autism spectrum disorder F84.0 (299.00) – low support needs. Family reported concerns with anxiety and depression. Therapist observed social anxiety and self-worth needs, parent/child relationship issues, and neurodivergent identity needs
Medication(s): None reported
1) Current Symptom(s)/Needs for Therapy: Anxiety-related dysregulation, social anxiety.

Long Term Goal(s):

Ronan will be able to encounter socially related dysregulating situations, environments, and emotions and will not have dysregulated meltdowns but be able to regulate through the experiences.
Short Term Goal(s)/Objective(s): Become aware of dysregulation triggers. Learn 5 regulation techniques.

Decrease dysregulation meltdowns from 2–3 per week to 1 per week.

Intervention/Action:

Structured play therapy interventions to address regulation (integrative play therapy). Understanding the regulatory system (psychoeducation, humanistic reflection).

Parent and child appreciation and acceptance of the child's social navigation preferences (psychoeducation, humanistic reflection).
Involvement of Client/Family: Parents will bring Ronan to all his therapy appointments. They will share regular updates about Ronan regarding home and school issues. They will participate in family sessions with Ronan when requested.
Review Date/Progress Toward Goal(s): 0/00/00 Making progress toward goals.
2) Current Symptom(s)/Needs for Therapy: Parent/child relationship strain, self-worth, and neurodivergent identity awareness struggles (child and parent).

Long Term Goal(s):

Ronan will be able to understand, appreciate, and accept his neurodivergent identity. He will feel positive about himself and display improved self-worth. Ronan and his parents will be able to explain the neurodiversity paradigm and value-affirming ways of parenting and being in a healthy parent/child relationship.

Short Term Goal(s)/Objective(s):

Become aware of the neurodiversity paradigm, affirming beliefs, and possible ableist beliefs. Learn 5 self-worth/empowerment interventions.

Parent and child will read and discuss a book about neurodivergence written by a neurodivergent author.

Intervention/Action:

Structured play therapy interventions focused on self-worth (integrative play therapy).

Bibliotherapy (selected by the therapist) and psychoeducation regarding neurodivergence. Participate in psychoeducation with the therapist (understand the difference between an affirming practice and an ableist practice).

Involvement of Client/Family: Parents will bring Ronan to all his therapy appointments. They will share regular updates about Ronan regarding home and school issues. They will participate in family sessions with Ronan when requested.

Review Date/Progress Toward Goal(s): 0/00/00 Making progress toward goals.

Support Services/Other Agencies Working with Client/Family:
None at this time.

Services Needed Beyond the Scope of this Therapist/Organization and Referrals Made:
None at this time.

Response to Other Concurrent Therapies:
N/A
Method & Duration of Therapy: Weekly Ind. 90834 and Family 90847 as needed.
Estimated Completion Date: 0/0/00

_____   _____

Robert Jason Grant Ed.D, LPC, NCC, RPT -S   Date

CCPT Example Treatment Plan

NAME: Sonia Example   **DOB:** 12/12/17   **CLINICIAN:** Rosie Newman
DATE: 1/1/22

DIAGNOSIS & JUSTIFICATION

Adjustment Disorder, Unspecified (F43.20). Client presents with daily outbursts lasting over 2 hours since starting a new school 3 months ago. Symptoms significantly impact functioning at home and at school.

PRESENTING PROBLEMS:

- Outbursts daily for 2 hours "when something doesn't go her way"
- Problems following directions at school
- "Bosses around" peers and younger sibling

LONG-TERM TREATMENT GOAL

Improve sense of harmony at home and improve functioning at school.

SYMPTOMS OBJECTIVE (SHORT-TERM)

- Decrease outbursts from daily to 4–5 times per week and decrease duration from 2 hours to 30 minutes or less per parent report
- Decrease noncompliant behavior at school from daily to 3–4 times per week per teacher and parent report
- Decrease "bossy" behaviors with peers and younger sibling from daily to 4–5 times per week per parent report

GROWTH OBJECTIVES

- Increase sense of self, self-regulation, frustration tolerance, flexibility, and problem solving
- Increase social awareness, social engagement, healthy boundaries, and reciprocity in plan

THEORY OF CHANGE

As progress toward growth objectives increase, Sonia's behavioral symptoms will decrease. When Sonia feels better about herself, can regulate her emotions, shows greater frustration tolerance, and can exercise flexibility and problem-solving, her meltdowns and non-compliant behavior will decrease.

When, in addition to meeting the above growth objectives, Sonia gains awareness of others, improves personal boundaries, and can engage reciprocally, she will have positive peer relationships.

INTERVENTIONS & FREQUENCY

- Child-centered play therapy, weekly
- Caregiver consultations, every 3–6 weeks

CCPT Example Treatment Plan

NAME: Sonia Example   **DOB:** 12/12/17   **CLINICIAN:** Rosie Newman
DATE: 1/1/22

DIAGNOSIS & JUSTIFICATION

Adjustment Disorder, Unspecified (F43.20). Client presents with daily outbursts lasting over 2 hours since starting a new school 3 months ago. Symptoms significantly impact functioning at home and at school.

PRESENTING PROBLEMS:

- Outbursts daily for 2 hours "when something doesn't go her way"
- Problems following directions at school
- "Bosses around" peers and younger sibling

LONG-TERM TREATMENT GOAL

Improve sense of harmony at home and improve functioning at school.

SYMPTOMS OBJECTIVE (SHORT-TERM)

- Decrease outbursts from daily to 4–5 times per week and decrease duration from 2 hours to 30 minutes or less per parent report
- Decrease noncompliant behavior at school from daily to 3–4 times per week per teacher and parent report
- Decrease "bossy" behaviors with peers and younger sibling from daily to 4–5 times per week per parent report

GROWTH OBJECTIVES

- Increase sense of self, self-regulation, frustration tolerance, flexibility, and problem solving
- Increase social awareness, social engagement, healthy boundaries, and reciprocity in plan

THEORY OF CHANGE

As progress toward growth objectives increase, Sonia's behavioral symptoms will decrease. When Sonia feels better about herself, can regulate her emotions, shows greater frustration tolerance, and can exercise flexibility and problem-solving, her meltdowns and non-compliant behavior will decrease.

When, in addition to meeting the above growth objectives, Sonia gains awareness of others, improves personal boundaries, and can engage reciprocally, she will have positive peer relationships.

INTERVENTIONS & FREQUENCY

- Child-centered play therapy, weekly
- Caregiver consultations, every 3–6 weeks

Sonia Example Progress Note for Session 12

CLIENT: Sonia Example   **DOB:** 12/12/17   **DATE:** 1/1/22   **TIME:** 4:00 p.m.
DURATION: 48 min
CPT CODE: 90834   **CLINICIAN:** Rosie Newman, LMHC   **NPI:** xx
DIAGNOSIS: Adjustment Disorder, Unspecified (F43.20). Client presents with daily outbursts lasting over 2 hours, impacting functioning at home and at school. Symptoms began when she started attending a new school 3 months ago.
DESCRIPTION: Sonia arrived with her mother and transitioned easily into the playroom. Sonia initiated the ball maze for the first few minutes. She then shifted to the dollhouse and created a scene in which the doll family was preparing for the birth of a baby. The doll parents were "stressed out," and the older son "got to play a lot of video games." At the end of session, Sonia sat at the sand tray, moving her hands throughout the tray, talking with the therapist about various likes and dislikes. Sonia transitioned out of the playroom easily.
ASSESSMENT: Play themes–family, mastery, relationship

PROGRESS TOWARD GOALS/OBJECTIVES:

Symptom Objectives	Growth Objectives
Decrease outbursts from daily to 4–5x/week. Decrease "bossy" behavior from daily to 4–5x/week. Decrease non-compliant behavior at school from daily to 3–4x/week per teacher and parent report. **Measurable progress will be assessed in caregiver session next week.**	Increase sense of self **Progress evidenced by play going deeper symbolically with baby doll in doll house.** • Increase sense of self, self-regulation, frustration tolerance, flexibility, and problem- solving. **Evidenced by creating tracking systems for taking turns.** **Evidenced by involving therapist in maze-making and turn-taking. Increase social awareness, social** engagement, healthy boundaries, and reciprocity in plan

INTERVENTIONS:

Child-centered play therapy–*Established structure and frame to allow Sonia to safely process feelings through play, tracked play to increase self-awareness, reflected feelings to increase feelings awareness, returned responsibility to improve self-agency, provided esteem-building statements to increase sense of self.*

PLAN:

Meet with caregivers next week to assess progress toward symptom reduction. Continue CCPT.

Digital Play Therapy Example Therapy Plan

Presenting Concerns – Anxiety, existential dread, and relational disconnections

Behavioral Indicators – Hypervigilance, such as feeling constantly on edge, concentration difficulties, trouble falling and staying asleep, a general state of irritability, and avoidance and rejection of peer relationships

Goal 1 – Reduce frequency, intensity, and duration of the anxiety so that daily functioning is not impaired.

- **Objective 1** – Learn and implement coping strategies and calming skills to reduce and manage anxiety symptoms.
- **Objective 2** – Express (through verbal dialogue and/or nonverbal play processing) perspective experiences of specific fears, prominent worries, and anxiety symptoms and identify its impact on functioning and methods for reduction/resolution

Goal 2 – Establish meaningful peer interactions and relationships that align with a genuine and authentic sense of self

- **Objective 1** – Freely explore personal interests, values, desires, and needs through play- based experiences and enhance self-concept through a safe and connected therapeutic relationship
- **Objective 2** – Confront fears of peer rejection and improve trust in and reliance on others through positive play-based relational experiences

Therapy Interventions

1. Facilitate non-directive play therapy to allow themes to emerge through Embry's natural communication method of play to gain insight into problematic thoughts, feelings, and experiences and to assist in addressing and decreasing the frequency, intensity, and duration of psychological distress.
2. Provide unconditional positive regard, reflect content and feelings in a nonjudgmental manner, and display trust in Embry's capacity to work through issues to increase their ability to cope with anxious feelings and enhance their relationship with self and others.

Of note, since digital play tools are one of many play therapy toy options in the playroom, and the client leads in non-directive play therapy, there are no specified goals, objectives, or interventions that identify digital tools specifically. Digital Play TherapyTM naturally emerged in sessions for Embry, so this became the primary treatment modality. The therapy plan, however, aligns with humanistic theory.

Family Systems Sample Treatment Plan

Goal One: Detriangulate both kids from parental distress

Objectives:

1. Parents continue processing long-avoided underlying wants, needs, and injuries in couple therapy;
2. Alexander will make a s different attribution to Brody's resistance to spending time with him. It will is no longer viewed as rejection, but instead as a reaction to family distress;

3. Alexander develops special monthly ritual just for him and Brody;

4. Monique identifies at least three people / pets she can go to for comfort and support, including cuddling;

5. Monique and Brody will experiment with separation, particularly at night;

6. Parents make overt positive statements about each other at least 3 times a week in front of their kids;

7. Attachment will be enhanced between each parent and child by engaging them in

Theraplay activities;

Goal Two: The family will process recent parental conflict.

Objectives:

1. Each family member will express thoughts and feelings related to recent parental conflict.;

2. Each parent will express understanding of each kids' thoughts and feelings;

3. Parents will assure children that they are getting support for their relationship;

4. Family will engage in creating shared family identity;

Goal Three: Brody complies with school attendance and improves grades.

Objectives:

1. Parents adopt a reward system in which Brody is rewarded for schoolwork with family activities, such as a family game night;

2. Alexander takes Brody to school at least three days per week;

3. Brody will be able to attend school successfully three out of five school days initially; and eventually, attend school successfully five days of the week (or 100% of the time).

Treatment will include two individual sessions with Brody each month and two family sessions. Individual sessions will be designed to support Brody to identify and process feelings related to family distress and school. Additional parent sessions will be held as needed. The therapist will coordinate with the couple therapist as needed and at least once every two months.

A Neurobiological Relational Approach

Sample Treatment Plan

Presenting Problem *(What brings them to treatment?)*
Janelle's parents are struggling with her behavioral response when things don't go the way she expects them to. She becomes angry and argumentative, followed by expressions of despair.

Goal(s) *(How will we achieve healing?)*
Increase Janelle's sense of interpersonal safety through repairing the implicit wounds from her early life, leading to a greater capacity to maintain relational connection when disappointed.

Objectives *(How will we know things are better?)*

- Janelle will have fewer tantrums and the ones she does have will be more congruent with the situation. Stan and Felicia will feel successful if she has no more than two per month, measured via parent report, understanding that the frequency can fluctuate as more trauma comes to the surface for healing.

- Janelle will enjoy improved peer relationships, needing less support of adults to help her navigate inevitable disappointments, measured via parent and teacher reports.

Interventions *(How will we get there?)*

- Offer attuned listening, reflective responding, and empathic communication to Janelle and her parents.

- Offer non-directive play therapy opportunities for Janelle.

- Offer Janelle the qualities of secure attachment in our play therapy sessions (presence, contact, reflection, responsiveness, and delight).

- Offer a non-judgmental space for both Stan and Felicia to describe their emotional and behavioral responses to Janelle, exploring the influence of unhealed relational wounds that arise in response to Janelle's distress.

- Offer care and disconfirmation for the parents' wounded parts. Consider referring for individual therapy as needed.

- Offer psychoeducation to Stan and Felicia about relational neuroscience and brain-based parenting to support their capacity to offer attunement and experiences of secure attachment for Janelle.

Sample Treatment Plan for Sexual Abuse Cases

- Goal #1: Reduce clinical scores on the TSCC and TSCYC (Briere, 1996)
    - Objective: Utilize expressive therapies to identify and process emotional and somatic reactions secondary to CSA
    - Objective: Utilize expressive therapies to process and integrate posttraumatic emotional and behavioral regulation
- Goal #2: Build and strengthen social support and adaptive coping strategies
    - Objective: Utilize expressive therapies to facilitate the development and use of progressive muscle relaxation (PMR)
    - Objective: Utilize expressive therapists to facilitate the use of deep breathing exercises to reduce posttraumatic stress reactions
- Goal #3: Process and integrate the history of CSA to reduce posttraumatic stress symptomology
    - Objective: Utilize expressive therapies to explore traumatic memories
    - Objective: Utilize expressive therapies to identify and process sensory reactions to trauma triggers
- Goal #4: Process and integrate the history of CSA
    - Objective: Utilize expressive therapies to identify and reframe cognitive distortions related to CSA
    - Objective: Utilize expressive therapies to provide meaning- making through the creation of a trauma narrative relating to CSA

Family Systems Sample Treatment Plan

Goal One: Detriangulate both kids from parental distress

Objectives:

1. Parents continue processing long-avoided underlying wants, needs, and injuries in couple therapy.
2. Alexander will make a different attribution to Brody's resistance to spending time with him. It will no longer be viewed as rejection but as a reaction to family distress.
3. Alexander develops a special monthly ritual just for him and Brody; Alexander demonstrates a willingness to discuss race, white supremacy culture, and unearned privilege non-defensively so that both parents can explore how racial bias and colorism may be impacting how they relate to their children.
4. Monique identifies at least three people/pets she can visit for comfort and support, including cuddling.
5. Monique and Brody will experiment with separation, particularly at night.
6. Parents make overt positive statements about each other at least three times a week in front of their kids.
7. Attachment will be enhanced between each parent and child by engaging them in Theraplay® activities.

Goal Two: The family will process the recent parental conflict.

Objectives:

1. Each family member will express thoughts and feelings related to recent parental conflict.
2. Each parent will express understanding of each kids' thoughts and feelings.
3. Parents will assure children that they are getting support for their relationship.
4. The family will engage in creating a shared family identity.

Goal Three: Brody complies with school attendance and improves grades.

Objectives:

1. Parents adopt a reward system in which Brody is rewarded for schoolwork with family activities, such as a family game night.
2. Alexander takes Brody to school at least three days per week.
3. Brody will be able to attend school successfully three out of five school days initially and eventually attend school successfully five days of the week (or 100% of the time).

Treatment will include two individual sessions with Brody each month and two family sessions. Individual sessions will be designed to support Brody in identifying and processing feelings related to family distress and school. Additional parent sessions will be held as needed. The therapist will coordinate with the couple's therapist as needed and at least once every two months.

APPENDIX C

Sample Session Notes

Example Play Therapy Session Note

Client Name: Jose Ruiz   Session Date: 04/13/2023   Start & Stop Time: 4:00-4:47pm

Session Arrival:

Eager__ Hesitant__ Resistant__ Agreeable__ Other_____

Affect:

Happy__ Reserved__ Sad__ Agitated__ Tearful__ Demanding__ Anxious__ Calm__ Angry__ Curious__ Hyper-vigilant__ Flat__ Blunted__ Labile__

MotorActivity Level:

High__ Low___ Medium__ Other__

Status/Stageof Therapy:

Exploratory__ Testing Limits__ Connecting__ Growth__ Termination__

Quality of Play:

Fantasy__ Dissosicative__ Regressive__ Trauma__ Expressive__ Exploratory__

Play Themes:

Nurturing__ Aggressive__ Disaster__ Power__ Family__ Creative__ Building__ Mastery/Competence__ Sensory__Game__ Cheating/Winning__Betrayal__ Strong vs. Weak__ Bad vs. Good__ Death__ Fixing/Repairing__ Protecting__ Rescuing__ Victim__ Helpless__ Positive/Affirming__ Negative/Denying__ Sexualized__ Messy__ Cleaning__ Sorting__ Mapping__ Other_____

Attention/Interactions:

Focused__ Distracted__ Oriented__ Disoriented__ Delusional__ Realistic__ Impulsive__ Interrupting__ Cooperative__ Collaborative__ Isolating__

Session Ending:

Agreeable__ Cooperative__ Uncooperative__ Resistant__ Tearful__ Happy__ Other_____

Therapist Signature:

Lynn Louise Wonders, LPC, RPT-S, CPCS, Psychotherapy
04/13/2023 6:02 pm

Example SOAP Session Note

Client Name: Jose Ruiz   Session Date: 04/13/2023   Start & Stop Time: 4:00-4:47pm

Subjective:

Child brought his a sketch he made at home with him to session. Client said, "I feel good about this. I made this myself." Child chose to draw with the pastels and as he drew he said, "Drawing helps me feel more together inside like I'm not so jumbled.." Child's mother waved to therapist with a big smile in the waiting room. after session.

Objective:

Child and mother arrived to session on time in therapist's office. Therapist provided client-centered therapeutic approach, tracking and reflecting client's expressions and choices to validate client's feelings and thoughts. Therapist provided cognitive-behavioral approach, identifying automatic negative thoughts and providing invitation for client to reframe and restructure those cognitions in line with reality testing. Child presented as feeling hopeful and empowered through experiences of drawing at home and in session..

Assessement:

Risk assessment: no concerns.

Status assessment: all within normal range - nothing notable

Progress: Client's presentation was more confident and hopeful than in past sessions.

Plan:

Continue weekly sessions. Provided child and mother with encouragement to establish daily drawing time together since this is an activity they both have skills and interest in.

Therapist Signature:

Lynn Louise Wonders, LPC, RPT-S, CPCS, Psychotherapy
04/13/2023 6:02 pm

Example DAP Session Note

Client Name: Jose Ruiz   Session Date: 04/13/2023   Start & Stop Time: 4:00-4:47pm

Data:

Client arrived with mother on time for 6th session for play therapy to address symptoms of social phobia, school refusal, anxiety and depression. Client was well-groomed and fully oriented. The client showed therapist a sketch and reported, "I feel good about this. I made this myself. Drawing makes me feel more together inside, like I'm not so jumbled.." Client noted that they are still having trouble sleeping at night. Client chose to draw with pastels in session. Therapist used client-centered reflection and tracking to support and validate client's thoughts and feelings. Therapist challenged the client's automatic negative thoughts about no one liking him at school. Client invited Therapist to draw with him. Client's mother waved and smiled widely to Therapist after session.

Assessement:

Risk assessment: no concerns.
Status assessment: all within normal range - nothing notable
Progress: Client's presentation was more confident and hopeful than in past sessions. Client was receptive to Theraipist's CBT interventions and appeared to enjoy the process of free-expression through the chosen drawing activity.

Plan:

Continue weekly sessions in office. Provided child and mother with encouragement to establish daily drawing time together since this is an activity they both have skills and interest in.

Therapist Signature:

Lynn Louise Wonders, LPC, RPT-S, CPCS, Psychotherapy
04/13/2023 6:02 pm

Example Family Session Note

Client Name: Jose Ruiz   Session Date: 04/27/2023   Start & Stop Time: 4:00-4:56pm

Family Members Present:

Mom, Brother, Grandmother and Cousin

Family Intervention/Activity:

All family members arrived for session together and participated in building a world together in the over-sized sandtray.

Relationship Dynamics Observed:

Jose appeared subdued through most of the session. Cousin Pedro 2 years older than Jose was domineering and bossy toward Jose and Jose's brother Pablo. Jose's mother and grandmother did not correct Pedro. Jose's mother coddled Jose, attempting to show affection but Jose was resistant and wriinkled his nose as if smelling a foul odor when she did. Pablo was hyper-active during the session and chatted to everyone, shrugging off Pablo's attempts to dominate.

Other Observations:

Pablo insisted the world to be built needed to be a family on vacation. Pablo led the activity assigning figures for each of the family members and directing each member where to place their figures. Pedro rebelled against Pablo's directions with his own ideas and laughed when Pablo became angry with him. Grandmother and mother listened to Pablo and Pedro and both laughed when the boys were in disagreement. Jose remained in one corner of the sandtray, isolating his figure and creating a fortress around his figure with the fencing and walls.

Interpretations and Plan:

Jose's isolation of his own figure and his quiet and subdued demeanor during the family session fits with his mother's concerns about resisting and isolating at home. Jose's cousin Pedro and grandmother have been living with Jose, Pablo and their mother since Pedro's mother became ill with cancer and could not longer take care of Pedro and the grandmother. After Jose's grandfather died of COVID in hospital, the family has been shifting around in terms of living arrangements. Therapist will recommend therapy for Pedro with another therapist and for Pablo as well. Therapist will provide some parenting guidance for mother and grandmother regarding co-regulation activities, validation of emotions and limit setting as needed for he boys at home.

Therapist Signature:

Lynn Louise Wonders, LPC, RPT-S, CPCS, Psychotherapy
04/27/2023 6::05 pm

Sample Progress Notes for Sexual Abuse Cases

Sample Progress Note for Reducing Clinical Scores On the TSCC
The client attended a session in the office. Her mood was sad with tearful affect. The client denied active or passive suicidal ideation. The session emphasized the reduction of post-traumatic symptoms by facilitating emotional expression and identification surrounding CSA. The play therapy intervention Revealing Your Feelings (Kenney-Noziska, 2008) was employed. The intervention presented the client with various emotions commonly experienced by victims of CSA and encouraged the processing of those feelings. Emotions were written with changeable markers inside various shapes. As the client colored in each shape, emotions about CSA were revealed and processed. Progress was made toward treatment Goal #1. The therapy plan is for the client to return to the office next week.

Sample Progress Note for Reframing Cognitive Distortions
The client attended a session in the office. Her mood was euthymic with congruent affect. No suicidal ideation was noted. The session emphasized identifying, challenging, and reframing distorted cognitions of guilt, blame, and responsibility for CSA. The play therapy intervention Blameberry Pie (Goodyear-Brown, Riviere, & Shelby, 2004) was utilized. The intervention allowed the client to identify beliefs surrounding the causality of CSA. Beliefs were written on strips of paper and placed into a pie pan. Each identified belief was explored for accuracy and reframed into smaller tort tins as needed. Distortions regarding self-blame for post-disclosure changes were noted. This area will continue to be explored. Progress was made toward treatment Goals #1, #2, and #4. The therapy plan is for the client to return to the office next week.

CCPT Sample Progress Note

CLIENT: Sonia Example   **DOB:** 12/12/17   **DATE:** 1/1/22   **TIME:** 4:00 p.m.
DURATION: 48 min

CPT CODE: 90834 **CLINICIAN:** Rosie Newman, LMHC **NPI:** xx

DIAGNOSIS: Adjustment Disorder, Unspecified (F43.20). Client presents with daily outbursts lasting over 2 hours, impacting functioning at home and at school. Symptoms began when she started attending a new school 3 months ago.

DESCRIPTION: Sonia arrived with her mother and transitioned easily into the playroom. Sonia initiated the ball maze for the first few minutes. She then shifted to the dollhouse and created a scene in which the doll family was preparing for the birth of a baby. The doll parents were "stressed out," and the older son "got to play a lot of video games." At the end of session, Sonia sat at the sand tray, moving her hands throughout the tray, talking with the therapist about various likes and dislikes. Sonia transitioned out of the playroom easily.

ASSESSMENT: Play themes–family, mastery, relationship

PROGRESS TOWARD GOALS/OBJECTIVES:

Symptom Objectives	Growth Objectives
Decrease outbursts from daily to 4–5x/week. Decrease "bossy" behavior from daily to 4–5x/week. Decrease non-compliant behavior at school from daily to 3–4x/week per teacher and parent report.	Increase sense of self *Progress evidenced by play going deeper symbolically with baby doll in doll house.* • Increase sense of self, self-regulation, frustration tolerance, flexibility, and problem- solving.
Measurable progress will be assessed in caregiver session next week.	*Evidenced by creating tracking systems for taking turns. Evidenced by involving therapist in maze-making and turn-taking. Increase social awareness, social engagement, healthy boundaries, and reciprocity in plan*

INTERVENTIONS:

Child-centered play therapy–*Established structure and frame to allow Sonia to safely process feelings through play, tracked play to increase self-awareness, reflected feelings to increase feelings awareness, returned responsibility to improve self-agency, provided esteem-building statements to increase sense of self.*

PLAN:

Meet with caregivers next week to assess progress toward symptom reduction. Continue CCPT.

APPENDIX D

Other Documentation Samples

Example Caregiver Feedback Form

Date: 04/04/2023   Child's Name: Jose Ruiz   Caregiver Name: Juanita Sanchez

1. Child's behavioral changes/improvements/regression the past week:
   Jose has been staying in his room a lot and hasn't wanted to talk or eat at the table with the rest of the family.
2. Child's sleep patterns the past week:

   He has had nightmares and is tossing and turning a lot in his sleep.

3. Child's eating patterns the past week:

   Only wants to eat by himself. Eats in his room.

4. Child's social interactions the past week:
   Has been keeping to himself and doesn't have interest in playing wtih his friends.

5. Child's school/academic behaviors/patterns this past week:
   His teacher sent a note home saying he has not been turning in his homework this week and doesn't participate in class.

6. What other concerns or achievements would you like to share?
   I'm worried that he is more depressed this week than before but I'm glad at least he is going to school again.

7. What questions or requests do you have for your child's therapist?
   If you have recommendations for how I can help hiim at home I would like to know.

Therapist's Notes About Above Info:

-Consider referring out for a psychiatric consultation to see if medication may be appropriate.
-Consult with mother and provide suggestions for how to encourage Jose to engage with her and other family members at home.

Sample Letter to Caregivers for Adjusting Treatment Plan

Wonders Counseling Services, LLC

Lynn Louise Wonders, LPC, CPCS, RPT-S
789 Broad St. Suite 201
Atlanta, GA 30328

June 1, 2023

Dear Stacey and Sam,

As we discussed in our last parenting session over telehealth on May 29, the presenting concerns you expressed about your son Jimmy at the beginning of our therapy together in November have escalated to a level that is beyond my present capacity to address therapeutically. For this reason, I will need to schedule three (3) closing sessions with Jimmy this month and provide referrals to other potential therapists who can better address the most present concerns in therapy.

I am providing below names and contact information for three (3) psychotherapists in the metro Atlanta area I believe will be a good fit for your family's present concerns and needs. They are all licensed and extensively trained in the subject of current concerns. Please reach out to them and see who you feel will be the best fit for your family at this time.

- John Smith, LPC, RPT-S – 404-555-4567
- Marita Longoria, LCSW, RPT-S 678-555-1234
- Kisha Phillips, LMFT, RPT-S 404-555-6789

I am happy to provide one 20-minute consultation with the therapist you choose to work with at no cost about your family's experience in therapy with me and current concerns. Please fill out and sign the attached Release of Information and fax to me at 404-555-7676 once you've chosen your new therapist.

Sincerely,

Lynn Louise Wonders, LPC, RPT-S, CPCS

INDEX

Made in the USA
Monee, IL
08 April 2024